BEYOND JAPAN

A volume in the series
Cornell Studies in Political Economy
edited by Peter J. Katzenstein

A full list of titles in the series appears at the end of the book.

BEYOND JAPAN

THE DYNAMICS OF EAST ASIAN REGIONALISM

. . . .

EDITED BY

Peter J. Katzenstein

and **Takashi Shiraishi**

Cornell University Press ITHACA AND LONDON

First published 2006 by Cornell University Press
First printing, Cornell Paperbacks, 2006

Printed in the United States of America

Library of Congress Cataloging-in-Publication Data

Beyond Japan : the dynamics of East Asian regionalism / edited by Peter J. Katzenstein and Takashi Shiraishi.
      p. cm. — (Cornell studies in political economy)
   Includes index.
   ISBN-13: 978-0-8014-4400-5 (cloth : alk. paper)
   ISBN-10: 0-8014-4400-4 (cloth : alk. paper)
   ISBN-13: 978-0-8014-7250-3 (pbk. : alk. paper)
   ISBN-10: 0-8014-7250-4 (pbk. : alk. paper)
   1. East Asia—Relations—Japan.   2. Japan—Relations—East Asia.
3. Regionalism—East Asia.   4. Regionalism—Japan.   5. East Asia—Economic conditions.   6. Japan—Economic conditions—1989–
7. East Asia—Social conditions.   8. Japan—Social conditions—1945–
I. Title: Dynamics of East Asian regionalism.   II. Katzenstein, Peter J.
III. Shiraishi, Takashi, 1950–   IV. Series.
  DS518.45.B49 2006
  327.520509′051—dc22

                2005025672

Cornell University Press strives to use environmentally responsible suppliers and materials to the fullest extent possible in the publishing of its books. Such materials include vegetable-based, low-VOC inks and acid-free papers that are recycled, totally chlorine-free, or partly composed of nonwood fibers. For further information, visit our website at www.cornellpress.cornell.edu.

Cloth printing   10 9 8 7 6 5 4 3 2 1
Paperback printing 10 9 8 7 6 5 4 3 2 1

Contents

Preface

This project extends a fruitful collaboration that dates back more than a decade. Soon after the publication of the predecessor to this volume (Katzenstein and Shiraishi 1997) we were both struck by the many hard-to-notice changes that were transforming Japan and East Asia. Over dinner in a fine Tokyo restaurant we hatched the plan for a book that would look at how the cracks in the Japanese model were shaping and being reshaped by a vibrant Asian regionalism.

It took us some time to move from this initial insight to the assembling of a group of authors who we thought had the in-depth knowledge and analytical skills to help us. Many, though by no means all, are former students and colleagues with whom we had worked at Cornell, both before and after Shiraishi's move to Kyoto University.

Initial draft outlines were presented at the Japan into Asia workshop that we convened in Kyoto in January 2003. Full drafts were discussed in a follow-up workshop at the East-West Center, Honolulu, in January 2004. We thank the Research Institute of Economy, Trade and Industry (RIETI), where Shiraishi serves as a faculty fellow, for funding and the Center for Southeast Asian Studies at Kyoto University for hosting the first meeting. And we are greatly indebted to RIETI, Cornell's Walter S. Carpenter, Jr. Professorship of International Studies, and the staff of the East-West Center for funding and staffing the second meeting.

Peter Gourevitch and Miles Kahler gave generously of their time and acted as discussants of many of the papers at the second meeting. Far beyond helping the authors sharpen the arguments of individual papers, their comments were invaluable in helping us to clarify our thinking on the project's key components and in articulating more accurately the central ideas driving it. All the project participants, and especially the two editors, owe Peter and Miles an enormous debt of gratitude.

Two anonymous readers for Cornell University Press gave the draft manuscript a close and insightful reading. Roger Haydon acted with the customary speed and humor that have created for him a large and devoted following among scholars of all stripes and in all parts of the world. Stephanie Hofmann readied the final version of the manuscript before we submitted it to the Press. Finally, Karen Hwa oversaw the final stages of production. To all of them we are grateful.

We also thank the contributors to this volume for putting up so willingly with our various demands. Without their intellectual engagement this project would not have been possible.

Finally, we are grateful for an intellectual friendship that has lasted now more than a decade and that geographic distance has not been able to dull.

PETER J. KATZENSTEIN

Ithaca, New York

TAKASHI SHIRAISHI

Kyoto

BEYOND JAPAN

1

East Asia—Beyond Japan

PETER J. KATZENSTEIN

East Asia is on the move, merging different national strands into a new regional fabric. No longer are regionalism (defined here in terms of institutionalized practices) and regionalization (defined here as a process that engages actors) projections of specific national models. Instead they are combining such models into something new and different, extending well beyond any national model.

This is an important change. Pundits and politicians have traditionally thought about region-making in terms of the ups and downs of different national models. Since the mid-1970s, for example, Japan and the United States have traversed different roads. While Japan was riding high in the 1980s, the United States was consumed by premonitions of national crisis; East Asia was widely believed to reflect that shift in national fortunes as pax nipponica was just around the corner. The 1990s witnessed a sharp reversal. Now it was the United States that crested, Japan that faltered; and East Asia again was a screen on which to project shifting national fortunes, this time in the era of pax americana. Meanwhile China's rise has signaled the arrival of a new regional power, and India lurks in the wings. If our infatuation with regional extensions of national models continues, then China's and India's moments will come, and they too will pass. Undue admiration of national models has been

I thank all the authors in this volume for their helpful comments on prior drafts of this chapter; Peter Gourevitch and Miles Kahler for acting as incisive commentators at a workshop at the East-West Center in Honolulu; the participants of Cornell's Political Economy Research Colloquium seminar for a spirited critique; Roger Haydon for his perennially sharp pen and good humor; and two anonymous reviewers for Cornell University Press for their trenchant comments.

transitory—each model, it seems, witnesses its brief moment of glory before declining.

The time is ripe for a shift in perspective. East Asia is moving rapidly beyond any one national model to the coexistence of several viable alternatives and the emergence of a truly hybrid form of regionalism. This book develops this argument with specific reference to the relations between Japan and East Asia. It would be a monumental research project to examine region-making in all its facets. Such a project would require us to track processes from the perspective of the United States and Americanization, China and Sinicization, Indonesia and Islamicization, and other Asian polities that are also creating distinctive terms of engagement with the region. So this book adopts a narrower empirical focus. If, however, it succeeds in making the case that, from the perspective of Japan, East Asian regionalism defies traditional understandings, other scholars can then inquire into hybrid regionalism from other national vantage points.

This argument may not convince those who think of Japan as a fading political and economic power. Contradicting Ezra Vogel's *Japan as Number One* (1979), Japan's best-selling song in 2002 had the title "It's O.K. Not to Be No. 1" (Onishi 2004a). Has not China displaced Japan as the leader in East Asia? Is not China the most likely challenger of U.S. primacy? Why then analyze East Asian regionalism from the perspective of Japan? These questions are rendered plausible by the favorable coverage China now receives in the media, reminiscent of the breathless adulation that was reserved for Japan in the 1980s. They are, however, unconvincing.

In terms of economic size Japan outranks China and will continue to do so for some time to come. In 2002 Japan accounted for 13.5 percent of global national income, compared to China's 3.5 percent (Beattie 2004). In terms of market exchanges, which best indicate regional power dynamics, Japan's GDP lead over China is roughly 4:1—about 40:1 on a per capita basis.[1] And after more than a decade of economic recession and deflation, Japan is still the second largest national economy in the world. China's GDP as a proportion of Japan's increased from 13 to 23 percent in the 1990s, and Japan's share of the combined regional GDP of Northeast and Southeast Asia declined from 72 to 65 percent.[2] This shift is significant, and all of China's

---

[1] GDP estimates vary widely between those calculated in market prices (as an approximate measure of relative power in the international economy) and those calculated in purchasing parity power (as a measure of comparative levels of total consumption). In terms of purchasing power parity China's GDP in 2000 exceeded Japan's by about one-third, whereas Japan's per capita income was six times larger than China's. See McNicoll 2004, 57–59.

[2] Calculated from the UN Common Data Base (http://unstats.un.org.//uns/cdb/, accessed February 9, 2004) as well as the National Statistics Office of Taiwan (http://www.stat.gov.tw, accessed February 9, 2004).

neighbors, Japan included, are taking due account of it. Yet these figures show that playing economic catch-up with Japan will take time.

Despite increases in its defense budget, China is a regional military power that lags well behind Japan in its total defense outlays and the technological sophistication of its military forces. China could easily take the Mischief Reef in the South China Sea from an impotent Philippine navy, but it is in no shape to take on the much better armed Japanese navy at the Senkaku Islands. China may be a serious threat to Taiwan, but it is highly doubtful whether it could successfully invade. China can pose regional military threats, but it is not a global rival for the United States and won't be for a very long time (Council on Foreign Relations 2003; Segal 1999, 29–32). This fact tilts the power imbalance even more toward a Japan that for half a century has enjoyed a durable alliance with the United States. Since Japan is likely to hold the middle ground between the United States and China, future power transitions in East Asia will be shaped decisively by how Japan and East Asia engage each other.

Finally, the technological sophistication of the Japanese economy and society continues to exceed China's by a large margin. China's entry into world markets is based on dependence on foreign firms for investment and technology. This fact circumscribes China's ability to become a technological rival to Japan or the United States. Since starting economic reform in 1978, China has taken in roughly $500 billion in foreign direct investment, ten times the amount Japan accumulated between 1945 and 2000. Foreign-funded firms accounted for 55 percent of China's exports and 85 percent of high-tech exports in 2002–3. Wholly owned foreign enterprises account for 65 percent of new foreign direct investment in China and dominate high-tech exports; they are less willing to transfer technology to Chinese firms than are joint ventures (Gilboy 2004, 36–41). The Chinese model of development thus differs radically from Japan's and Korea's in that it gives foreigners substantially more control over China's technology base.

In short, there is a difference between giving China its due and declaring Japan for all intents and purposes irrelevant. In the shifting balance of prestige China clearly has bested Japan since the mid-1990s. But a very large economic, military, and technological gap continues to divide where Japan is today and where China would like to be tomorrow.

In this chapter I address four issues. First, how do processes such as Japanization and Americanization combine, and what are the effects of increased Sinicization for an East Asian region that is truly hybrid? Second, which are the most important actors and mechanisms in East Asia's regionalization? Third, in which policy domains is a regional extension of national models still discernible, and in which have such models become fully fused? Finally, how can we think about East Asia and analyze its new dynamics of region-making?

Region-Making in East Asia: Beyond National Models

East Asia is more than the extension of specific national models. In some ways Japan and the United States are shaping East Asia through a variety of bargains. In others East Asia is being created by processes that make it virtually impossible to untangle distinct national influences. With specific reference to questions of technology, popular culture, and democracy, I illustrate both situations and so recap the main conclusion of chapters 4–9: East Asia is moving beyond the influence of national models.

Japanization

The concept of Japanization is an abstraction that refers to diverse empirical patterns (Elger and Smith 1994b, 37–38). Japanization does not offer fixed benchmarks by which to measure its spread. Rather, it involves open-ended processes of diffusion, emulation, and the adoption of distinctive patterns of production, consumption, and behavior. It thus does not yield clear copies of a template replicated in different national or local settings. The combining of patterns can result from deliberate organizational design, from ongoing gradual change in shared cognitive schemas and normative orders, and from political conflicts driven by competing interests. The most intensively studied instance of Japanization, the American automobile industry, indicates the importance of all three mechanisms (Westney 1999b, 385, 402–3). What holds for the Japanization of the U.S. auto industry also holds for the Japanization of East Asia.

In the 1980s the term "Japanization" was used to characterize the shift from an old to a new paradigm of production. It refers to the particular talent of Japanese firms in creating large productivity gains in the export of manufactured goods, such as cars, auto parts, and electrical products. It describes also the setting up of Japanese factories abroad, which has revolutionized the global automobile industry. More generally, "the notion of Japanization," Tony Elger and Chris Smith (1994a, 7) write, "has become a label for a fairly open-ended agenda of investigation rather than a set of strong claims about the scope and character of the spread of Japanese production techniques." Yet the awareness of a "Japanese model" increased with the spread of its foreign direct investment, especially after the mid-1980s. East Asian governments and automobile producers sought out Japanese investment and encouraged the introduction of new products and processes. The threat of U.S. protection encouraged Japanese firms to create new production platforms outside Japan. Furthermore, the Japanese government favored foreign direct investment as an attractive way of recycling Japan's large trade surplus. In the 1980s various actors with complex motivations pushed the process of Japanization.

By the early 1980s Japan began to challenge the leading position of the United States in key technologies. By the 1990s Japan had become a world leader in important technologies, making deep inroads into areas where U.S. firms had held unassailable positions only a couple of decades earlier (Hatch and Yamamura 1996, 97–98; Yakushiji 1986). Japanese policymakers regard technology as a precious national asset that needs to be guarded jealously (Katzenstein 1996, 138–42); Japanese producers are very eager to acquire technology and very reluctant to part with it. Richard Samuels has carefully analyzed this process. Since 1945 Japan has licensed tens of billions of dollars of technology developed elsewhere at the cost of hundreds of billion dollars. "What once was purchased," Samuels (1994, 187) writes, "soon was licensed for coproduction. What had been coproduced was then codeveloped. Budgets and politics willing, what is now codeveloped will be indigenized." In contrast to all other industrial economies, where the foreign share in patent applications increased, in Japan between the mid-1970s and mid-1980s it *declined* by about 50 percent. The foreign share in total patents is five to eight times larger in the United States and in Europe than in Japan.

On the export side the situation has been quite different. Japanese firms are reluctant to part with any technology until it has been fully commercialized, and the proportion of Japanese technology exports going to unaffiliated firms has declined (Hatch 2000, 356). This is a long-standing complaint among Japan's East Asian trading partners whose trade statistics reveal a deep technological dependence on Japan, their main supplier of crucial components. Taiwan's chip industry, for example, depends fully on Japanese equipment manufacturers. Korea's car industry is fully integrated into international production chains in which Japanese corporations often dominate. Product specialization and backward integration tighten the links between East Asian trading partners and Japan. While industries evolve dynamically, as Dieter Ernst shows in chapter 7 the unwillingness or inability of Japan to open its technological base is an irritant in Japan's relations with its neighbors (Bello 1993; Katzenstein 2003b). Japan remains remarkably insular and resists the pull of a global technological order—a stance that has regional ramifications.

Throughout East Asia during the 1990s a new wave of Japanization occurred that had little to do with the earlier one. As David Leheny (chapter 9) and Takashi Shiraishi (chapter 10) argue, Japanese popular culture has been increasingly embraced by the newly affluent younger "middle mass" in all of East Asia's major metropolitan areas. Japan's affluence and technological prowess have made deep inroads, and Japanese department stores and supermarkets have altered consumer cultures (Igarashi 1997, 7–9). In the 1990s the products of Japan's popular culture industries—songs, television shows, comics, toys, Pokemon games, fashion, and food—swept across East Asia with truly astounding speed. Japanese today is the most popular foreign language in Singapore. No longer is it viewed as a passport to a job with a Japanese company. It is instead the magic key that opens the door to Japan's popular culture. Student exchanges between Singapore and Japan have been small, but the creation of the Japanese Studies department at the National University of Singapore has served a growing student demand, even after Singapore's government began playing down its policy of learning from Japan. The department's pedagogical mission has been to learn about Japan from Singapore's cultural context rather than simply to foster the transplanting of Japanese social practices.

Today, Japan's popular culture has global appeal. "Hello Kitty" is Western so she will sell in Japan, and she is Japanese so she will sell in the West (McGray 2002, 50). Part of the attraction of Japan's culture industries is their flexible and absorptive character. Japan's cultural products and idiom facilitate regional spread, and not conveying a distinctly Japanese message is their greatest commercial strength. As Anne Allison (2004, 47–48) concludes:

> Japan's cultural industries have touched a pulse in the imaginations and lives of millennial children in this era of cybertechnology and postindustrial socialization. They have done this by blending flexibility and fantasy into technology that is conveniently portable, virtuality that is intimately cute, and a commodity form that is polymorphously perverse. And, as its stock in the marketplace of children's entertainment rises (slowly) around the world, Japan is moving itself closer to the center of global culture. One consequence of this is the decentering of cultural (entertainment) trends once hegemonized by Euroamerica (and particularly the United States).

This conclusion fits with what we know about Japan's stance on democratization in Asia (Inoguchi 2000). As the largest or second largest aid donor in the world, Japan typically eschews an explicitly political stance (Miyashita 2003; Arase 1995; Orr 1990). Japanese policy aims instead at improving the conditions for sustained economic growth, often in a manner that helps Japanese business interests as well as East Asian economic growth and political stability. When the United States asks for a more politicized approach to economic issues, for example by imposing sanctions to express political disapproval, Japan tends to follow if it must but not because of a conviction that such policies are sensible.[3] The creation of vibrant export markets in Asia is a core interest of Japan's aid policy in the short and medium term, but the government considers the creation of vibrant democracies a long-term affair that cannot be accelerated by the economic instruments of statecraft.

---

[3] Japanese skepticism about the overt politicization of economic aid is supported, amply, by Thomas Carothers's (1999, 171, 181–82, 250–51, 308, 332) conclusion regarding the extremely limited accomplishments of American policies seeking to export democracy.

The experience of Singapore illustrates how Japanization works under relatively favorable conditions. Singapore started its well-orchestrated "Learn from Japan" campaign in the early 1980s. Because it is small, in relative terms the number of Japanese investors and the amount of Japanese foreign direct investment in Singapore has loomed large. If any place in East Asia was exposed to the concentrated influence of Japanization, it was Singapore. Furthermore, Singapore had modernized without losing its identity and had refurbished Western models of modernity to suit East Asian contexts, so officials there considered Japan especially relevant.

Some Japanese practices and models were not suited to Singaporean conditions. Japanese-style management, for example, was inappropriate even for Japanese-affiliated enterprises. Singapore's individualism, lack of company loyalty, limited reliance on big manufacturing plants, and ethnically heterogeneous society provided too stark a contrast for the successful adoption of unmodified Japanese management. With the family as the cornerstone of Singaporean society, it seemed impossible to switch to Japan's group culture with the company as the basic cultural unit (Thang and Gan 2000, 11). Japanese institutions and practices were of greater relevance on other issues. Quality control circles, for instance, were introduced in Singapore on a large scale in the 1980s. So was Japanese-style neighborhood policing, for which demand was high despite a crime rate lower than Tokyo's (Katzenstein 1996, 93).

Singapore's various experiences with Japanization reveal some regularities: initial assistance from Japan and at times close emulation of Japanese institutions and social practices yield eventually to modifications to suit local circumstances and, later, to growing indifference. Far from worrying about the pervasive influence of Japanization, Leng Thang and S. K. Gan (2000, 21) conclude that "it is paradoxical that Japanese influence is extremely modest when compared with the prominent Japanese presence in Singapore since the 'learn from Japan' era." More generally, the movement to learn from Japan slowed dramatically in the second half of the 1990s. "There is widespread skepticism in much of Asia," writes T. J. Pempel (1997, 76), "about the wisdom of emulating any alleged 'Japanese model,' following Japan's leadership, or allowing Japan to be Asia's main bridge to the West." In a nutshell, in the making of an East Asian region, "flying-geese-style Japanization" is out, "beyond Japanization" is in.

Americanization

What is true of Japanization is also true of Americanization. More than a century ago William Stead (1901) argued that the New World was having a big impact on the Old. Even then Stead's argument contained only a half truth: America was indeed affecting the world, but the world was also affecting America. *Webster's Third New International Dictionary* defines "Americanization" as the process by which immigrants were made into Americans. Not any longer. The processes that link the United States, East Asia, and the world have become increasingly complex in fusing different national influences.

Americanization is a close cousin to globalization and Westernization, but it is analytically distinct. Globalization results both from generic modernization and from specific adoptions of U.S. products and practices (Nye 2000). Since the seventeenth century globalization created America, rather than the other way around, primarily by bringing peoples, both free and enslaved, in large numbers to the New World. Today, because of the size of the U.S. domestic market and its leading position in information technologies, many of the products of modernity appear in other countries in American guise and thus are easily mistaken as products only of Americanization. They are not. Furthermore, because of the U.S. openness to immigration, many products—pizza, hamburgers, and frankfurters among them—appear to be genuinely American even though they are in fact imports.

Americanization is marked by the legacy of two hundred years of Anglo-American preponderance in world politics. Preponderance can be measured in terms of both material capabilities and institutional and ideological appeal. This is as much true of American preponderance in East Asia today as it was half a century ago. But the present is distinctive because of the growing importance of processes no longer defined by the logic of traditional power politics.

The United States emerged from World War II as the undisputed global technological leader. Since the early 1970s, one study reports, about two-thirds of the international supply of disembodied proprietary technology has been of U.S. origin, with the United Kingdom running a distant second (Ernst and O'Connor 1989, 29).[4] U.S. corporations increased their overseas R & D expenditures from 7 to 10 percent between 1977 and the mid-1990s, dwarfing corresponding figures for German and Japanese corporations (Howells and Wood 1993, 22–23; Pauly and Reich 1997, 13–15). As Dieter Ernst (chapter 7) shows, after a Japanese surge in the 1970s and 1980s, the technology gap between the United States and Japan has again widened since the mid-1990s.

Americanization refers also to the appropriation of American popular culture by different social strata, groups, and generations, each creating specific subcultures and all together constituting a national culture (Jarausch and Siegrist 1997, 14–16). Research into the Americanization of the young, everyday life, gender roles, generational change, literature, popular music,

---

[4] This estimate is based on an imperfect statistical indicator, the national technological balance of payments, which covers only a part of international technology flows (including the sale of patents, licensing agreements, provision of know-how, and technical assistance).

film, and television gives us insight into complex processes of cultural and social change in East Asia. Americanization has both positive (affluence, modernity, tolerance, enlightenment) and negative (non-Asian, culturally inferior,
superficial, materialist, profit-hungry) connotations. Positive and negative
connotations are indelibly fused in the concepts of democracy and capitalism. In the 1950s and 1960s the American way of life became accessible to a
thin strata in East Asia. A generation later pervasive changes in the major metropolitan areas in East Asia have transformed accessibility into familiarity. Students of popular culture use concepts such as "cultural creolization" (Kroes
1996, 164) to underline the active role that local actors play in the selection
and appropriation of American mass culture. "Self-Americanization" (Maase
1997, 223–26) is not a bad way to capture the repertoire of practices open to
numerous recombinations by those who operate not in homogeneous national societies but in complex networks of variegated cultural affinities.

"Americanization," writes Gerd Gemünden (1998, 17), "is far from being
a unified or unifying process." Hollywood, for example, is to a substantial degree owned by non-Americans and many of its most famous directors and actors are non-American. Paralleling developments in the recording industry,
in the early 1990s only three of the seven major Hollywood studios were controlled by U.S. corporations: Disney, Paramount, and Warner Brothers. Yet
national ownership had little impact on the way films were conceived and
made in Hollywood. Indeed, the influx of foreign movie makers stretches
back to the 1920s and 1930s. In terms of ownership and artistic talent, Hollywood is the world. "Odds are good," writes James Verniere (1999), "that
your favorite American movie classic was directed by someone from somewhere else." Like "Self- Americanization," the "Other-Americanization" of the
contemporary U.S. popular culture industries illustrates the hybridity and
polymorphism of the United States and its global entertainment industry.

Democracy is a third aspect illustrating Americanization. Since its beginning perhaps the most important aspect of America's mission in world politics has been Wilsonian—to make the world safe for democracy through both
emulation and war. Other actors in world politics have also tried to strengthen
the forces of democracy: Britain in some of its former colonies in the 1950s
and 1960s; the European Union in southern and central Europe in the 1970s
and 1990s; and nongovernmental organizations ranging from the Catholic
Church to Amnesty International in Latin America, Asia, and central and eastern Europe. In historical and comparative perspective, however, the American effort, and the ambiguous results it has spawned, stands out (Smith 1994;
Carothers 1999; Diamond 1999; Rose 2000–2001). President Reagan's insistence on effecting a global "democratic revolution," starting with Central
America and Central Europe, preceded the U.S. attempt to spread democracy on a worldwide scale. Among the numerous and often contradictory rea-

sons the Bush administration advanced to justify its attack on Iraq in 2003, the expected benefits of democracy in Iraq have figured prominently.

The spread of democracy in Asia has been an integral part of this American-inspired revolution. The Philippines (1986), South Korea (1987–88), Taiwan (in the 1990s), and Indonesia (1998) have adopted democratic systems of government. In China and Burma democratization movements were suppressed. In other Asian countries hard or soft authoritarian governments persist even though economic and social transformations proceed at an extraordinarily rapid pace. Although the decisive impetus for democratization in Asia came from domestic politics, external support for democratic opposition movements made some difference at specific times. South Korea's democratization was helped by the political support that the U.S. administration gave to the objective of democratization after the mid-1980s (Muravchik 1991). Though long a stout supporter of the authoritarian Marcos regime, at its very end the U.S. government switched sides and facilitated the transition to democracy. Moreover, the Suharto regime fell in the wake of the Asian financial crisis. Tough economic and political demands from the International Monetary Fund helped topple a repressive regime the U.S. government had supported for decades.

"The rise and dominance of America," writes Fareed Zakaria (2003, 3), "has made democratization seem inevitable." But democracy Asian-style contradicts the American preconception that free markets and democracy work hand in hand (Smith 1994, 291–97). As both doctrine and policy, for example, Reaganomics held that shrinking the role of the government in the economy would strengthen both civil society and political democracy. Whatever the merits of the U.S. model may be, the East Asian economic miracle did not support this central claim. It demonstrated instead that democratization can occur with market competition flourishing despite government intervention (Zakaria 2003, 55–57, 87). In Asian democratization, political and social hierarchies have been redefined, and mass-based politics has become an important engine of social change. East Asia thus points to the relevance of a democratization that plays itself out as much in the shopping mall as in the voting booth.

Hybrid Regionalism and Sinicization

In East Asia the processes of Japanization and Americanization have fused to create regionalization that goes beyond any one national model. In the 1950s, 1960s and 1970s American GIs, the first demands for the liberalization of trade and capital, growing foreign direct investment, jazz, rock music, and chewing gum, cartoons and Disney animation, sitcoms and chocolates, Coca-Cola and Lucky Strikes all spread the promise of the American way of life. The growing relative power of the United States in world politics, increasing liberalization in trade and capital flows, the spread of cross-border production networks and technology flows, environmental degradation and the political countermovement it spawned, fast-food chains, Hollywood action movies, and American pop music deepened the Americanization of East Asia in the 1980s and 1990s.

This Americanization has fused with Japanization. Japan's underlying cultural similarity with other East Asian societies and Japan's longer exposure to Americanization have given it a central role in mediating connections between East Asia and the United States. Japan's popular culture industry, for example, often acts to rework Western sensibilities to fit East Asia. This is true also in fashion, where Japan translates American and European ideas into "senses of pitch, color, taste, and emotion that it shares in common with East Asia" not with the West (Igarashi 1997, 11). Because of its special relationship with the United States, Japan also mediates the geostrategic and commercial demands and expectations of U.S. governments in East Asia. In this mediation, Japanization leaves a less clear imprint on individual consciousness and collective ideology. Japan's popular culture products, for example, are perfect vessels for transporting a common cultural experience across East Asia. Japanese comics are becoming East Asian comics. The mixing of Americanization and Japanization is not so much transmitting distinctive national models as it is helping to spark hybrid regionalism.

The rise of China and East Asia's "Sinicization" is reinforcing that trend. Sinicization refers here to both the growing importance of China *and* the social, economic, and political reassertion of the Chinese populations living in Southeast Asia.

In the last two decades China has made great strides, and today a growing number of observers are speculating about the coming of a pax sinica: East Asian states will not balance against China but bandwagon with it as China rises. The recent track record of such speculations does not inspire confidence. An impending pax nipponica ended when the financial bubble burst; pax americana yielded in a few short years to a deficit-addicted, nervous United States trapped in a war of its own choosing. China's sheer size is having a large effect on East Asia, it is true, and that effect is growing quickly (Kokubun and Wang 2004). Yet Sinicization is not remaking East Asia in the likeness of China. Takashi Shiraishi's analysis in chapter 10 points us instead in another direction. The Sinicization of Southeast Asia has worked itself out in different ways in different countries. Ethnic Chinese make up large parts of the professional classes in Southeast Asia and control large segments of the business sector in various countries. The influx of Japanese capital after 1985 affected these Chinese strata differently, yielding a Sinicization that has proved remarkably variable at the regional level. Sinicization is important because it results in a hybrid regionalism that makes it virtually impossible to disentangle different national strands. The important role that the overseas Chinese play in East Asia reinforces the hybrid nature of the region.

The overseas Chinese suffered greatly in the middle of the twentieth century. They were devastated by the effects of the Great Depression, the Pacific War, Japanese occupation, and nationalist anticolonial revolutions. Politically cut off from China between the 1950s and the 1970s, the Chinese in Southeast Asia were subject to assimilationist policies that Southeast Asian governments imposed as part of nation-building. The economic power of Chinese businessmen began to grow once again in the 1960s as they eventually moved beyond national into regional and global markets, increasingly as trusted supporters of rather than despised pariahs in Southeast Asian polities. In a carefully calibrated strategy Chinese businessmen invested in roughly equal proportions in Southeast Asia, China, and the United States. Upper class and upper-middle-class Chinese, especially in Indonesia and Thailand, began sending their children to high schools in Hong Kong and Singapore, for better training in Mandarin and English, and to the United States and the United Kingdom, for university and professional education. Even though they retain Hokkien, Cantonese, or Teochew as their mother tongues, Chinese businessmen no longer rely on local dialects for business. Nor does this new generation of Chinese use clan or regional ties to build social networks. Trilingual in Mandarin, English, and a mother tongue, they use their Chineseness as the key to their networks. Sinicization is a market-driven phenomenon intimately connected with the rise of China, for the overwhelming share of the foreign investment that has helped catapult China forward is owned by ethnic Chinese who live in Southeast Asia.

What do the case studies in this book suggest about Sinicization? On questions of security (chapter 4), it is clear that China's sheer size is beginning to create novel security predicaments on issues such as the organized smuggling of illegal immigrants and drugs as well as the encroachment of Chinese gangs in national and regional markets for gambling and prostitution. On the more conventional issue of military security China also looms large. The highly volatile Taiwan issue is a powder keg for the entire region. Historical memory also provides ample sources of animosity, and not only in relations between China and Japan. In the summer of 2004, Chinese-Korean relations soured dramatically when China attempted to claim the Koguryo kingdom (37 BC to AD 668) as a Chinese vassal state rather than acknowledge it as the forerunner of the Korean nation (Brooke 2004). On financial questions (chapter 5), in October 2003 the combined reserves of China ($406 billion), Hong Kong ($112 billion), and Taiwan ($197 billion) were larger than Japan's ($617 billion), exceeded those of the European Union ($350 billion) by a factor of two, and dwarfed those of the United States ($73 billion) by a factor of ten. Still it seems far-fetched to envision the Sinicization of East Asian financial relations after the response of the United States and Japan to the Asian financial crisis and its aftermath was found to be so inadequate (Bowles 2002). The formal or informal pegging of the Chinese currency to the dollar and agreements to participate in regional currency swaps are noteworthy, yet far removed from imposing anything like a Chinese model on East Asia's financial arrangements. On trade questions (chapter 6), China's agreement with the Association of Southeast Asian Nations (ASEAN) to negotiate a free trade agreement has accelerated Japan's movement in the same direction, complemented by a growing number of bilateral arrangements linking Japan to Southeast Asian economies. Because many trade relations between China and Japan continue to be complementary, and because China will confront problems with the implementation of international agreements for many years to come, it seems likely that Sinicization will blend in, rather than supplant, a hybrid mixture (Pilling and McGregor 2004; Perlez 2002). Region-wide trade arrangements are moving well beyond specific national models.

Taiwan and the overseas Chinese have been central in creating East Asia's regional production networks (chapter 7). This development was spurred less by Chinese initiatives and more by shifts in the competitive position of Japanese and American firms in specific sectors. Still, the rise of the Chinese electronics industry—as a base for export production, as a sophisticated growth market, and as a source of innovation and specialized skills—is likely to have lasting effects on East Asia. In electronics China will contribute to the synergistic processes that are central for the continued expansion of Japanese exports and economic growth. These will define East Asian regionalization beyond any specific national model. China's market size and dynamic adjustment have also played a large role in the reorganization of East Asia's ecology (chapter 8), displacing to China, in some instances in only a few years, the large ecological shadow Japan once cast over Southeast Asia. China's trade with Japan in resource-intensive products, from poultry to furniture, and its vegetable exports have increased disproportionately, creating a serious problem for Japan's traditional agro-export zone in Southeast Asia. It also saddles China with serious ecological problems. Finally, with the opening of China's popular culture market to imports, the emergence of an East Asian popular culture is well under way (chapter 9)—complementing rather than substituting for the Japanization that has rapidly altered East Asia's urban economies, especially among the young. In popular music, for example, the songs of Hong Kong stars such as Jacky Cheung show the strong influence of Japanese pop. Virtually unknown in Japan, a Japanese pop star groomed for East Asian markets, Chiba Mika, has had tremendous success in China, Taiwan, and throughout Southeast Asia. Hong Kong's comic book industry, personalized by Tony Wong, the founder of Jademan, has rested for years on pirated editions of Japanese manga (comic books). The same is true of Taiwan where the Tong Li Publishing Company, run by Fang Wennan, released more than one thousand titles over a fifteen-year period (Schodt 1996, 306–7). And Hong Kong and Taiwan are gateways to China's domestic market, which has shown enormous receptivity to Japanese manga and anime.

What is true for popular culture is true more generally. In the emergence of East Asia it is impossible to untangle Japanization, Americanization, and Sinicization. North of Beijing, for example, upscale homes at the "Orange County" development cost upward of half a million dollars (Rosenthal 2003). And Japanese-style convenience stores (*konbini*) are spreading rapidly in South Korea (Fukunaga 2003). International markets versus state control, cultural cosmopolitanism versus postcolonial nationalism, urban versus agricultural life, maritime-coastal versus interior-continental geographies—such oppositions do not capture the hybrid East Asia that is emerging. A new social foundation for East Asian societies does, as Takashi Shiraishi argues in the concluding chapter. "About a dozen metropolitan regions in East Asia—representing a fraction of one percent of the region's land area and less than 7 percent of its total population—collectively account for about 80 to 90 percent of the region's international activities," projecting a bubbling consumerism that reflects "a networked regionalism which in turn rests on global capitalism" (Rohlen 2002, 8, 9). National models no longer supplant one another in sequential fashion. Instead they fuse and yield unexpected regional patterns. Such hybridity undermines established preconceptions about the differences that separate Japan from China, or Orient from Occident. From Tokyo and Los Angeles to Singapore and Seattle, from Shanghai to Ho Chi Minh City, extending beyond all national models and fusing into a new regionalism, East Asia offers us a glimpse of a future marked by unexplored opportunities and new challenges.

Actors and Mechanisms

Regionalism beyond national models yields a complex picture. Explicit attention to the actors and mechanisms that create regionalization in East Asia helps us understand the processes by which the region is moving beyond specific national models.

Actors

Actors include governments, corporations, nongovernmental organizations, and individual citizens and consumers. Governments are central in the politically directed domains dealing with security, finance, and trade. The prime minister, Ministry of Foreign Affairs, the Defense Agency, and the National Police Agency, as well as the U.S. departments of State and Defense, are all central to the evolution of Japanese security policy in an East Asia that remains greatly influenced by the United States. Chapters 5 and 6 show that the same is true to different degrees in finance and trade. The Asian financial crisis in 1997 and the Seattle meeting of the World Trade Organization in 1999 revealed a far-reaching politicization that makes governments rather than bureaucrats the drivers of Asia's financial and trade orders. Governments are also the central actors in intergovernmental organizations that operate at the global or regional level, such as the IMF, the World Bank, and ASEAN, as well as the World Trade Organization.

In contrast, as the case studies in electronics, ecology and agribusiness, and popular culture illustrate, transnational and multinational corporations are much more important in regional production networks. The distinction between these two types of corporate actors is not a hard-and-fast one, either analytically or empirically. Viewed from the perspective of either "national business systems" or "global corporate governance" they are both vitally important actors in East Asia.

In terms of ownership, control, top management, and legal nationality, only a handful of corporations are truly *trans*national. They have headquarters mostly in the small European states and include a few binational corporations. Transnational corporations are shaped by globalization and face the problem of coordinating activities across far-flung markets. They must cope with global requirements of best practice, nationally specific sets of institutional constraints and opportunities, and specific corporate histories and cultures (Dörrenbächer 1999, 21–62). To survive in global markets such corporations often create complex, hierarchical networks. With financial and physical capital increasingly mobile, and with technologies compressing both time and space, protective national cushions are increasingly stripped away. Such corporations are transforming the global economy into an island that in the words of Kenichi Ohmae (1990, x–xi) "is bigger than a continent— the Interlinked Economy (ILE) of the Triad (the United States, Europe, and Japan), joined by high-growth economies such as Taiwan, Hong Kong, and Singapore." Chapter 7 offers some evidence to support this view.

Competition between *multi*national firms is driven by the worldwide expansion and integration of core corporate functions, including R & D, and the growth of strategic alliances among different producers. Multinational corporations continue to be shaped primarily by the national ideological and institutional context in which they started operations. In their activities they largely target markets in North America, Europe, and East Asia. By whatever indicator one chooses—productivity, value-added, employment, or profits— these corporations have grown disproportionately during the last two de-

cades. Their success creates new forms of competition between and cooperation among national economies. By the early 1990s, their operations had
reached levels of importance that were last seen before World War I. Yet "stateless operations," writes Yao-Su Hu (1992, 108), "do not necessarily mean
stateless corporations." For the most part the national base of corporations
with far-flung international operations remains unquestioned. Robert Gilpin
(1975) argued this point long ago when he observed that the primacy of U.S.
multinational corporations was due not to a liberal international economic
order but to the political power of the United States. With an impressive array of empirical evidence, Paul Doremus and his colleagues (1998) provide
confirmation of this: enduring national political structures shape the operations of those corporations. This is true in East Asia. Supported by the political foundations of a liberalizing regional economy and backed by smart
corporate and governmental policies, Japanese corporations have spread
throughout East Asia, as chapters 7 and 8 show.

Consumption politics, for example in the areas of food and popular culture (chapters 8 and 9), primarily reflect the choices of individuals. Changes
in work and family life, for example, have cultivated individual tastes and developed markets for frozen foods and foreign travel. Such developments are
having a profound impact on East Asia's political ecology. This is not to deny
the role of individuals in other issue areas: professionals from a broad array
of backgrounds attend the track-two and track-three meetings through which
governments, think tanks, and private institutions exchange information on
issues of security. Criminals organize the smuggling of illegal immigrants and
the illegal trade in drugs. Businessmen and academics attend innumerable
conferences and workshops to discuss pressing issues of finance and trade.
And social movement activists and individual consumers typically meet in the
virtual space that the World Wide Web offers to debate how to further social
change. In one way or another, they all are participants in region-making in
East Asia.

Mechanisms

A variety of mechanisms help make a region in contemporary East Asia, and
the six case studies provide rich illustrations. The studies span only a decade
or two and so do not offer sufficient data for tracing extended causal chains
of regional processes. No such explanation is offered here. Yet the cases suggest some interesting preliminary results. On questions of security, chapter 4
argues that the U.S. government relied in the 1990s on a mixture of coercive
and persuasive bargaining to extend Japan's policy to broader regional interests. On some aspects of internal security, such as Japan's counterterrorism policy, Japanese policy is evidently learning from U.S. police practices. By

contrast, East Asian governments have had only a minor influence on Japan and Japanese policy. Tentative movements toward multilateral security arrangements point to possible changes in the future based on techniques of persuasive bargaining that might help overcome South Korea's and China's painful historical memories. In sharp contrast, Japan's response to the threat that North Korea poses to its security contains strong elements of coercive bargaining. In sum, on questions of national and international security, emulation as well as bargaining shape region-making, rather than outright coercion, mutual interests, or pure persuasion.

On questions of trade policy, chapter 6 argues that interest-based rather than coercive or persuasive bargaining is the typical mechanism in region-making. In trade, in sharp contrast to security, one striking innovation of the last five years has been a move by the Japanese government and others, such as Singapore, to complement cumbersome multilateral with more flexible bilateral free trade agreements. The decision to pursue such an agreement with South Korea in the summer of 2003 is the most important illustration of this trend to date. Because differences in market size inevitably create asymmetric vulnerability, moves toward trade liberalization may heighten rather than flatten political hierarchies in East Asia. Volatility and vulnerability loom even larger on questions of finance, as chapter 5 demonstrates. The absence of bilateral or multilateral policy coordination, unlike that on national security and trade issues, has left East Asian governments open to large-scale disruptions, as the financial crisis of 1997 so clearly illustrated. In response, persuasion, information sharing, crisis-based learning, knowledge-based bargaining especially in and around the IMF, and mutual standard-setting have defined region-making in East Asia, linked to the instabilities of global financial markets and a policy consensus that continues to be defined largely, though no longer exclusively, by the U.S. government. In sum, most important in these three cases are different types of bargaining and different types of learning, standard-setting, and information sharing. Furthermore, the cases illustrate movement toward some multilateral arrangements in domains where bilateralism still reigns supreme. They also illustrate movement toward bilateral deals where multilateralism prevails.

In the other three cases competitive collaboration and emulation are prominent mechanisms. Regional production networks, chapter 7 shows, are marked by both technology competition and collaboration; and a regionwide organization of manufacturing mixes rivalry, imitation, and joint technology development. On questions of ecology, chapter 8 demonstrates, Japanese corporations are finding new ways of organizing trade and transferring technology to other East Asian firms. Japanese supermarkets and convenience stores are experimenting with new marketing strategies. And Japanese consumers are developing new tastes and consumption patterns. Furthermore, environmental change has a direct effect on the way East Asia's regional political economy is organized. In region-making the specific modalities of actor bargaining and crisis-based learning interact with the material and unmediated effects of environmental degradation. Finally, on questions of popular culture, chapter 9 shows how market competition and social imitation are mechanisms that bring about social and economic change.

Although these observations are insufficient for systematic inferences about region-making in East Asia, they yield one preliminary finding. Sectors experiencing different rates of change and marked by the practices of different actors reveal different mechanisms. East Asian regionalism is widely acknowledged to rely on informal market institutions more than on formal political arrangements. New, market-based mechanisms centering on competition and imitation now yield a hybrid outcome that differs greatly from the traditional "flying geese" model that once characterized the relationship between Japan and East Asia.

Beyond National Models

Japan and East Asia are embarking on a new phase of their mutual engagement. A precise dating of the current transition remains a matter of some controversy, but most would agree that it falls somewhere between the bursting of the Japanese economic bubble around 1990 and the Asian financial crisis of 1997. Whatever date we choose, one thing is certain: Japan no longer offers other East Asian states an appealing, state-led model of economic and social development.

Part I argues that a new regionalization is emerging from a Japan that exhibits new political, economic, and social patterns of behavior but that has not, as of yet, experienced a structural transformation (Pempel 1998; Schwartz and Pharr 2003). In Japanese politics a dominant socioeconomic coalition, a set of formal institutional arrangements, and a particular policy mix no longer reinforce one another, ending Japan's famed developmental state. Furthermore, the model of Japanese society as one wholesome family has been eviscerated by social practices increasingly at odds with public ideology. A myriad of changes marked Japanese society in the 1990s: a new style of political leadership, more professionalism and less pork in party politics, a shift in generations bringing about a rise in the importance of independent voters, a decline in the power of bureaucrats, and new roles for women, immigrants, the media, consumer advocacy groups, and the nonprofit sector. At the same time political and social structures evince a great deal of institutional stickiness. The combination of behavioral changes and institutional continuities has hollowed out what was once a coherent national model.

Part II analyzes changes that primarily engage governments and corporations on questions of security, finance, and trade. After a moment of uncertainty in the early years of the Clinton administration, Japan's alignment with the United States on questions of security has deepened. At the same time, the Japanese government became intent on defending a supposedly homogeneous and crime-free Japan against regional threats posed by illegal immigrants, organized crime, and drug trafficking. In the construction of East Asia's financial order, meanwhile, Japan has straddled half-hearted resistance to and half-hearted support of the "Washington consensus" promoted by the IMF and the U.S. Treasury Department. Finally, in East Asia's evolving trade regime Japanese initiatives in promoting trade liberalization bilaterally have complemented the United States and the World Trade Organization's efforts to liberalize multilaterally. Across all three domains governments and corporations create practices shaped in variable proportions by the United States and Japan.

Part III focuses attention on issues that involve not only governments and corporations but a large number of other actors dealing with technology, ecology, consumption, and lifestyle issues that reflect the emergence of an urban middle class in East Asia's major metropolitan areas. The growth of regional production networks in East Asia's electronics industry, for example, reflects a slippage of Japanese and a reassertion of American corporations—and the rise of Taiwanese, Korean, and other producers throughout Southeast Asia. Rather than substitute one national model for another, however, a more complex regionalization is emerging, marked by new actors, an overall pattern of persistent diversity marked by partial convergences and multilayered regional networks that are more or less hierarchical in their control over technology, product development, and marketing. In resource-intensive sectors, shifts in Japanese consumer demand shape the exploitation of renewable resources. An extended chain connects the choices of Japanese consumers at the microlevel with ecological outcomes at the macrolevel, mediated by markets and politics. Changes in lifestyle, the evolution of agro-industrial sectors, and environmental degradation are all part of a seamless web. The same is true of Japan's popular culture industries. Individual lifestyle choices have created a strong demand for the creativity of Japanese pop artists and fast-changing products in East Asian markets. The government's media policy seeks to exploit these regional developments to Japan's national advantage. Japanese politicians seek to exploit the notion that Japan is accumulating "soft power"[5] in East Asia—a dubious claim that nonetheless resonates with the durable notion that it is Japan's special role to mediate between East Asia and the West.

---

[5] Joseph Nye (2002, 8–9) defines soft power as "getting others to want what you want" because of admiring one's values and emulating one's example.

The book ends with the argument that East Asia's new regionalism is both the creation and the product of a new class structure in East Asia's major metropolitan areas. A common lifestyle and consciousness is emerging, with political consequences that remain largely undefined.

The End of the Japanese Model? Institutional and Behavioral Disjunctures

T. J. Pempel addresses in chapter 2 one notable development of the 1990s: the puzzling convergence of democratic institutions, political stasis, and negative economic performance. Under conditions that seem to merit at least a change in government, perhaps even in regime, Japanese politics has been marked by institutional continuities. Poor economic performance throughout the 1990s failed to spur far-ranging institutional experimentation. Procedural change did occur in Japan's electoral system, in the structure of the party system, in the system of bureaucracy, in the strengthening of executive powers, in the unwinding of long-standing, interlocking business ties, and in Japanese finance. The political struggles over institutional and policy reforms have pitted different factions of well-established insiders against one another. Yet Japan's "uncommon democracy" (Pempel 1990) did not witness a phenomenon normal in other democracies that have run into hard times since the late 1970s: well-organized outsiders battling entrenched insiders. Instead, Japanese insiders, locked into an old but no longer viable model of political economy, have prevented significant policy change. External pressure from the United States declined together with Japan's international standing, but various government agencies, especially the Ministry of Economy, Trade, and Industry (METI, formerly the Ministry of International Trade and Industry), are now using their own versions of pressure (*naiatsu*) to force the pace of domestic reform, for example, by pursuing bilateral free trade agreements that will expose sheltered economic sectors to foreign competition. At the same time, underlying structural change includes the growing role of foreign direct investment, the aging of Japan's population, and a changing international security environment. These developments are bound to have institutional consequences. Chapter 2 suggests that Japan spent a decade establishing a new political balance, one that seems better poised to cope with longstanding economic problems.

In their analysis of Japanese society in chapter 3, William Kelly and Merry White point to a similar disjuncture between behavioral change and institutional immobility. Their starting point is the public ideology of Japan as a familial nation focused on a competitive economy and unique cultural values. Over time this ideology has become increasingly irrelevant to the way many Japanese lead their lives—individuals are now freer to experiment. Have powerful actors lost control over the formulation of compelling ideological images? Or has their position eroded in central institutions such as the family, school, and workplace? Whatever the answer, a once-persuasive public ideology has much less effect on lifestyle now than in the past. Social institutions are losing their capacity to enforce the conventional ideology and the behaviors it prescribes. When a twenty-year old, Hitomi Kanehara, shared Japan's top literary prize in 2004 with a nineteen-year old, Japan had two best-selling novels that grappled with the first post-bubble generation's lack of expectations and its intense desire for personal satisfaction (Onishi 2004b). Japan's definition and enactment of ideas of social normality now have an unmistakable brittleness.

Looking at the experience of five groups typically viewed as outside the ideological mainstream, Kelly and White illustrate the range of everyday choices for ordinary Japanese. These choices undercut, counteract, and in the end hollow out a public ideology that is less and less in touch with social reality. Students, slackers, singles, seniors, and strangers are experimenting with new social practices that erode a national middle class and the agreement about what the national mainstream looks like. In doing so they stretch, and at times shatter, the carefully nurtured official ideology of Japan as a harmonious family. Rather than wait for potentially cataclysmic change in the political sphere, individuals are bringing about important change in the interstices of society even when Japan lacks social institutions to support such behavioral innovations.

Moving beyond One National Model

The hollowing out of Japan's political and social models has transformed region-making in East Asia. The United States and Japan supply alternative models that inform policy in domains such as security, finance, and trade. In Japan national security is conceived in "comprehensive" terms, encompassing both traditional military and novel social issues, as chapter 4 shows. Political and social changes have yielded at best marginal institutional and policy change. Such change has not depended on regional developments. The disintegration of Japan's Socialist Party removed a major domestic roadblock to a redefinition of Japan's military policy (something the United States has ardently pushed for since the early 1980s). In deploying troops in Iraq, Japan's government finally crossed a postwar watershed. Although the decision seems to cement Japan's security relationship with the United States, in fact the terms of deployment are carefully circumscribed. Nor is it clear what the consequences will be for pressing regional security issues in East Asia: North Korea's missile program and possible production of weapons of mass destruction, the Japanese commitment to a theater missile defense program, and most important the conflict over Taiwan. Will Japan continue to rely strongly on the United States as it wages a global war on terrorism? Will it seek a regional response through government-to-government negotiations in the Asian Regional Forum, military visits and exercises, and participation in track two? Or will it continue to combine the two options as it did throughout the 1990s?

On issues of internal security, the Japanese police have reacted defensively to regional developments. Because the police lack good contacts with resident communities of foreigners, their job is made even more difficult by the declining role of Japan's crime families, the yakuza. The threat that regional developments pose to Japan's homogeneity as a family nation, moreover, no longer offers the political traction it once did. Still, the police have been quite successful in making their definition of the threats from the region help define Japan's defensive stance. In an era of increasing regional security cooperation Japan continues to favor bilateral arrangements with the United States and other states. Finally, Japan's counterterrorism policy points to high variation in the political definition of threat. The police did everything to downplay the first use of weapons of mass destruction by a terrorist organization, Aum Shinrikyo's sarin gas attacks in the Tokyo subway in 1995. It is now seizing a central role in a war on terrorism that the United States has chosen to fight primarily with military means.

Besides state security, no other problem is as centrally connected to all domains of political, economic, and social life as finance. Natasha Hamilton-Hart argues in chapter 5 that as with external security, the regionalization of the financial sector is intimately linked to global developments. The cooperative realignment of the dollar-yen exchange rate after 1985 set the stage for the growth of regional trade and production links. It also prepared the ground for Japan to seize the initiative as the United States failed to respond to the Asian financial crisis in the summer of 1997. Convinced of the correctness of economic fundamentals in most of East Asia, Japan saw that the greatest need was the provision of short-term liquidity—the $17-billion rescue package for Thailand was put together under Japanese leadership and without U.S. participation—rather than fundamental economic restructuring and far-reaching liberalization. In 1997, Japan thus asked that the quotas of the East Asian members of the IMF be increased, to allow the IMF to respond to future crises in a more orderly fashion. In addition Japan asked for the creation of an Asian monetary fund. The United States and the IMF strongly opposed Japan's initiative. Instead the IMF mobilized sufficient reserves to stabilize the finances of South Korea and Indonesia.

Japan's policy initiative did not get off the ground, but only fourteen months later U.S. policymakers were conceding that the Japanese approach would probably have been better than the harsh structural reforms imposed by the Washington consensus. The IMF and the U.S. Treasury forced on Indonesia macroeconomic fiscal policies so restrictive, and microeconomic structural reform policies so inappropriate, that they hastened the downfall of the Suharto regime. Yet in 1997–98 Japan was aiming not at global but at regional financial reform. After the initial clash with Japan, the United States and the IMF made sufficient adjustments to satisfy the minimum needs of the Japanese government. At bottom, however, the coercive aspects of their policies could not be concealed by a veil of "soft-speak."

Japan has continued to adhere cautiously and furtively—and largely in cooperation with the IMF—to the approach that it outlined in 1997 on issues of liquidity, financial standards, and surveillance. Under novel conditions, with numerous governmental and nongovernmental actors participating and often disagreeing, the resolution of the Asian financial crisis was both a full victory for the United States, in terms of control over policymaking, and a partial victory for Japan, in terms of substantive policy prescriptions. It thus yielded a regional division of labor between the United States and Japan. Yet national responses taught unforeseen lessons. The relative success of the Japanese-supported Malaysian policy during and after the crisis has reinforced the view that in unpredictable financial markets policy experimentation beyond the Washington consensus can be an asset. Yet the room for maneuver remains restricted, and the activities of American rating agencies have preempted Japanese attempts to address the country's moribund financial institutions on preferred, national terms (Sinclair 2005, 89–91, 128–32, 142–44). As capital becomes more readily available to their own consumers, moreover, China, Japan, Taiwan, and the other East Asian economies may have less cash to finance ballooning U.S. trade and budget deficits.

American primacy is not of equal importance to all aspects of East Asia's changing financial relations. Monetary cooperation and currency regimes, for example, provoke a remarkable amount of discussion and joint research. Admittedly, such proposals are still a long way from being implemented through ad hoc or institutionalized policy coordination—market and political incentives as well as the weakness of Japan's domestic financial institutions stand in the way. At the same time the withdrawal of Japanese corporate capital, specifically bank loans, from East Asia illustrates that regional cards are being reshuffled (Hamilton-Hart 2004). At the end of 2004, Japan, China, South Korea, and Taiwan held about 40 percent of the American government's public debt, a total of about 1.8 trillion dollars (Brooke and Bradsher 2004, B2). Future financial crises may well result in experiments, without U.S. leadership and on terms not necessarily to Washington's liking.

During the last two decades East Asian trade has experienced explosive growth. Naoko Munakata shows in chapter 6 that this growth results from the regional initiatives of governments and the regional activities of firms. More clearly than in finance, Japanese policy and the behavior of Japanese firms complement the liberalization program of the WTO. Regional free trade initiatives are supporting regionwide Japanese as well as Taiwanese, Korean, U.S., and Southeast Asian production networks. In the case of Japan these regional initiatives also seek to accelerate structural reforms in the domestic political economy. Export-oriented and import-competing sectors and their political allies are thus affected directly by Japan's foreign trade policy in East Asia. Since 1997 regional trade initiatives have been occurring in East Asia as much as in a broader Pacific and a narrower Southeast Asian context (Jonquières 2002; *Economist* 2003). This shifting geographic scope has the potential to move East Asian trade beyond American control. Growing numbers of bilateral trade initiatives may put Japan and China at the center of the region's trade arrangements.

Trade arrangements may be achieved through global, regional, and bilateral negotiations, and the differences have important implications for the exercise of political power. With the exception of China, Japan has by far the largest market in East Asia. As a result its negotiating power is much greater in bilateral and regional than in global trade negotiations. It remains, of course, a matter of political interpretation how trade asymmetry influences policy. Naoko Munakata argues in chapter 6 that it prompted China to propose a free trade agreement with ASEAN member states. Trade negotiations also provide the Japanese government with instruments useful in dislodging powerful domestic groups that resist reforms. Japan signed an Economic Partnership Agreement with the Philippines and is well along in bilateral negotiations to reach similar agreements with Thailand and Malaysia. The most ambitious of these new initiatives is the Japan–Republic of Korea free trade agreement that would join two economies with a combined GDP of $5 trillion. In all of these negotiations the liberalization of specific markets presents challenges: Japanese agriculture in negotiations with Thailand, Malaysian automobiles in negotiations with Malaysia, and Japan's labor markets for nurses and professional caregivers in negotiations with the Philippines. Furthermore, an ongoing ASEAN initiative goes much further, seeking to create a free trade area linking ASEAN with China, Japan, and Korea. Possible tensions between continued American leadership in multilateral trade negotiations and the increasing importance of newly fashioned bilateral and regional trade arrangements in East Asia are likely to increase. The prospect of a Japanese-Chinese-Korean free trade area, which Chinese premier Zhu Rongji proposed in the fall of 2002, for example, would surely move trade issues from the business section to the front page of the U.S. daily press, and it would force the United States to react to, rather than to lead, trade policy developments in East Asia.

Hybridization of Different National Models

In a wide range of domains corporations and individuals often undercut or sidestep governments and create, at the regional level, true hybrids of different national models.

In the 1970s and 1980s Japan provided the technology, capital, components, and strategic management models for the evolution of regional production networks in East Asia's burgeoning electronics industry. Dieter Ernst argues in chapter 7 that the 1990s saw a substantial erosion of Japan's dominant role. Concentration in the industry, fueled by a deep recession in Japan and by the New Economy boom in the United States, shifted technological and market power: the U.S. lead over Japanese corporations grew particularly in the industry's technologically most advanced segments. Ernst demonstrates that this industry is no longer experiencing competition between distinct national models. Hierarchical relations between firms and growing complexity in the terms of their relationships are more important. Single firms can no longer manage the new and complex relationships brought about by both the rise of China as an important producer and consumer of electronic products and a change in the organization of international business aiming at vertical and often regional specialization within global networks of marketing, production, and innovation. Far from withdrawing from East Asian operations, Japanese firms are restructuring, expanding, and upgrading their production. In short, the Asianization of production networks is superseding their Japanization and Americanization.

The watchword for this process is *hybridization*. Japanese firms must now organize along lines that fully tap the creativity of their non-Japanese skilled workers and engineers. This is a formidable task, as the familial model of the firm retains a much stronger grip over Japanese corporate culture than does the familial model of the polity over Japanese society. Rather than reflect strength, as it once did, an adherence to Japanese ways now signals serious weaknesses of Japanese management in the utilization of local skills and human resources, in penetrating local markets, in outsourcing support services, and in using advanced communication technologies. Such weaknesses reflect core features of Japanese corporations and deeply entrenched constraints on their East Asian operations. Familiar concepts such as "technonationalism" or "technoglobalism" no longer capture the painfully slow efforts at the reinvention and adaptation of Japanese firms (Keller and Samuels 2003). The industry is blurring distinct national models in regional processes marked by hybridization rather than by the move to global standards of best practice.

Similar developments, Derek Hall argues in chapter 8, occur with environmental questions. Historically, Japan's relations with Southeast Asia were uncomplicated. Japan used Southeast Asia as a resource sink, exporting polluting industries there and extracting key resources. Shrimp farming and eucalyptus plantations, for example, can have devastating consequences for fragile local ecosystems. The people who depend on those ecosystems have to get out of the way when production for export markets begins in earnest. Site degradation is of some concern in manufacturing industries such as electronics, but the sustainability of production is crucial for East Asia's agribusiness. The deep domestic slump of Japan's entertainment industry during the prolonged illness and eventual death of Emperor Hirohito in 1989 caused a sharp drop in Japanese shrimp consumption and a crash in prices. Sharp retrenchment in the Southeast Asian shrimp industry illustrated the unmediated relationship between Japanese demand and Southeast Asian production.

In the 1990s cause-and-effect relations between Japan and Southeast Asia became much more complex and less easily traced. Ecological sustainability, Hall argues, is the result of complex regional chains that start with shifts in Japanese consumer demand. However large Japan's "ecological shadow," the 1990s brought important changes rooted in Japan's economic stagnation, Japanese consumer demand and retail trade, trade and investment liberalization, and the rise of China as a major exporter of fresh and frozen vegetables as well as wood products. The result is unexpected: rather than witnessing a deepening of Japan's ecological effects on Southeast Asia, we find that Japan's shadow ecology has become more global on the one hand and more China-centered on the other.

Complexity is also evident in David Leheny's analysis of Japan's popular culture industries in chapter 9. Japan's cultural presence in East Asia is a striking one. The influence of the old, uncool, hierarchic, and economically focused Japan has declined in East Asia, but the influence of the new, cool, chaotic, and culturally dynamic Japan has risen. Joseph Nye (1990) originally coined the concept of soft power, but it was Douglas McGray (2002; Nye 2004) who popularized the notion. In an article cleverly titled "Japan's Gross National Cool" McGray analyzed the enormous successes of Japan's various entertainment industries across East Asia. The idea that Japan has soft power is deeply attractive to Japanese journalists, politicians, public intellectuals, and bureaucrats. When other, harder types of power are waning, soft power evokes an attractive alternative for elites who feel threatened by adverse developments. This was as true of the United States in the late 1980s as it is for Japan today. A "cool" Japan may describe a country that is liked and trusted.

Yet, as Leheny argues, it is impossible to measure Japan's gross national cool and misleading to emphasize its potential to reshape East Asia. The discussion of Japanese (or American) soft power tells us more about the conflicted identities of political actors and nations than it does about the presumed effects of popular culture. Japan's popular culture industries have clear economic benefits. Japanese corporations market the products that emerge from the creative energies of artists working in different sectors of pop culture. Shaping the lifestyle dreams of young people living in East Asia's major metropolitan areas has given Japanese firms and artists a regional stage on which to perform—and to make a lot of money. Japanese punk bands and anime artists, however, cannot lift the nation from economic distress to new heights of cultural preeminence. Instead they both influence and are influenced by developments in other societies and markets, both in East Asia and in North America. Thus they help create a hybrid regional pop culture, encompassing segments such as popular music, video games, TV dramas, cartoons, and movies.

Creating the Social Foundation for a New East Asia

In the book's concluding chapter, Takashi Shiraishi analyzes the social foundations of East Asia's hybrid regionalism. Under the umbrella of the U.S.-Japan security arrangement, and in a world economy liberalizing under U.S. leadership, since the mid-1980s regional processes have been creating a cosmopolitan mainstream in different national contexts. The rise of new professional strata has facilitated the spread of a regionwide consciousness, shaped by far-reaching commonalities in lifestyle, consumption, popular culture, university education, professional training, travel, marriage, and language qualifications. All of these factors are laying the social foundations for a market-centered regionalization in East Asia.

The emergence of these social foundations shapes a new East Asia. In 2002 personal consumption in East Asia stood at about $5 trillion, on a par with the figure for the EU, and not so far behind the $6.9 trillion figure for the United States. Consumption growth is very high, helped along by the fact that consumer banking is one of the few profitable areas left for the growth of East Asian financial institutions. The use of credit cards in East Asia is exploding. In 2001 Visa International, which controls half of the regional market, reported that the volume of retail sales and cash withdrawals grew by 44 percent, to $310 billion. Total consumer debt in South Korea rose by 28 percent (Thornhill 2002). Once the East Asian countries fix their lingering banking crisis, this region will become the leading source of demand for consumer goods in the world economy. Such a development will have far-reaching consequences for the position of the dollar, the financing of U.S. trade and budget deficits, and U.S. interest rates and economic growth.

Equally uncertain are the effects of this new, cosmopolitan mainstream for a democratic, prosperous, and peaceful foreign policy. In other regions and historical periods the middle class has occasionally hitched itself to the wagon of xenophobic nationalism. Because of the exposed political position of the Chinese middle classes this is an unlikely outcome, at least in Southeast Asia.

The rise of East Asia's new middle classes can be credited less to Japanese influence and more to complicated and multiple sources. They are reinforcing East Asia's hybrid regionalism.

Regional Processes beyond Hierarchies and Dualisms

Concepts underlining hierarchies in political power and binary distinctions between civilizations pose barriers to our recognizing what is remaking contemporary East Asia. Titles like "Asia, a Civilization in the Making" (Yamazaki 1996) and "The Asianization of the World" (Friedman 1997) help us focus instead on variegated processes well beyond the regional extension of specific national models.

Power Hierarchies: Japan in the American Order

A little more than a century ago Japan embarked on building a formal empire in East Asia. Japan's policy was bound to collide with the British, Dutch, French, and American colonial empires in Southeast Asia and with the crumbling Sinocentric order in Northeast Asia. Military security was a paramount concern for Japanese elites. After the Sino-Japanese War Japan acquired its first colony, Taiwan, through annexation in 1895. After winning the Russo-Japanese War, Japan colonized Korea starting in 1911. Later Japan expanded onto the mainland, projecting its power into Manchuria and Northeast China. In the 1930s it embarked on making Japan, Korea, and Manchukuo into an autarchic regional empire strong enough to wage total war. Japan provoked virulent anti-Japanese and anti-imperialist Chinese nationalism that drew it into a wider and far more costly war in China proper. Japanese policy set in motion a process that ended in the collapse of the British-led, informal empire in China, and it put Japan in direct conflict with the United States. Southeast Asia was outside the original scope of the East Asia Co-Prosperity Sphere. As Japan got bogged down in China, however, the only way not to give in to Chinese nationalism and the Western powers was to move south into the Dutch East Indies, which was rich in natural resources, above all in oil, and make the Japanese empire self-sufficient. "Greater" was added in 1939 to the original strategic vision, to save the by then bankrupt idea that had initially informed the establishment of Manchukuo. It was a risky gamble: Japan went to war against the United States and Britain. That war ended in Japan's catastrophic defeat and in the dismantling of its colonial empire.

Since 1945 Japan has moved within an American-centered order in East Asia. Wars in Korea and Vietnam were driven by an anticommunist impulse that defined U.S. foreign policy between 1945 and 1975. In Korea and South

Vietnam the United States chose to fight communism in what turned out to be a stalemate in the first war and its worst defeat in the second. American policy supported staunchly conservative and anticommunist regimes not only in Japan but also in South Korea and South Vietnam, Thailand, Indonesia, and the Philippines. In this initial period after 1945 Japan was a shrewd client state, seizing the opportunities that the Korean War and, to a lesser extent, the Vietnam War offered. War jump-started economic recovery in Japan, America's East Asian armory, and turned it into an astonishing story of economic growth and transformation—a model for other East Asian states to emulate.

Preoccupied with a bitter domestic conflict over the character of its polity in the 1950s, Japan in subsequent decades became one of the world's leading trading states. By the early 1970s the consolidation of its domestic political order and the rebuilding of its economy and society had set the stage for reengagement with East Asia. The publication of *Asia's New Giant* (Patrick and Rosovsky 1976) captured Japan's rapidly improving position. The book's cover depicted an orange sun above the horizon. All readers understood that this sun was rising, not setting, for in the golden 1970s Minerva's owl was flying at dawn, promising Japan as a technological superpower in the next millennium. It was, in fact, not an owl but a goose. Heading a "flying V" formation of East Asian geese, Japan was to pull the region forward with its unparalleled successes in manufacturing. East Asia's newly industrializing countries were poised, in succession, to replicate Japan's success, moving steadily forward in manufacturing sophistication and economic development. Japan was to remain the unquestioned leader in the region, controlling all critical technologies and core industries, yet other countries would quickly benefit too.

Japan thus occupied a central economic position in the security order that the United States had fashioned for East Asia. With the exception of North Korea, East Asian states have created perhaps the biggest economic miracle in the history of capitalism. For most of these East Asian states Japan was the model of how to move from Third to First World status. Rates of economic transformation have been telescoped, and prosperity has spread at a rate unimaginable half a century ago. Japan, South Korea, and Taiwan, ASEAN's members (such as Singapore, Malaysia, Thailand, Indonesia, and the Philippines), China, and most recently Vietnam all have experienced, or are now experiencing, economic and social change so compressed in time that it is tantamount to revolution. These changes, furthermore, helped bring about the creation of a linked regional political economy. Alice Amsden (2001) speaks with justification of *The Rise of "the Rest"*.

In the 1990s this model of Japanese influence in East Asia came to an end (MacIntyre and Naughton 2004). Japan's economy stagnated while that of China and the United States rose. Instead of an economic hierarchy organized around Japanese regional production networks, competing Japanese and Chinese production networks were now creating a new environment open to both the reality of increasing competition and the promise of greater cooperation. Furthermore, the United States, from a position of unrivaled military superiority, pushed hard for liberalization and deregulation in the 1990s. Japan was in no position to offer a challenge, in part because of its special security arrangements with the United States, in part because U.S. initiatives served important Japanese interests, and in part because U.S. markets continue to be the preferred outlet for East Asian exporters. The resulting asymmetry in relations continues to give U.S. economic policy initiatives a disproportionate weight, further accelerating the decline of the Japanese model in East Asia.

Civilizational Dualisms

Orientalism and Occidentalism describe deeply engrained patterns of thought that make us view the world in terms of binary distinctions: "us-them," "rational-irrational," "modern-traditional." Clashing civilizations are the latest incarnation of a style of thought that views civilizations as neatly bordered units. Such dualisms applied to East Asia and its relationship to the world lead to a blind alley of slogans and simplifications. They prevent us from recognizing the complex interweaving of processes that are remaking contemporary East Asia.

Occidentalism and the disparaging or admiring attitude toward the West that it reveals is not the same as affinity or distaste for the United States. Ian Buruma and Avishai Margalit (2004) identify four features shared by most versions of Occidentalism: the City, the Bourgeois, Reason, and Feminism. Each connotes feebleness, greed, and decadence, which typically are invoked as Western and negative. Other accounts stress positive traits—Owen Harris (1993, 46–47) writes of "the glory that was Greece and the grandeur that was Rome, Christianity, the Renaissance, the Reformation, the Enlightenment, the French and industrial revolutions, representative democracy, the rule of law, the market economy." In a totally different vein Xiaomei Chen (2002) stresses the liberating effects of Western discourse on post-Maoist China. In either its negative or its positive version, however, the Occident should not be conflated with America. "The image of an emerging homogeneous, universally Western world," writes Samuel Huntington (1996, 28) is "to varying degrees misguided, arrogant, false, and dangerous." As studies of contemporary welfare capitalism too numerous to be recounted illustrate, within the West there exist different ways of becoming modern without necessarily becoming American. Supporters of American exceptionalism insist that a gulf separates the United States from the West. Others recognize a family resemblance just as they recognize a resemblance between, for example, Norway and the West, without insisting on a perfect match (Jackson n.d., 48–65, and 2001; O'Hagan 2002).

The concept of Orientalism (Said 1978) also reveals both critical and admiring views. Oswald Spengler (1933), for example, warned between the world wars that Japan's Yellow Peril was threatening to engulf the civilized world, and shorn of its explicitly racial imagery, such language remains a powerful undercurrent in American and European commentaries on the rise of Japan and China in contemporary world affairs. Proponents of "Asian values," in sharp contrast, extol the virtues of the collectivist, Confucian mind-set that marks East Asian polities and sets them apart from the decadent and overly individualist politics of the West. Political authority derives not from the dry, cold, rationalist, democratic individualism that marks the West but from the moist, warm, emotive, soft authoritarian collectivism that constitutes the East. Malaysia's former prime minister, Mahathir Mohamad, and Ishihara Shintaro (1995), nationalist politician and now governor of Tokyo, encapsulate contemporary Orientalism. They elide the fundamental differences that separate Malaysia's openly acknowledged, multiethnic polity from a Japan that has erased (much smaller) ethnic divisions from its public ideology. Their argument disregards altogether the fact that Singapore originally invented the Asian values ideology in the 1970s as part of a self-conscious strategy of state building. Whether deployed by critics or supporters, however, Orientalist vocabulary is too broad, too abstract, and too static to capture the social and political processes that are remaking East Asia.

Porous Regionalism: Beyond Power Hierarchies and Civilizational Dualisms

The processes now remaking East Asia fuse national models. They break down such models into fragments available for novel recombinations and complex cause-and-effect relationships.

East Asia is, of course, shaped by major states such as Japan, the United States, and China, and the national models they project—this much is familiar. More novel is the fact that regions are made porous by the fusion of international and global processes (Katzenstein 2005). These two concepts refer to different processes (Hirst and Thompson 1996, 8–13). Globalization is transforming East Asia; it highlights the appearance of new actors and novel relationships. Internationalization affirms basic continuities in the international system; it draws attention to the continued relevance of traditional actors and the intensification of existing relationships. While internationality is embedded in territorial space, globality transcends geography (Scholte 2000, 49). Global processes create pressures toward common standards and the convergence of different national practices while leaving room for local adaptations. International processes reinforce different national practices, orchestrated by powerful national institutions. The strategy and structure of large corporations illustrate the basic difference. In a global economy transnational corporations tend to undercut national policies, adjust corporate practice to one preferred global standard, and give rise to a broad array of local reactions. In an international economy national governments continue to adapt local economies to the operations of multinational corporations.

Globalization and internationalization interact and typically occur simultaneously. We can track their complementarity as regions become porous while preserving distinctive institutions. The September 11 attacks on the World Trade Center and the Pentagon provide a telling illustration. That a global network of terrorists could wreak such massive destruction confirmed the increasing importance of new actors and new relations, as even the United States succumbed to the surprise attack. Yet al Qaeda's power rested substantially on its symbiotic relation with the Taliban government of Afghanistan, and removal of the Taliban regime deprived al Qaeda of a territorial safe haven. Moreover, the combined effect of global and international processes has meant different things in different regions (Katzenstein 2003a). In the eyes of Washington September 11 was an act of "war" directed against the United States and justifying a military response. In European eyes the attacks were a "crime" that required patient police work and coordinated international action. In East Asia the attacks were viewed as a "big event" that needed careful attention because of its effect on the United States.

East Asian regionalism encompasses both material and imagined dimensions. It is "given" by geography and "made" through politics. Geographic proximity shapes the intensity of social and economic exchanges, the salience of political and other relationships, and the pressures to coordinate government policies. Yet regions are also shaped by cognitive practices and political discourse. Contest about boundaries is part of the politics of regionalism. From the perspective of China, for example, Saudi Arabia and Iraq are part of West Asia; from the perspective of the United States they are part of the Middle East. Rarely acknowledged, such differences in perception are consequential.

Porous regions emerge from the interaction of various processes. In naming them we tend to reduce their complexity and risk erring in one of two directions. First, we drain global processes of their specific national content. More than two centuries of Anglo-American preeminence, for example, have imbued core institutions and widespread practices in the world polity with the aura of being "natural." Private property, human rights, the free flow of scientific ideas and, more recently, legal restrictions on their technological applications—yet such taken-for-granted matters always reflect power struggles, victories and defeats, and distinctive policy choices. Second, we tend to reduce international processes to national labels such as Japanization, Americanization, and Sinicization. Such terms contain the important insight that polities seek to shape the regional neighborhood they inhabit, with what Arnold Wolfers (1962, 67–80) has called "milieu goals." Yet such goals yield in reality to novel combinations and new hybrids. The sum of these processes creates an East Asia that undercuts the heroic simplifications and the limited insights that thinking in terms of power hierarchies and civilizational dualisms promises. It is when we look beyond the extension of national or civilizational models toward their regional hybridization that we shall start to recognize the emergence of a new East Asia.

The first part of this book analyzes political and social processes in Japan that have hollowed out the model it once offered to East Asia. Yet Japan remains a major force in East Asia and, together with the United States, China, and other polities, offers a broad range of political alternatives to the region. The second part shows that regionalization in East Asia is occurring in a space that leaves room for the coexistence of alternative national models in various policy domains. On questions of security Japan remains a close ally of the United States, and it persists in defending a purportedly homogeneous and crime-free Japan. In finance Japan engages in competitive collaboration with the United States. On trade questions Japanese and American policies show far-reaching complementarities. On other issues, as the third part illustrates, regionalization in East Asia is marked by growing complexity and variable links among actors. This is true of domains as different as regional production, ecology and agribusiness, and popular culture. Regional outcomes in these domains transcend clearly distinguishable national models and permit the emergence of a hybrid regionalism. The book concludes with an analysis of the social foundations of this hybrid regionalism—which still lacks a firm political definition.

Over the past generation we have been asked repeatedly to train our sights on still another rising sun promising to paint Asia in still another national color. It is time for a shift in perspective. East Asia is readying itself for the emergence of something new and different. At the beginning of the twenty-first century East Asia is being remade by many different kind of actors and in ways that display many unforeseen and complex connections. The result is a hybrid. Regionalization is taking place beyond clearly marked national footprints. Whether we analyze this process from the perspective of Japan, or of China, the United States, or any other country, this book argues, may affect the tone of some of our arguments. It would not, however, change its central tune: regionalism and regionalization in East Asia are occurring in a space beyond all national models.

I

JAPAN

2

A Decade of Political Torpor: When Political Logic Trumps Economic Rationality

T. J. PEMPEL

Japan's political economy presents a tantalizing puzzle. The country has all the formal trappings of democracy, including a free and frequently critical press; a diversity of densely organized and often competing interests; a party system that includes a multitude of independent, ideologically diverse, and competitive political parties; and regularly held elections that are by any comparative measure relatively free and fair. Yet, despite such democratic institutions, the country underwent the industrial world's deepest economic slump from 1990–2005 with no substantial change in government nor any mixture of public policies that reversed the economic downturn. Japanese democracy meted out no substantial electoral punishments to those who presided over the national economic meltdown until perhaps the election of September 11, 2005. This combination of democratic institutions mixed with political stasis in the face of overwhelmingly negative economic performance poses, I believe, the most overarching puzzle concerning Japan's recent political economy.

This combination of economic stagnation and phlegmatic politics contrasts with Japan from the early 1950s until about 1990. Throughout that period the country had a stable set of political institutions, social forces, and public policies, all of which were fused into a powerful and stable political regime closely associated with world-class national economic dynamism. Various labels—"1955 system," "developmental state," "embedded mercantil-

In addition to the two symposiums held at Kyoto and Honolulu, I benefited from presenting earlier drafts of this chapter at Harvard University, the University of California, Berkeley, and as the Henry Luce lecture at Southwestern University. I wish to acknowledge the many useful comments made on each of these occasions. In addition, Ellis Krauss, Steven Vogel, and an anonymous reviewer made extensive and helpful suggestions for revision.

ism"—were affixed to this mixture. Moreover, as William Kelly and Merry White make clear in chapter 3, during this period Japanese society was informed by, and operated in resonance with, a minimally questioned "family model." Virtually all major actors behaved as if they were mutually dependent on, and mutually supportive of, one another. Economic growth, long-term conservative rule, social stability, and individual satisfaction reinforced one another, creating a long-term positive spiral.

Japan's model of economic development was not only widely supported at home, it spawned imitators abroad, particularly across Asia. Driven by a sequence of war reparations, tied-aid, investments, and production networks, Japan's economic and financial predominance in Asia generated unmistakable benefits for Japanese-owned companies, while catapulting the country into a position of unchallenged primacy throughout the region. The country acquired an unmistakable attractiveness to a diversity of regional Asian political and economic elites who sought to reconfigure their political economies by adopting core Japanese practices.

Three decades of propitious economic circumstances make it superficially simple to understand why Japan's structures of political power retained such impermeability at home and such preeminence and appeal throughout Asia. Domestically, voters and interest groups had little incentive to challenge officeholders who, legitimately or not, claimed credit for the country's tremendous economic success. And Japan's "creative conservatives" were adept at co-opting potentially appealing opposition proposals and local governmental initiatives, thereby adjusting policy specifics so as to ameliorate citizen discontents. If there is one "law" that has credibility with both practicing politicians and political scientists, it is that a vibrant economy enhances the likelihood that government officeholders will retain their positions. Moreover, admiration for one's most prosperous neighbor should occasion little surprise.

Far more puzzling has been the persistence of the conservative government with its lack of social or policy overhaul during the country's economically "lost decade" (Hiwatari and Miura 2002). The puzzle takes on added interest because, since the early 1990s, Japan witnessed major alterations in what are usually taken to be the most critical vehicles linking citizens to governments—the national electoral system and the political party system. The electoral system was substantially restructured in 1994, and in the wake of these changes, Japan's party system went through a plethora of combinations and recombinations. Although Japan's voters were at no loss for electoral alternatives, Japan's rulers held their seats despite numerous claimants anxious to replace them.

These seemingly big changes in the electoral and party system did not result in any quick realignment of key socioeconomic groups and their respective privileges and disadvantages. Nor did they lead to either new economic policymakers or successful economic policies. The same ruling party clung to power relying on the same major socioeconomic blocs for support as it pursued a sequence of demonstrably ineffective economic policies year in and year out. There was little evidence of political learning or political realignment by political leaders nor of political retribution against them by voters. Hence the prevailing image of Japanese politics throughout the last fifteen years has been that of continuity rather than change.

The only parenthesis in conservative national control came with the seven-party coalition government that held office for nine months starting in 1993. That coalition's success, however, was short-lived; its policy agenda did little to address national economic problems; and, by the following summer, the Liberal Democratic Party (LDP) was back in government as the result of a previously unimaginable alliance with its formerly most implacable ideological adversary, the Japan Socialist Party (JSP). That alliance gave Japan its first socialist prime minister since 1947, Murayama Tomiichi, but the LDP remained the dominant party in parliament and in the governing coalition. Since then, at least as of this writing, the LDP has remained the largest party within each subsequent government, controlling the prime minister's office, the cabinet, and the national political agenda since 1994 (most recently in coalition with New Komeito). Nor has there been any major shift up or down in the relative power of key socioeconomic blocs. Conservative dominance has continued despite the changes in the electoral and party systems, and despite the fact that a host of statistical indicators—GNP growth, unemployment, productivity, the Nikkei stock market, corporate bankruptcies, nonperforming bank loans, shares of world exports, public sector debt, and foreign credit ratings to name but the most prominent—provided stark and unmistakable indicators of the massive deterioration of Japan's economy. (For details, see Pempel 1998, 138–45.) A number of these indicators—such as unemployment, bankruptcy, growth, pension erosion, and stock prices—exerted a direct influence over the lives of large segments of the citizenry. Others wreaked havoc on the fortunes of key support groups. To the extent that these data remained negative and public policies did not reverse them, one might have expected citizen mutiny or internal conservative revolt. In fact, even though sequences of different and sometimes competing economic policies have been tried, all proved ineffective; yet, political revenge and revolt were minimal and socioeconomic realignment was slight. Why didn't these changes happen?

Democracy and Policy Change

It is possible to envision at least two radically different linkages between democracy and political change. The first of these involves a variety of outside pressures that lead to the replacement of one government and its policy agenda by an alternative set of officials advocating new policies. The most widely recognized of these occurs when voter power punishes incumbents deemed insufficiently responsive to new or changing citizen preferences. Unhappy with the policy directions taken by a sitting government—possibly as a consequence of major social changes and socioeconomic realignments— a sufficient number of voters shift their prior electoral preferences, voting to throw the incumbents out and replacing them with an opposition party whose alternative policy program is seen as more appealing. These are among the most classic transformations in government portrayed in textbooks on democracy. The electoral victories of Margaret Thatcher, Ronald Reagan, Ariel Sharon, and Kim Dae Jung provide classic instances of such electoral shifts followed by redirections of public policy.

A very different, but similarly citizen-centric, linkage involves preemptive policy changes undertaken by incumbent governments. In those instances, government officials, their political antennae sensitive to some potentially volatile mixture of existing policy inadequacies and changing citizen or other constituent preferences, modify or reverse past policies in advance of overt voter revolt. Less dramatic than electoral revolt, such preemptive government action is tougher to analyze, but it was by far the most frequent pattern of policy change in Japan from 1955 until 1990. And as a particularly important variant of this elite-led model of change in the case of Japan are instances in which action by local governments or by the Japanese courts, not just shifts in voter mood, have been vigorous catalysts, goading the national government to adopt new measures.

During the 1990s, however, Japan saw neither citizen revolt followed by new parties coming to power nor preemptive government policy shifts that alleviated the underlying problem. Why, after all those years, did Japan's elected leaders not put forward policy programs laying out new economic directions? Alternatively, why, despite changes in many aspects of politics, including all the changes in electoral rules, voting patterns, and new parties, and its own unmistakable lack of voter popularity, did Japan's conservatives manage to hold on to power so tenaciously? Equally perplexing, why did opposition politicians not capitalize on the country's continued economic downslide? Why, despite the efforts of alternative contending power bases, did no alternative leadership emerge to challenge the dominance of the elected politicians in Nagatacho? Why did the business community and the voting public not unite in a revolt to demand political change? Why, in short, did Japan's political system not beget either more effective economic policies or electoral revenge? The answer, I contend, lies in the deeply institutionalized roots of a political economy structured to resist the Schumpeterian process of "creative destruction." It is not that no efforts were made to restructure political power and public policies over the last fifteen years; rather, it is that those endeavors continually confronted more powerful forces of resistance. That new forces were slow to take root and spawn rapid changes was in part a tribute to the rock-hard political terrain on which they fell. To understand Japan's decade plus of political rigidity one must appreciate the staying power of the structures of the past.

Socioeconomics and Constituent Politics

When it was formed in 1955, a period in Japan that Samuels (2003b, 230) astutely characterizes as one of "fluid ideological borders and political desperation," the Liberal Democratic Party was cobbled together out of highly diverse constituencies that were united less by some agreed-upon policy agenda and more by common opposition to the newly unified Japan Socialist Party (JSP), combined with a shared desire to divvy up the spoils of office. Formally and institutionally united, the newly merged conservatives were nevertheless cleft by numerous issues including security, rearmament, ties to China, education, and constitutional revision, among others. These continued to differentiate party groupings for the subsequent three and a half decades.

On economics, however, several important tensions among the party's competing constituencies were resolved by particularly fortuitous compromises. Economic nationalism remained an overarching umbrella—improving the national economy's competitive standing was a sweepingly accepted goal— but there were sharp divisions over the specific mechanisms by which to do so. Big business had been a major catalyst in the party's formation; also supporting the new party were many former bureaucrats such as Ikeda Hayato, Kishi Nobusuke, Fukuda Takeo, and Sato Eisaku. Generally speaking, such interests leaned heavily toward bureaucratically led industrial policies, tightly balanced budgets, and rapid technological improvement of large-scale firms, domestic oligopolization, and the aggressive pursuit of export markets. Equally important, however, many of the new party's most powerful politicians represented areas where small businesses and farming were the strongest economic voices in the constituent choir. As such, they were less hospitable to the policy orientations of the first group, instead demanding local protection from both urban Japanese businesses and from overseas imports. Such constituent interests drove these politicians to embrace classic pork barrel politics, interregional redistribution of governmental tax revenues, and the maintenance of a social safety net that would prevent market forces from undercutting the businesses and employment bases in their districts. If such policies meant little collective worry about tightly balanced budgets, so be it. Rapid economic growth was far less important to this latter group than was ensuring the economic viability of their district's farms and small businesses (for comparative perspectives see Frieden and Rogowski 1996).

The ingenuity of the LDP's economic policies lay in their ability to accommodate these competing socioeconomic and political elements through a combination of high growth and local protection. This fusion built into Japan a strong "welfare" component, radically different from the welfare state model prevalent in much of Western Europe. The Japanese safety net provided public assistance less for disadvantaged individuals and more for economically depressed or slow-growing geographical areas and economic sectors. In theory, such assistance allowed such areas and sectors the time needed to make difficult transitions; in fact, in the same way that many individual social welfare recipients in other countries became increasingly dependent on public subsidization for their livelihood, so numerous Japanese regions, economic sectors, and individual corporations turned into semipermanent wards of the Japanese treasury with their LDP parliamentarians serving as welfare officers.

The shotgun marriage of these two broadly different constituencies was facilitated by conservative control over governmental offices and annually expanding budgets. Numerous front and back channels with varying degrees of legality and illegality enriched party coffers, financed party leaders, and held potential opponents at an impoverished distance from the ever-more-lucrative public money spigots. Mutual recognition by all party members of the incalculable political benefits that accrued from the LDP's perennial hold over public office eased the resolution of any intraparty disputes over economic policies. Schlesinger (1997, 109) captures this resulting inclusiveness by suggesting that the party was a vehicle for both "the bagmen and the statesmen."

The LDP's diverse constituencies were represented by relatively comprehensive and sector-specific corporatist networks. Numerous sector-specific, and often regionally comprehensive, associations existed for agriculture, different types of businesses, and for associations of professionals such as doctors, dentists, lawyers, and the like. Most such associations included exceptionally high proportions of their potential members and could speak with relatively cohesive voices in national interest-group politics; some even enjoyed direct representation in the upper house of parliament; the most important were virtually guaranteed a seat at bureaucratic investigations of policy initiatives affecting them. Meanwhile, virtually all national bureaucratic agencies enjoyed tightly delimited spheres of regulatory control over, and regularized interactions with, competing socioeconomic constituencies. Thus, the Ministry of Finance had virtually sole responsibility for the country's banks and financial institutions, the Ministries of Agriculture and Construction provided powerful links to the rural areas, MITI (Ministry of International Trade and Industry) was the agency most closely tied to big firms and oligopoly, but it included the Agency for Small Business, which had an explicitly different representational mandate.

Bureaucratic links to powerful economic interests were further connected to subsectors of the ruling LDP through the party's functionally specific committees on its Policy Affairs Research Council. The council was organized into a series of committees parallel to the various cabinet offices and bureaucratic agencies. Horizontal coordination and integration of separate spheres of economic activity was far less in evidence than was their vertical separateness (e.g., Yamamoto 1972, 115). Essentially, policy oversight and any tentative proposals for change involved a number of "iron triangles," each composed of a bureaucratic agency, one or more interest groups, and selected LDP politicians. Only after agreement was reached within these functionally specific triangles were any new proposals submitted to the cabinet and to parliament. The system thus provided little room for free-ranging civil society groups, for independent cabinet initiation, or for extensive horizontal coordination among agencies or affected interests. Over time, such policy-specific networks became ever more deeply entrenched and difficult to dislodge.

Elsewhere (Pempel 1999) I have characterized the resultant mix of economic policies as "embedded mercantilism." Japan's domestic markets were effectively closed to most foreign products and investments capable of challenging Japan's domestic industries. At the same time, while the home market was largely closed to outside penetration, over time Japan spawned numerous globally competitive firms in a host of sectors from machine tools and consumer electronics to automobiles and robotics. Originally dominant in the home market, such firms gradually moved on to exporting their best products to global markets, creating first-class multinational production networks with manufacturing and marketing facilities in numerous countries worldwide. These firms, along with their smaller domestic subcontractors and distributors, were the major engines of Japan's high-growth economy for the first thirty-five to forty years after the end of World War II. Meanwhile, firms and sectors lacking such global competitiveness and whose primary markets remained domestic nevertheless survived by virtue of the entrenched system of politically enhanced protection and oligopolistic privileges at home. The resultant "national economy" was in fact an oil-and-water combination, with some parts highly sophisticated, productive, and closely integrated with the rest of the world and other parts highly dependent on protected national markets and almost totally buffered from global challenges and competition.

Long-term LDP rule was crucial to the fusion of these two dramatically different streams. Control of the government apparatus allowed conservatives to pursue economic politics that avoided hard choices between potentially competing constituencies. High growth by large globally competitive firms generated sufficient treasury income to allow the ruling politicians to dole out extensive portions of pork and protection, both for smaller businesses and for the rural areas. The party grew accustomed to, indeed it thrived on, economic policies driven by the rather antagonistic logics of growth and redistribution.

Blisteringly hot GNP growth rates kept government revenues expanding automatically upward. This in turn allowed officials to undertake new policy initiatives without making offsetting cutbacks in older policies or cutting off support for inefficient sectors. Although they became progressively more costly over time, the policies that provided economic protection to Japan's least competitive sectors—construction, distribution, financial services, air transport, road freight, food, agriculture, and small business generally—could be sustained without automatically undercutting the broader competitiveness of firms in areas such as automobiles, consumer electronics, and machine tools.

In softening intraparty economic tensions, the ruling party was helped by Japan's multimember, single-ballot electoral system. Under that system successful candidates to the lower house (House of Representatives) could be elected with as little as 12–15 percent of the district's total vote. Hence, two, three, four, or sometimes five LDP-supported parliamentarians could be elected from the same district, even if (perhaps particularly if) they embraced somewhat different constituencies and supported different policy goals. By voting their most narrow preferences, voters from even the most particularistic groups (dentists, veterans, grocers, and so forth) could ensure themselves a parliamentary representative. National party policy positions were largely removed from electoral competition while personalistic and clientelistic politics drove most campaigns (Flannagan et al. 1991; Miyake 1985; Kobayashi 1991; Kabashima 2004).

Extensive gerrymandering ensured rural overrepresentation. Rural districts could often elect parliamentarians with one-third or less the number of votes that were needed to win in urban areas. And rural areas continue to account for roughly one-third of all the seats in the lower house of parliament. It is there that the conservatives were strongest and where the new opposition parties—and any demands for economic liberalization, deregulation, and an end to subsidies—faced their greatest hurdles. Meanwhile, the most vigorous social changes came in the expanding urban and suburban areas, so that rural overrepresentation militated against the easy translation of such social changes into political power.

Of particular importance was the fact that the system made it all but impossible to vote *against* the party in power. With only one ballot per voter and as many as five representatives per district, it was far more common to vote against a disliked individual by shifting one's vote to another candidate of the same party or to a nominal independent who, post election, would often affiliate with the ruling LDP. It was extremely difficult to mobilize allegedly unhappy voters against a party with more than one representative in the district.

In all of these ways, Japan's political system provided deeply entrenched structures that privileged many of the country's least economically viable geographical areas and economic sectors. Control of government office, internal oligopoly, protectionism, and high growth by the country's globally competitive firms and sectors buffered such areas and sectors from the extremes of market competition.

Unending Economic Torpor

The conservatives' fusion of globally competitive and nationally protected economic constituencies was jolted but not derailed by the Plaza Accord of 1985 (Pempel 1999). As the yen doubled in value, Japan was given strong incentives to shift its national economy from its protected, export-oriented bias in a new direction represented by far less regulation, more reliance on domestic demand, and a greater openness to foreign imports and investments. Various proposals were made by Japanese government committees, most notably the Maekawa Committee, to pursue precisely such a direction. But such a shift in policy would have come at the expense of powerfully invested domestic sectors, bureaucratic agencies, and politicians—all of whom were able to wield considerable electoral and economic clout against such a shift.

The potentially stark confrontation between alternative courses of economic action was skirted, however, as numerous Japanese firms expanded their manufacturing and banking investments around the world, with roughly 40 percent of foreign direct investment (FDI) going to North America and 25 percent going to other areas of Asia. In 1989, 5.7 percent of the manufacturing capacity of Japanese-owned companies took place outside of Japan; by 2000 that number had jumped to 14.5 percent. The figures were vastly higher in key sectors such as electronics (25%) and autos (33%) (Pacific Council 2002, 17). In numerous areas, as Dieter Ernst explores extensively in chapter 7, many Japanese companies became fully integrated into world production networks.

Such outgoing FDI, in conjunction with an exceptionally loose monetary policy, vented a great deal of the accumulating pressure within Japan for hard choices between a continued focus on domestic protection plus exports or a shift to a more open economy driven by incoming investments and imports along with enhanced domestic consumption. Japanese banking and financial institutions continued to make relatively poorly secured but initially profitable and rapidly expanding loans, fueled by collateral in the rising asset prices of land and stocks. An artificially inflated economy resulted, which continued to mask the underlying tensions between Japan's internationally competitive firms and sectors, on the one hand, and the rural areas, small businesses, and protected sectors (including banking and finance) on the other. In short, Japan's policies post-Plaza and into the early 1990s avoided hard choices among policies or economic sectors, instead reinforcing the strengths of these dual economic constituencies. The result was the incredible asset bubble that enveloped Japan during the second half of the 1980s.

Once that bubble burst in 1990–91, the tensions among competing economic policy choices came starkly to the political surface. Yet, under slower growth, any particular course of action proposed as a "solution" to Japan's economic troubles was sure to generate clear-cut winners and losers within different economic sectors and geographical regions, thereby undermining the delicate political balance of diverse constituencies that had long been at the heart of conservative political rule. With potential losers so well networked into the national political system and with bureaucratic and interest-group power structured to prevent the imposition of policies that might cause severe disadvantages to any privileged constituency, the result was a well-entrenched and collective resistance to any hard choices against vested interests, no matter how beneficial particular choices might have been for the national economy as a whole. The holders of power had little incentive to engage in, and strong structural barriers to prevent them from pursuing, rapid policy reorientations that would cut out old power holders in favor of new ones.

Impediments to Voter Revolt

Social changes and voter discontent should have made Japan ripe for electoral revolt during the 1990s. The anemic economy and its negative consequences were an overwhelming source of voter unhappiness. And they were accompanied by an ongoing series of corruption scandals implicating some of the nation's highest elected officials and civil servants. Additionally, Japan witnessed several demonstrations of an inept governmental emergency capability involving timidity in the face of sarin gas attacks on major cities by the religious terrorist group Aum Shinrikyo and a feckless governmental response to the devastating 1995 earthquake in Kobe. The ruling LDP saw substantial drops in its popularity. Indeed, public opinion polls occasionally showed the LDP to be among the most unpopular of Japan's major parties, and several incumbent LDP prime ministers during the mid- to late 1990s registered only single-digit popularity levels.

Growing voter uneasiness rode atop much deeper currents of social change that swept through Japan before and during the period of economic torpor. The Japanese population has undergone a major demographic shift from rural to urban and suburban areas. Voter identifications changed as fixed loyalty to particular parties gave way to a rise in independent voters. In the 1960s, less than 10 percent of Japan's electorate identified themselves as "independents." By the 1993 election this figure was up to 38 percent, and by January 1995 it was 50 percent (Pempel 1998, 159). Such voters were disproportionately concentrated within Japan's urban areas, had different lifestyles than many of their rural or older predecessors, and were presumably ripe for mobilization by new challengers.

In chapter 3, Kelly and White make clear that Japanese society has been undergoing a series of other more particularistic changes since the late 1980s. Within at least five major groups—students, slackers, singles, seniors, and strangers—they argue, new social behaviors signaled the waning power of the earlier "mainstream consciousness" to channel citizen aspirations and efforts. Yet the combination of macrodemographic shifts and the rise in independent voters did not translate into victory for opposition political parties. Nor have the social groups examined by Kelly and White taken explicitly political organizational forms aimed at achieving major political changes. Instead, long-standing structural impediments have worked against converting Japan's extensive societal changes into politically meaningful forms, most particularly into coherent and consistent support for an opposition party with an alternative economic agenda. Indeed, rather than pursuing politicized activities, or forging dynamic civil organizations or socioeconomic blocs with a coherent political agenda, the groups identified by Kelly and White have remained internally and personally focused, and consequently, they have been politically marginal.

The former electoral system for the House of Representatives worked against clear choices between candidates from different parties as well as choices between policies. Party and candidate differences were blurred, not sharpened. The Japanese electoral system changed in a number of fundamental ways during the early 1990s, but those changes did not result quickly in sharp party and policy contestations.

The seven-party coalition of Hosokawa Morihiro that took power in 1993 put in place an extensive series of changes in the electoral laws. Four laws established new campaign regulations along with a complete overhaul of the electoral system for the House of Representatives. The latter was again modified before the 2000 election. It now consists of 300 single-member seats plus 180 chosen by proportional representation. The electoral system for the upper house (House of Councillors) was further revised in 2000.

Under the new electoral system, the party system changed dramatically. New parties formed and party reorganizations occurred with perplexing frequency. With time, there was a consolidation in the number of what Reed (2000) has called "viable parties." At least two of these—the New Frontier Party and the Democratic Party of Japan (DPJ)—presented highly credible challenges to the LDP. In the 1996 lower house election, for example, the two combined to win over 44 percent of the proportional representation vote compared to 32.8 percent for the LDP. Meanwhile, the LDP and the combined opposition drew almost identical percentages of the single-member-district vote. The 1998 upper house election saw the LDP drop from 61 to 44 seats while the Democratic Party and the Japan Communist Party both doubled their seats, giving the combined opposition a majority. In the 2003 lower house election, the DPJ defeated the LDP in proportional representation balloting and became the most successful opposition party in postwar history with 177 seats (37%), and the party system appeared to consolidate around two large parties, the LDP and the DPJ. Such changes should have been conducive to enhancing the chances for successful voter revolt.

At the same time, none of these changes, powerful as they were in capturing Japanese and foreign newspaper headlines, resulted in dramatic changes in party rule, in the underlying structures of power within the country, or in the basic thrust of central policy directions, particularly in economics. Japan experienced no deep structural power shifts. Instead, Japan's prior model of political economy—its "embedded mercantilism"—was tweaked but not fundamentally reconfigured. Electoral politics, socioeconomic blocs, and the top rungs of governance proved highly effective in resisting fundamental changes; the structures put in place over the long decades of conservative rule continued to hinder rapid change. Thus, despite gaining larger proportions of the total vote in 1996, the opposition parties still saw the LDP outpoll them as the latter gained nearly 48 percent of the seats while the opposition won only 42 percent. The apparent opposition victory in the 1998 upper house election was short lived, generating at best limited lasting electoral momentum, while in the 2000 House of Representatives election the LDP managed to win 48.5 percent of the seats while the DPJ gained only 26.5 percent. Indeed, in the 2001 upper house election, the LDP, led by its new leader Koizumi Jun'ichiro, scored a substantial victory, one Koizumi repeated in the 2003 lower house election. Only in the 2004 House of Councillors election did it begin to appear that perhaps a major opposition party, with an electoral constituency not wedded to the old regime, had developed the momentum that might propel it into governmental power.

Certainly, during the decade or more when Japan's economy was in its worst shape, no sustained political opposition appeared with a compelling and electorally attractive economic vision to challenge that of the governing party. As Scheiner (2002, 18) put it, "Since the late 1980s, the Japanese public appeared to grow eager to latch on to new party alternatives, but while new party threats were quick to rise up, they did not find a way to maintain voter allegiance, and the LDP is yet to face a serious sustained challenger."

The changes in the voting system and in the patterns of party organization were slow to erase the massive impediments facing potential new parties and candidates. As a consequence, rapid electoral revenge and victories by opposition parties were tough to achieve. As Robert Weiner (2002) points out, the weakness of the party opposition in Japan is *not* in itself particularly unusual. Elections in most democracies favor incumbents, making the mounting of any serious opposition a formidable undertaking. (Americans can remind themselves of the simple fact that in the 2004 elections for the 435 seats in the House of Representatives, no more than twenty-five seats were truly competitive.) The barriers to running credible opposition candidates remained enormous—the advantages of incumbency, name recognition, the powers of office, the high costs of campaigning, and the difficulty any new opposition party faced in fielding politically experienced candidates, to name only several of the most striking. Japanese parliamentary incumbents do extensive case work for their individual constituents and for their financial backers. One study (Iwai 1990) showed that most LDP parliamentarians provide $100,000 per month in support to their constituents—in the form of gifts for weddings, funerals, and the like—more than three times their monthly salaries. And the longer a single party is in power, the more it becomes the vehicle of choice for aspiring young politicians, making it progressively more difficult for opposition parties to develop a rich reservoir of talented potential national candidates.

The tremendous advantages enjoyed by incumbents remained particularly valuable in the rural areas where longstanding personal electoral machines (koenkai) and hereditary conservative politicians were most well-entrenched. In 1996, for example, there were seventy LDP incumbents in rural areas compared to only twenty-eight from the new opposition parties. In contrast, within urban districts those new opposition parties were able to field sixty-eight incumbents to only thirty-three from the LDP. The LDP drew 47 percent of the rural vote in the single-member districts compared to only 30 percent for the new opposition parties in 1996, and in 2000 the gap was an even wider 50 percent to 7 percent (Scheiner 2002, 295–300). Indeed, the big city problems of the LDP were made most obvious in 1998 when the LDP did not win a single seat in the most metropolitan prefectures of the country. Still, despite the fact that Japan's population lives disproportionately in urban and suburban areas, the rural grip of the LDP remained exceptionally tough to break, and the conservatives' rural strongholds made it even more difficult for the opposition parties to gain power. Scheiner (2002, 258) effectively summarizes this dilemma for the opposition: "Even if an opposition party won 30 percent of the rural SMDs [single-member districts] and one-third of all PR [proportional representation] seats—results greater than the DPJ was able to achieve in 2000—it would still need to win 75 percent of the remaining seats (mixed and urban SMDs) in order to win a [parliamentary] majority."

Incumbent protection was ironically bolstered—at least in the short run—by creative manipulation of the newly revamped electoral system. Conservative candidates who lost in single-member districts were able to remain parliamentarians by gaining sufficiently high spots on the proportional representation lists of their party. Thus as many as eighty-four district losers were "rescued" by "winning" through their overlapping candidacies on the party lists in 1996.

Opposition parties faced particular difficulties in Japan's combination of clientelism and fiscal centralization, both of which favor LDP incumbents. To the extent that the national government exercised preponderant control over local financing for multiple decades, newly formed opposition parties found it almost impossible to develop bastions of local power from which they could groom candidates while simultaneously developing pockets of support from which to test out new policies and to launch a credible challenge against the national ruling party. For such reasons, aspiring politicians had compelling incentives to affiliate with the party or parties that controlled the purse strings at the national level. The newly reorganized parties that came into being during the 1990s had to struggle mightily to overcome the legacy of these long-standing barriers.

Similarly, although Japan has seen a burst in new nongovernmental organizations (NGOs, or NPOs—nonprofit organizations—as they are more usually called in Japan) these too faced considerable official opposition. Roughly one-half of Japan's six thousand NPOs did not exist before the Kobe earthquake of 1995. That newness, plus a weak national tradition of public philanthropy, means that most remain thinly funded and weakly staffed. In addition, a public access law, enacted in 1998, gave a major boost to Japanese "civil society," as a variety of citizens groups gained access to previously inaccessible public records and the biases of no-longer-secret bureaucratic actions were unveiled (Pekkanen 2000). Yet NPOs continued to confront massive official opposition to their activities. Thus, before the January 2002 international conference to generate funding to rehabilitate war-ravaged Afghanistan, one powerful LDP leader, Suzuki Muneo, successfully pressed the Ministry of Foreign Affairs to prevent NPO participation. And various government agencies have conducted extensive and secret background investigations on individuals and NPOs that have sought government data under the new sunshine laws. If "civil society" is gaining some strength in Japan, and serves as a potential counterweight to the party-bureaucratic nexus that has long dominated policymaking, it is doing so slowly and in the face of tremendous official resistance (contrast with Schwartz and Pharr 2003).

In summary, long-standing rule by the LDP along with gerrymandered districts and budgetary control created and sustained overwhelming obstacles that prevented the rapid translation of social changes or voter frustration into opposition party success. More than a decade of economic torpor might well have warranted political retribution in the abstract, but anyone attacking from outside the well-constructed castle of conservative dominance had to overcome deep institutional moats, towering protective walls, and an arsenal of conservative weaponry. That opposition electoral success was consequently far from instantaneous should occasion little surprise.

Structural Impediments to an Alternative Economic Agenda

The barriers to opposition success from outside the ruling circles of power also help to explain why the ruling conservatives themselves were in no great rush to jettison their past economic approaches in ways that would have challenged established constituent groups. Instead, within the conservative camp, a large number of deeply vested interests—banks, farmers, bureaucrats, and potentially bankrupt companies to name only the most obvious—had every economic reason to resist changes that might threaten their guaranteed place at the public trough. And so, of course, did many elected officials. More significant, all of these groups maintained strong structural controls over key veto points in the political system that allowed them to mount an effective campaign of resistance to changes they opposed.

Japan's biggest economic problem, as has been well documented, was the country's massive problem of nonperforming loans (NPL). This problem grew out of Japan's 1985–90 asset bubble and the subsequent collapse of that bubble in 1990–91. Economists offered competing analyses of how best to deal with the NPL problem. Monetarists called for easy money; neo-Keynesians preferred budgetary stimulation; many structuralists argued in favor of a massive internal reorganization of the entire economy. Not surprisingly, this last suggestion was the one most strongly resisted by those with a stake in the existing system.

Most of Japan's NPLs were secured by land or stock held by the borrowers. When stock and land prices collapsed, the loans became virtually worthless. Yet, for the banks to write off these loans and attempt to sell off the collateral at their new but drastically reduced values would have meant bank failures, massive bankruptcies, and unemployment among the borrowing firms, even if such actions might eventually have led to an economically positive reallocation of national resources in favor of more highly productive and internationally competitive firms and sectors. Failure to write off the loans kept numerous so-called zombie firms on life support. They were Japan's walking dead, unable to utilize capital profitably. But clearly, numerous LDP constituents would have been hurt by radical financial measures to end the NPL problem through structural reforms that would have eliminated the zombies. Equally vulnerable would have been electorally sensitive LDP officeholders, who were anxious to avoid the politically damaging consequences of firm failure, unemployment, and further collapses in stock prices.

Economic reform proposals that arose from within the conservative camp thus confronted barriers at least as serious as those confronting challengers from outside the ranks of the rulers. Numerous constituent supporters of the old regime retained strong interests in preventing an unraveling of those policies that privileged them. And in their opposition to change they had strong allies in bureaucratic and LDP circles as well as control over numerous policy-making veto points. Even conservative reformers were forced to confront the tightly closed and functionally organized policy-making process described above, a system that privileged individual bureaucratic agencies, corporatized interests, and functionally oriented parliamentarians. As a consequence, it was a mixture of easy money pushed by the Bank of Japan, and expansionary budgets pushed by politicians and many bureaucrats, that became the policy mixture of choice throughout most of the 1990s. The expectation was that national and corporate growth would be stimulated, even at the expense of inflation, so that the NPLs could eventually be paid down by companies returning to profitability, rather than written off or monetized. More importantly, if such stimulation had the desired effects, there would be no need for deeper structural reforms of the economy as a whole, nor any direct penalties being paid by key conservative constituencies.

Particularly valuable in holding conservative constituents in line was the government's control over the public budget. Even during the worst of the country's macroeconomic difficulties, the LDP continued to use this budgetary power to provide all manner of clientelistic benefits to constituents, seeking to keep them quiescent and electoral opponents at bay.

Throughout the 1990s, the ruling conservatives relied on Keynesian fiscal stimulation, combined with low interest rates, and not a little bit of electoral self-interest to lard out publicly funded pork to valued constituents. The *Economist* (April 23, 1998, 107) showed that between 1994 and 1998 public spending as a percent of GDP shrank in almost all rich democracies. The biggest drop came in Sweden where it fell from 68 percent to 59 percent of GDP.

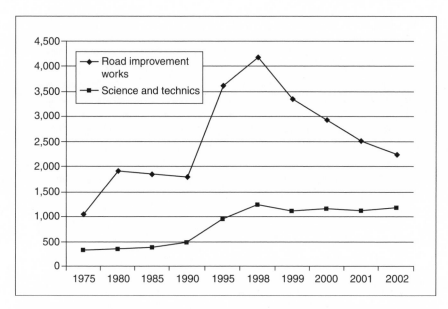

Figure 2.1. Budget expenditures (selected years). Note: Value in yen (billions).

Britain saw a large 6.1 percent drop. In contrast, the only country where public spending increased during this period was Japan, which saw a growth of 2 percent.

For most of the 1990s, government expenditures went heavily to large-scale construction projects in rural areas while spending for science and technology languished (see figure 2.1). Until at least 1998, Japan's government officials continued to pursue classical pork over investments in potentially high-payoff technologies, new firms, or innovative manufacturing procedures. The Bank of Japan, meanwhile, pursued exceptionally low interest rate policies, making it easier and cheaper for the government to issue debt. With little public money going into projects likely to generate enhanced labor or capital productivity or to exert a strong multiplier effect throughout the economy, government debt levels soared to approximately 160 percent of GDP, by far the highest levels in the industrial world. Public debt service in Japan was chewing up nearly one-quarter of the annual national budget in 2004. Japan was the only major country running a bigger budget deficit than it had four years earlier. Such boondoggles exacerbated Japan's economic difficulties even as they provided an unmistakable political benefit to the party in power. Fiscal and monetary looseness became key tools in the LDP's retention of power, retaining constituent loyalty at the expense of future generations. Moreover, conservative control of the budget also meant that the opposition, lacking the ability to control the national treasury, entered each electoral battle armed with a metaphoric slingshot against incumbents wielding howitzers.

Ironically, even the Japanese big business sector did not demand radical changes in economic policy. The major big business federations along with the always budgetarily conscious Ministry of Finance remained strong opponents of expanding government debt; indeed, the ministry pressed for tax hikes to offset any stimulus packages—hardly a politically palatable proposal or one likely to resolve the nation's NPL or deflation problems. Yet, most arguments about reducing public works, redirecting the budget in other directions, or tight fiscal austerity faced political stonewalling in the interests of policies designed to shift public resources to well-entrenched and generously contributing, if not always internationally competitive, supporters.

Keidanren, Japan's largest and most prestigious business association, has traditionally aligned itself with the principles of "deregulation" and "economic reform." And when the coalition government came into power in 1993, Keidanren eliminated its previously automatic electoral support for the ruling conservatives (Pempel 1998, 140–41). But like the LDP, Keidanren is made up of both globally competitive and protection-dependent firms and sectors. Consequently, it too has been a less-than-consistent advocate of new policies and structures. Japan has thus seen nothing like a massive mobilization of business pressure against the undeniably inefficient policies the government pursued for fifteen years.

Business quiescence on economic policy was facilitated by the large numbers of Japan's most internationally competitive corporations that had already transferred substantial portions of their productive facilities offshore. As a result, such companies were no longer so directly affected by the costs of slow-to-no reform economics at home. Furthermore, domestic business demands for programs of enhanced economic efficiencies were muted because many of their remaining domestic operations depend on their smaller (and often less efficient) subcontractors. Moreover, many of Japan's largest corporatist business associations, which might be expected to favor tighter fiscal policies, bank restructuring, and resolution of the NPL issue, are hemmed in because memberships of national peak associations are so comprehensive that constituent firms advocating such changes are often counterbalanced within the organization by firms likely to oppose them. Toyota and Canon, in effect, are offset within Keidanren by Mizuho Holdings and Daiei (Vogel 1999). Japan's business community more generally was further split, with Keidanren's influence offset to a large extent by that of the Japan Chamber of Commerce, whose members are predominantly small and medium-sized firms with primarily domestic markets.

Thus, much as was the case with the institutional rigidities mitigating against changes from without, the institutions and political glue that had long held the conservative regime together also worked to impede rapid preemptive policy changes from within the conservative camp.

Nevertheless, as the economy spiraled downward, more of Japan's ruling conservatives began to seek the mantle of "economic reformer," advocating new economic policy directions. Since 1993, a host of political leaders, at the national, prefectural, and city levels, have wrapped themselves in the reformist cloak, issuing challenges to the prevailing political system and promising radical structural overhauls across an array of policy arenas. Among the more prominent have been former prime ministers Hosokawa and Hashimoto and current prime minister Koizumi as well as governors in a dozen or more prefectures. As a result, for much of this period the real battle over "reform" versus "resistance" in Japan has taken place primarily within conservative ranks, rather than between conservatives and outside opponents or between the government and citizen-voters. Yet, at least until Koizumi's rule—and many would argue, even through most of it—intraconservative reformers faced formidable obstacles in their effort to gain control of the policy agenda and to redirect the economic balance of costs and benefits.

In some noneconomic areas, policy change was rapid. As Richard Friman and others make clear in chapter 4, long-standing sacred cows of policy have been slaughtered in the defense and security areas. On September 23, 1997, the U.S. and Japanese governments put in place a set of revised guidelines for Japan-U.S. defense cooperation. These changed the basis for Japan-U.S. security cooperation to include a specific section on Japan-U.S. defense cooperation in surrounding areas, not limited only to Japanese territory. Previously, any such substantial revision and rearticulation of the treaty would have been the subject of major street demonstrations; this time they were passed with only minor public debate. Similarly in 1999, the national flag and anthem were officially and rather quietly reintroduced, ending decades of hitherto ideologically charged animosities on both sides of the issue. Similarly, the government moved quickly at U.S. behest after September 11, 2001, to institute extensive antiterrorism legislation. Japanese ships were dispatched to the Indian Ocean as part of the war against al Qaeda in Afghanistan, and Japan sent troops to support U.S. actions in Iraq. All represented major breaks with the past. A systematic liberalization of wide swaths of the financial sector, labeled the Big Bang, after the Thatcherite changes affecting the City of London, was instituted in 1998. Substantial changes also took place in, among others, labor policy, social welfare, and education.

Economic changes were far slower to materialize. Although the reformist voices within the conservative camp grew louder with time and as the old ways failed to remedy the economic situation, actual changes in policy demanded

numerous slow and not-always-visible changes in the structures of policymaking as a prelude to actual policy shifts. Just as Japan's electoral system and
party system underwent important changes that did not result in instant
change, so too did the country's national bureaucracy and the broader policy-making structures. In January 2001, Japan's twenty-odd ministries were re-
combined into thirteen, with an important redistribution of functions and
powers in many of the most important.

Many of the previously tight links between agency and constituent interest
group were broken and the longstanding system of vertical administration was
challenged. Previous powers of bureaucratic officials to testify before the parliament were checked. Political appointees previously held only the top two
posts in any ministry, leaving agencies free to pursue their internal agendas;
that number was more than tripled for most agencies, providing additional
layers of political checks over earlier bureaucratic autonomy. In addition, as
part of the 1996 Big Bang the Ministry of Finance lost its previously complete
control over licensing of financial institutions to a new agency, the Financial
Supervisory Agency (later Financial Services Agency).

Perhaps most important, the new and well-staffed Cabinet Office, plus a
bolstered Cabinet Secretariat, gained substantial muscle within the general
policy-making process. At the end of 1999 the Prime Minister's Office had a
staff of 582 and the Cabinet Secretariat had 184. By the end of 2001, the new
Cabinet Office had nearly 2,200 staff and the Cabinet Secretariat had more
than tripled to 487 (Prime Minister of Japan 2002). Under 1999 legislation,
the prime minister was also given explicit authority to engage in policy planning and to initiate legislation. The new Council on Economic and Fiscal Policy gained considerable leeway to generate a mixture of policies that would
address the NPL problem, banking problems, deregulation of public sector
corporations, and a host of related issues. All of these measures shifted the
previous balance of power between elected officials and senior bureaucrats.
Individual agency autonomy declined as the power of elected politicians rose.
Even more important, the power of individual LDP leaders, including the
once-formidable faction leaders, has been reduced as the prime minister and
the cabinet have gained more policy-making oversight and decision-making
power. Overall, the rigid vertical policy-making structures of the past have
been slowly trumped by new and powerful initiatives by the prime minister,
the Cabinet Office, and the Cabinet Secretariat.

Additionally, a series of changes took place in laws governing corporate organization that encouraged large numbers of private companies to reduce
their crossholdings of stock shares with one another; reduce their links to so-
called main banks; change their patterns of internal employment and promotion; and give greater emphasis to corporate profitability. At least as
important, the Industrial Revitalization Law passed in 2003 setting up the In-

dustrial Revitalization Corporation, which was given a host of powers to force the internal restructuring of "zombie companies" that were deeply in debt and showed little sign of near-term returns to profitability.

These new structures of power have been vital to structural economic reform efforts, particularly those undertaken by Prime Minister Koizumi. Koizumi took office promising "reforms with no sanctuaries" and laid down an explicit challenge to many of the underlying structures and power holders blocking political and economic change. Koizumi's critics would argue that he has been quicker to generate slogans and promises than to deliver comprehensive reforms. They suggest that the underlying structures remain largely unchallenged by his actions (Mulgan 2002).

Yet the numerous changes in structures and policies, some put in place by his administration, others in place before he took office, have provided Koizumi with a reconfigured policy-making process, enabling him and his supporters to push through changes in economic policy that will force substantial structural reforms and an end to many old patterns. Most notably, he has utilized the Council on Economic and Fiscal Policy, which has broad economic advisory powers and reports only to the prime minister. On June 21, 2001, it proposed sweeping changes in a host of politically sensitive areas. Koizumi has since carried out reforms in many of these areas, including road construction, the postal savings system, the NPL problem, the privatization of various public sector corporations, and caps on the issuance of new bonds for public works (Amyx 2004a).

Koizumi was constantly opposed on many of his policy proposals by well-entrenched party leaders. For four years, Koizumi and his allies jousted on a tightrope with anti-reformist party leaders. Still, he held on to office much longer than his ten immediate predecessors; he bypassed major faction leaders in his cabinet choices and in many of his policy proposals, thereby weakening their long-term power capabilities. Koizumi proved that his real sources of strength lay outside the party, largely with a public that had grown frustrated with the slow pace of political and economic reform and with a media savvy that allowed him to bypass traditional party channels. Then, with surprising boldness, Koizumi's party reform effort bore political fruit. When his postal reform bill was blocked in parliament, he dissolved the Lower House, purged thirty-seven of his LDP opponents, and dispatched new LDP "assassins" to challenge them in their own districts. Making "reform" the keystone issue, he led the LDP to a romping victory on September 11, 2005. Koizumi's partially purged LDP won two-thirds of the seats, decimating both his intra-party resisters and the opposition DPJ. The balance of power has shifted definitively in favor of a structural reform agenda, and it is difficult to see these being quickly reversed by any successor to Koizumi.

Important changes, most of them unlikely to be reversed by changes in government, have also begun to occur at the corporate level in Japan. These often appear to be slow and episodic, but collectively they have been monumental. The experiences of Nissan under Renault control are particularly telling; massive restructurings made the president of Nissan, Carlos Ghosn, a national economic hero. Other foreign firms have successfully penetrated the previously closed financial and insurance sectors and increased their influence over broad business practices within the entire sector. Similarly, numerous foreign corporations such as Citicorp, IBM, and Carfours have entered Japan with competitive vigor, forcing widespread reorganization by their Japanese-owned competitors. Numerous firms once considered too big to fail have gone bankrupt; others are likely to follow. Meanwhile, many of Japan's longstanding corporate success stories—Honda, Toyota, Sony, and Canon, for example—retain their high levels of profitability, while other newer firms, such as Uniqlo, Softbank, or Rakuten Ichiba, are laying the groundwork for long-term success pursuing new business models. Such evidence suggests that Japan is undergoing substantial microlevel economic changes that complement the moves away from macrolevel political rigidities and the introduction of new reformist policies to deal with NPLs and zombie firms. In the long run, such microlevel changes will almost surely have a transformative effect on the overall economy, particularly to the extent that they are bolstered by macrolevel structural and policy changes such as those being pursued by Prime Minister Koizumi. The result is likely to be a substantially restructured national political economy.

Looking Ahead: Reform versus Resistance

It became increasingly clear at both the elite and mass levels that economic choices under slow growth could no longer be made with expectations that there would be no losers, as had been the case under Japan's earlier rapid economic expansion. Enhancing national productivity now demands radical alterations in numerous sectors of the economy. Yet Japan's political system long resisted opposition challenges from the outside as well as policy changes from within the ruling circles. Old rigidities softened slowly. Over a decade of low interest rates and generous government subsidies and spending did little to revitalize national economic productivity or to stimulate structural changes. Instead, they reflected the power of existing structures to keep important LDP constituencies permanently dependent on the public treasury in exchange for their votes.

For a decade there was little change in office holders or public policies. Conservative power brokers used well-entrenched structures of power to prevent the adoption of new economic policies that would have harmed domestic and politically protected sectors. The residues of Japan's 1955 system remained deeply entrenched through much of the last fifteen years, despite their obvious interference with policies of economic growth.

Nor were elections quick to uproot Japan's entrenched and economically inefficient sectors. The numerous revampings of the electoral and party systems led to few clear-cut electoral choices on national economic policy. The longstanding weakness of opposition parties reduced the seriousness of threats to conservative power through voter revolt. Clearly, the LDP, often with the support of the Japan Communist Party, the Clean Government Party, and the Democratic Socialist Party of Japan, supported the economically inefficient status quo while the new opposition parties by and large favored far more deregulation and economic liberalization to benefit urban areas and Japan's more competitive sectors (Uchida et al. 1996). But this cleavage was far from clear-cut. Voices of structural reform began, with time, to swell inside LDP ranks as well. And meanwhile, the gradual rise in the electoral appeal and parliamentary strength of the Democratic Party of Japan increased the external pressure on the LDP to continue dismantling the old system in ways that would allow for a revitalization of the national economy.

As of this writing, it has become clear that many of the longstanding structural impediments to changes in economic policy are slowly being dismantled. And new economic policies have been pushed, particularly by Prime Minister Koizumi, while Japanese corporations have themselves been moving away from longstanding behaviors that impeded productivity growth, adopting instead methods that hold greater promise of improved global competitiveness. The 2005 election results should spur further reforms.

That Japanese society is undergoing a series of wide-ranging changes that portend substantial breaks with the past is clear from Kelly and White's evidence in chapter 3. Yet those social changes were not mirrored by equal changes in politics or economics. Among other reasons, the new social groups that Kelly and White examine have been far quicker to opt out of politics than to opt in. To what extent, and with what speed, such changes will eventually filter into the political arena is not clear. Yet beyond the groups they stress, other changes are restructuring Japanese society. Broad demographic changes are certain to continue making Japan's citizenry more urban rather than rural, older rather than younger. The work force is likely to become more female, more part-time, and less committed to long-term careers within a single firm than it has been over most of the postwar period. Previously dominant elite tracks to power are almost certain to be paralleled by equally powerful alternative paths that challenge previous monopolies over powerful posts. Local governors, mayors, and civil servants are almost certain to con-

tinue challenging their Tokyo counterparts as they seek to advance particularistic policy solutions across a range of issues. Japan has seen an explosion
of nongovernmental organizations since the Kobe earthquake in 1995, and
many are anxious to exert policy-making influence or to take on new tasks or
those previously handled by the public sector on a variety of issues.

That many of these social changes will find reflections in the political arena
is highly probable. It is, for example, hard to imagine a Japan twenty-five years
from now as protectionist of agriculture or small business, or as devoid of public policies dealing with the particularities and demands of large numbers of
women or part-timers in the work force as is currently the case. Meanwhile,
the potential for serious political change through the electoral and party system is being enhanced because of changes within the LDP and particularly
the 2005 victory of "reformer" Koizumi.

Thus, the catalysts of serious change have been winning out since the turn
of the century. But in the long tortured process that has preceded this apparent shift in movement, three points demand attention. First, substantial
overhaul of an extensive and deeply entrenched set of policies, procedures,
and institutions takes considerable time. It is well for an American audience,
for example, to recall that in the late 1980s the United States was widely seen
as being locked into a spiral of declining productivity, loss of jobs and markets to overseas competitors, constantly expanding budget deficits, and a permanent underclass of unemployables. Yet a decade later the picture had been
radically reversed. The shift came not through any single policy measure or
electoral shift but as the outgrowth of a series of linked and reinforcing
changes in corporate behavior, the Internet revolution, changes in national
welfare and immigration policies, a host of deregulation measures, and the
positive effects of a rising stock market on government revenues. That some
of these changes have now been slowed in no way negates the substantial reversal in America's economic fortunes from the 1980s to the present. But any
assumption that changes in public opinion swiftly and automatically lead to
reform must be weighed against the capacity of well-entrenched structures to
impede that process.

Second, although the decks may have long been stacked against the newer
opposition parties or against intra-LDP advocates of economic reform, politically generated change is proving possible. The LDP lost power in 1993 not
because of electoral defeat by an opposition party but because of dissention
and splits within its own ranks. The proclaimed principles of political parties
and the interests of individual parliamentarians are frequently at odds. As was
noted above, the LDP in 2005 continued to contain a disjunctive mixture of
pro- and antireformers. Yet, the internal balance then shifted dramatically in
favor of the reformers. Moreover, under the new electoral system, many in-

dividual politicians in Japan are able to act with less fear of internal party or factional retribution. Therefore, if breaking with the ruling party promises a plausible chance of a parliamentarians' becoming part of a winning coalition, the incentives to split go up. Many of the conservatives who broke party ranks in 1993 were undoubtedly convinced that staying with an LDP that had been broadly labeled as "antireform" might well threaten their own electoral fortunes while they stood more of a chance of being reelected by making a break with "corruption" to join something "reformist" (Otake 1995; Kabashima 1994). A similar threat from within conservative ranks occurred when Kato Koichi challenged the leadership. For the moment there are few incentives for party reorganization from within the LDP. A super majority for the party should reduce the incentives for individual members to bolt in search of greener political pastures. But the devastating loss for the DPJ will surely generate internal finger-pointing and possible reorganization. And while the LDP currently looks to have regained its "one-party dominance," there are few guarantees against either future splits or an opposition party comeback.

This leads logically to the third point, and the reasons for expecting long-term change. Japan has gone through major changes in policymaking structures, the centralization of power in the cabinet and in the prime ministership, the microlevel changes in corporate behavior, and most particularly in the policies advanced by Prime Minister Koizumi. It is not yet clear how extensive these reforms will prove to be and to what extent recent shifts will be permanent and establish a new, less protectionist regime. But structural changes have allowed substantial economic reforms that are being generated from within the LDP itself.

Japan continues to confront a deeply rooted battle between those sectors of its economy that are globally competitive and that will benefit from and embrace market deregulation and greater liberalization versus those forces heavily dependent on a politically protected domestic economy and public works. In the long run, almost certainly, the former will "win," and certainly political momentum now favors a quickening of the pace of reform. But it is likely to come with continued government support to the country's more dependent sectors. They are unlikely to be abandoned completely even as reforms progress.

Since the turn of the century the combination of structural changes within the political world, new policy initiatives that challenge the most retrograde elements of Japan's protectionism and oligopoly, along with rapid microlevel changes among many of Japan's individual corporations, suggest that after a long decade of torpor the forces of change have gathered sufficient momentum to overturn the major forces of resistance. The old system that was so politically and economically beneficial to the country from the early 1950s into the very early 1990s proved incapable of delivering the same mixture of political or economic benefits under altered global and domestic conditions. It is a system that is slowly being dismembered, and recent evidence suggests that the pace at which it will change, and be replaced by new patterns, is rapidly increasing.

3

Students, Slackers, Singles, Seniors, and Strangers: Transforming a Family-Nation

WILLIAM W. KELLY AND MERRY I. WHITE

Have new forms of engagement between Japan and Asia overtaken processes of Americanization in the region? Answering this question requires looking within Japan itself to identify domestic sites of social institutional reorganization. Given over a decade of economic stasis and retrograde politics, it may seem odd to foresee significant societal changes. Nonetheless, we believe there are potentially far-reaching developments emerging in today's society, driven by domestic, regional, and global forces and with consequences not only for Japan but for its influence in other parts of Asia. Many of these developments have been enabled by the break that the 1990s created from the mass middle-class society, the conservative politics of prescriptive familism and cultural nationalism, and a government- and corporate-led economic agenda of aggregate growth that marked the post–World War II decades.

The events that roiled Japan during the 1990s surprised most analysts. We all witnessed—but few had foreseen—the decomposition of central elements of both the international system and the domestic arrangements that had sustained Showa Japan through its postwar decades. The breakup of the Soviet Union, the death of the Showa Emperor in 1989, the collapse of the 1980s bubble economy into a prolonged economic stasis and recession, the continuing disarray of the post-1955 political system—these and other developments present us in the early twenty-first century with a far more chastened and anxious object of contemplation than the confident Japan of the late

This chapter has been jointly and equally prepared by the two authors. Both of us have drawn on, revised, and updated several recent publications, especially White 2002 and Kelly 2002.

1980s. What many Japanese have taken to call the "lost decade" (*ushiwareta junen*) stretches into a new century.

Many argue in retrospect that Japan was only able to recover and prosper in the half century between 1945 and 1990 because it was nurtured by a special and now-defunct hothouse international political economy that included an undervalued yen in a dollar-denominated world economy, a U.S. security umbrella in a bipolar superpower struggle, and an edge in high-value manufacturing technologies in an era of industrial capitalism. Such analysts conclude that the disappearance of these conditions precipitated the malaise and crisis in which Japan now lingers. Although it is undeniable that these fundamental shifts had structural consequences, we would add three further developments that are more domestic but equally significant in shaping the conditions of daily life and individual behavior.

First, mid- to late-twentieth century Japan was ideologically marked by a historically unique generation, the so-called single-digit Showans, those born in the first nine years of the reign of the Showa Emperor, between 1926 and 1934. This generation, set in a demographic profile with a youthful bottom-heavy age pyramid, with stable but low fertility, was marked as rooted in but not responsible for Japan's fifteen-year Pacific War, and it came of age in a society made youthful by the immediate postwar baby boom. As the single-digit Showans die off, that age pyramid has begun to reverse, as the larger population at the base of the pyramid moves up into retirement. We are still seeing gaps between generations, even as most of the population was born or mainly raised in the postwar period, and even as consumer culture tends to blend rather than to distinguish generational experiences.

Second, in important respects the societal arrangements and inducements that were consolidated by the mid-1960s have, ironically, proven too successful for their own good. They have produced what William Steslicke (1987) once called the "dilemmas of success." The educational arms race—that is, the continuing escalation of parental investment and student effort to gain one of the limited number of prestigious educational credentials—and the hyperconcentration of resources and population in metropolitan Tokyo are two examples of the power of this monocentric urban society to focus on one locale—be it an educational apex or a geographical center—as the source of power and value.

Third, many argue that Japan's present arrangements cannot accommodate its present realities. Contradictions and resentments have surfaced publicly, and private discontents have become public critiques. The population has had enough of an economy that produced "rich Japan, poor Japanese" and a political system that combined Confucian welfare and its stringent demands on families with corrupt cronyism. The government's sloganeering about "expanding leisure," "promoting privatization," "internationalization," and "our beautiful family culture" draws wry smiles from an increasingly cynical citizenry. Of course the rhetoric of social policies has never matched the lives of the constituencies they claim to serve, and discontent has broken through the polite veneer of official representation, revealing families and individuals who never approximated the "unique and beautiful social culture" politicians extol. These people have found that the unconventional may be the only way ordinary people can survive, convention having served them poorly.

Japan is thus at a moment both of residual dysfunction and of emergent understandings and arrangements. Still, even these three domestic developments do not in themselves specify the shifts in people's lives and actions that might actually be producing these restructurings. We want to propose five tendencies that are challenging the social formation of contemporary Japan:

- Among students, (a) the increasing success of private secondary schools with six-year middle and high school programs to place their students in elite universities and (b) the declining ability of public high schools to find jobs for their graduates going to work through the formal job placement procedures that have operated so successfully in recent decades.
- Among young workers, the increasing numbers who choose or are forced to accept part-time or temporary employment.
- The rapidly rising percentage of women who are postponing marriage and parenting, many of whom remain living with their parents while continuing to work.
- Among the elderly population, the rising percentages who are living alone or with a spouse for longer periods of their later years.
- Among the large numbers of nonethnic permanent residents and ethnic Japanese return migrants, a new visibility and assertiveness that are making these "strangers" to the mainstream more familiar in daily life and a more effective testament to the fallacy of ethnic homogeneity that centered twentieth-century Japan's cultural nationalism.

It is risky to speculate on vectors of change, and we certainly do not claim that these five diagnostics exhaust the possibilities. We are intrigued by them, however, because each poses alternatives and exposes contradictions that cannot be easily contained by present arrangements. Students, slackers, singles, seniors, and strangers: five social types whose actions, though certainly constrained, rarely collective, and seldom animated by political objectives, nonetheless are harbingers. They are categories of actors, not social groups; they differ widely in their room for maneuver and range of choices; and all five are marginal categories to the ideological mainstream, though less marginal in economic or political terms. But to anthropologists such as ourselves, who have long been concerned with the nature of Japan's "new middle class" modernity, they signal the waning power of a "mainstream consciousness" to channel aspirations and effort.

Japan in a Family Way

These particular emergent actions all bear on the official representations and everyday realities of families in present-day Japan. Although families are critical in framing individual lives in every society, the family has played an especially strategic role in modern Japan, in policy, discourse, and action. Even more than other advanced industrial nation-states, twentieth-century Japan has officially and popularly represented itself as a family-nation, in political, economic, and social terms and forms (Ochiai 1997). Over the century, these formulations have had different ideological tones (from the aggressively political to the economically stolid), and the family idiom has been applied to various locations(e.g., the family emperor-state, the corporation as family, and family as social bedrock of the state). Formulations and exhortations of family have even been fundamentally contradictory; sometimes the family form exhorted has been the multigenerational *ie* and at other times it is the family as nuclear unit (e.g., White 2002).

Family talk has often been paired with family critique, however, as new motivations, actions, and realities among students, singles, slackers, seniors, and strangers are fracturing the bedrock of the ideologically approved family. To protect an image of the family most useful for social policy, the critiques have focused on those who appear to deviate from the model, and thus, in themselves, seem to be breaking up the unit into errant or deviant components. Thus, the critiques often tend to ignore the family unit itself as a social force and focus on elements of families—youth, women, and the elderly in particular—as paradoxically putting the families to which they belong at risk. The "good family," the social service institutions, media, and politicians agree, should take care of its own, and in doing so take care of the nation.

For instance, one problem that critics locate in the family is a steady downward trend in birthrates, which is affecting the national demographic profile, the economy, schooling, and family life itself. To some, it is evidence of women's self-sufficiency and power to choose, but to critics it signals a decline in family values and a serious risk to the future of society. The rising number of elderly people and their increasing dependence on family and society are framed within the falling birthrate as a future burden on revenue-deprived social services. The increase in temporary employment among the young, called "furita" in the press, is taken as a lack of broader commitment to social responsibility among youth, rather than as a product of job shortages in the permanent employment sector. And, continuing the theme of selfishness among the young, the "parasite singles," unmarried young people who live with their parents past the usual entry into marriage or bachelor independence, shout "Immaturity! Lack of self-sufficiency!" to some observers. As for the husbands and fathers in such families, they alone appear immune from most criticism: hard-working and selfless, they continue to provide the resources to maintain at least the image of family, or so it is said.

Among the student youth, the supposedly meritocratic link between schooling and occupation is attenuating as more of them seek out private secondary schools that have better placement records in elite universities and thus in elite employment than the public high schools, whose graduates represent the larger percentage of school leavers in ordinary jobs. The premise in the past was that the student's hard work would assure success; increasingly, it is the family's ability to pay for educational enhancements that makes some children more "equal" than others (Kariya 2001).

For those young adults whom some might call slackers, the entry point into lifetime employment has narrowed even further than in the 1970s, when "examination hell" and the "credential society" were first noted. Many youth who previously would have been slated for assured futures in white-collar work are now forced into part-time or temporary employment. It is true that many call themselves "furita" (a new term that combines the English "free" and the German "Arbeiter") as a choice rather than a necessity, but, as one young man noted, "It's not a lifestyle choice; it's all there is for me."

The point of entry into work has become especially problematic for young women. Although in the past women graduating from middle school or high school were seen as "golden eggs," desirable as well-trained, docile low-wage clerks or factory workers, now they have a harder time finding work. Those with higher education, in fact, now see an "ice age" in employment chances as they are frozen out of the market for desirable jobs even harder and faster than males.

Family forms and relations are further affected by the increasing numbers of young women beyond school age who remain living with their parents and staying with their jobs (however dead-end) longer, thus delaying marriage and childbearing. Although the popular press and government officials may say that women are on a "birth strike" and selfishly putting Japan's future at risk, women (married or unmarried) who delay mothering for the most part need to work rather than "choose" to work. Indeed, the cost of raising a middle-class child is so high that much of the paid work done by married women is devoted to paying education costs. And the choice to have only one child (leading to the much-discussed *hitori-ko mondai* or one-child problem) is most often explained by this fact.

For women, too, the care of the elderly looms as a burdensome prospect.

With families bearing most of the cost and time for supporting dependent elderly, and with ever-lengthening life spans, more women find themselves in middle age or even old age caring for their husbands' or their own parents. As people have fewer children, the care of the elderly can no longer be shared among several siblings. The family member whose work is seen as most disposable and who is seen as having the most free time is the housewife, and it is she who finds herself doing the caregiving.

Among seniors, there is a recent trend to live apart from family, or to live in housing dedicated to the elderly, for so long as it is possible. Seniors increasingly have more community services available, such as senior centers, adult day care, activity groups in ward offices, and the like for either occasional respite activities or as more fulltime hobbies and passions. Volunteer work for and among the elderly has increased, and nongovernmental organizations are now trying to fill the gap left by social policies (Nakano forthcoming). These emergent patterns can offer rewarding alternative routines and satisfactions to a family-embedded old age, but because most are only available for elders who are physically fit, they do not resolve but perhaps only postpone the intractable issue of who is to care for the infirm and the dependent elderly.

Thus, each of these trends is grounded in and is reshaping the official representations and the everyday realities of family that stand at the heart of contemporary Japan. In specifying these emergent actors we are also mapping new tensions and new connections between publicly sanctioned typifications of "Family" and popular forms of "families."

To be sure, even the distinction between such conventionalities and the multiple realities in which people live is often difficult to make because people are drawn to use the rhetoric of typifications of family form and school success and work careers, and endeavor to conform to their promise and demands. But those of the Japanese population enumerated by our alliterative title (and others) are not blind to that difficulty, and in their own ways they are challenging the present conventions of their society. They are seldom unconstrained by the force of social norms, rarely collective in their actions, and hardly animated by political objectives, but they are nonetheless harbingers of new alliances and strategies that may well break up of what has long been considered a mass society. At the very least, these trajectories may signal the waning power of a "mainstream consciousness" to channel aspirations and effort and force a revision of the "Family" talk that has been so literally and metaphorically central to official talk about private lives, economic activity, and national representations for so long.

Students: Private Shortcuts to Academic Success and Failed School-Work Links

The severe recession throughout the 1990s intersected with a shifting population profile to pose serious threats to higher education and the school-to-work transition. The entry-level hiring scale of major corporations shrank dramatically in that decade. Newspapers were full of anecdotes about elite graduates in "job shock" accepting ever-lower entry positions as overqualified recruits to gain entrance to first-tier corporations, or resigning themselves to less prestigious company openings, with ripple effects on down the educational prestige ladder. At the same time, the number of eighteen-year-olds in the population was declining sharply, from 2.05 million in 1992 to 1.51 million in 2000, putting enormous pressures on the already shaky finances of lower-tier, tuition-dependent private universities and junior colleges, and encouraging some to strategize on services to offer to nontraditional students, companies, and the elderly.

In spite of a shrinking college age population, declining job opportunities continue to produce strong competition for elite universities. The consequence may well be the collapse of the tense balance between public- and private-sector secondary education that has held for the last three decades. A complement to public high school education thought to be sufficient for elite university entrance was a heavy dose of after-school cram classes, home tutoring by college students or faculty, and possibly a postsecondary year in a private examination-preparation school. In only the last five years or so, the more assured—and expensive—route is through the emerging tier of elite private high schools that offer six-year secondary programs. Some are attached to private universities, access to which is all but assured by attendance in the high schools. In 1993, the percentage of applicants who were admitted to the various faculties of Tokyo University, the pinnacle of the top tier, from private high schools had reached nearly 50 percent. Of the top thirty placement high schools, twenty-one were private institutions. This trend has continued for a decade. Preliminary figures for the 2005 entrance exams show that all but one of the top 23 placement high schools were private (the only exception was #15; figures from Nii 2005).

Admitting their students by highly competitive exams at the end of their sixth-grade year (somewhat analogous to the fateful "eleven-plus" exams in Britain), these schools, in effect, combine the three years of junior high school with the three of high school. They move their students through the Ministry of Education secondary curriculum in four and a half to five years, leaving the balance for preparation for specific university entrance exams.

The particular school-to-work transitions of contemporary Japan have depended on the tight calibrations of school and work prestige hierarchies

(Rosenbaum and Kariya 1989). For several decades, the widely discrepant outcomes of the individuals moving through school into workplaces have been accepted without public outcry or collective resistance (though sometimes frustration, grief, and personal tragedy receive public attention). In large part, the successful have claimed legitimacy for the principle of effort = achievement, and the failures have been cooled out through the public belief that the process is egalitarian. Ostensibly, secondary facilities are equally funded, the national curriculum is equally distributed, and the exams are for the most part equally demanding and equally "fair." The present school-to-work complex is threatened, however, by the increasing privatization of the system and the increasingly inegalitarian streaming of students with more family resources into the most prestigious establishments.

The effect is to more starkly reveal what the long-supposed meritocracy has never been able to provide: reward for ability. The sociologist Ishida Hiroshi has shown that elite higher education did not have a statistically significant social mobility effect in the last thirty years (Ishida 1993, 2001). Government policies, teachers' union agitation, public opinion, and private expectations notwithstanding, children of advantaged parents were consistently overrepresented in elite universities. The word "elite" itself, which used to imply equal opportunity for prestige, now means reproduced parental social status among the advantaged. Private secondary students have disproportionately filled the ranks of Tokyo University's entering classes at least since the early 1970s, a result of the 1967 Tokyo metropolitan university reforms (Rohlen 1977). Indeed, what Kariya and Rosenbaum (1999) call "bright flight," the exodus of better students from public secondary schools to private secondary schools, has been most advanced in those prefectures like Tokyo that implemented deliberate "detracking" policies. Clearly, public education has been "misrecognized" as meritocratic for a long time, and it is possible that a thoroughgoing privatization of the upper tier of secondary education will neither fundamentally shake the institutional linkages nor challenge the legitimacy of school outcomes or workplace destinations. This is unlikely, though, and if the present tendencies become future trends, a very different public-private tension will develop. The stage will be set for a new educational arms race on much more transparently unequal class and regional terms.

The bottom end of the secondary education hierarchy is similarly changing rapidly. Educational officials and researchers have long highlighted not only the quality of training in Japan's technical and commercial high schools but, more important, the extensive job counseling and placement of school graduates by their schools, who maintain direct connections with employers and actively broker their students into jobs (Dore and Sako 1989, Okano 1993). Mary Brinton and others have documented the serious and rapid shrinkage of such school-work links, which have underpinned the stable labor force entry for vast numbers of blue- and pink-collar workers at least since the early 1970s (Brinton 2000, Tang and Brinton 2003, Honda 2003). This shrinkage, combined with the shrinkage of the school-age population, may mean that the present sense of the equity and utility of public education will collapse across the spectrum.

Slackers: Youthful Furita in the Ice Age of Employment

At the height of Japan's speculative frenzy in the 1980s, the notorious temporary work agency Recruit coined the neologism *furita* to designate and valorize the very category of temporary worker whose supply and demand the company brokered so profitably. These workers were the job hoppers, the fast labor of fast capitalism, and part of the media spin was to attribute a hip lifestyle to these insecure and inconstant workers. Software developers, anime illustrators, and other independent knowledge workers were glamorized, while their résumé-free counterparts in fast food and other less prestigious service industries seldom seemed trendy.

Interestingly though, the uses of the term survived, indeed proliferated, after the bubble collapse. By the late 1990s, *furita* had become a media buzzword of more complex connotations, an official category of labor for the Ministry of Labor, and a term of self-identification (and sometimes self-deprecation) for large numbers of twenty- and thirty-somethings. In March 2002, the Japan Institute of Labor (JIL) estimated that the number of furita had reached 1.9 million, largely in the tertiary service sector. In its survey of eighteen- to twenty-eight-year-olds—half of whom were furita—the furita were polled about their hours and income. They worked on an average forty hours per week, with monthly earnings of 100,000 to 150,000 yen. Fully 70 percent had never been employed as regular employees since leaving school.

There may be little that is novel about this phenomenon except the term. Irregular workers of all varieties have always been crucial to the labor force. In the past, temporary workers (usually women) provided a cushion for industries; they could expand in good times, contract in bad, and not endanger the positions of "permanent" employees. The 1990s, though, saw a significant increase in the casualization of the labor force; Osawa (2001) cites government figures showing that in 1990 roughly 20 percent of all employees, including 38 percent of female employees, were in some form of "irregular employment" (defined as work that was not full-time); by 1999, those proportions had increased to 25 percent of all employees, including 45 percent of all female employees (see also Goka 1999; Nishitani 2003; Weathers 2001; Sato 2001). This has been accompanied by a proliferation of categories of the irregular: beyond what Osawa calls the full-time part-timers (*paato*), there are contract workers (*shokutaku* and *keiyaku sha'in*), fixed-term workers (*kikanko*) dispatch workers from temp agencies (*haken*), and side jobs (*arubaito*).

It is in this workscape of para-employment that those whom the government now defines as furita are distinguishing themselves—by their youthful age profile, educational backgrounds, job categories, and career aspirations. No doubt the numbers are inflated by the sustained serial recessions of the past twelve years, creating an "ice age" of hiring freezes, downsizings, and bankruptcies, "chilling" applicants out of regular line employment. But the furita are not a simple consequence of economic forces. To be sure, in the March 2002 JIL poll, 40 percent reported that they had no choice and 45 percent reported no particular reason for opting for freelance jobs, while 15 percent said they were working toward their ultimate goal with this kind of employment. Most expressed the desire for regular employment. However, the longer one is a furita, the less likely one is to find regular employment. The Japan Institute of Labor poll indicated that roughly half of furita who sought regular positions were successful within the first year, but after two or more years that dropped to 28 percent. There are of course other variables affecting this drop besides time alone.

The furita and other irregulars portend changes in workplace relations, corporate human resource policies, and individual career tracks. What now is changing is the view of the labor force: no longer can it be said that one's life chances are determined by one's educational achievement; no longer can adulthood be confirmed with a permanent job (as corporate warrior or professional housewife); no longer can workplace relationships, corporate training, and the configuration of advancement and hierarchies be predictable and stable. What was always the case for some, from day laborers to women doing piecework at home to job changers who have always offered flexibility to the corporations, is now true for more people. The issue is not whether greater numbers of job transfers are positive or negative (what is mobility and freedom for some is insecurity and low wages for others—"fast" labor is cheap labor). Rather, it is whether the recruitment, training, and retention of a growing spectrum of semiskilled, skilled, and professional workers are destabilizing the enterprise structures of the past several decades. The evidence to date—including cutbacks in in-house training programs that are less useful for stimulating corporate loyalty, restructured pay and promotion scales to favor performance over seniority, and early retirement programs to shed older core managers—suggests they are taking their toll on the images and claims of existing large enterprises.

Singles: Women Who Can Say "No!" [1]

Two developments of the 1980s have been frequently assayed for their subsequent effects on marriage, family, and gender relations in the 1990s and after. First, for much of that decade, the growing labor shortages in blue-collar, clerical, and low-level technical work opened up opportunities for women as companies sought to avoid hiring foreign guest workers. Despite the heated controversies over the Equal Employment Opportunity Law, its passage in 1986 led to only indirect effects on women's employment. Women had jobs, not careers. Women who had completed a four-year university program were strongly affected in the 1990s by the "ice age" in employment: the more education they had, the higher their aspirations, and the more likely those aspirations were to be dashed. Most women who work, and that includes most housewives by the 1990s, say that they need to work, either to sustain their households or to provide for the costs of their children's educational preparation. Few see it as a choice, especially the kind of choice that male officialdom deems selfish.

Second, the ballyhoo over the lack of marriage-prone women for men eager for matrimony at the end of the 1980s was at its most strident in its predictions of a birth crisis. Japan became the incredible shrinking country, and the fertility rate of the week, prefecture by prefecture, became a television staple. The "1.57 shokku" of 1990 was a media boom and the title of Tanimura Shiho's best-selling novel, *Kekkon shinai ka mo shiranai shokogun* (The Maybe-I-Won't-Get-Married-after-All Syndrome) seemed to say it all. A popular magazine for young women, *Croissant,* ran a series of profiles of popular and successful women singles in their thirties and forties, and social critics derided its seeming support for female singlehood, calling it the "Croissant syndrome" (White 2002, 137–40).

Croissant magazine soon went back to extolling housewifery and romance, but in fact large numbers of women in this age group remained unmarried, most of them highly educated middle-class women. By 1995, 48 percent of women and 67 percent of men aged twenty-five to twenty-nine were unmarried, and in metropolitan Tokyo well over half of women turning thirty had not yet married. Those who did marry seemed to be delaying having children: in 1997, 40 percent of couples married for four years did not have children. And in 2003, the national birthrate was down to 1.32 (and much lower than that in Tokyo), far below replacement rate.[1]

[1] Ministry of Public Welfare, ed., *Shoshi shakai o kangaeru.* The most recent reports put it at 1.31. The most recent government population projections are available online at http://www.ipss .go.jp/Japanese/newest02/newest02.html. In English, James Raymo (2003a, 2003b) offers the most recent statistical analysis of marriage patterns. Japan is hardly alone with its rapid fertility rate decline; Krause 2001 is an anthropological study of struggles precipitated by a similar drop in Italy.

We must add a cautionary note about the data and their representation. The age group surveyed in the national birthrate study is "women of reproductive age," which is defined as those between 15 and 49. This is a much broader group than those married and of reproductive age, so naturally births measured against this broader base would be at a lower (and more alarming) rate given that teen pregnancies and births are extremely low in Japan. There is no doubt, however, that married couples are delaying childbearing and that the consequent one-child problem is having an impact on families, schools, and workplaces that will only increase in the future.

Government responses to this have included the four-ministry Angel Plan, which took flight with a flourish of trumpets in 1994 but has since been grounded by inadequate funding and halfhearted implementation. This program aimed to establish day care centers with convenient hours and locations so that women could work and raise children without having to rely on family members or expensive private facilities. One female day care teacher, in line with male leadership hand-wringing, told a mother, "You should really raise your baby yourself at home; do you really need day care?" Without support, the Angel Plan is faltering, but more day care centers are now being built. A more recent initiative, the Plus One campaign, asks parents to consider their reproductive plans and then "add one" child to the goal! While officials in the Ministry of Health deny active pronatalism, they say "we don't need to have such heavy-handed approaches . . . as they did in wartime with 'umeyo, fuyaseyo ' [give birth and multiply]. We let the local areas [suffering from rural to urban population drain] do it for us." One young man in his thirties, eldest son of rice farmers in Okayama, lamented that "my brother and I must stay to work the farm, but it looks like we cannot get married: all the young women go to work in Niimi (the nearest large town) and don't want to farm." The women who leave gain a degree of independence earlier in such urbanized areas and may be less fettered than their brothers.

The sense of crisis (among the largely male officialdom) was met on the local level with calls for women to reproduce. Prefectural and municipal offers of stipends and subsidies for housing and education for mothers who have more than one child—with higher stipends for more than two—were supported with posters such as one seen in Okayama, picturing a child with a tear running down his cheek that was captioned, "Is your only child lonely? Doesn't he want a brother or sister?" The model of family behind these campaigns was the middle-class model of the economic boom decades—the separate-spheres household of the corporate-employed husband and the housewife managing the home and children.

Despite such official anxiety and crude propaganda, there is little evidence that it is children and child rearing that women seek to avoid when they postpone marriage. When wariness of family obligations shapes a woman's resistance, it is much more likely these days to be nervousness about elder care than child care. Most families at some point must face caring for their elders, and it is rare that a family can slip smoothly into this function these days. What it takes, with increasing longevity and more years of potential disability, is a daughter or daughter-in-law who is willing to serve as the full-time family-based caregiver. David Plath (1975) refers to the stage of life when care of the young and care of the elderly are in the hands of women as the "middle-aged Confucian sandwich." More so than in Europe or the United States, caring for dependent elderly is overwhelmingly treated as the responsibility of a female relative. The major concern of women over forty is said to be aging— and even more than their own aging, it is that of their parents, in-laws, and husbands. It is often said that a woman experiences three "ages": in her fifties, the care for her parents and her husband's parents; in her sixties the care of her husband; and in her seventies and eighties, her own care. The other side of this picture is that men experience three childhoods: in their youth, nurtured by their mothers; in their middle years, dependent on the domestic arrangements created by their wives; and in their old age, dependent on their wives' caregiving.

Caregiving responsibilities have never been easy and are exacerbated by the factors discussed here: mass longevity, state efforts to keep primary care a family responsibility, more nuclear households, fewer siblings with whom to share care of parents, and rising female workforce participation (now well over 50 percent for all married women and about 70 percent for women in their forties). These factors ensure that a substantial number of women will face the dilemma of Akiko, the middle-aged woman protagonist in Ariyoshi Sawako's popular 1972 novel *Kokotsu no hito* in which Akiko as daughter-in-law is pressured to quit her job to care for her senile father-in-law. She tries everything, but the available social and community services are not open to a person with advanced senility. After complaints from the police who returned him from his wanderings, Akiko resigns herself to caring for him. The book is an indictment of the lack of institutional support for the elderly and their families and something of a celebration of Akiko's commitment to care for her father-in-law, a commitment met with cynicism by younger women today (Ariyoshi 1984).

In short, for Japan as a self-designated aging society, the increasingly public tensions between the genders are potentially even more significant than those between the generations. Women's organizations in Japan are far larger and more assertive than the national associations for older citizens. It is likely that future public policies and programs for older Japanese will have to accommodate the private choices that individual women are now making about marriage and children as much as they seek to address the needs of the burgeoning elderly population.

Seniors on Their Own: Independent Lives or Lonely Hearts?

Many of the most demanding social issues facing Japan today cluster around women-related crises that have strong causal linkages: women having fewer children → shrinking birthrate → diminished labor force → lowered tax base → insufficient funds for social services → women working longer → elders left without support. We have heard so much about Japan as an "aging society" that the phrase is itself a bit long in the tooth. Still, preemptive crisis-talk has proven in the past to be an effective technique of power, and visions of an aging society may rank among the most effectively preemptive of all. Official talk about aging began in the early 1970s when Japan still had the most youthful population profile in the Organisation for Economic Co-operation and Development (OECD). Only in the 1990s did Japan's broad-base population pyramid become a tall, thin rectangle. Now there is talk of an inverted pyramid (*gyaku piramido*), in which the age ladder bulges at the top and not at the bottom. The Japanese press has trumpeted several doomsday narratives, by which in the year 2500 there will be only fifty thousand or ten thousand or other unthinkably small numbers of Japanese left. One paper declared a Shaker scenario: that in the year 3000 there will be only two Japanese left, both old women!

Geometric images are backed by a barrage of arithmetic. The number of youth age ten to nineteen declined 25 percent in the 1990s. The number of people over sixty has increased 35 percent. The year 1995 marked the first-ever decrease in the total labor population (workers age fifteen to sixty). By 2013, about one-quarter of the population will be older than sixty-five, making Japan the "oldest" nation in the world, and it is estimated that pensions, social insurance, and medical costs will require 23 percent of GNP. Over half the elderly population at that point will be over seventy-five years old.[2] The birthrate in metropolitan Tokyo is projected to fall to 1.1, pushing the "dependency ratio" of workers to nonworkers to unsustainable heights.

Japan's aging society is seen as resting on the twin pillars of private care and public resources, and both are already showing signs of having reached the limits of personal and political tolerance. Now in their seventies, the single-digit Showans are graying into Japan's first "mass longevity" elders. For the moment, the moral stature of this particular historical generation is extremely significant, at least for their middle-aged children, in mitigating re-

---

[2] The United Nations defines an aged population as one in which at least 7 percent of citizens are at least sixty-five. It took the United States seventy years for the percentage of elderly to climb from 7 percent to 14 percent; the same increases took forty-five years in Great Britain and Germany, eighty-five years in Sweden, but only twenty-five years in Japan. These and other statistics are drawn from the Ministry of Public Welfare 1998.

sentment about the escalating costs of an aging society. As these "honorable elders" pass, however, it becomes much less likely that public entitlements and private caregiving will be adequately extended (Campbell 1992).[3]

Programs such as the Golden Plan (aimed at supporting caregivers with respite care and home services for elders within three-generation households) and other incentives to maintain the elderly within a family environment are scarcely sufficient to provide what families need, which means, usually, what the daughter-in-law (now usually working at least part-time) needs to maintain the high standard of care expected for everyone in the household. In this generation of elderly at least, there is still a relatively high rate of living with children—about 60 percent of Japanese over the age of sixty-five live with their children (and two-thirds of those households also include their grandchildren). About one in four elderly live with a spouse, and only 15 percent live alone. Thus, Japanese elderly live with their children at four to five times the rate in the United States, and eight times the rate in Great Britain. And yet, it is difficult to distinguish between preference and necessity. For some, the high rate of living with children represents the clear superiority of families taking care of their own members; for others, it is forced on them by a shortage of quality public- and private-sector long-term care facilities and by the legal and ideological presumptions of family responsibility (Hashimoto 1996; Long 2000).

Families engage in a variety of strategies to cope with the gap between what they have and what they need (Long and Harris 2000). Their necessary and creative adaptations of normative family forms show the flexibility families require to accomplish what public systems will not. For example, patrilineality falls by the wayside when care must be sought from any available family member, and daughters are preferred by many elderly people over their daughters-in-law. Relationships in those three-generation households may not always be smooth. The shock of a sudden move to live with children when care is needed is both physical and emotional. The former "U-turn" phenomenon, in which an adult child lives away from his or her natal home for work and family rearing and then moves back when parents need care, has changed; now it is the dependent parents who move to what is to them a new home in a child's family, under the care and direction of a daughter or daughter-in-law. This "emergency Confucianism" leads to stress on all sides. What David Plath (1988) called the "intimate politics of co-residence" are much more frequently concerned with social relations than financial abilities. For that reason, an important diagnostic may be the rising rate of elderly who live alone or with only a spouse. In 1980 these numbered only 6 percent of all house-

---

[3] Campbell (2000) does take an optimistic view of the potential of the new Long-Term Care Insurance program instituted in 2000.

holds, but by 1992 the figure had risen steadily to 11 percent of all house-holds and fully 40 percent of the over-sixty-five population.

Other strategies, clearly socially and emotionally unfortunate, include a kind of *tarai-mawashi,* a rotation of the grandparents from sibling to sibling, over a year's time. In Yasujiro Ozu's 1953 film *Tokyo Story,* the famed director portrayed with pathos and sentiment the passive dependence of the older generation at the mercy of their uncaring and even abusive married children. It need not be that harsh today. One family keeps its elderly parents in the na-tal home, and it is the sibling caregivers who in turn move to their parents' house for a few months at a time. Others help their active elderly relatives find group homes, some of which are very nice indeed, serving the interests of the residents with such programs as painting, gardening, and cooking.

Individual solutions can be expensive, however, and economic resources govern the possibilities for comfort in old age. Where there are local volun-tary groups and "time banks," there are meals-on-wheels and other supports for people in their homes. The time banks promise that for every hour you volunteer to help an elderly person, you will receive one hour in return when you yourself need care. Time itself will tell if these can provide sufficient sup-port and reassurance.

Life expectancy in Japan is now the highest in the world for both sexes—84.93 years for women and 78.07 for men. Those considered "old" now fall into several "cohorts": the young elderly, fit enough for work or hobby activ-ities and travel (and a prime target for marketers); the middle elderly, able to maintain themselves alone but not quite as actively; and the old elderly. The rate of "old elderly" is increasing, including the bedridden elderly among them. Confucian justification for home-based care, insufficiently supported by the Golden Plan that emphasizes home care of the elderly, wears very thin, especially when programs have scant resources or are unreliably staffed. Fam-ilies complain that the admission choices of programs are idiosyncratic and that there should be better and more available nursing homes as well as staged-care living facilities. Good nursing homes have long waiting lists; one must apply before the care is actually needed, which again puts emotional strain on families. People who place their elderly relatives in such places are often tagged as "selfish" and unfilial, as children who "throw away Granny." Old peoples' homes are sometimes indeed dismissed as *obasute-yama,* after the legend in which old people are taken to the top of a mountain to endure a "good death" by exposure to the elements.

Strangers in the Midst: Unveiling the Myth of Ethnic Homogeneity

If the first "shock" of an aging population profile is the stress it is putting on the country's social welfare system, the second shock is in the prognosis for the workforce. Now that the number of over-sixty-five elders exceeds the number of persons fifteen and under, policymakers are bracing for an eventual labor shortage. This seems a perverse statistic in the face of the current job shortage, but few doubt that recovery from the recession will expose the inevitable demographic future.

One solution officially and popularly debated is to import foreign labor, but even as it addresses an economic need it exposes a central prop of national political ideology. For much of the twentieth century, Japan believed itself to be ethnically homogeneous, but the Japanese population and its leaders must now face the reality of heterogeneity, both in the present and, if they seriously embrace increased labor migration, the future (Douglass and Roberts 2000). Of course Japan's labor force has long been ethnically plural; legal and illegal migrant laborers have been in Japan for over a century. The largest numbers of non-Japanese ethnics are the resident Koreans, who now exceed three million; their "ethnic enclaves" center on the Kansai area, but they live throughout Japan (Ryang 1997, 2000; Fukuoka 2000). In 2000, 335,575 Chinese were registered as foreigners in Japan, with perhaps another 30,000–40,000 illegally in the country. Tsuda Takeyuki (2003, x) estimates that there are 280,000 Japanese-Brazilian return migrants, with another 45,000 migrants of Japanese descent from other South American countries. These persons, considered Japanese by race, often do not speak Japanese and do not share much of Japanese culture. Still, they are considered Japanese enough to be suitable employees, often in work that most young Japanese would not choose (Tsuda 2003; Roth 2002). There have also been large numbers of people from Southeast Asia (Thailand, Malaysia, Singapore, and elsewhere), and in the 1980s and early 1990s, many men from Bangladesh, Pakistan, Iran, and Iraq. Many of these were people without work visas who entered Japan on student visas and slipped from sight, becoming illegal laborers. Sex workers also arrive on student or training visas, brought by agents (often connected to organized crime) who provide some Japanese language training in their home countries, such as Thailand and the Philippines, before they come. It is estimated that there are over a million illegal workers in Japan. Obviously, needed labor must become regularized and recognized labor and be provided social services, schooling for children, and health insurance—and their wages must be taxed to provide more revenue for such provisions. Japan has been praised for long-term planning: Will it demonstrate the political will to apply it to its diversifying labor force?

The larger question is what pluralism will mean to Japan as a society. Among the largest population of non-Japanese ethnics, the permanent Korean residents, faced with continued discrimination for their Koreanness and with using hard-won legal avenues to obtain opportunities in the mainstream, the trends have been strongly for assimilation. But assimilation, even with full legal equality, is the erasure of all difference, not the forthright embrace of plural ways of living. And if new foreign laborers continue to grow in numbers, will it mean classes of workers and residents going to the bottom of the social ladder, adding ethnicity to the stigma of poverty? The challenge of pluralism, therefore, is whether differences in personal identity and lifeways are respected within the mainstream.

Are there other routes to pluralism? One possibility is that intermarriage, producing acculturation or even assimilation, between Japanese and people of non-Japanese origins will become more frequent. In rural Okayama and elsewhere, wives for farmers come from Southeast Asia, Taiwan, and elsewhere in Asia, making mixed marriages when local women refuse a farm life; will this route to multiculturalism make a difference in the profile, and the consciousness, of society (Suzuki 2003)? Others foresee changes as alternative families begin, slowly, to include gay and lesbian couples, as the elderly begin to create their own group homes, and as young and old live alone in greater numbers. One accommodation that brings generations together in a novel way is the assisted-living/nursery school residence in which elders participate actively in the nursery school attached to the home for the elderly, bringing "grandparents" together with children who rarely see their own, and providing the older people with feelings of family that they no longer can experience in their own (Thang 2001).

Japan's Future: In a "Families" Way?

Japan is at a moment when social problems have created circular name-calling and when conservative officials and policymakers have tended to lay these issues at the feet of families—most particularly at those of the women of the family who are accused of not acting "in a family way." The political scientist Steven Reed (1993, 8) has used the phrase "common sense" to describe the ordinary understandings of life in Japan as a sense that belies the constructions of policymakers and observers and that incorporates the idea of internal diversity and change. If one takes the commonsensical and plural families as units of inquiry, and if we call unorthodox and unscripted units "families," two revelations follow: one, that the failures of public policy to support people are the result of a unitary construction of family seldom met in reality; and two, that families, truly supported in their own plural, flexible, and cobbled-together choices, have the ability to be families still, embracing students, slackers, singles, seniors, and strangers all.

Structurally, it is ironic that generational cohorts, gender roles, and educational outcomes are among the axes of difference that are helping to unbind Japan's postwar social contract and restructure relationships and expectations. After all, the moral force of the single-digit Showans, the complementarity of gendered role dichotomies, and the fairness of educational outcomes were key ideological tenets of the "mainstream." These have now become fault lines that expose the tenuousness of the mainstream arrangements.

Will these new trends in social behavior—such as students taking new directions, women not marrying, and young adults seeking or being forced to seek new work—bring about new institutional *forms* of educational pathways, work structures, and families? T. J. Pempel's discussion of politics and economics during this same decade in chapter 2 concludes that there has as yet been no transformation in these sectors, despite significant procedural reforms in the electoral system, in the organization of the national bureaucracy, and in the financial industry. He finds instead that entrenched political and economic interests muddled through the decade and up to the present, inhibiting rather than initiating implementation. He suggests, however, that the institutional and procedural reforms may well have laid a foundation for inevitable "regime shift." We are proposing a parallel argument about new social behaviors that are anticipating a society that may well come to reflect and support that behavior. As yet, there is no societal "regime shift," in part because those who are acting in new ways have not yet mobilized as interest groups or as collective political voices, and their frustrations have not been addressed. If they do mobilize, change is ever more certain, but even if they do not, it is nonetheless likely.

The formulation of social action underlying our approach demonstrates that each of the five social diagnostics we have described represents a point where private action rubs against and begins to unravel the delicate skein of ideologies and institutions. And there need not be organized activism to collectivize such individual decisions. Indeed, in all five dimensions, structural change is resulting from the cumulation of disparate and parallel personal actions in quite understandable, "commonsense" realities governing choices and options. This is not a claim premised on a rational-choice voluntarism, which takes individual intentionality as the independent causal agent of structural outcomes and a universal rationality as the presumed basis of that intentional choice-making. Rather, the recursive structuring of individual agency, cultural meaning, and institutional form, as well as the multilayered consciousness and historical experience of actors, produce the actions we have described, performed under varying constraints and with subtle degrees of reflective knowledge, discursive articulation, and tacit understandings—withal, effective actions.

Most public commentary, domestic and foreign, about Japan in the new millennium paints a dark picture of a nation adrift, plagued with social malaise, political sclerosis, and economic stagnation. We have mapped social trajectories that lend support to such pessimism. But Japan is transforming—

along the lines and as a consequence of the actors and actions we have noted. And the adaptability, creativity, and flexibility shown in these emergent forms are cause for some optimism that many in Japan have envisioned and are enacting new lifeways that may yet produce a society whose vibrancy is based on pluralism and inclusion.

The thin shell of ideologically supported convention, we suggest, is about to crack—and when it does, and institutions are forced to recognize makeshift and novel social engagements as being within the range of "normal," the actual diversity of life strategies and choices will become more apparent in Japanese society. Moreover, the struggles of people to do more than get by will have to be addressed in social policies framed by those who have heretofore comfortably ignored them. The new Japanese "normal" in all its nonconsensual diversity will be seen in the rest of the region as perhaps a sign that Japan is no different from its neighbors.

As a result, Japanese influence in the region may in fact increase—not through policies aimed at doing so but through changes made to accommodate the diverse range of youth, women, elderly, and immigrants and their needs. After all, many of the phenomena we have described for Japan (an aging population, a shrinking birthrate, and a changing and diversifying educational system, labor force, and expectations for women and families) also obtain in other nations in the region. When Japanese leaders can demonstrate their willingness to create an adaptive set of social policies supporting the country's changing population, they may well help to provide models for others.

II

BALANCING AMERICA AND JAPAN

4

Immovable Object?
Japan's Security Policy in East Asia

**H. RICHARD FRIMAN,
PETER J. KATZENSTEIN,
DAVID LEHENY,
AND NOBUO OKAWARA**

The external and internal security environments confronting Japan are changing. Japan faces new challenges such as missile defense, the spread of weapons of mass destruction, relations with North Korea, and, significantly, the deployment of the Self-Defense Forces (SDF) in Iraq and the broader war on terrorism. Internally, Japan faces an array of challenges to stability and order including illegal immigration and illicit drug trafficking, both of which are becoming more diverse and less amenable to control. Despite challenges to both security environments Japan's policies have not adjusted evenly. In the post-9/11 world, Japan's external security policies—purportedly the sacrosanct hallmark of postwar Japanese pacifism—appear to have changed more than its internal policies.

On questions of external security, tight constitutional constraints on Japanese military operations abroad and Japan-U.S. defense coordination continue to frame political debates. In this context, the government's support for U.S. activities in the war on terrorism remains highly qualified and contingent. But international events, combined with political and social change in Japan, have undermined the strength of the pacifist side in the domestic struggle over Japan's security. Conservatives have pushed successfully for a larger military role for Japan, in accordance with American requests. The government also has sought to embed itself in a multilateral security framework while remaining fully attuned to domestic political constraints on the terms in which Japan is prepared to engage the world.

Japan's internal security policies remain deeply rooted in notions of a Japanese homogeneity and uniqueness that should be defended in distinctive ways. As noted by William Kelly and Merry White in chapter 3, Japan's social dynamism has been an uneasy fit with prevailing notions of the country's timeless homogeneity and enduring national character, ideological motifs that also mark the political immobilism described by T. J. Pempel in chapter 2. Asia's dramatic social changes have not left Japan unaffected. With the rise in immigration to Japan, the police have been exceptionally keen on clamping down on drug trafficking and the growth of foreign crime syndicates. Officials continue to cling to the image of Japan as a society that, by virtue of its homogeneity, guarantees an exceptional level of safety to its citizens. The image persists even as important domestic institutions, such as the traditional, order-enhancing role of organized crime (*boryokudan,* or, more commonly, the yakuza), have sharply diminished in the 1990s, and police links to immigrant communities remain tenuous. Internal security policy thus seems more like a faithful mirror of the public ideology of Japan than it does of changing social practices that are altering Japanese society.

Operating within the political constraints of Article 9 of its peace constitution and shielded for decades from possible external attacks by a security treaty with the United States, the Japanese government is continuing to put close relations with the United States at the center of its broadly conceived security policy. The disintegration of the Japan Socialist Party in the 1990s has given Japan's government political space to adjust to changing external demands that the country play a larger international and regional role, within the constitutional restraints that are always open to continuous reinterpretation. And because it shies away from unilateral initiatives on military matters, Japan's government is in general fully supportive of newly emerging multilateral security institutions in Asia.

Counterterrorist policies, especially after the September 11 attacks, illustrate how external and internal security are linked inextricably. Until recently, anticommunism at home and case-by-case efforts marked Japan's counterterrorism policies, and even the 1995 Aum Shinrikyo attack provoked only limited policy and administrative changes, due to resistance by domestic religious organizations and parties. Police and diplomatic efforts that focused primarily on the safety of Japanese from depoliticized overseas threats also reinforced the idea of Japan as a family polity, with a benevolent and protective government willing to step in to protect citizens from a world they did not make and cannot understand. Since 9/11, however, Japanese conservatives have successfully mobilized domestic fears, especially of North Korea, to justify an expanded antiterrorism role alongside the United States. Legitimized by U.S. efforts to remake security as a comprehensive phenomenon, the government has successfully pushed for a more muscular presence overseas while maintaining institutionalized motifs of homogeneity and state responsibility at home to keep at bay fears of a changing region and a changing nation.

In an Asian security environment increasingly marked by porous boundaries between internal and external security, limited change in Japan's external security policy has outpaced changes in Japan's internal security policy. Japanese officials have adopted a comprehensive approach to the country's national and societal security that extends well beyond marshalling the military force necessary to defend against external military threats. The effects of the 9/11 attacks thus have not forced any fundamental rethinking about Japan's security policies. Continuity in policy rather than dramatic policy change marks Japanese security policies both abroad and at home. For most Japanese security policymakers, an ideal Asian security environment would feature atomized nation-states that are open to legal trade but have tight controls on migration and trafficking and are tied in loose multilateral networks under American security guarantees. While promoting multilateral cooperation in the Asia Pacific region, however, Japan has taken incremental steps toward expanding the military's international role. Furthermore, Japan's internal security initiatives betray durable though outdated notions of Japanese homogeneity. The government's policy thus is caught between building an Asia that requires a further opening of Japan and maintaining the illusion of a Japan that never really was and never will be.

Japan's External Security Policy

Japan's comprehensive definition of security enjoys broad social and political support. It is embedded so deeply in domestic institutions that political actors in the foreign policy establishment, the national security apparatus, the police, and the economic bureaucracy regard it as normal and acceptable. What is normal in Japan, however, is not normal in Washington. And as the junior partner in the security arrangements between the two countries, Japan's approach to security thus needs to be multidimensional. Mike Mochizuki (1997, 37, note 2) has noted that attention to the nuances of language matters on this vital point. The Japanese government translates the term *takakuteki* as "multilateral," but it could also be translated as "multidimensional." The latter translation conveys that Japanese policy aims at embedding its bilateral security ties with the United States in a broader, multifaceted set of security relations rather than moving some distance from bilateralism toward multilateralism. Bilateralism, multilateralism, and the relation between them thus cut to the core of Japan's security policy as it complements its vitally important ties to the United States with an Asia of increasing economic and political relevance, and relates the military security concerns of the United States to a more comprehensive Japanese conception of the same term. This is the crux of Japan's adaptation of its security policy in a changing regional context.

Compared to the United States and Europe, Japan's security policy thus has a distinctive cast. The United States has command of the full register of multilateral, bilateral, and unilateral policy instruments in its arsenal. Europe takes pride in having overcome unilateralism and bilateralism and is a champion of multilateralism as the constitutive principle of modern statecraft. Japan's approach differs from both. Because it lacks the social purpose and the necessary capabilities, Japan strongly devalues unilateralism. It prefers bilateral arrangements, both with the United States and also with its partners in Asia Pacific and other parts of the world. Yet general developments in the international society of states, as well as in the Japanese polity, have created an embryonic multilateralism during the last two decades that has begun to complement rather than substitute for Japan's traditional bilateral approach (Okawara and Katzenstein 2001; Kim 2004; Krauss and Pempel 2004).

In the early years of the Clinton administration, growing bilateral trade conflicts, Japanese uncertainty about U.S. strategy in Asia Pacific, and an increasing emphasis on Asia Pacific in Japanese foreign policy all pointed to a possible loosening of bilateral ties between Japan and the United States. Despite these potential signals, a series of reevaluations of strategic options in both Tokyo and Washington culminated in the April 1996 signing of the Japan-U.S. Joint Declaration on Security and the September 1997 Revised Guidelines for Japan-U.S. Defense Cooperation. The joint declaration calls for a review of the 1978 Guidelines for Japan-U.S. Defense Cooperation, and the revised guidelines spell out the roles of the U.S. military and Japan's Self-Defense Forces in the event of a crisis. The latter refers specifically to "situations in areas surrounding Japan that will have an important influence on Japan's peace and security" as the context in which the two governments could provide each other with supplies and services (Gaiko Forum 1999, 134–35, 141; Defense Agency 2000, 236). The 1995 revised National Defense Program Outline (which calls for the SDF to acquire the capability to cope with situations in areas surrounding Japan that could adversely affect its peace and security) and the revised guidelines have effectively broadened the mission of the SDF (Araki 2000). The mission of Japan's military is no longer simply the defense of the home islands against a direct attack, thus securing Japan's position in a global anticommunist alliance. In the eyes of the proponents of the revised mission of the SDF, Japan's military is also committed to enhancing regional stability in Asia Pacific and thus, indirectly, Japan's own security.

In the wake of the attack on the United States on September 11, 2001, the mission of the SDF has expanded further. In October 2001 the Diet passed the Anti-Terrorism Special Measures Law, which permitted the dispatch of the SDF to the Indian Ocean and the support of U.S. combat troops in Afghanistan with water and fuel. Subsequently, between December 2001 and mid-September 2003 SDF ships supplied U.S. and other ships with fuel worth twelve billion yen (*Asahi Shimbun* 2003d). The law, effective for two years only, was extended in 2003 for another two years.

Furthermore, in July 2003 the Diet passed the Iraq Special Measures Law. Effective for four years, it authorized the SDF to provide humanitarian relief to Iraq and logistical support to U.S. and other militaries operating in that country. The law limited SDF operations to noncombat zones, but allowed the forces to transport weapons and ammunition for other militaries. The director of the Defense Agency gave dispatch orders to the SDF in January 2004. After the first troops of the main contingent of the Ground Self-Defense Force left for Iraq the government raised its terrorism alert to the highest level, tightening security around government buildings, nuclear power plants, and other sensitive locations throughout the country. Compensation for families of members of the SDF killed in Iraq was raised by about 40 percent to $926,000 (Onishi 2003; *Asahi Shimbun* 2003c; Onishi 2004c). Richard Samuels (2004, 10) is on the mark in calling the Iraq operation an "epochal" decision.

Thus, for the first time Japan's SDF were playing a security role outside of the "area surrounding Japan" that was ambiguously denoted in the Guidelines for Japan-U.S. Defense Cooperation. Because the Indian Ocean and Iraq clearly fall outside of even a generous definition of the security region surrounding Japan, new legislation was required to enable Prime Minister Koizumi Jun'ichiro to assist the United States as he and his American counterparts wanted. This cooperation thus required a redefinition in the U.S.-Japan security arrangements that had gradually taken shape during the 1990s (Katzenstein and Okawara 2001–2002; Okawara and Katzenstein 2001). The two new laws enacted to adapt to the post-9/11 world have expanded the geographical scope of Japanese-U.S. military cooperation in a way few people thought politically possible before September 11, 2001 (Midford 2003; Samuels 2004).

One element of the security arrangements between Japan and the United States that is of increasing importance is missile defense. Accommodating requests that the U.S. government had made since 1993, and responding to the strong sense of worry of the Japanese public over the 1998 North Korean missile test, in 1999 Japan started a joint research project on missile defense with the United States. This further complicated Japan's relations with China, which had already been clouded by the new defense guidelines. With uncertainties about North Korean intentions not dissipated, the Japanese government, while continuing with the joint research project, decided in December

2003 to purchase a five hundred billion yen missile defense system from the United States. Deployment of the system is scheduled to begin in 2007, making Japan part of the regional missile defense network in the Asia Pacific region envisaged by the United States (*Asahi Shimbun* 2003a, 2003b).

Okinawa remains one of the most volatile issues in Japan-U.S. security relations (Johnson 1997; Shimada 1997; Yamaguchi 1997; Institute of Social Science 1998). American bases occupy about 20 percent of the main island. A staging area for the U.S. military in Asia Pacific, Okinawa suffers from a variety of social ills and missed economic opportunities. After a twelve-year-old Okinawan schoolgirl was raped by three U.S. servicemen in September 1995, in October the American government agreed to give "favorable consideration," prior to indictment, to Japanese requests to take into custody those suspected of committing murder or rape. Japan was not happy with how the 1995 agreement was implemented, and in July 2003 a lower house committee on Okinawa issues unanimously passed a resolution calling for considering the revision of the 1960 Japan-U.S. Status of Forces Agreement, which requires the turning over of servicemen to Japanese authorities only after indictment. The U.S. concern has centered, however, on extending legal protection for its military personnel in Japanese custody. Another contentious issue has been the relocation of U.S. bases in and from Okinawa. In a prefectural plebiscite held in September 1996, 89 percent of those who turned out to vote supported both consolidation and reduction of the U.S. military presence and a reform of the 1960 agreement. In December 1996, the United States agreed to remove eleven of its military facilities in Okinawa. But at the end of 2003, only two had been removed, primarily because of the difficulty of relocating the facilities (Kumagai 2003). Thus, for the time being, the operational side of U.S.-Japan security relations exists on a politically fragile basis of support.

The importance of bilateralism is not restricted to Japan's security relations with the United States. For example, with only a few lapses since 1993, senior Japan Defense Agency (JDA) officials have met annually with their Chinese counterparts to discuss a variety of issues of mutual concern. In addition, Japan has initiated regular bilateral security talks with Australia (since 1996), Singapore (since 1997), Indonesia (since 1997), Canada (since 1997), and Malaysia (since 1999) (Boeicho 2000, 187). With the tightening of U.S.-Japan security relations after 1994, Japan has become more self-conscious in developing a broad set of bilateral defense talks and exchanges that both complement its persistent dependence on the United States and cement the U.S. presence in the region. By 1999 Japan had committed to about ten regular bilateral talks, too many for the two officials assigned by the JDA to this task. In brief, the JDA is increasingly engaging Asia Pacific in a broad range of bilateral security contacts.

The 1990s also witnessed the gradual emergence of a variety of Asian-Pacific multilateral security arrangements involving track-one (government-to-government), track-two (semigovernmental think tanks), and track-three (private institutions) dialogues (Stone 1997; Wada 1998, 154–83; Green 2001, 193–227). Japan's interest in and support for strong multilateral arrangements dates back to the 1960s when its neighbors in Southeast Asia rejected several Japanese proposals to create multilateral economic arrangements (Katzenstein 1997, 12–20). Looking for a new diplomatic initiative in the wake of the Gulf War and convinced that the cause of Asia Pacific regionalism was ready to be advanced further diplomatically, Foreign Minister Nakayama Taro proposed a new multilateral security dialogue as part of the ASEAN Post-Ministerial Conference in July 1991. By the end of the decade, Japan's Ministry of Foreign Affairs and Defense Agency had become interested in moving from "confidence- and security-building measures," based on nations sharing information about each other's defense posture, toward "preventive diplomacy" as one way of solving some of the harder security problems in the Asia Pacific region. With varying degrees of enthusiasm the Japanese government has supported all of the new multilateral initiatives.

The trend toward security multilateralism in Asia Pacific is reflected in several track-two dialogues. Since 1993, for example, Japan, seeking to enhance mutual confidence on security, economic, and environmental issues, has participated with China, Russia, South Korea, and the United States in the Northeast Asia Cooperation Dialogue. In addition, since 1994 the Japan Institute of International Affairs has cosponsored with its U.S. and Russian counterparts (the Center for Strategic and International Studies and the Institute of World Economy and International Relations, respectively) the Trilateral Forum on North Pacific Security, which is regularly attended by senior government officials from all three countries. Furthermore, since 1998 Japan has conducted semiofficial trilateral security talks with China and the United States (*Asahi Shimbun* 1998; Sasaki 1997). Important track-two talks also occur in the Council for Security Cooperation in the Asia Pacific, whose predecessor was the ASEAN-affiliated Institutes for Strategic and International Studies (Stone 1997, 21–25; Simon 1998, 207–9; Wada 1998; Job 2000; Simon 2002). In the early 1990s, the institutes played a crucial role in encouraging ASEAN to commence systematic security dialogues. And with the establishment of the track-one ASEAN Regional Forum in 1994, the track-two activities of these institutes have grown in significance.

That track-one and track-two activities can be closely connected is clearly illustrated by recent developments in dealing with sea piracy. Alarmed by the increase in the number of pirate attacks in Southeast Asian waters that could affect Japan's oil imports, in April 2000 the Japanese government convened a track-one conference on sea piracy in Tokyo (Gaimusho 2002, 129–30).

The conference established loose frameworks for bilateral and multilateral cooperation on this issue. To put additional teeth into multilateral cooperation, the Japanese government hosted a track-two conference in October 2001. The participants came to share the view that an intergovernmental group should be set up to develop a regional antipiracy agreement. The first meeting was held in Tokyo in July 2002. Track-two activities shape the climate of opinion in national settings in which security affairs are conducted. They can also help decision-makers in articulating new ideas. And they also help build transnational coalitions of elites with considerable domestic influence. Over time, they may socialize elites either directly or indirectly to different norms and identities. In brief, they have become an important feature of Asian-Pacific security affairs.

Japan's Societal Security Policy

Japan's societal security policy has long sought to ensure domestic order by embedding the police in society and relying on the police and, to a lesser extent, other agencies in the enforcement bureaucracy to prevent inroads by foreign threats (Katzenstein 1996). The policy draws heavily on an institutionalized norm of collective identity that links Japan's successes in domestic social order to the country's ethnic homogeneity. The homogeneity myth shapes expectations of how policing can link the state and society in a shared enterprise as well as how Japanese society is able to resist threats to social order that have plagued other advanced industrial countries (Hoshino 1994; Friman 2001). The social and economic changes discussed in chapters 2 and 3 increasingly pose challenges to the homogeneity myth, but rather than exploring new paths to social order, the enforcement bureaucracy has redoubled its efforts to preserve homogeneity and embed the police in society.

The police have long maintained the image of Japan's social order by isolating minority populations such as the *burakumin* (a lower caste facing continuing discrimination) and permanent foreign residents from Korea and China (Weiner 1997). They have relied on Japanese organized crime groups (the yakuza) to facilitate this image by acting as paths for socioeconomic opportunity for marginalized Japanese youth and some minority groups, such as permanent foreign resident Koreans, while curtailing the activities of others (De Vos 1992; Kaplan and Dubro 2003). During the 1990s, revenue shortfalls in the post-bubble economy weakened accommodations between and within the major crime syndicates. The result was a wave of gang violence that spilled over into the broader public sphere and eroded an unspoken public and police tolerance of organized crime. Antigang legislation introduced during the 1990s, the Botaiho (Boryokudan Taisaku Ho—Organized Crime Countermeasures Law), increased state scrutiny of criminal groups, criminalized a range of gang activities, and led to increasingly intrusive law enforcement techniques. Though the impact of the measures should not be overstated, they had the intended effect of decreasing the public profile of organized crime (Friman 1999; Herbert 2000; Kaplan and Dubro 2003; Hill 2003). Combined with the economic downturn, however, the legislation also had unintended effects on illegal immigration and the transnational drug trade into Japan.

During the 1980s, immigration policies and a booming economy had encouraged new waves of legal and illegal migration. Initially, Japanese law enforcement officials expressed only limited concern over the potential threats to social order from the new migrants. National Police Agency reports in the early 1980s noted an increase in violations of immigration regulations, work permits, and laws prohibiting prostitution. The reports did not conceptualize this increase as a major threat. In the context of increasingly visible foreign populations and a broader national debate over immigration policy reform during the late 1980s, however, the police position became more strident. The 1987 *White Paper on Police* (*Keisatsu Hakusho*) prioritized threats posed by Japan's internationalization and explicitly focused on the problems posed by the new foreign workers (Keisatsucho 1987; see also Herbert 1996, 196). This pattern continued during the 1990s, with law enforcement officials often making little distinction in the legality of the migrant status of foreign workers and stipulating linkages between the new wave of visiting foreigners (*rainichi gaikokujin*) and organized foreign crime groups. By 2003, the linkage between foreigners and crime had reemerged as part of a broader national politicization of crime as a challenge to social order.

The interrelated threats of the transnational drug trade and illegal immigration have received special attention in Japan. Japan has long been a transshipment point for the Southeast Asian drug trade into Europe and the United States. And it is one of several money laundering centers for transnational crime in Asia (Friman 1996; State Department 2003, 2004). Although Japan's domestic drug market is relatively small by international standards, drug trafficking remains an issue of domestic concern. Stimulants, especially methamphetamine, are the primary drugs of choice, while marijuana and hashish, cocaine, heroin, and various psychotropic drugs attract more limited interest. The police, and to a lesser extent narcotics officers of the Ministry of Health, Welfare, and Labor are responsible for drug enforcement. Due in part to the legacy of extensive police penetration of Japanese society during the 1930s, Japanese enforcement methods have been less intrusive than those in other advanced industrial countries. Authorities have moved only slowly to introduce undercover operations, paid informants, controlled delivery, money laundering investigations, and wiretapping (Friman 1996; Katzenstein 1996; *Japan Times* 2002b; *Japan Today* 2002f).

The yakuza play a dominant role in the transnational drug trade, integrating methamphetamines from Asian suppliers, most recently China, North Korea, the Philippines, and Taiwan, into extensive domestic distribution networks (Friman 1999; State Department 2004). Drug distribution networks in stimulants that exclude the yakuza are relatively rare. Due in large part to the limited interest of the yakuza in extending their networks to dealing in other drugs, external suppliers of narcotics, marijuana and hashish, and psychotropic drugs have made only limited inroads into the Japanese market. This pattern began to shift during the 1990s. Apprehensions of foreigners for drug offenses increased dramatically, especially those involving narcotics and marijuana. However, these patterns partially reflected Japanese law enforcement's refocusing of resources and manpower on foreigners. And they revealed a deep reluctance to use controlled delivery practices to trace drug shipments from point of entry to upper- and middle-level Japanese wholesalers. Still, large-scale, foreign-controlled distribution networks remain relatively rare (Friman 1999, 2004).

Emigration to Japan has been influenced negatively by immigration regulations that restrict access by unskilled workers, especially those of non-Japanese descent, and positively by the pull effects of the economy's growing structural dependence on such labor (Mori 1997; Sellek 2001). Island geography and the relative ease of exploiting inconsistencies in the country's enforcement of visa practices have made overstaying more common than illegal entry with false documents or by clandestine means (Herbert 1996, 43–45; Friman 2003). During the 1980s, migrants exploited tourist visa exemption accords and precollege student visa programs to gain access to the country. Tighter monitoring of these programs by the early 1990s shifted migration to other paths. Chinese snakehead (*jato*) smuggling networks emerged as sources of altered Japanese passports, Taiwanese identity cards, and assistance in identity theft and deception. The latter included arranging fake marriages and applications for entry as "war-orphan" spouses or relatives of Japanese stranded in China after 1945 (e.g., *Mainichi Daily News* 1997; *Daily Yomiuri* 2001b; *Japan Today* 2002b). Through the 1990s, these networks also turned to large-scale migrant smuggling into Japan using fishing boats and cargo ships (Mo 1994; Friman 2001; *Daily Yomiuri* 2001a).

The police responded to these challenges by adding, and shifting existing, resources into task forces that prioritized international crime, emphasizing foreign crime in annual and biannual reports, and stressing the foreign crime threat in media and public relations campaigns (Herbert 1996; Friman 2001). The police academy introduced foreign language training and study tours. Metropolitan police departments turned to a combination of a limited pool of civilian language interpreters and digital translators to facilitate basic investigations. The National Police Agency also turned to the selective deployment of police officers abroad for experiential training (Keisatsucho

1999; Friman 2001). These programs were geared primarily toward aiding the police in dealing with foreigners who, disturbingly from the police standpoint, did not follow the idealized Japanese pattern of interaction with authority. The results through the 1990s were uneven at best. Especially missing from these efforts was a systematic exploration of how to build better police ties with new immigrant communities.

The combination of Botaiho and economic pressures also facilitated the fragmentation of illicit drug and migrant trafficking networks. In the case of methamphetamine, the yakuza began to move upstream into smuggling while reducing their public profile at home by clandestinely subcontracting retail distribution operations to networks of non-Japanese. Those yakuza less well placed in dominant drug distribution networks also began to expand into the smuggling and distribution of marijuana and synthetic drugs (Friman 1999; Kaplan and Dubro 2003; Friman 2004). Long active in the smuggling and trafficking of women for the Japanese sex industry, the yakuza also began to diversify into the issuing of illegal work permits and the smuggling of male migrant labor. Drawing on new ties with yakuza organizations, Chinese smuggling networks began to offer package deals for transportation, employment, and accommodation in Japan (Friman 2001, 2003).

Although not so well acknowledged by the police, the intersection of diversification, syndicate infighting, and yakuza efforts to avoid greater public scrutiny also began to erode the ability of Japanese organized crime to help regulate public order. Operating on a smaller scale and better able to prey on new migrant communities, groups of mainland Chinese and other foreigners soon began to displace the yakuza from protection, gambling, and prostitution rackets in major entertainment districts. Faced with what appeared to be reckless threats and acts of violence from Chinese gangs, and already under public scrutiny, the yakuza began to retreat from these traditional strongholds. Highly publicized police crackdowns in areas such as Tokyo's Kabuki-cho district led some Chinese to leave Japan, others to move out of Tokyo into other Japanese cities, and still others to temporarily lay low as the yakuza sought to reassert themselves into the vacuum. This pattern was repeated several times at the beginning of the new millennium (Mo 1998; Friman 1999; *Mainichi Daily News* 2001; *Japan Times* 2002a, 2002f; Kaplan and Dubro 2003).

By 2003, a combination of crime rates rising to postwar highs and arrest rates falling to postwar lows focused public and political attention on the erosion of social order. Facing public scrutiny, police officials sought to explain crime and arrest patterns as stemming from increasing juvenile, organized, and foreign crime and from a police force lacking the necessary resources to facilitate order. Organized foreign crime, however, soon emerged as the primary threat in official discourse and the need for the protection of homogeneity and the increased embedding of the police in Japanese society as the

primary solutions (Keisatsucho 2003; Reynolds 2003). In August 2003, the National Police Agency (NPA) announced that it would be adding ten thousand new police officers by 2006 to restore public safety, on top of an additional ten thousand officers already scheduled for 2002–2004 (*Asahi Shimbun* 2003e). In the same month Tokyo governor Ishihara Shintaro announced the formation of a new security task force headed by Tokyo's vice-governor for security, the former NPA official and noted Hiroshima police official Takehana Yutaka. By September, Ishihara also was pledging to deploy Tokyo police and immigration authorities to seven area prefectures to help decrease crime by foreigners (Utsunomiya 2003a, 2003b).

Foreign crime emerged as a central theme in the September 2003 LDP internal party elections and the national parliamentary elections the following month. Leading candidates in both emphasized the need for a stronger stand on crime, especially foreign crime (Reynolds 2003; *Japan Today* 2003a). In the Japanese National Diet campaign, top LDP officials blanketed the media with the party's pledge to address the threat of foreign crime. Justice Minister Nozawa Daizo pledged to make Japan safe again so that "women and children can walk alone on the streets at night," through the introduction of new law enforcement measures, additional prisons, and biometric identifiers in foreign passports to curtail illegal immigration (Matsubara 2003; *Japan Times* 2003a). By December 2003, the Tokyo Metropolitan Government had begun to act on a provision in the LDP platform, announcing new joint task forces with the Ministry of Justice's Immigration Bureau intended to "halve the number of illegal residents in Tokyo in five years" (*Japan Today* 2003b). The Ministry of Justice also announced tighter regulations on residency permits for Chinese students seeking to study in Japan and the introduction of profiling measures aimed at identifying likely illegal foreigners (*Mainichi Daily News* 2003; *Asahi Shimbun* 2004). The NPA announced a major institutional reorganization through amendment of the Police Law in 2004 that would "integrate divisions that focus exclusively on crime syndicates, foreigners, drugs, and guns" (*Daily Yomiuri* 2003). Amid the politicized uproar and anecdotal evidence of rising foreign criminal activity, little attention was focused on the relatively small amount of crime committed by foreigners as a percentage of overall crime, potential flaws in statistics on crimes by foreigners, and the rather limited and declining numbers of illegal immigrants.

It is unsurprising in this domestic context that the international response of Japanese law enforcement to societal security challenges also has reflected an emphasis on preserving homogeneity as the path to societal security. In general, the Japanese government has sought international assistance to impede the entry of persons posing potential threats while deflecting foreign pressure for more extensive cooperation that could lead to potential interference in the Japanese approach. On drug control issues, Japanese compliance with U.S. requests for greater formal cooperation, especially at the enforcement level, traditionally has been slow (Friman 1996). Japanese authorities have sought to extend bilateral ties with drug source countries, especially those in Northeast and Southeast Asia. These ties have consisted of occasional government missions, temporary deployment of Japanese enforcement personnel abroad, and limited steps toward cooperative law enforcement. More commonly they have entailed training programs for foreign law enforcement personnel in Japanese policing methods. Japan's multilateral drug control efforts include participation in major United Nations drug control treaties as well as task forces and conferences, including those organized under the auspices of the UN, G8, OECD, Interpol, and the ASEAN Regional Forum. The gap between such Japanese participation and the implementation of treaty and task force provisions in practice remains, however, in bilateral as well as multilateral relations (Friman 1996; State Department 2004).

On illegal immigration issues, Japan has turned to bilateral efforts primarily with migration source countries in Asia. Deliberations over visa exemption accords and student visa programs, and to a lesser extent lax entertainment visa programs, initially distinguished these negotiations. By the mid-1990s bilateral negotiations were focused on China. In an attempt to curtail incidents of large-scale migrant smuggling, in March 1997 a Japanese delegation of enforcement and foreign ministry officials met with Chinese counterparts in Beijing and Shanghai. In 1998, Japanese and Chinese officials completed negotiations on a framework agreement of cooperation that included provisions for the deployment of Japanese police officials to Beijing, Fuzhou, Guangzhou, and Shanghai (*Japan Times* 1997a, 1997b; *Daily Yomiuri* 1998). More recent cooperation has focused on tracking down Chinese perpetrators of violence in Japan (*Japan Times* 2003b; *Japan Today* 2003c). Though solutions do lie in coordinated efforts between source and host countries, the bilateral efforts with China illustrate a broader pattern of Japanese authorities failing to adequately address the domestic dynamics that influence illegal immigration (*Japan Today* 2002a). In brief, Japan's policy has been aimed at enhancing its societal security, bilaterally where it can and multilaterally where it must.

Japan's Counterterrorism Policies before September 11, 2001

Because Japan, like many other advanced industrial nations, has largely treated terrorism as a law enforcement rather than as a military or political issue, it is unsurprising that the country's pre-2001 counterterrorism programs would resemble its approach to crime. By working within unyielding political and legal constraints and a conceptual frame emphasizing a safe, conservative core for Japanese society, the police have shifted from isolating and expelling citizens with radical leftist leanings toward the careful management of such domestic threats as new religious movements. Without a clear sense of how best to deal with the threat of international terrorism, police and diplomats have traditionally operated on a case-by-case basis. Although they have tried to adhere to international conventions on terrorism they have been more concerned with maintaining some flexibility to save Japanese lives in specific terrorist incidents. The consistent notion here has been that Japan's unruly elements could be expelled or controlled, thereby creating a safe and untroubled social core for Japanese security; foreign terrorist threats were, as much as possible, seen as uncoordinated, nearly random intrusions of a dangerous and chaotic world from which Japan required protection.

Throughout the 1970s, the Japanese government found itself plagued by uncoordinated but coinciding threats that left the impression of a nation under siege. Organized in the late 1960s and early 1970s, the Japanese Red Army (JRA) became one of the world's more fearsome terrorist organizations, its small size notwithstanding. In the 1970s, JRA operatives massacred twenty-four people at Lod Airport in Tel Aviv, following it with airplane hijackings that netted the group large ransoms from the Japanese government, and even tried to take over the U.S. embassy in Kuala Lumpur. In the face of heavy pressure from international police organizations, JRA members were largely forced to stay in a small number of countries (North Korea, Syria-controlled Lebanon, Libya) that were willing to give them cover, but during the 1980s the bulk of Japanese counterterrorism activity focused on the group.

During the JRA's exile, a homegrown crisis developed, as the Japanese government sought to use farmland in Chiba Prefecture to build a new airport. It inspired an odd but surprisingly durable alliance between conservative farmers and radical students convinced that the government's efforts were directed at helping the U.S. prosecute the war in Vietnam. The government tried for years to remove the farmers from their land, by force if necessary. The standoff has ultimately ended only because of the old age of the remaining farmers and because of intensely unfavorable press associated with some of the government's early strong-arm tactics. The situation endured as a tense fact of life in Narita rather than as a full-fledged insurgency or crackdown. Even occasional bombings of the homes of government bureaucrats associated with the plan did not lead the police to react with overwhelming force against the farmers (Keisatsucho 1988, 7–85; see also Apter and Sawa 1986).

Japan's police have been able to take advantage of their community relations—perhaps best symbolized by the *koban* (police box) system—to monitor the development of antigovernment organizations with violent capabilities in postwar Japan. Of critical importance was the antisystemic bent of the leftist groups, whose motives were seen as more threatening than those of violent right-wing organizations. Though constrained in part by constitutional protections of civil liberties and by restrictions on the use of force, the Japanese government has occasionally been able to pull off extraordinary shows of force, including the massive search of apartments in Tokyo along the parade route for the funeral of the Showa Emperor in 1989 (Katzenstein 1996).

Partly because of its experience during the tumultuous 1960s and 1970s, the NPA focused nearly exclusively on leftist radical movements, a strategy whose limitations became painfully apparent in 1995 when the government suffered a massive intelligence failure culminating in Aum Shinrikyo's sarin gas attack on Tokyo's Kasumigaseki subway station. This millenarian cult had, in the process of building a fanatical base around its leader Asahara Shoko, apparently been involved in a 1989 murder of a Japanese lawyer and a "test case" sarin gas attack in Matsumoto in 1994. They are also suspected of attempted attacks with botulinum toxin, anthrax, and VX gas, in addition to various and sundry cases of extortion, murder, and possibly even the 1995 shooting of NPA chief Kunimatsu Takaji. Moreover, by 1995, the cult had global assets in excess of $1 billion, operated more than thirty branches in six countries, and claimed fifty thousand members worldwide. The resourceful cult used its connections, especially those in Russia, to build significant chemical and biological weapons capabilities, acquire an attack helicopter, and get a model for an AK-74 assault weapon, which it may have been readying for mass production (Sansoucy 1998, 3–4, 11–16, 19, 27; Miyasaka 2001, 1, 78). Even without direct evidence of its various crimes, the police might have been expected to find it worrisome that a large, rich religious cult with millenarian overtones and end-of-the-world fantasies might have counted among its members so many science graduates of Japan's top universities.

Since 1945 the taboo against police interference in the affairs of religious sects has run very deep in Japan. While the police were extremely attuned to the activities of left-wing radicals in the 1970s and 1980s, they were less concerned with the potential criminal activities of religious organizations. Aum Shinrikyo is one of fifteen hundred religious organizations officially recognized by the government between 1984 and 1993. These sects fill the political space left vacant when Shintoism disappeared as the conservative state religion after 1945. Once granted recognition, these groups have generally enjoyed numerous privileges, tax exemptions, and de facto immunity from any form of political oversight (Sansoucy 1998, 17–23). Resistance to government interference in religion has been institutionalized largely through the emergence of the political party Komeito (from 1998 New Komeito, Clean Government Party), tightly linked to the Soka Gakkai, a "new religious movement" that claims twelve million members. Although the Soka Gakkai and other optimistic, life-affirming offshoots of Buddhism and Shintoism share little ideologically with the "new-new religions"—usually called *karuto* (cults) in Japanese—Komeito's determined efforts to protect the financial and political privileges of its parent religion have likewise made it easier for groups such as Aum to escape scrutiny (Hardacre 2003).

The Aum attack was therefore a massive intelligence failure deeply steeped in politics. Although there was ample evidence of its criminal behavior and despite numerous complaints about the cult, the Japanese police "studiously avoided investigating Aum" (Steinhoff 1996, 17). The Public Security Intelligence Agency, responsible for investigations connected with the Anti-Subversive Activities Law, had almost invariably focused on left-wing movements, and had virtually no experience with surveillance of religious groups; before the 1995 attack, it had virtually no information on Aum (Hardacre 2003, 148–49). Although the group's attacks revealed it to be heavily anti-state in its goals, its status as a religious movement and its distance from traditional left-wing groups had shielded it from the government scrutiny that almost certainly would have shut down a similarly destructive communist organization.

When prosecutors drew up charges against the offenders, they chose to treat the attacks as individual murders and assaults rather than invoking Articles 77 (carrying out civil war) and 78 (preparing for civil war) of the Japanese Criminal Code. The prosecution thus sidestepped an investigation of the group's extensive transnational links, especially with Russia (Miyawaki 2001, 2–3). While in the opposition, Komeito had been unable to prevent revision of the Religious Corporations Law, which required religious groups to provide the government with more information about group activities and finances; in theory, this afforded the government the means to pursue organizations suspected of criminal activity. Indeed, the LDP had forced through the revisions in part to link Komeito with Aum and thereby discredit the opposition (Hardacre 2003, 146–48). But if politics makes for strange bedfellows, Japan's political promiscuity in the past decade has been truly remarkable. Komeito has been a member of the LDP-led ruling coalition since 1999, and it has apparently enforced some restraint on the creation of new post-Aum laws. The most important piece of legislation, passed in late 1999, has been the Law to Control Organizations That Have Committed Acts of Indiscriminate Mass Murder. Though written ostensibly to provide the government with the authority to investigate "all" such organizations, the law's convoluted title and the surrounding politics make it clear that it was designed specifically to permit government scrutiny of Aum (now renamed Aleph)—and of virtually no other Japanese organizations.

After the Aum attack, many observers have been struck by the tepidness and the slow pace of the government's response. This was in agreement with the Japanese public's view of Aum as a bizarre religious cult with no clear political objectives and little likelihood of a repetition of future terrorist attacks with weapons of mass destruction (Japan Society 2001, 21; Miyasaka 2001, 76). The LDP government tried to strengthen the counterterrorist capabilities of the police by revising the basic legislation governing the National Police Agency and by adding new laws facilitating the detection of future terrorist attacks. Yet the opposition, which was rooted in a deep suspicion of the potential abuse of executive authority, prevented any comprehensive measures against suspicious organizations. With the support of the Japan Federation of Bar Associations, human rights activists and the mass media argued against the invocation of the Anti-Subversive Activities Law, and Aum was permitted to survive as a religious organization (Mullins 1997; Miyasaka 2001, 69, 77; Pangi 2003, 40).

In fact, most of the government's responses should be categorized not as "counterterrorism" but rather as the more politically neutral "crisis management." Coming shortly after the Kobe earthquake, in which the Japanese government manifestly failed to act quickly enough to save at least some of the more than six thousand people who ultimately perished in the quake (Pekkanen 2000), and in the midst of embarrassing financial debacles that it seemed powerless to prevent, Aum Shinrikyo's attack seemed to be more evidence that the Japanese government was incapable of dealing with crises. Critics seemed preoccupied with the roots of Japan's crisis management problems, whether in the Japanese national character or in organizational culture (Sassa 1997, 183–85).

Responsibility for crisis management was assigned to the Cabinet Office for National Security Affairs. A subsequently enacted radical administrative reform program makes it virtually impossible to gauge how and in what agency Japan's crisis management policy might be conducted in the future (Itabashi, Ogawara, and Leheny 2002). Even when the NPA, for example, succeeded in developing new capabilities, it has found itself unable to make much use of them. After the Aum attack, the NPA cooperated with prefectural police to create *tokushu butai* ("special units," but generally known by the acronym SATs, for Special Assault Teams) designed to handle terrorist crises such as hijackings. Although the NPA announced the creation of the SATs in a white paper written in the midst of the Peru crisis, when the Japanese ambassador's house was occupied for four months by Tupac Amaru members, the connection was tenuous; no one suggested that the SATs should have taken part in a rescue effort (Keisatsucho 1997). Not even Japan's hawks have seriously proposed that SATs should be allowed to operate in overseas crises. Instead, they tend to save their political capital for the promotion of larger-ticket military items for Japan's national defense.

If the Japanese government's counterterrorism efforts at home have been marked by tightly focused investigations of specific and publicly acknowledged threats, overseas they reflect a case-by-case approach that does not focus on specific movements but on protecting the lives of Japanese citizens in specific incidents. Keenly aware of the difficulty of preventing attacks before they occur or of handling crises with the use of force, Japanese policymakers have become extraordinarily sensitive about their inability to protect Japanese citizens. Japan publicly maintains a "no concessions to terrorists" policy in accordance with international conventions, but the Japanese government has found itself with a reputation as a bargainer. To be fair, the most visible instance of Japan's willingness to negotiate with terrorist groups—its payment of $6 million to the JRA to end a 1977 hijacking in Bangladesh—took place before international conventions proscribed deals. But Japanese newspapers reported in 1997 that the Japanese government paid a ransom of between $2 million and $5 million to the Islamic Movement of Uzbekistan to release several Japanese aid workers who had been taken hostage in Kyrgyzstan (Leheny 2001–2002). The government's decision to work nonstop for the release of the hostages reveals a little-discussed component of Japan's counterterrorism policy: whether correctly or incorrectly, Japanese policymakers believed that the political costs of allowing hostages to die would be unacceptably high.

This approach was, until recently, further reinforced by the structure of Japanese counterterrorism policymaking in the Ministry of Foreign Affairs (MOFA). Unlike the United States, where the Office of the Coordinator for Counterterrorism operates as an independent section within the State Department, the Japanese counterpart organization was nested in the Consular and Migration Affairs Department—the division chiefly responsible for the protection of Japanese citizens overseas. Although known in English as the Anti-Terrorism Office, the Japanese title—Hojin Tokubetsu Taisakushitsu—is better translated as the Office for Special Measures for Our Citizens Overseas. With the NPA able to play only a limited role in counterterrorism overseas due to stringent restrictions on the exercise of police or military force outside of Japan's borders, the Consular and Migration Affairs Department was the primary actor in Japan's overseas counterterrorism efforts.

Hamstrung by constitutional and normative constraints, however, MOFA's office pushed as much as possible the idea that Japanese had to take better care of themselves overseas because the Japanese government might be unable to do so. MOFA's offices helped to publicize several "kaigai anzen animeshon bideo" (overseas safety animation videos) that depict the world as a menacing place, especially to the trusting and therefore vulnerable Japanese. These videos, made by the Council for Public Policy—an NPA-affiliated think tank—feature a rich variety of themes. The humorous *Sakusen Kodo Tokyo* (Battle Code Tokyo) follows a Japanese man who has been kidnapped and

tricked into believing that he is in Tokyo, when he is in fact in a cheap facsimile made by foreign spies. The facsimile fails because the foreigners are
simply unable to make it safe enough to keep the man (and apparently, his
kidnapped predecessors) from being killed on roads and beaches that, unlike
the real Tokyo, are actually unsafe. A more dramatic video, *Kidnap*, follows
the efforts of a Japanese salaryman overseas to rescue his boss, who has been
taken captive by terrorists. The message is clear: the Japanese state makes the
Japanese secure at home, but the world is not Japan. Paradoxically, of course,
it is the state's responsibility to make Japanese aware of its inability to protect
them overseas.

The Impact of 9/11

Judging by the Japanese government's rhetoric, al Qaeda's September 11
strikes on New York and Washington changed everything. Japan was firmly on
the side of the United States in the war on terror, and Foreign Minister
Kawaguchi Yoriko argued that Japan would need to make changes in its laws
to align its policies with those of the United States and Great Britain. In December 2001, MOFA added a new counterterrorism organization, the International Counterterrorism Cooperation Office, within the Foreign Policy
Bureau. Its members complement the staff still in the Hojin Tokubetsu
Taisakushitsu, but they now have responsibility for promoting Japan's counterterrorism work with the United States, the G8, the United Nations, and
other states.[1] Although the Diet was slower than Prime Minister Koizumi in
promising Japanese support for the U.S. campaign against the Taliban and al
Qaeda in Afghanistan, it ultimately responded with the Anti-Terrorism Special Measures Law. This law was not an effort to engage in counterterrorism
per se, but rather to support American activities in this specific instance. The
law does little, if anything, however, to prepare either the government or the
public for the possibility that the war on terror may have implications for Japanese interests, especially in Southeast Asia (Leheny 2001–2002).

Some of the government's other "counterterrorism" initiatives may have
longer-term security implications, and they have been built on Japanese concerns over more proximate threats, such as Chinese criminals and North Korean spies, rather than a barely understood specter called al Qaeda. Long
haunted by the concerns over clear North Korean violation of Japanese waters for drug smuggling, espionage, and most disturbingly, kidnapping Japanese citizens, the LDP used the opportunity posed by 9/11 to link a revision
of the Japan Coast Guard's governing law to the overall threat of terrorism

---

[1] Interview, March 2004.

(Maeda 2002, 187–88; Shinoda 2002). In so doing, it essentially loosened restrictions on the Coast Guard's use of force against the euphemistically named "unknown vessels" (*fushinsen*) that constantly violated Japanese territorial waters. Not two months later, in December 2001, Japanese Coast Guard vessels surrounded and fired on a presumed North Korean spy boat, which then exploded and sank, presumably because of a self-destruct mechanism. Although the incident actually ended in China's economic zone (Valencia and Ji 2002, 724), rather than Japan's, criticism at home was muted largely because of the increasing visibility of numerous North Korean menaces.

Japanese security specialists argued that Japan's support of U.S. counterterrorism permitted Japanese actions overseas, a bizarre mismatch with the government's inability to use the SDF effectively at home in the event of an invasion or similar incursion. In the words of one of Japan's leading international relations specialists, Akihiko Tanaka, "We have laws for when there is a crisis in the region, and now we will probably have a law when there is a crisis far overseas. But the laws for when Japan is attacked are inadequate" (Harney 2001, 2). In the spring of 2002 the cabinet also approved a package of three bills addressing the eventuality of an armed attack on the home islands of Japan (Nabeshima 2002). The unexpected admission by Kim Jong Il, during a state visit by Koizumi to Pyongyang, that agents of his government had kidnapped fifteen Japanese, and that a majority of them had died while working as language teachers to North Korean spies, had by this time left little doubt in the minds of many Japanese about where the threat lay. When a March 2002 poll by Central Research Services (Chuo Chosasha) inquired about threats to Japan, the four most popular answers—"terrorism," weapons of mass destruction attacks, overseas guerrillas (specifically including those onboard "suspicious boats"), and missile attacks—were all clearly or arguably tied to North Korea (MOFA 2002b).

The most important of the three bills defined more precisely the responses that would be permitted in the eventuality of a direct attack. The other two bills amended the Self-Defense Forces Law and the law governing the Security Council of Japan. At issue, politically, was not preparation for the most acute of Japan's security threats, North Korean spy ships (already covered by the Coast Guard law revision) and missile or terrorist attacks. Although the government's interpretation of Article 9 clearly recognizes Japan's right to use military force to stop an external attack, thereby allowing the emergency legislation, critics saw the legislative package as a Trojan horse designed to chip away even further at constitutional restrictions. With many legislators quietly uneasy in the governing coalition and vociferously critical in the opposition, the government made no attempt to push the bills through the Diet in 2002. In May 2003, the governing coalition accepted some of the amendments to the main bill proposed by the Democratic Party of Japan (DPJ), the largest opposition party in the Diet. They included a government commitment to maximum respect for the constitutional rights of citizens in countering any armed attack and giving the Diet the power to terminate the military operations covered by the bill. Compromise effected, all three bills passed the lower house in May and the upper house in June 2003, with the support in each house of over 80 percent of the members. Prime Minister Koizumi thus successfully instituted an emergency security law, something that was not feasible when his father, Koizumi Jun'ya, headed the Defense Agency in the 1960s (Samuels 2003a).

For military matters, the post-September 11 security environment became an opportunity for the LDP to achieve policies it had long wanted to pursue but believed to be impossible. Using the demands of an attacked and enraged ally as a foot in the door, and then relying on widespread public fears of a dangerously unbalanced neighbor, the government took steps that had long been planned. Rather than using the issue of terrorism to reassess societal security, however, Japanese authorities remained focused on foreigners and eroding homogeneity and the challenges posed by organized crime. By late 2002, the authorities had made explicit their view that terrorism was inextricably linked to transnational drug trafficking, illegal migration, and North Korea (*Asahi Shimbun* 2002c; *Japan Today* 2002e, 2002d, 2002g). Police expansion and NPA reorganization, as well as NPA and Ministry of Justice calls for prison and detention house expansion, were the solutions enacted to the challenges to homogeneity (*Daily Yomiuri* 2001c; *Japan Times* 2002c). Former NPA official Sassa Atsuyuki neatly captures the prevailing police mood in a 2004 article in the influential opinion monthly *Chuo Koron*. Japan is unprepared for international terrorism, he argues, because there were too many restrictions placed on the government by liberals who have ignored the need for public safety. He proposes that what Japan needs, therefore, is a much larger police force that can ensure that police boxes are always staffed, that people be appropriately searched at public locations, and that special attention be paid to Arabs and Muslims. He admits that this requires racial discrimination but calls it *sezaru o enai* (unavoidable) (Sassa 2004, 89). In effect, terrorism becomes one more in a larger constellation of threats for which the prescription is always the same: more police, larger budgets, and, where possible, fewer restrictions on investigations.

Some of the NPA's activities reflect direct pressure from the United States as well as the provisions of UN conventions on terrorism. Japan has signed on to, and begun to implement, new international conventions on suppressing terrorism and curtailing the financing of terrorist organizations. Following Prime Minister Koizumi's announcement of a seven-point antiterrorism plan in September 2001, President George Bush noted with appreciation Japanese measures to "strengthen international cooperation in sharing information and immigration control" (U.S. Department of State 2001; MOFA 2002a). To date, Japan has frozen the assets of terrorist organizations and has tried to align its money laundering laws with the international convention on the financing of terrorism. The government also ordered its embassies and consulates to be more assiduous in screening visa applicants, doubled the number of visa and immigration trainees (MOFA 2002a), and exchanged customs officials as part of the Container Security Initiative designed to protect the United States from the smuggling of terrorist weapons via container vessels (*Japan Today* 2002c). Japan also has joined the United States in six-party talks with North Korea on nuclear threats and in broader multilateral cooperation as part of the 2003 Madrid Initiative aimed at curtailing North Korean weapons of mass destruction as well as drug and currency smuggling (Kim 2003; Kralev 2003; Nabeshima 2004). The most visible evidence of this cooperation has been Japan's large-scale monitoring and inspection of North Korean ships entering Japanese ports (*Asahi Shimbun* 2003f; *Japan Times* 2003c).

On occasion, however, Japanese policy had resisted as much as accommodated the demands of the United States, illustrated here by the longstanding negotiations over concluding the Mutual Legal Assistance Treaty (MLAT). Such treaties allow for direct communication and cooperation between law enforcement authorities rather than requiring them to work through diplomatic channels. Initial negotiations had proved time consuming, with some observers speculating that the Japanese government was loath to allow direct U.S. intervention in Japanese investigations (*Japan Times* 2002d, 2002e; U.S. Embassy 2002). While delaying on the MLAT, the Japanese government took incremental steps to protect the Japanese from foreign criminals and drugs. Finally, facing heavy and consistent pressure from the United States, the Japanese government concluded the MLAT negotiations and signed the treaty in August 2003, stipulating that it was aimed primarily at terrorism and crimes involving the Internet (*Yomiuri Shimbun* 2003a). U.S. government interpretations of the MLAT, however, appear to be much broader than those held by Japan, suggesting that the pattern of Japanese resistance and accommodation will continue (Department of Justice 2003).

Observers have frequently commented on the constitutional and political constraints on Japan's security approach, but they have been far slower to notice the comprehensiveness of Japanese policies. In the aftermath of September 11, Japan now faces a world more attuned to the interrelationship between internal and external security, as well as a changing region replete with myriad dangers for citizens and policymakers alike to consider. Changes in the international environment have complemented political and social transformations in Japan. Yet in the post-9/11 world, Japan's external and internal security policies appear to be shifting unevenly.

The blueprint for a more assertive Japan has existed for decades, especially since the Nakasone years in the 1980s. Though deeply controversial, hopes that the Self-Defense Forces would be given an expanded international role have animated political debate, especially since the end of the Cold War, and with the atrophy of the traditional Japanese left there are fewer brakes than ever before on government action. In contrast, the constraints on internal security policy change are as much intellectual as they are political. The only way to deal fully with the challenges of the transnational drug trade, illegal immigration, and terrorism is to acknowledge that security is not served by seeking to re-create Japan as a hermetically sealed, homogenous nation. Put simply, there is no blueprint in Japan for looking beyond the defense of homogeneity as the path to internal security.

Ideally, a Japanized security environment in Asia would consist of atomized, independent nation-states, all cooperative, economically open but physically distinct, and able to trust in one another's good intentions. By promoting multilateral cooperation, the Japanese government has sought to mitigate domestic and Asian concerns over the iron-clad U.S.-Japan alliance, which it sees as the ultimate guarantor of Japanese security. In the post-9/11 world, security specialists around the globe are grappling with what a U.S.-led war on terror means for different regions and for the world in general. For the Japanese government, it provides an opportunity to harness wider and more comprehensive national fears over security, using them to justify a more assertive international stance. But the government shows few signs of peering too closely at what rapid social and regional transformation will likely mean over the long term. Staring into the abyss of the changes might reveal something about Japan's future that the government would rather not see.

5

Creating a Regional Arena:
Financial Sector Reconstruction,
Globalization, and Region-Making

NATASHA HAMILTON-HART

Two images of financial markets and policies in East Asia since 1997 continue to circulate. The region's financial systems have either been subject to large doses of disciplinary globalization, if not outright Americanization, or they have been quietly influenced by Japanese policies of region-making. Japan can either be seen as suffering "abject defeat" or as achieving a quiet postcrisis victory (Hughes 2000). In the first view, the crisis discredited Japan's model of finance and proved its incapacity to provide international leadership. Its banking system was on the brink of collapse and massive withdrawals of Japanese loans were blamed for exacerbating the regional crisis. Stripped of the cushion provided by easy Japanese finance and any residual admiration of Japanese economic strategies, Asia no longer offered covert resistance to the forces of globalization: financial systems were becoming more fully liberalized and financial policies and institutions were being remade to reflect global regulatory standards. In the second view, Japan was staging a comeback in the region through its postcrisis aid, advice, and diplomatic activity. Internationally, it was assuming a newly assertive profile in the global institutions assigned the task of strengthening the rules governing the global financial system. It was willing to challenge U.S. views and demand greater voice in these arenas, not only for itself but for Asian countries collectively.

The persistence of both these images reflects the unsurprising reality that postcrisis reforms in Asian financial systems and policies are not uniform. The direction of regional financial polices remains contested, domestically and internationally, and neither side in these debates has won a clear victory. More important, however, the dichotomy of globalization (with its implications of convergence and Americanization) opposed to Japanization conceals the ways in which some forms of convergence can provide for greater national resilience and regional space. Global market forces and outright political pressure have constrained Japanese initiatives to influence financial arrangements. But if Japan's region-making initiatives are to succeed it must implement institutional and policy reforms that are commonly described as reflecting forced convergence on global market and regulatory norms.

In this interpretation, the crises of 1997–98 signal neither a reversal of Japanization nor a shift toward exclusive regionalism in finance. Elements of Japanization in Asian finance before 1997 were, if not illusory, precarious and subject to firm limits set by American political and financial power. The crises made these limits obvious but also precipitated a series of reconstructions within Japan and in the region. These as yet incomplete transformations have the potential to support meaningful financial governance frameworks in Asia. Significant steps have been made in this direction, even if regional frameworks are still in the early stages of development and most are nonoperational. The fact that the foundations of a formal regional architecture for managing finance now exist marks a real change from the situation before 1997. However, while the foundations for reform in Japan and more formalized regional arrangements have been laid, there is no clear or uncontested trajectory along which they will develop. Asia as a region figures increasingly in Japan's positioning in international economic affairs, but it does not define Japanese policy or self-interest.

Japan's financial policies and capacities for regional engagement are related to developments in its domestic financial system. The apparent strength of Japanese banks as they built up staggering assets during the bubble economy years was closely connected to the surge of Japanese investment in Asia. With the bursting of the asset bubble in 1990, market and political pressures to conform to global liberalization trends and American regulatory models intensified. But it took nearly a decade of banking system paralysis, culminating in a near crisis, before these pressures produced significant reform. The dismemberment of the Ministry of Finance and foreign takeovers of failed financial institutions starting in 1998 signal the death of the Japanese model and the ascendance of American modes of financial governance. Yet, if this process of financial reform succeeds and Japan's extremely weak banking system emerges in a stronger position, subject to more effective regulatory oversight, the transformation may be counted as a shift that will allow for more coherent financial policies and region-making on more autonomous terms.

Domestic financial weakness in the 1990s mirrored Japan's relative weakness in shaping international financial governance arrangements centered on global institutions. As negotiations on a supposedly "new international financial architecture" played out in the second half of the 1990s, Japan lost the visible contests over what this architecture would mean. International financial reform proceeded in ways that reflect the dominance of American-oriented financial markets, regulatory systems, and international institutions that govern global finance. Market pressures in the form of competition, exchange rate imbalances, and capital account vulnerabilities affected perceptions and national capacities for influencing global reform. These constraints, however, have been less important in determining the course of international financial reform than political muscle and enduring institutional legacies. European and American influence combined to produce reforms that amount to an intensification of efforts to make surveillance in a liberalized system work, rather than structural change of that system. The sources of U.S. influence in international finance include continued veto power (but not full control) in the International Monetary Fund and the World Bank, the international role of the U.S. dollar, and ongoing dominance in constructing the ideational yardsticks used to define global standards. The United States has also continued to press bilaterally for countries in Asia to adopt standards and policies that further processes of globalization on American terms.

Japan scaled back its attempts to influence international financial arrangements starting in 2000. After that, head-to-head contests in global arenas became less relevant, as political efforts to forge more effective financial arrangements shifted into a different gear. Regional initiatives, which had been pursued since 1997, occupied a more central place in Japan's foreign financial policies. Regional arrangements are not attempts to retreat from processes of globalization or aimed at "keeping the United States out" (Bowles 2002). Rather, we can see a Japan-led attempt at constructing a more resilient regional financial system that will be integrated globally. Its toolkit for region-making in finance includes efforts to build up "soft" or ideational power as much as financial resources. Although these regional arrangements have made progress, their development remains subject to intraregional political dynamics and the successful reconstruction of Japan's domestic economy and financial system.

Japan's Financial System: Crisis and Change

Just as Asia's currency and financial crises broke, Japan's domestic banking system was experiencing acute stress after more than seven years of delay in dealing with the problem of nonperforming loans (NPLs) caused by the bursting of Japan's bubble economy. Japan's financial sector regulator, the

Ministry of Finance (MOF), had for years avoided decisive action to force the banks to write off their NPLs, since write-downs would have pushed bank capital ratios far below international levels and in many cases would have meant outright bank failure (Amyx 2004a). Dealing with the NPLs would thus require the injection of substantial public funds into the banks and a radical restructuring of the banking system, with attendant destabilization of the economic sectors that account for much of the NPL problem. As T. J. Pempel discusses in chapter 2, borrowers in (or exposed to) these sectors—particularly the construction industry, agricultural cooperatives, and small businesses—are key constituents of the LDP. For this reason, the MOF faced strong political reluctance to precipitate changes that would damage these interests. In addition, Japanese banks were of course resistant to moves that would force bank closures, major restructuring, and opening up the still-protected banking market to foreign competition and takeovers.

The path that offered the least resistance was for the major banks and the MOF to continue their cooperative but increasingly uneasy partnership, papering over the problems in the industry by turning a blind eye to NPL reporting standards, arranging takeovers of distressed smaller banks, and hoping that economic growth and the reflation of asset values would restore bank balance sheets. It was no coincidence that overseas lending by Japanese banks, which had soared during the bubble economy years, continued at only a slightly slower rate in the 1990s. Japanese banks were trying to outgrow problem loans at home and, given the lack of quality domestic borrowers, their only option was to focus on expanding overseas assets. Japanese bank loans were a significant component of the precrisis capital flows to Asia that contributed to economic distortions there and made much of the region vulnerable to a reversal in investor sentiment. And the sharp reversal of these loans—in some accounts a trigger for the crisis (King 2001)—aggravated conditions in the crisis economies.

Rather than outgrowing the NPL problem, Japan's economy and financial markets remained depressed, and Japanese banks' Asian assets proved not to be any solution at all. By 1998, a string of increasingly large domestic failures threatened the stability of the Japanese financial system. The major banks were not in any position to absorb more failed institutions—their own NPL problems were growing worse even as failures in the financial sector were starting to involve larger firms. Over the decade starting in 1991 more than 170 banks and depository institutions went bankrupt, and although 130 of these involved small-scale credit cooperatives (Horiuchi 2003, 89), failures beginning in 1995 involved larger institutions. These included forced closure of housing and loan institutions in 1995 (which required the disbursement of public funds in addition to commercial banks bearing some of the costs of dissolution) and MOF-arranged rescues of some larger commercial banks by the major banks from 1996. In late 1997 the tenth largest commercial bank and one of the "big four" securities houses both effectively collapsed.

This critical period for the banking system came against a backdrop of other pressures for financial reform. U.S. demands that Japan open its financial services markets and reform its regulatory codes produced some changes in markets such as insurance. But market pressures created by the growing ability of Japanese borrowers to access global financial markets more effectively and insistently raised the costs of delaying reform (Laurence 2001; Posen 2001). The old system of financial governance through market segmentation, informal administrative guidance, and personalized networks linking the MOF and the financial sector was becoming increasingly unsustainable. Not only was the condition of the banking sector a sign of its failure, a series of scandals involving MOF personnel meant that the once-respected and powerful ministry was increasingly the object of public disgust, vulnerable to growing demands for wholesale bureaucratic and political reform (Laurence 2001, 147–55, 173–75; Amyx 2003a; Amyx and Drysdale 2003). MOF assessments of the condition of the financial sector were no longer believed to be accurate. For example, in 1996 the MOF figure for NPLs was thirty-eight trillion yen, while unofficial estimates put the volume of bad loans at seventy-five trillion yen (Laurence 2001, 178). MOF information was increasingly contested by an influx of new private sector analysts and rating agencies producing their own estimates. Official denials and outrage at ratings downgrades (Sinclair 2005) only added to perceptions that the old alliance that had presided over Japan's financial system was corrupt, out of touch with reality, and flailing desperately.

In November 1996 a major financial reform package known as Japan's Big Bang announced plans for changes that would make the system more efficient, transparent, and competitive. Over the next three years a series of laws were passed that implemented these goals, providing for further capital market deregulation, corporate finance and accounting reform, securities industry liberalization, and bank recapitalization (Horiuchi 2003). New domestic and foreign entrants to the financial sector, and the new readiness to allow financial firms to fail, increased competition. Foreign direct investment in Japanese financial institutions rose from $242 million in 1995 to $8.6 billion in 1998, and by 1999 foreign investors had dramatically increased their presence in Japanese financial markets, accounting for almost 25 percent of trading on the stock exchange (Laurence 2001, 183).

Major institutional change and the injection of substantial public funds into the banking system came in 1998. In April, authority over monetary policy was transferred from the MOF to the Bank of Japan, making the central bank more formally independent and thus bringing it into line with prevailing beliefs in Europe and the United States that central bank independence is essential for proper economic governance. New laws also broke up the MOF and established a separate Financial Supervisory Agency (FSA, renamed as the Financial Services Agency in 2000, when it took over another finance-related bureau from the MOF). Importantly, along with these administrative reorganizations came a decisive change in Japan's style of financial regulation: from a personalized system based on opaque networks and informal guidance, regulation became much more transparent and rule-based (Amyx 2003a). The new FSA showed itself willing and able to take a proactive and resolute approach to banks that were experiencing difficulties: in addition to nationalizing two major banks and imposing administrative penalties for regulatory violations, by May 2001 it had issued fifty-nine "corrective action" orders requiring banks to raise additional capital and make management changes (Amyx 2003b).

The cumulative effect of these reforms has been to make Japan's system of corporate governance and financial regulation look much more like America's (Laurence 2001; Posen 2001; Horiuchi 2003). Changes since 1998 are more than cosmetic moves designed to preserve the old networks linking banks, the MOF, and the LDP. This alliance, a key feature of Japan's old system of industrial finance, has been broken. Major restructuring has occurred in the banking sector, due to nationalizations, foreign acquisitions, and domestic mergers. Since 2000, five new banks have been created from mergers of fourteen of Japan's largest banks (Amyx 2003b). On the other hand, although the financial system has been transformed, it has not been cured. Despite write-offs of some bubble-era loans, NPLs remain a burden on the banks, which continued to incur huge losses through 2002 (*Business Times* 2003a). Their condition was so weak that the FSA was forced in early 2003 to ease its requirements regarding capital ratios and profit targets (*Straits Times* 2003a). By the end of 2003 the major banks reported positive earnings outlooks and the government was credited with having taken decisive action in its bailout of Resona Bank in June (*Business Times* 2003c; Tsuru 2003). The banking system as a whole remained weak in 2003 but the major banks had significantly reduced their bad loan problems by the time the government announced another reform plan for the financial sector at the end of 2004 (IMF 2003b; *Business Times* 2004).

Japan's financial reforms have been prompted by market pressures, but financial reform in Japan (as elsewhere) is more a case of reregulation than deregulation: new rules and oversight mechanisms mean that a greater role for market competition is combined with an *increased* role for government regulation and enforcement (Vogel 1996, 16–18). The players and institutions of "organized capitalism" in Japan have not disappeared and may be engineering their reorganization rather than their demise (Vogel 2003). A new body, the Industrial Revitalization Corporation, was established in May

2003 with a mandate to spend up to ten trillion yen to buy up bad loans. There are suspicions that it will simply help the banks delay making unpopular operational changes (*Straits Times* 2003b; *Business Times* 2003b). However, officially, the Industrial Revitalization Corporation aims to promote debt restructuring that will allow fundamentally sound companies to regain competitiveness. Its chances of success are increased by the genuine changes that have occurred since 1998. Although the old links between the MOF, the LDP, and the banks have been severed, as Pempel shows in chapter 2, the LDP has not yet broken free of its constituents in the uncompetitive sectors of the economy. It is the political influence of these groups that is at the heart of not only the NPL problem but Japan's larger problems with its public finances and economic competitiveness. These problems remain a factor shaping the type of influence Japan exercises in global and regional arenas.

Global Forces: Markets and International Rules

Global market pressures have exerted a steady structural influence on financial systems in many Asian countries. The region is relatively open to global financial markets and therefore has a major stake in the global regime governing international finance. This regime—used here to mean the rules and multilateral institutions with a global mandate in the financial sector—works in tandem with national regulatory practices to provide the regulatory context in which financial markets operate. The dramatic crises in Asian and other emerging markets at the end of the 1990s put the issue of reforming systems of financial regulation high on the international agenda. Japan became publicly engaged in criticism of the global financial regime and advocated major reforms to both the substantive rules governing international finance and the institutions that implement them. Some change has occurred on both counts, but Japan and other Asian countries had relatively little influence on the process.

Japan's proposal to manage the crisis using a regional liquidity facility that became known as an "Asian monetary fund" was shelved, in part due to strong U.S. objections, in favor of IMF programs for the crisis economies (Amyx 2004b). Under the aegis of the IMF, these countries embarked on major structural and institutional reform programs aimed at bringing them into line with global standards as defined by the multilateral institutions. Most financial markets in East Asia are now more open than they were before the crisis. Net flows of private capital to non-Japan Asia have been positive in recent years (see table 5.1), with the most significant form of private capital being foreign direct investment, most of which is accounted for by FDI inflows to

Table 5.1. Capital flows to non-Japan Asia in US$ billions

	2001	2002	2003f	2004f
Private flows, net	55.4	66.6	84.3	87.4
direct investment	51.7	55.9	60.4	64.8
portfolio investment	12.4	2.6	11.6	13.3
commercial banks	−10.7	3.1	8.5	5.5
nonbank creditors	2.0	5.0	3.8	3.8
Offical flows, net	−8.3	−15.1	−12.8	−5.2
Resident lending/other	−25.1	−12.9	−4.2	−13.7
Change in reserves[a]	−70.3	−110.1	−131.2	−120.5

Source: IIF 2003, 7.
Note: Includes China, India, Indonesia, Malaysia, Philippines, South Korea, Thailand. f = forecast.
[a]Minus sign equals an increase in reserves.

China (IIF 2003, 7). Japan too has experienced much higher levels of FDI inflow since 1997, albeit from an extraordinarily low base: FDI inflows to Japan averaged $9 billion per year from 1999 through 2002, while for the same period FDI inflows to the United States averaged almost $193 billion per year. However, the gap between the two countries is narrowing: in 2002, the United States registered $30 billion in FDI inflows, compared to $9 billion to Japan (UNCTAD 2003, Annex table B.1).

Direct investment inflows to Japan are overwhelmingly from Europe and the United States. U.S. investors have also made some significant purchases of Korean assets since 1997 (Hamilton-Hart 2004). However, in the rest of Asia FDI flows have a significant regional aspect. Intraregional FDI flows in East Asia excluding Japan rose from 37 percent of total FDI inflows to Asia in 1999 to 40 percent in 2001 (UNCTAD 2003, 46). Combined with Japanese FDI flows to East Asia, which remains substantial despite a sharp decline since 1998, this means that non-Japan East Asia gets more than half of its inward FDI from regional countries. Hong Kong, Singapore, Taiwan, and Japan are the region's largest outward investors, with Korea, Malaysia, and China investing smaller but still significant amounts abroad (UNCTAD 2003, Annex table B.2).

Net bank lending to East Asia turned positive in 2002, ending the massive drawdown of bank loans to the region from 1997 (Hamilton-Hart 2004, 142–43). However, the trend varies from country to country: foreign bank loans outstanding have declined in the last two years in the case of China, Indonesia, and Thailand, while foreign bank lending has increased to Japan, Korea, Taiwan, and Malaysia (BIS 2002, table 9). Japan is by no means the dominant lender to the region: that role is played by European banks (see table 5.2). U.S. banks have stepped up their lending to Asia in recent years, overtaking

Table 5.2. Foreign bank claims on Asia, 2003

	Total	Europe[a]	U.S.	Japan
China	55.4	29.5	4.7	9.7
		(53%)	(8%)	(18%)
Indonesia	34.7	21.9	3.0	6.0
		(63%)	(9%)	(17%)
Malaysia	54.6	24.5	8.2	5.3
		(45%)	(15%)	(10%)
Philippines	22.3	11.7	4.5	2.5
		(53%)	20%)	(11%)
Korea	94.5	45.7	15.4	12.1
		(48%)	(16%)	(13%)
Taiwan	47.0	24.6	15.5	3.1
		(52%)	(33%)	(7%)
Thailand	35.6	14.9	4.0	8.6
		(42%)	(11%)	(24%)
Vietnam	3.0	1.8	0.3	0.3
		(59%)	(12%)	(8%)
Japan	658.9	358.2	70.4	—
		(54%)	(11%)	
Hong Kong[b]	254.9	171.0	18.5	24.9
		(67%)	(7%)	(10%)
Singapore[b]	136.8	69.6	16.6	18.4
		(51%)	(12%)	(13%)
United States	3,393.5	2,384.2	—	485.3
		(70%)		(14%
Total foreign claims		8,548.1	788.6	1,201.5

Source: BIS 2003, table 9 (foreign claims of reporting banks on individual countries by nationality of reporting banks).
Note: US$ billions, as of June 2003.
[a]Europe: Austria, Belgium, France, Germany, Netherlands, Switzerland, United Kingdom.
[b]Lending to the offshore market.

Japanese banks in several markets. Although Japanese banks continue to account for a significant amount of foreign lending to countries such as China, overall they are much less important creditors to the region than in the mid-1990s when Japanese lending accounted for 35 percent of total foreign lending there (Hamilton-Hart 2004, 135).

Capital flows to Asia have recovered from the sharp reversals associated with the financial crisis, and the region is buffered by large current account surpluses and foreign reserves. On a net basis, direct investment is the most significant form of external financing and this has been much less volatile than other forms of capital flow. Portfolio flows remain volatile throughout the region. In some countries, notably Indonesia, foreign investor activity is now less significant than it was: foreign trading accounted for an average of 18 percent of total trading on the Jakarta stock exchange from 1998 to 2003, compared to 60 percent from 1994 through 1996 (JSE 2003, 13). The sharp rises on most regional stock markets in 2003 involved substantial trading by foreign investors with relatively short time horizons, even though net purchases were not that high in most markets. Portfolio flows and currency trading still have the potential to be destabilizing in the event of any loss of confidence. Together with the return of bank lending to some countries, this means that while many of the specific weaknesses present before 1997 have been addressed, the region remains vulnerable to future financial disturbances.

Reforms of the international regime governing finance have the objective of mitigating this vulnerability. In the wake of the crises of 1997 and 1998, efforts to promote financial stability aimed to create a "new international financial architecture" to govern global finance (Kahler 2000). The main organizations involved are the IMF, the Bank for International Settlements (BIS), and the World Bank, and the main changes involve revised procedures for IMF lending, standard-setting, and surveillance in a liberal international financial system. No fundamental changes have been made to the underlying policy regime governing finance, the crisis management capacity of the IMF, or the structure of control over the IMF (Lee 2002). Despite some initiatives that aim to "bail-in" private sector actors in crisis situations, the international financial architecture places the burden of responsibility for ensuring system stability on public authorities by significantly increasing the information gathering and surveillance tasks required of regulators. By eschewing alternative mechanisms to promote stability, such as endorsing a return to more segmented markets, it is ultimately taxpayers, not globally active financial investors, that pay most of the costs of this type of regulatory approach (Laurence 2001, 16–17).

Japan's activism and challenge to the prevailing global financial regime was most pronounced between 1998 and 2000, when it issued frequent and strongly worded statements regarding the need for substantive reform of the IMF and the international rules governing the financial system. Public criticism of the way the IMF handled the crises in Asia by individuals closely associated with the government was unprecedented, but rather than withdraw from global institutions the government became more vocal in its attempts to reform them and to set new financial governance standards (Katada 2001). After receiving a lot of attention at the G7 summits in 1999 and 2000, high-level interest in reforming the international regime governing finance receded in 2001 and 2002 (Fratianni, Savona, and Kirton 2002). The extent to which the outcome represents a defeat for Japan is somewhat contentious. Some Japanese officials were relatively satisfied with the direction of reforms and believed that the IMF and the U.S. administration, as well as Japan, had modified their original positions (Amyx 2004b). Further, as a major creditor nation, Japan's interests overlap to some degree with those of Europe and the United States, whose banks and investors also have large international portfolios. Nonetheless, very little of Japan's agenda for change articulated during and after the crises was adopted. It did win some concessions on the issue of crisis management, and the United States dropped its objections to Japan's revised bailout scheme for Asia. On institutional reform, however, Japan "deferred to U.S. leadership and signed on to a G-7 proposal of IMF reform that closely follows the U.S. blueprint and does little to address the issues raised by Japan" (Searight 2002, 181).

The new financial architecture has introduced changes to financial regulation and the IMF. The Fund has undergone a series of internal makeovers and reviews of its procedures, and has been the subject of several external studies aimed at providing blueprints for reform (Lee 2002). As well as an increased role in financial regulation, the IMF has been handed two new issues as a result of mainly U.S. and European influence: debt relief for highly indebted poor countries and safeguards against money laundering and terrorist financing. The Fund as an organization has made a commitment to be more transparent, and an independent evaluation office has been established.

The Fund's resources and procedures for lending have also been amended. Its resources increased as a result of a quota revision in 1998, but no further increases have followed. Some new lending facilities have been established to allow members access to financing beyond their quota in "exceptional" circumstances. Another postcrisis change to IMF lending was the establishment of the Contingent Credit Line (CCL) facility, aimed at allowing more rapid disbursement of Fund resources to prequalified countries that are facing genuine liquidity crises. This, however, has had minimal impact because members have been reluctant to negotiate CCLs. One controversial aspect of IMF lending, the conditionality requirements imposed on borrowing countries, has also been revised (IMF 2002a). In response to widespread criticisms that Fund conditionality was too intrusive and wide-ranging, the new guidelines for conditionality assert that it will now be more focused, with an emphasis on country "ownership" of the program. This declaration of intent may have done little to narrow the focus on conditionality in practice, however, since the inclusion of governance and institutional factors that underlie macroeconomic management opens the door to very broad interpretations of appropriate areas for Fund conditionality. The scope of Fund surveillance has explicitly been increased beyond its original focus on macroeconomic indicators to include "institutional requirements for economic development" (IMF 2002b).

The Fund's ideas regarding what counts as appropriate and sound macroeconomic, exchange rate, and regulatory policy have undergone some revision. For example, support for capital account liberalization is now more nuanced, generally accompanied by the phrase "gradual and sequenced" in recommendations for liberalization. A former Indonesian central bank official posted to the IMF during and after the crisis confirmed that opinions there had shifted slightly on issues such as the sequencing of financial liberalization and the appropriateness of some Fund actions in borrowing countries (interview, Jakarta, February 2003). On the other hand, the Fund's initial postcrisis retreat from unconditional endorsement of capital account and financial liberalization has been a limited one. The option of capital account controls does not figure at all in its proposals for promoting financial stability, and Japan's repeated calls for IMF reform to pay greater attention to large-scale and abrupt capital movements (for example, Miyazawa 2000) has only been addressed by support for greater capital account monitoring. This is very much in line with U.S. preferences, as it continues to seek commitments to forego the use of capital controls, pushing both Chile and Singapore on this issue during bilateral trade agreement negotiations.

On other financial policy issues, the Fund has endorsed a financial governance approach that emphasizes liberalization combined with increased prudential oversight and transparency. Commitments to privatize banks and allow sales of financial assets to foreigners were included in its crisis lending programs to Thailand, Indonesia, and South Korea. In recognition that liberalized markets are subject to certain types of failure, the global financial regime has greatly increased the amount of attention given to standard-setting and surveillance. The Bank for International Settlements has been the focal point for developing new capital rules for international banks, while the IMF has taken the lead in developing early warning models, technical assistance, new mechanisms for monitoring, and the formulation and standardization of disclosure requirements. In general terms, the new regime for promoting international financial stability is based on perfecting market functions, not replacing market mechanisms. Any post–Washington consensus as to the content of appropriate and sound economic and financial policies, which inform the elaboration of financial standards and surveillance models, continues to be defined by U.S.-dominated institutions (Wade 2001; Kapur 2002).

Another element of continuity in the "new" financial architecture is that little has changed in terms of who exercises control over the IMF. It remains a European- and U.S.-dominated institution in its voting structure, representation on the executive board, and management. By common assent, Asia is underrepresented in the organization and this issue has been taken up by Japan (for example, Henning 2002, 72–73). One indicator of Japan's determination to redress this imbalance was its nomination of Sakakibara Eisuke, the champion of Japan's proposal to establish a regional liquidity fund in 1998 and whose strong views regarding the problems created by capital mobility were well known, to be the IMF's managing director in 2000. The nomination gained some support from Asian countries but was widely considered symbolic (Noland 2000), something that was acknowledged in Japan's statement that the move reflected its view that the position should not be based on a candidate's country of origin (Miyazawa 2000).

Another illustration of how Japan has been frustrated in its attempts to influence the evolution of financial reform based on the IMF and World Bank is the issue of quota allocations and representation on the IMF executive board. Japan was insistent in pushing for increases and reallocation of quota shares, repeatedly raising the issue at IMF meetings. Although a general quota increase was secured in 1998 and an exceptional reallocation to increase China's share was granted in 2001, Asia remains collectively underrepresented compared to Europe both in terms of quota allocations and representation on the executive board. As late as September 2002, Japan argued that "the IMF's usable resources are at a very low level, and we hope for an immediate decision on the quota increase" and, simultaneously, that reallocations should be examined (Hayami 2002a). When the deadline for negotiations over the review of quotas was reached, however, no increase or reallocation was agreed to. The official executive board position (which reflected that of the United States but directly contradicted earlier Japanese statements) was that the IMF's liquidity "remains adequate" (IMF 2003a).

After this it appears that Japan, at least for the moment, has turned its attention elsewhere. In contrast to its previous longer and more detailed arguments on the issue, its April 2003 statement to the International Monetary and Financial Committee (IMFC) of the IMF merely noted briefly that "discussion on a quota increase should resume soon" and that the quota distribution should "reflect the current situation of the world economy" (Shiokawa 2003). Another possible sign that Japan is reducing its emphasis on IMF reform is the progressively shorter official statements made at the biannual meetings of the IMFC, and the much reduced scope of discussion items included in official statements at the joint annual World Bank–IMF meetings. For example, the Japanese statement at the 2000 joint annual meeting includes quite lengthy sections on regional cooperation in Asia and reform of the World Bank (Hayami 2000), but both items were absent from the 2002 statement (Hayami 2002a). At a meeting of the IMFC in 2002 Japan appeared to suggest that the need for such meetings should be reconsidered (Hayami 2002b).

Overall, international efforts to reduce vulnerabilities and develop more effective crisis management mechanisms have done little to alter the structural vulnerabilities associated with open financial markets. The thrust of the "new international financial architecture" has been to develop market infrastructure, with a strong emphasis on information and the promotion of global standards. What these standards mean, however, remains loosely defined in many areas. Much technical work on, for example, how bank capital ratios should be calculated or capital account transactions recorded has proceeded in the BIS and the IMF. But on substantive policy issues, official IMF specification of the principles of the new financial architecture generally goes little further than motherhood statements, calling for things such as "responsible" macroeconomic policies and "appropriate" exchange rate regimes. Although the generally unmodified commitment to open markets, central bank independence, and American-style financial governance is clear from both much of the IMF's research output and its country programs, this vagueness in the wording of key principles means that the IMF can potentially be quite elastic in its application of lending criteria and standards on the ground.

There are signs that the IMF has relaxed its earlier emphasis on governance and structural reform issues in countries such as Indonesia. Since 2000, it has issued generally positive reviews of Indonesian progress under its program, pointing to improving macroeconomic indicators and sales of nationalized assets. Little has been said about the way asset disposals have occurred, or the fact that Indonesia has made no tangible progress on trade liberalization or dealing with the corruption-related problems that were identified as critical for reform in earlier programs. Although corruption and general governance issues are the province of the World Bank not the IMF, the IMF has avoided making public statements that are critical of Indonesian regulatory practices even in the financial sector. In private, it has continued to be engaged in efforts to reform and influence change at the central bank, which remains the main financial sector regulator (interview, central bank official, Jakarta, February 2003).

Asian countries are showing signs of retreating from the very close relationship with the IMF brought about by its crisis-related lending. Korea and Thailand announced their intention to complete repayments of IMF crisis loans in 2003. In February 2003 the Philippines announced its intention to exit from IMF supervision by the end of the year, declining to renew its post-program monitoring arrangement once its current loan facility expired in September. Although this decision was later reversed and IMF monitoring continued, at the time the central bank governor said that international rating agencies would provide adequate monitoring, without the costs of hosting IMF officials twice a year (*Manila Times* 2003). Concurrently, demands that Indonesia exit from its IMF program in 2003 also built up. The IMF had of course been unpopular in Indonesia and an easy target for politicians since 1998, but by early 2003 a growing number of local economists as well as politicians were arguing that renewal was not desirable. The Japanese government was also supportive of an exit strategy for Indonesia, not, officially, because it had a quarrel with the specific content of the IMF program there but because it recognized the political unsustainability of continuing the program. That is, given the IMF program's unpopularity and the upcoming general and presidential elections in 2004, if the government renewed its program its commitments would lack credibility, which could actually worsen investor confidence (interview, Japanese official, Jakarta, February 2003). While insisting that Japan would not restructure Indonesia's sovereign debt in the absence of an IMF program, support for a controlled exit strategy was nonetheless a move toward embedding recovery policies within local political realities.

Creating Regional Space for Financial Cooperation

Initiatives to develop regional financial arrangements for crisis prevention, management, and currency coordination are related to concerns in Asia that global-level management centered on the IMF and the BIS is inadequate. Proposals for financial cooperation form part of the new regional cooperation agenda in Asia after 1997 described by Naoko Munakata in chapter 6. Along with Japan's substantial crisis-related lending to Asia and other official moves to disperse advisers and extend support to industry in the region, Japan's promotion of regional financial cooperation has been interpreted as an outright move to regionalize a Japanese system of "developmental" state guidance, hence as something of a direct challenge to globalization in general and the United States in particular (Hughes 2000; Bowles 2002; Hatch 2002a, 2002b). However, current modes of Japan-led region-making rely on nonconfrontational tools and are based on principles that have little in common with traditional models of Japan's so-called developmental state.

Implicit criticism of the IMF's crisis management in the region was a factor motivating regional cooperation to promote financial stability, but the development of a regional crisis management capacity is at least as much informed by the view that, given regional contagion effects and interdependence, there are advantages to regional facilities as a complement to IMF crisis management. To date, the capacity for regional crisis management remains modest, but it has grown rapidly considering that the region had virtually no mechanisms at all for crisis management before 1997.

Before the crisis, Japanese officials had been considering the merits of some kind of regional crisis management facility and had, along with Hong Kong, signed some repurchase agreements with regional central banks (Hamilton-Hart 2003). In the early stages of the crisis they raised the idea of an Asian monetary fund privately with Asian governments (Amyx 2004b). Although they failed to establish such a fund, countries in the region were

clearly receptive to the idea of developing some kind of regional support facility and Japan was the main force driving more low-key initiatives to this end.
Increased financial cooperation since 1997 has mainly taken place under the
umbrella of the ASEAN Plus Three (APT) group, consisting of ASEAN countries, China, Japan, and South Korea (Stubbs 2002), although Japan also supports initiatives associated with the Manila Framework Group of Asia Pacific
Economic Cooperation (APEC) and ASEAN itself (Rajan 2001). Regular
meetings of APT finance and central bank deputies have taken place since
1999, and APT finance ministers began to meet officially in 2000.

In May 2000 APT finance ministers announced a plan to expand the
ASEAN Swap Arrangement and to establish a network of bilateral currency
swap agreements, known as the Chiang Mai Initiative (CMI). The aim was to
develop some regional crisis management capacity that would provide emergency foreign currency liquidity support in the event of a future financial crisis. The ASEAN Swap Arrangement was enlarged from $200 million to $1
billion in November 2000. Over the next three years, a series of bilateral swaps
were negotiated, amounting to $31.5 billion in potential liquidity support.
The first of these swaps were mostly one-way arrangements with Japan as the
potential creditor. Korea and China, however, soon began to anchor bilateral
swaps and, by 2003, seven of the thirteen swap arrangements under the CMI
did not involve Japan (ADB 2003).

Taken together with the additional $7.5 billion in bilateral swaps provided
by Japan to Korea and Malaysia under the New Miyazawa Initiative, the CMI
could mobilize substantial funding. One point of comparison is the amounts
made available in the IMF bailout packages of 1997. Although the total available to any country under the bilateral swap arrangements (BSAs) is less than
the amount pledged in the IMF packages, these packages need some interpretation. Although they were widely described as providing $17 billion for
Thailand, $35 billion for Indonesia, and $57 billion for Korea, this included
substantial "second line of defense" commitments that in many cases were not
disbursed.

CMI support is intended to provide additional support for recipient countries, not to replace crisis lending from the IMF. At the moment this is ensured
by an official link to the IMF. The BSAs provide for "automatic" disbursement
(subject to the provider's agreement) of up to 10 percent of the total facility.
Beyond this, countries drawing from the facility must have an IMF program
in place, a stipulation that China and Japan succeeded in embedding in the
agreement, against the objections of Malaysia in particular (Amyx 2004b).
This linkage to IMF conditionality has been criticized for undermining the
independence of the CMI (Dieter and Higgott 2003), and it certainly binds
the facility much more tightly to IMF approval than bilateral or regional swap
facilities in Europe and North America (Henning 2002, 49–62). The linkage

does not mean, however, that the CMI will be nothing more than a regional arm of the IMF.

Some countries, particularly Singapore, have no wish to promote a regional facility that would ever be independent of the IMF, but the reasons behind the linkage vary. It was the main donor countries that insisted on the linkage to the IMF, which offers them a way of deflecting criticism of bailout exercises that are likely to involve unpopular or intrusive measures. The main reason for retaining a link to the IMF is that the region currently lacks any system of surveillance, which is a necessary counterpart to liquidity support. IMF surveillance and conditionality is thus necessary to protect the credibility of the new regional facility. Without it, the BSAs could have perverse effects if they were drawn by countries perceived to need some kind of structural adjustment policies: in such circumstances, disbursements would simply line the pockets of currency speculators and do nothing to halt a loss of investor confidence. Surveillance is also necessary to reduce the inevitable moral hazard element generated by commitments of support: the risk that expectations of rescue will reduce incentives for taking adequate prudential measures.

The CMI may in fact outgrow its formal link to the IMF. There are real divisions of opinion as to whether this is desirable but, officially, the link to the IMF is a temporary measure, agreed to with the condition that a regional study group be established to examine issues associated with a regional surveillance system. In November 2001, the study group met in Kuala Lumpur and discussed reports prepared by Malaysia's central bank and Japan's finance ministry (Bergsten and Park 2002, 31, 33). Although no agreement was reached on specifics the group did agree to a two-phase approach to continue the process of developing regional surveillance. There is no time frame for completing this process, but the end point envisaged is a regional group or institution that will be able to make independent assessments of regional countries (Bergsten and Park 2002, 48–49).

Supporting this process, new initiatives for information-gathering and analysis have been located within the Asian Development Bank (ADB). It has developed a prototype for a regional early warning system, which may be the beginning of some regional surveillance capacity (ADB 2002a). The ADB is among the players contributing to the intellectual process of developing frameworks and technical analyses of financial cooperation trajectories (ADB 2002b). The Asian Development Bank Institute in Tokyo is also serving as a regionally based source of technical knowledge on financial policy and economic management more generally. Such regional monitoring and research capacities, established largely as a result of Japanese efforts, could develop the knowledge-generating capacity to supply credible versions of "appropriate" financial standards and economic policies independently of the Washington institutions.

Japan is also leading the intellectual effort to develop acceptance of currency coordination in Asia. The academic and ideational groundwork for monetary cooperation in the region began to build only after 1997. Japan gave more attention to the idea of increasing the use of the yen as an international currency starting in the late 1980s, and in 1994 and 1995 the Japanese Ministry of Finance, the Ministry of International Trade and Industry, and the Economic Planning Agency all released reports mentioning the desirability of greater international and regional use of the yen (Kwan 1996, 3). However, the reforms to Japan's financial system that would make this feasible were not adopted until the late 1990s, when some of the obstacles to internationalizing the yen were addressed.

In addition to endorsing the idea of coordinated currency basket pegs in the region, Japan has also supported (and funded) a number of ongoing research projects investigating the viability of monetary cooperation in the region. One of these, the Kobe Research Project, was endorsed by the finance ministers' conclave of the Asia Europe Meeting held in January 2001 and presented its reports in July the following year. Led by Japanese academics working in cooperation with officials and academics from Europe and Asia, the Kobe Research Project's reports contain several technical studies pointing to the benefits of greater monetary cooperation, as well as discussions of preconditions and modalities. The Japanese Ministry of Finance has also cosponsored a three-year research project based in the Australian National University on future financial arrangements in East Asia, which includes studies of cooperative currency arrangements in the region.

Because coordination means a managed exchange rate regime, the first test of feasibility for the options currently being explored is whether "intermediate" managed exchange rate regimes are desirable. Current economic orthodoxy holds that anything other than "hard corner" exchange rate regimes are unsustainable in financially open systems: countries should either follow a free float or commit to an irreversible currency peg and give up monetary policy independence. This would rule out the kind of currency basket systems that most analysts of currency coordination are working with. However, like many countries (Calvo and Reinhart 2002), most of the region appears to be extremely reluctant to follow orthodoxy and adopt a free floating exchange rate regime. Hence in addition to Malaysia's introduction of a formal peg to the U.S. dollar, China and Hong Kong have maintained their de facto pegs, and several other countries appear to have reverted to precrisis exchange rate regimes that accorded the U.S. dollar predominant weight in revealed currency baskets.

There is no strong consensus regarding the benefits of currency cooperation in the region, but the common assumption that countries in Asia are too diverse to gain from currency cooperation is increasingly contested by recent research (for example, Brouwer 2002; Kwan 2001; Ito 2002). Clearly, the more economies are similar in terms of trade structure, sensitivity to external shocks, and inflation rates, the fewer trade-offs they face in adopting similar monetary policies. Further, models of monetary cooperation that take into account its dynamic effects suggest that many of the preconditions for monetary cooperation as set out in optimum currency area theory are in fact endogenous (Frankel and Rose 2002). In this light there are fairly strong grounds for suggesting that currency coordination in the region would yield gains (Shin and Wang 2002).

Cooperation could also allow the region to reduce its extremely high foreign reserve holdings. East Asian countries together hold foreign reserves of more than $1 trillion—compared to $171 billion held by the European Monetary Union countries and $29 billion held by the United States (Shin and Wang 2002, 28). Since about three-quarters of global reserves are held in U.S. assets, this suggests a potential political obstacle to future currency cooperation in Asia. The United States enjoys unique advantages as the issuer of the world's most widely used currency, and the U.S. dollar-based international financial system generates many lock-in effects.

Shifting to an alternative regime would require a high degree of coordination of a type that has not even been attempted in recent initiatives for regional financial cooperation. Unlike regional crisis management facilities and governance projects, which in their current forms are complementary to continued globalization defined largely in American terms, currency cooperation runs against the more immediate market and political incentives faced by most countries in Asia. Coupled with the weakness of Japan's own financial system and economy, these conditions place significant constraints on its venture into region-making.

Globalization, in the form of capital mobility and market pressures for liberalization, is an important structural force affecting Asia's financial markets and regulatory systems. Global pressures are also the product of institutional legacies and direct political power, which privilege certain rules, standards, and players in multilateral arrangements governing finance. The U.S. dollar's role in the international financial system and Europe's disproportionate voice in the IMF are two elements of globalization that persist because of the collective action problems associated with institutional redesign. Global and, in particular, American influences in the region remain the most significant external forces shaping Asian financial systems.

Japanization, in contrast, remains mostly incipient. Japanization is only superficially related to the amount of Japanese money poured into the region. In the decade after the revaluation of the yen that started with the Plaza Accord of 1985, Japanese direct investment and bank lending in Asia dramatically increased in tandem with Japan's domestic "bubble economy." Many observers detected the emergence of a Japan-centered regional economy sustained by Japanese finance, Japanese models of development, and Japanese production networks. Reality was always more complex, of course, and this image of a Japanized system of Asian finance vanished in 1997, when the region's extraordinary financial vulnerability became visible. At the same time, Japan's own financial system came close to collapse and the reverse side of Japan's precarious and asymmetric financial relationship with the rest of the region came to the fore: Japanese banks, having contributed to the massive inflows of finance to the region, then exacerbated the crisis and subsequent contraction of regional economies by their sharp withdrawal of loans from the region.

Japan's role in postcrisis initiatives to create regional financial support arrangements marks a different form of Japanization, one that again reflects both global forces and conditions in Japan's financial sector as it undergoes regulatory reform and partial reconstruction. Japan is the structural mainstay in most initiatives for the development of a more regionally based approach to financial management. Japan's approach to developing new modes of engagement in the region has also been pursued in nonstructural terms: Japan is the primary actor driving the development of policy consensus and intellectual validation of new regional arrangements. However, Japanese investment in global institutions and its relationship to the United States have prevented it from taking regionalism in a direction that directly competes with them.

The search for regional financial governance frameworks has achieved modest advances that, to date, have avoided provoking contests with the global financial regime or the United States. In this sense, they have been cost-free and, possibly for that reason, some observers have dismissed them as insignificant. Regional arrangements could develop in a direction that would threaten global institutions with a relative loss of influence, but this trajectory is very far from being clear or uncontested within Japan or the rest of Asia. It certainly does not represent the path of least resistance: it would require overcoming obstacles to collective action in the region and further financial sector recovery and revitalization of Japan's economy.

The evolution of regional arrangements and the global regime governing finance has mostly been the product of politically directed processes. Market pressures and private sector initiatives sometimes reinforce government preferences and sometimes work at cross-purposes to official initiatives. Crises have obviously been important in altering perceptions and creating demands for official action. But insofar as elements of any authoritative governance structure exist at either regional or global levels, there are no credible alternative providers of key stabilizing functions apart from official actors. Moody's may move markets (when it does not follow them) but it is not in the business of providing liquidity in a financial panic, enforcing regulatory standards, or coordinating exchange rates. Although private sector assessments in the form of bond ratings were formally incorporated into global financial standards, as stipulated in the "Basel II" capital accord for international banks finalized in 2004 (King and Sinclair 2003), the basic regulatory framework and enforcement system depends on governmental and intergovernmental organizations.

The mechanisms by which official actors have developed these financial governance systems have varied. The interest of the United States and Britain in forging a liberal global financial regime that emphasizes transparency rather than structural segmentation of markets is straightforward: as countries with long-term balance of payments deficits and large, internationally integrated financial industries, they gain from the approach to financial governance that is embedded in global institutions (Blyth 2003, 255–56). They have been able to veto proposals for fundamental change to the global financial system that were raised in the immediate aftermath of the crises. In these negotiations, Japan initially attempted to project influence in a rather confrontational way, with its proposed Asian Monetary Fund and open criticism of IMF conditionality in Asia. This approach was followed by a period of negotiation and interest-based bargaining within global institutions over the content of reforms to the global financial regime. Japan achieved little of its initial agenda and, in the main, the "new international financial architecture" reflects American and European priorities. Although the result was a compromise among these players, it was largely reached through processes of bargaining, although there may have been some instances of individual learning and voluntary adjustment.

The influence enjoyed by American and European powers in the global financial regime is largely due to their privileged position within key international organizations, their role as hosts to the world's largest financial markets, and America's position as the issuer of the primary international currency. This structural position of strength has been combined with preeminence in knowledge-generation and standard-setting. Overt political muscle-flexing surfaces occasionally, but, more often, the elaboration of global rules for finance appears as a highly technical, knowledge-intensive process with no open acknowledgement of its political underpinnings or implications (Porter 2003). Particular ideas and technical knowledge legitimate the approach to financial governance that is embedded in the current global financial regime (Blyth 2003). For the time being, most of the technical knowledge that counts is generated and promoted by organizations based in the United States or dominated by U.S. and European influence. Although in one sense obviously knowledge-based, the standard-setting powers of organizations such as the IMF gain their force through material incentives rather than persuasion: the IMF's seal of approval is the door not only to IMF financing but also to many other sources of official aid, debt restructuring, and private finance.

In contrast to the negotiated bargaining and sometimes coercive standard-setting that characterize the global financial regime, Japan's relatively quiet initiatives at the regional level have employed a different approach. Here, persuasion and learning as ways of trying to bring about consensus and the capacity for action are more evident. Japan's regional cooperation agenda has begun a localized process of articulating standards and developing new cooperative mechanisms. Even if the attempt is not meant to carve out alternative standards, it does seem to be a move to create alternative arenas of legitimate standard-setting and coordinated action. This would provide the infrastructure that could bring more concrete financial muscle to bear on future governing arrangements. Asia's impressive currency reserves and much more modest regional liquidity arrangements in themselves are not usable ammunition in any future reshuffling of influence between region-making (Japanese or other) and the entrenched U.S.-defined global regime for international finance. These hard resources will only come into play if an infrastructure of information, analysis, and formal interstate coordination develops further. Japan is leading moves to develop this infrastructure, but it is not in place, has no clear trajectory, and even its supporters are uncertain about how they want it to develop.

6

Has Politics Caught Up with Markets?
In Search of East Asian Economic Regionalism

NAOKO MUNAKATA

East Asia's dynamic economic growth since the mid-1980s has spawned market-driven regionalization processes that have deepened regional economic integration. Yet regional integration has not been accompanied by any significant politically directed, intergovernmental processes of regional institution building. For decades governments in the region did not actively pursue either preferential trade agreements or other formal institutions for regional integration.[1] In the wake of the Asian financial crisis of 1997–98 the situation has changed drastically. Governments are now actively exploring bilateral free trade agreements (FTAs). The idea of an "East Asian community" to promote "peace, prosperity and progress" through "cooperation in the economic, political, security, environmental, social, cultural, and educational arenas" (East Asia Vision Group 2001) has become fashionable. Has politics finally caught up with markets?

Though it looks as if change took place abruptly, it has in fact evolved gradually, starting well before the financial crisis. In this chapter I examine the evolution of East Asian regionalism by identifying three driving factors and three retarding factors and assessing their relative importance in each stage

---

[1] The word *regionalism* is occasionally used to emphasize the negative, mercantilistic attitude of the members of regional arrangements who narrow-mindedly pursue the interests of the region at the expense of other regions or international institutions. In this paper, however, *regionalism* merely refers to institutional frameworks set up by governments in the region to promote regional economic integration. Various arrangements of regionalism have different levels of commitment by the participating governments. The FTA is a solid form of regionalism. On the other hand, regional consultative bodies that do not involve legally binding agreements but aim to promote economic integration among the members are a looser form of regionalism.

of the evolutionary process.[2] This analytical exercise helps clarify how much influence major states—the United States, Japan, and China—have had in regional developments and how this influence has been shaped by a complex set of evolutionary processes.

Factors Shaping Regionalism

There are three factors that drive regional institution-building. The first is what might be called defensive reaction to extraregional pressures (henceforth referred to as defensive regionalism). This includes two elements. One is growing concern about discrimination caused by preferential trade agreements in other regions such as the European Union, the North American Free Trade Agreement (NAFTA), and the proposed Free Trade Area of the Americas. East Asian governments have felt pressure to counteract and strengthen their negotiating leverage in one way or another by forging a regional grouping of their own. This factor has increased in importance over time, as the trend toward regionalism expanded geographically as well as functionally. The second element is the frustration with unilateral U.S. actions and "market fundamentalism" (dubbed "the Washington consensus"), which has driven governments in the region to look for a greater leverage in dealing with the United States and U.S.-dominated institutions. This becomes important, for instance, when governments in the region are confronted with trade conflicts with the United States or when they had to deal with the International Monetary Fund in the Asian financial crisis.

The second factor is the shared desire of governments in the region to have an effective mechanism for cooperation, in order to promote de facto integration and to deal with common challenges (henceforth referred to as intraregional economic interdependence). East Asian economies have an incentive to reduce transaction costs among neighbors, to strengthen economic linkages with high growth areas in the region, and to participate in and facilitate the existing dense business networks of vertical intra-industry trade. Because they share such common challenges as rapid industrialization and the institutional transition from developmental states to more market-oriented economies, governments in the region are motivated to share their experiences. There is also a political incentive to include less developed

---

[2] The analytical framework of the evolutionary process of regionalism in Asia in four states with three driving forces and obstacles is based on the approach taken by Munakata (2002). The author will publish an updated analysis of the evolution of East Asian regionalism in Naoko Munakata, "Transforming East Asia: The Evolution of Regional Economic Integration," forthcoming from Brookings Institution Press.

neighboring countries in the network of economic interdependence, in order to promote their economic development and political stability and to maintain harmonious diplomatic relations. The political motivation is important in defining the boundary of a particular "region" that is to be covered by an institutional framework—but it is the intensity of economic interaction that creates its substance and depth. As globalization and technological progress have accelerated changes in the regional economic landscape, regional economies have developed stronger incentives to create an effective local mechanism (in addition to global institutions) to provide prompt and focused solutions to immediate regional problems.

The third factor is intraregional competitive dynamics. East Asian economies compete with one another for foreign direct investment and export markets. Once an influential country spearheads the implementation of measures to make it more attractive to foreign investors and more competitive in export markets, others are prompted to follow and thus neutralize its advantages. Depending on the situation, this dynamic has motivated East Asian economies to conduct unilateral and voluntary liberalization of trade and investment, as well as to conclude preferential trade agreements with economies in and outside the region.

In spite of these forces, the path to creating an institutional framework in this region has never been straightforward, due to three retarding factors.

The first is the lack of cohesiveness in the region: diversity in developmental stages, political systems, and cultural and religious backgrounds; and the centrifugal force of historical antagonism and political rivalry among regional powers. Although some aspects of diversity, such as developmental gaps, are instrumental in promoting interdependence through complementary economic structures, they have made it difficult for East Asian economies to pursue institutional frameworks for regional integration at the same pace.

The second factor is the regions' extraregional dependence, especially on the United States, combined with the U.S. focus on bilateral relationships as opposed to multilateral frameworks in Asia (Katzenstein 1997, 23–27; Hemmer and Katzenstein 2002) and its displeasure, explicit or not, with Asian frameworks in which it is not included. Governments in East Asia understand that U.S. interests need to be anchored in the region, since they need its security presence, technology, and capital, and that they must accommodate their biggest customer. This element offsets the impact of defensive regionalism. The balance of these two factors—dependence on the United States and defensive regionalism—has been largely determined by U.S. policy. When U.S. policy accommodates East Asian common interests and demonstrates a strong commitment to regional stability and prosperity, momentum for Asian-only forums through defensive regionalism will likely decrease, and vice versa.

The third factor is East Asian countries' hesitancy about institutionalization. Although they appreciate problem solving, they exhibit inherent skepticism towards rigid, top-down institutions (Katzenstein 1997, 27–31) and tend to prefer consensus building rather than confrontation. In addition, governments have at times demonstrated a lack of commitment or capacity to follow through with politically unpopular measures. Consequently, they tend to avoid institutionalization and opt for easier, more flexible, and (occasionally) less fundamental solutions. This hesitation offsets the impact of intraregional economic interdependence.

The extent and depth of this hesitation hinges on the nature and significance of the problems countries face, the availability of alternative solutions, and the potential gains provided by institutionalization. The more serious the problems and the less effective the solutions available elsewhere, the more momentum institutionalization is likely to gain, which might possibly result in legally binding agreements that constrain sovereignty and have discriminatory effects vis-à-vis nonmembers. The strong economic performance of East Asian economies until the Asian financial crisis made them uniquely confident of their economic dynamism and ability to attract FDI through unilateral liberalization of trade and investment, without depending on legal frameworks such as FTAs (Hashimoto 1995a, 1995b). The crisis, however, undermined this confidence. The hesitation also decreased over time as the political voice of the private sector, which had benefited from liberalization, strengthened. As East Asian economies became more mature in dealing with regional frameworks and began to appreciate the efficacy of institutional agreements in sending positive signals to foreign investors and giving political momentum to domestic reforms, they overcame knee-jerk rejections of institutionalization and started choosing the most effective ways of solving particular problems. Nevertheless, the lingering lack of willingness or capacity to thoroughly implement tough measures will slow the pace and dilute the substance of future institutionalization efforts.

The role of the United States and the reaction of East Asian governments to perceived U.S. policy intentions, once decisive in determining the shape of regional economic institutions, is now only one influential factor. At the same time, as the region became more exposed to the force of globalization and integrated through business activities including those of U.S. corporations (i.e., regionalization), intraregional economic interdependence has become more important.

I will first examine the characteristics of East Asia's regionalization that have been crucial in defining the shape and nature of regionalism and then review the four distinct stages of its evolution. The final section deals with the interaction between regionalism and the influence of the United States, Japan, and China.

Regionalization in East Asia

Forces and Actors

Regionalization in East Asia has largely been driven by the competitive activities of businesses and governments, under the pressures of globalization and technological progress. Global businesses have an economic incentive to choose the most suitable locations for particular operations in order to make the entire production process more efficient. Technological progress in transportation, information, and communications have enabled more effective integration and management of production networks at a distance from headquarters, expanding the freedom of choice for global businesses regarding the location of various types of operations. Individual talent and capital are also freer to go wherever they can maximize their value. The increased freedom in business locations causes unattractive areas to suffer from industry hollowing out and brain drain. Host governments, in turn, have come under strong pressure to compete with one another for FDI, as well as for productive resources such as individual talent and technology as an important driver of economic growth and development. Global institutions such as the World Trade Organization and the International Monetary Fund have also pushed host governments to liberalize their economies. These dynamics, while not unique to Asia, prepared the environment conducive to the creation of the production networks that have driven regionalization in Asia.

The sharp appreciation of the yen after the Plaza Accord in 1985 started the process of regionalization in East Asia in earnest. It first prompted Japanese firms to relocate their labor-intensive production process to lower-cost countries, causing a surge in export-oriented FDI to ASEAN countries. Manufacturers in newly industrializing economies, such as Korea and Taiwan, followed suit as their currencies also appreciated against the U.S. dollar. In 1992, when Deng Xiaoping underlined the importance of special economic zones for his reforms in his south China tour, China also started to attract FDI, putting competitive pressure on ASEAN countries. The flow of FDI led to the accumulation of manufacturing capacity in the region.

In the 1990s, world business leaders increasingly perceived East Asian economies as attractive investment destinations, not only for export-oriented operations but also for operations targeted at local markets. Particularly in the latter half of the 1990s, the information technology boom and fierce competition under the shorter life cycle of technologies and falling prices prompted Western newcomers to use Asian production capacities for greater production speed and price competitiveness. In the wake of the Asian financial crisis, lower purchase prices of corporations and deregulation of foreign capital accelerated cross-border mergers and acquisitions in the region. China's accession to the WTO made it particularly attractive as an FDI destination, as investors expected improvements in its investment environment. In the 1990s, and particularly in the latter part of the decade, FDI from the United States and Europe increased its relative weight in such sectors as automobiles, electronics, distribution, and finance in Asia as a whole (METI 2001, 6–9, 22–25). At the same time, Asian economies—not just Hong Kong, the largest source of FDI in China, but also Taiwan, Korea, and Singapore—increased FDI in China (JETRO 2003b, 181–87).

Characteristics

One of the most significant characteristics of the regionalization of trade and investment in Asia is the dominant role of production networks. Technological innovations and the elimination of trade and investment barriers helped reduce the cost and enhanced the availability of a service link, "a composite of activities such as transportation, insurance, telecommunications, quality control, and management coordination to ensure that the production blocks interact in the proper manner" (Arndt and Kierzkowski 2001, 4). This opened up new opportunities for fragmentation, "the decomposition of production into separable component blocks connected by service links" (Arndt and Kierzkowski 2001, 10) across national frontiers. In particular, the sophistication of the system to numerically control manufacturing processes lowered the skill levels needed to perform certain steps in the manufacturing process and allowed for the location of those steps in developing economies.

In addition, the "modularization" of the architecture of products—the division of a product into subsystems or modules with common design rules, which can thus be designed independently yet function together as a whole—became prevalent in the electronics industry (Baldwin and Clark 1997). Modularization opened new opportunities for suppliers at arm's length (without long-term relationships) to participate in existing production networks, further increasing the flexibility of the location of production blocks. In addition, the common design rules lowered the level of coordination necessary to integrate various parts into a final product, making assembly a low-value-added step (the so-called smiling curve phenomenon) (RIETI 2002). This prompted foreign companies, particularly in electronics manufacturing services, to set up assembly factories in China where there was a seemingly inexhaustible supply of cheap labor as well as low-cost electronics parts (Kuroda 2001, 79–133; Kwan 2002). This accelerated China's integration into regional production networks, increasingly making it a new link in those networks.

Thus, the accumulation of FDI led to dense production networks within the region, with parts and components going back and forth among factories for numerous processing and assembly tasks, with a tight schedule and a low inventory, before being shipped to final markets. This operation of the production networks has significantly boosted intraregional trade (METI 2002a, 15–16), particularly that of intermediate goods (such as parts and materials), which grew faster in the 1990s than that of finished goods (METI 2001, 10–11). The regionalization has turned East Asia into a tight network of economies that operates as the factory of the world, relied on by major world economies such as the United States and Europe to provide greater industrial efficiency and lower living costs for their citizens.

While businesses have greater freedom in choosing the locations of various production blocks, there are industrial clusters where certain types of industries are concentrated. Once an industrial cluster is formed, "agglomeration" of industries in that location tends to be accelerated, as long as such "centripetal forces" such as good access to markets (backward linkages) and suppliers (forward linkages) outweigh "centrifugal forces" such as immobility of necessary production factors and higher costs due to congestion. "The interaction among scale economies, transport costs and factor mobility" determine the balance (Fujita, Krugman, and Venables 2001, 11, 346). Increased freedom in choosing the locations of various production blocks seems to have affected this balance; in a relatively short period of time, new industrial clusters have emerged in locations without an existing technological or industrial base, but with other advantages such as cheap labor, lower costs of building new factories, and easy accessibility (Kuwahara 2004).

In this new environment of "more fluid agglomerations" (Kuwahara 2004), government policies have a greater impact on the formation of industrial clusters. Developing economies have new incentives to improve the attractiveness of their industrial sites, through such measures as building transportation and communications infrastructure, liberalizing trade and investment regulations, providing tax incentives to FDI, and providing better opportunities for educating and training the local workforce. In addition to seeking to form industrial clusters on their own, Asian governments also adopted policies to strengthen the linkages with high growth areas in their neighborhoods. In the 1990s, the governments of the more developed members of ASEAN, urged by private companies that had increased their roles in the economies of those countries, consciously adopted policies to create complementary relationships within its membership and with the emerging economies such as China and Vietnam, in order to capitalize on their growth potential and to position their own countries as a hub in the region (Kuwahara 2003b). The rise of China will continue to prompt ASEAN countries to create industrial structures that are complementary to that of China but that could be competitive with one another.

Another characteristic of regionalization in East Asia is the highly uneven degree of integration among different types of products. The electronics industry has spearheaded regionalization (METI 2002a, 15–17) due to the increase in vertical intra-industry trade and intra-product trade of intermediate goods. On the other hand, sectors with higher costs of service links (caused by, for example, protection by host and investing countries), or where the production process is not amenable to fragmentation, lag behind, as is the case with agricultural products (Fukao, Ishido, and Ito 2003). On the other hand, Fukao et al. (2003) show that in Europe, where barriers to intraregional trade are much lower due to institutional market integration, the shares of vertical intra-industry trade and horizontal intra-industry trade are higher—not only in the categories of "electrical machinery" and "general and precision machinery," as in East Asia, but also in the trade of many other manufacturing products such as chemical, wood, and paper products, as well as transportation machinery. This contrast suggests that East Asia has significant room for expansion of intra-industry trade in various products (Fukao et al. 2003). That Japanese farmers are more eager to expand exports as they see opportunities to sell high-end fruits and rice to increasingly affluent Asian consumers suggests that intra-industry trade will expand even in agricultural products (*Mainichi Shimbun* 2003; *Yomiuri Shimbun* 2003c).

Last but not least, the third characteristic of Asian regionalization is East Asian exports' dependence on final demand from industrial countries. As noted above, the operation of the production networks in the region, with ever-finer specialization among various countries, has boosted intraregional trade. The engines of the production networks (the final demands to which they supply), however, are in large part in extraregional markets. The Monetary Authority of Singapore (MAS; 2003, 64–65) estimates that, in 2001, approximately 78 percent of non-Japanese East Asian exports were directly (64 percent of total) or indirectly (after further processing within non-Japan Asia—14 percent of total) bound for markets outside the region.[3] Kim (2002) points out that the export growth of non-Japan Asia,[4] particularly that of the more developed Asian electronics exporters (Korea, Taiwan, Singapore, and Malaysia), has been tightly correlated to U.S. investment in information technology. He estimates that Asia's domestic demand, on average, accounted for only one-fifth of the total export growth of non-Japan Asia in the 1999–2000 cyclical expansion. These analyses do not deny that domestic demand in the region, particularly consumer spending, has been growing and has become an increasingly important driver of East Asian economic growth. At this point, however, the size of private consumption in East Asia re-

---

[3] The estimate was made using the detailed 1995 Asian Input-output tables by the Institute of Developing Economies of the Japan External Trade Organization.

[4] Non-Japan Asia includes China, Korea, Taiwan, Malaysia, Singapore, Thailand, Indonesia, and the Philippines.

mains relatively small compared to that of the G3 economies (the United States, Europe, and Japan) (MAS 2003, 65). Japan cannot absorb the growth of East Asian exports all by itself.

Thus, the integration of export-oriented Asian economies is substantially different from that in Europe or North America, where the most important markets are within the region. East Asia's extraregional dependence provides a strong incentive to remain open to other regions of the world. This incentive has informed these countries' efforts to institutionalize regional integration, the immediate goal of which is not to become a self-contained market but rather to make production networks in the region more competitive and investment more attractive.

In the future, higher standards of living in developing economies in the region, especially in China, offer long-term potential as a major source of demand (MAS 2003, 66). With other things equal, this could affect the relative U.S. influence in the region; but that will not necessarily be the case. In the first place, the United States has not been as dominant an absorber of products in East Asia as it has been in the Western Hemisphere. The rise of China as another important absorber will not bring about a drastic change to the East Asian quest for diverse markets in the world. Asian production networks have become such a large source of supply that they are more likely to continue to operate as the factory of the world than of the region. Moreover, the source of U.S. influence is not just its markets. The United States will continue to exercise its influence in the region with its technology and capital, its military supremacy (with largely benign strategic interests in the region), and its attractiveness to the citizens of increasingly democratic Asia as the most dynamic liberal democracy.

The Role of Japanese Business Networks

Some argue that Japanese manufacturers, supported by the government, have tried to extend their strong relational ties into Asia, that "the regionalization of Japanese manufacturing has helped block or inhibit structural change" and that it "is merely preserving the status quo" (Hatch 2002b). This argument is misplaced.

Regionalization of Japanese manufacturing has generally taken place as a rational reaction of the more outward-looking segments of the Japanese economy (particularly, as Dieter Ernst notes in chapter 7, the electronics industry) to the pressure of global competition—not as a way to preserve the status quo or to export the Japanese model to the rest of Asia. This does not mean that all their investment decisions have been sound. Many Japanese investors made bad judgments, particularly during the economic bubble in the late 1980s. Unprofitable investments, however, were mostly retrenched in the wake of the Asian financial crisis, if not before. The long-term relationship between Japanese manufacturers and their suppliers, which Hatch (2002b) calls "relationalism," has also been based on economic incentives. Japanese manufacturers have dismantled the relationship when it ceased to serve its purpose. Delays in needed changes were due to inertia, not a policy intention to preserve relational ties in Japan. On the other hand, businesses have preserved and adjusted the relationship where it continues to make economic sense.

In this connection, it is useful to recall an important distinction Fujimoto (2002) makes between the "Japanese supplier system" and the "keiretsu network." The Japanese supplier system is supported by three distinct characteristics: long-term business relationships; competition among a small number of suppliers for continuous buildup of capabilities; and outsourcing of interrelated works, allowing suppliers to improve capabilities to integrate those works and thus become better equipped to improve product performance. In the keiretsu network, on the other hand, equity is held by and executives sent from the parent company; it does not necessarily have the functional characteristics of the Japanese supplier system. According to Fujimoto, the Japanese supplier system is well suited for products of "integral architecture"—typically the automobile—where the integration of various modules of the product design or the production process is crucial for the performance of the product, and, therefore, its competitiveness. Fujimoto finds that the essential characteristics of the Japanese supplier system have remained intact in the automobile industry in the latter half of the 1990s, while "keiretsu" relations gradually disintegrated in the corporate world (Kuroki 2002).

Moreover, once extended to Asia, Japanese production networks have undergone significant changes in order to adapt to the local situation. For example, while first-tier parts suppliers rarely supply only one assembler even in Japan (Fujimoto 2002, 175), it becomes more important for them to deal with various assemblers operating in Asia to achieve the minimum efficiency scale. Furthermore, Japanese production networks do not consist exclusively of firms owned by Japanese corporations. For example, Japanese firms in China are increasing their procurement from Taiwanese or local Chinese suppliers as the quality of their products improves (Kuroda 2001, 86–94). Lack of discretion on the part of local subsidiaries, however, has often caused delays. As Ernst argues in chapter 7, "the strictly sequential procedure of corporate decision-making in Japan" explains the slow moves of Japanese electronics firms in Asia. Japanese firms are increasingly aware of the slow decision making that prevents them from keeping up with the rapidly changing business environment in host countries.

Japanese firms operating in Asia are also aware of the need to attract highly competent local employees. A survey conducted in China shows that college students give higher priority to opportunities for career development and personal growth than salary in making decisions about their jobs (ChinaHR .com 2003). Quoting this survey, Kwan (2003) argues that Japanese firms are not popular among Chinese students because local employees cannot expect promotion. This creates a vicious cycle in which the inability to attract competitive local human resources makes it difficult to promote local employees to managerial positions and to delegate decision-making authority to local managers, making companies less attractive to competent and ambitious people. A study by Japan External Trade Organization or JETRO (2003a) suggests that Japanese companies recognize this problem. The study shows that Japanese subsidiaries in Asia recognize the need to promote local employees to management positions, rather than relying on expensive Japanese expatriates, in order to enhance their competitiveness. Nevertheless, many Japanese firms have not been able to move as fast as they wish. For example, it is said that many hesitate to promote local personnel to the top management positions of local subsidiaries because of concerns about possible difficulties in communication between headquarters in Japan and the overseas subsidiary due to the language barrier or the lack of cultural understanding. The slow pace of change reflects their anxiety about the lack of needed organizational capacities—which could not be enhanced overnight—rather than a misguided intention to preserve the failing Japanese model in Asia.

It should also be noted that Japanese subsidiaries in Asia did not react uniformly to the Asian financial crisis. Fukao (2001) demonstrates with his empirical study that the larger the value-added per worker of a local subsidiary, the more likely it was that the affiliate maintained its workforce. The study also shows that the greater the parent company's vertical corporate network in the same host country, the more likely it was that its subsidiary kept its workforce. These results suggest that a subsidiary was more likely to receive assistance from its parent or firms within the same corporate network when it had a valuable skilled workforce or was an important part of an active production network in the host country. The result clearly suggests that keiretsu networks were not something to be preserved at any cost but have in fact been going through various changes. Japanese government assistance to help corporations maintain their operations in Asia in the wake of the crisis could not—was not intended to—override business decisions to withdraw from nonviable operations.

Japanese production networks continue to evolve and transform themselves, as manufacturers with varying abilities struggle to adapt their corporate strategies and capabilities to the competitive reality. Despite the differences in the forms of Japanese network organization in Asia as compared to those of their American and other Asian counterparts (see Ernst, chapter 7), Japanese firms do react to market pressures. The role of Japanese production networks, therefore, does not constitute an exception to the market-driven nature of the process of regionalization.

The Evolution of East Asian Regionalism

Regionalism in Asia has evolved since the mid-1980s in four distinct periods. Different forces identified in the introductory section came into play at each stage and determined the developments in a particular period, while forces that had been ignored or frustrated in a particular period caught up and affected the ensuing developments. The U.S. policy of promoting globalization in general and liberalization of trade and investment in Asia in particular initially had a decisive influence, but its relative weight was reduced as a result of its success in awakening the region's governments to adapt to globalization in ways that suited their social and economic conditions. In addition, the lack of consistent U.S. policy attention to this part of the world, and to its developmental needs in particular, helped diminish U.S. influence in designing regional institutions in East Asia. At the same time, Japan—which had initiated regionalization in the latter half of the 1980s and the regionalism of East Asia in the late 1990s—found itself under increasing pressure from the rest of East Asia to restructure its domestic economy and actively integrate itself into the region.

First Period: Competition and Interaction among Various Proposals

The first period, between 1985 and 1992, saw active competition among different regional framework proposals. It was in this period that the regionalization discussed in the previous section created the force of "intraregional economic interdependence."

The first actual stimulus for institutionalized economic integration, however, came from the United States in the form of an unofficial proposal for an ASEAN-U.S. FTA[5] ASEAN was not ready. In the late 1980s, the idea of bilateral FTAs with Japan, the Republic of Korea, and Taiwan considered in U.S. policy circles (USITC 1988, 1989), while not official, aroused considerable concern among Asian and Pacific policymakers due to "America's proclivity toward unilateral trade actions" (Funabashi 1995, 108). They were also concerned about the regionalism in Europe and North America.

These concerns, together with rapid economic growth and regionalization

---

[5] See the account of Singaporean scholar and diplomat Tommy Koh, quoted in "The Negotiator," November 23, 2002, channelnewsasia.com.

in East Asia, prompted Japan (MITI 1988, 1989) and Australia to initiate what later became the Asia Pacific Economic Cooperation (APEC). Unlike the proposal by the Japanese Ministry of International Trade and Industry (MITI), the Australian proposal initially did not include the United States and Canada. Also, it was more focused on trade liberalization, whereas MITI's idea was more focused on enlarging the economic pie through growth rather than simple market liberalization (Funabashi 1995, 66). The two countries did not iron out the substantive differences but concentrated instead on soliciting support for the launch of the ministerial meeting.

In the meantime, U.S. policy circles had also become more open to the idea of a multilateral forum on economic issues in the Asia Pacific region (for example, Shultz 1988). Secretary of State James A. Baker, in the George Bush administration, had also been considering a multilateral framework on economic issues (personal interview, former U.S. State Department official, Washington, D.C., October 2003). After Australia accepted the U.S. request for its participation, Secretary Baker expressed his support for "a new mechanism for multilateral cooperation among the nations of the Pacific Rim" (Baker 1989). Thus, the first APEC ministerial meeting was held in Canberra in November 1989.

In late 1990, frustrated by the difficulties in concluding the Uruguay Round of trade negotiations and APEC's apparent inability to check NAFTA regionalism, Malaysian prime minister Mahathir Mohamad proposed an "economic bloc . . . consisting of ASEAN, Indo-China, China, Taiwan, Hong Kong, South Korea and Japan . . . to countervail the other trade blocs" (Goh 1990; Aris 1990; Youngblood 1991). After Japan's immediate rejection of the notion of a "bloc," and China's suggestion that the initial cooperation should be "loose" (*Japan Economic Newswire* 1990), Malaysia clarified that the proposal was "a looser Asian economic grouping" consistent with the General Agreement on Tariffs and Trade (GATT) (Youngblood 1991). After consultation among ASEAN members (AEM 1991), the proposal was renamed the East Asian Economic Caucus to avoid further misunderstanding. Despite these attempts at moderation, the proposal met strong objections from the United States (Yoneyama 1990) as something that "draws the line down the Pacific" (State Department 1991) as well as undermining APEC.

East Asian policymakers, eager to anchor U.S. interest, did not have a compelling interest in promoting this idea; but the strong U.S. reaction left them feeling that they should be able to choose for themselves with whom they could meet and talk. There was also a sense that the U.S. reaction was hypocritical given the regionalism it promoted within its own hemisphere (Bush 1990). The United States responded that the proposed NAFTA would "not establish common barriers to those outside" (Baker 1991) and therefore would not become a "bloc." It was not clear, however, why a consultative body would undermine APEC when subregional FTAs such as NAFTA would not (State Department 1991).

While Malaysia struggled to gain support for its East Asian Economic Caucus proposal, ASEAN started a new economic integration initiative, the ASEAN Free Trade Area,[6] in 1992. Concerns about the competition for FDI with eastern European countries and China, and the possible loss of ASEAN identity and bargaining power as APEC became more established, prompted ASEAN members to agree on the first framework of comprehensive regional economic integration in East Asia.

In the meantime, APEC became gradually established as a regional forum. In 1991, China, Taiwan, and Hong Kong simultaneously joined APEC, significantly boosting its importance (Baker 1991–1992, 6). Under the Clinton administration, the United States renewed its interest in opening up Asian markets through APEC. This began the transition to the second period.

In this period, the main driving force was defensive regionalism. Intraregional economic interdependence stimulated the recognition of the need for some form of cooperation to deal with common challenges, but did not play a large role at this point. At the same time, all three obstacles (lack of cohesiveness, U.S. displeasure with an Asian-only framework, and the avoidance of institutionalization) were at work.

One characteristic of the regionalism in this period is the minimal focus on substance, despite an impulse to get together. With no regionwide framework in place, there was a tendency to try to find a single formula that would accommodate everybody's agenda and to focus on its membership.

Second Period: Primacy of APEC

The second period began in 1993 when the United States chaired APEC and ended with the Asian financial crisis in 1997. In this period, APEC became the primary vehicle for regional cooperation. Strong U.S. leadership (Clinton 1993) enhanced APEC's momentum and overcame members' residual resistance to pursuing trade liberalization within this forum. The United States hosted the first leaders' meeting in Seattle. The Eminent Persons Group assigned to draw up a vision for APEC went as far as to suggest the possibility of creating an APEC FTA (APEC-EPG 1993, 1994, 1995); however, there was no agreement on that point due to East Asian members' concerns about preferential trade arrangements, as well as about trade liberalization at a pace set by negotiations. Instead, the leaders adopted the Bogor goal of liberalization in 1994 (APEC 1994) and the Osaka Action Agenda (APEC

---

[6] The Agreement on the Common Effective Preferential Tariff Scheme for the ASEAN Free Trade Area was signed at the Fourth ASEAN Summit held in Singapore on January 27–28, 1992.

1995), choosing a mechanism based on members' voluntary efforts and peer pressure to achieve the ambitious target.

Although APEC became the primary economic forum in the region as a result of strong U.S. leadership, it did not fulfill most of the expectations that its members had at the forum's inception. First, APEC was not effective in checking the regionalism in the Americas (Summit of the Americas 1994), not to speak of Europe. In addition, the U.S. unilateral approach to trade frictions had "added to Asian ambivalence about the United States," while tensions between the United States and Asian countries, notably Indonesia, over human rights, workers' rights, press freedom, and so on made Asian countries view the U.S. role in APEC warily (Manning and Stern 1994, 86).

Second, the U.S. desire to open Asian markets was eventually frustrated. The implementation of the Bogor goal was left to voluntarism and peer pressure. The United States failed in its attempt, through early voluntary sectoral liberalization (EVSL), to change the modality of trade liberalization in APEC from voluntarism to tariff negotiations.

Third, the Asian desire for an effective framework of cooperation was not satisfied. Economic cooperation was given a lower priority in APEC. Project proposals proliferated, with few efforts to systematically follow up. Frustration culminated when the EVSL was the primary item on the 1998 APEC agenda in late 1997, shortly after the eruption of the Asian financial crisis.

In the meantime, Japan and ASEAN developed a cooperative framework. In 1992, the ASEAN economic ministers and the Japanese MITI minister started to hold meetings (AEM-MITI) on the fringe of the ASEAN economic ministers' meetings, with the chief objective of promoting integration within ASEAN. MITI provided technical assistance to the projects under this framework, to complement existing assistance on a bilateral basis (MITI 1993). The framework, however, was not effective in reducing Japanese tariffs on those sensitive items that ASEAN members wanted to export more of.

Rapid economic growth in Asia and the establishment of APEC also stimulated European interest in Asia. ASEAN played a coordinating role in launching the Asia-Europe Meeting in 1996. The meeting provided a new opportunity for East Asian countries to get together before meeting with their European counterparts, although Taiwan and Hong Kong were not included because of political issues on the upcoming agenda. While these forums were not necessarily successful in achieving specific, substantive results, they satisfied Asian countries' desire to try out various types of forums and further promoted mutual understanding.

APEC experiences laid the groundwork for the next period in two ways. First, the forum's fundamental problem was rapid growth without the solidification of core objectives. The lessons for its members were that they could not expect APEC to solve all the problems and, therefore, should have complementary forums, consisting of smaller numbers of members whose interests converge. At the same time, APEC has incubated regional cooperation in Asia. It has brought governments and businesses together in the region through many meetings and projects. It has increased awareness of common problems, new means of cooperation, and differing priorities.

In this period, the same driving forces that had brought about APEC in the first period were at work: a shared desire to enhance leverage against the European Community, to prompt it to come forward and conclude the Uruguay Round; Asia and Australia's desire to counter (in the case of APEC, by co-opting) U.S. unilateralism, protectionism, and intrahemispheric regionalism; and Asia's desire to deal with the challenges of development and increasing interdependence. The U.S. and Australian aim to liberalize Asian markets to further gain from the deepening interdependence, while not a driving force for "East Asian" regionalism, also remained at work. However, the United States was less patient than in the first period. It was less prepared to accommodate the region's diversity and the time needed to build a sense of community before achieving the desired tangible results (personal interview, former U.S. State Department official, Washington, D.C., December 2003). This impatience eventually heightened Asians' wariness of U.S. leadership in APEC, preparing for the surge of defensive regionalism in the third period.

Third Period: Breakdown of Taboos

The transition to the third period started with the Asian financial crisis that erupted in July 1997. It changed the landscape and mind-set of regional economies in several ways, bringing about a major turning point for the development of East Asian regionalism.

First, East Asian countries were reminded of their interdependence by the "contagion" of the currency crisis. In addition, they perceived that the United States and the IMF, seen as a tool of U.S. international economic policy, exacerbated the hardship of the countries hit by the crisis. This perception, combined with the fact that U.S. hedge funds substantially profited from the massive selling of Asian currencies, hurt the U.S. image in the region (Munakata 2003a). The experience convinced East Asian countries that they had to protect their own interests, since global institutions under U.S. leadership could not always be counted on. This conviction prompted them to build up foreign reserves and to initiate regional cooperation to promote financial stability in Asia; later, it nurtured a more comprehensive idea of regional integration. Stronger intraregional economic interdependence and defensive regionalism were at work.

Second, there was a loss of self-confidence in Asia's economic dynamism and rising anxiety about regionalism elsewhere. The Asian crisis brought down regional domestic markets and focused countries in the region on exports. They became serious about overcoming the discrimination caused by FTAs to which they did not belong, and began to seek FTAs that would strengthen their relations with major world markets not affected by the crisis. This attempt in turn reminded them, especially the small- and medium-sized economies, that their bargaining power largely depended on the attractiveness of the entire region. This seemed to create increased momentum for FTAs among neighboring economies (*Nikkei Business* 2000). Loss of confidence in Asia's economic dynamism thus strengthened defensive regionalism and reduced the hesitation about institutionalization.

Third, the crisis aroused a sense of urgency regarding economic reform. To obtain necessary financing from the IMF, agreed-upon reform measures had to be implemented. Foreign investors also watched with keen interest how far governments were willing to go. The need to restructure domestic economies and attract FDI heightened their interest in FTAs that would lock in domestic reform in legally binding agreements with foreign countries. Thus, hesitation about institutionalization weakened substantially.

Fourth, the influence of ASEAN was significantly reduced. China's relatively stable economic performance throughout the crisis, and the surge of FDI into Korea, contrasted sharply with the collapse of domestic demand and the slow progress of economic reform in ASEAN. The shift of gravity to Northeast Asia prompted Singapore to go it alone in strengthening relations with countries outside ASEAN. Singapore's move set off intraregional competitive dynamics and further reduced Asian countries' hesitation about institutionalization.

Fifth, other Asian countries' perception of Japan changed, as it lost its attractiveness as an economic model (Prestowitz 1997). The threat of Japanese economic dominance in the region disappeared. Now, Asian countries feared that the Japanese business commitment in Asia might decrease and that its economic crisis might deepen the Asian crisis. Asian and U.S. senior officials called on Japan to take responsibility for supporting the Asian economic recovery (Rubin 1998; Summers 1998). From the outbreak of the crisis, Japanese manufacturers tried to maintain their offshore operations in the region and retain well-trained local employees. The government took various measures to aid the crisis-hit countries as well as Japanese companies (Munakata 2001). Asian countries, however, seemed to also expect Japan to expand imports through the economic recovery. Thus, resistance to an increased Japanese role in the region was replaced by the expectation that Japan should lead the region out of the crisis and spearhead regional efforts to create a stable economic environment.

The loss of momentum in the APEC process disappointed the U.S. government, and the economic crisis further dampened U.S. enthusiasm for

Asia. The focus of U.S. trade policy shifted to the negotiations on China's WTO accession. At the same time, Washington, though lacking fast-track authority from Congress, maintained its interest in Western Hemisphere regionalism (Summit of the Americas 1998). Incidentally, a P5 (Project 5) initiative, a proposal for an FTA among five "like-minded" countries (the United States, Chile, Singapore, Australia, and New Zealand) was floated, indicating that liberalization-oriented APEC members had started to explore alternative ways to achieve regional trade liberalization. These developments convinced Asian governments that APEC should not be the only regional framework in Asia and that forums could exist without the United States.

The common experience of these changes fostered an interest in regional cooperation and removed the taboos regarding East Asia–only forums and preferential trade agreements. Suddenly, there was enormous interest in trying various alternatives as additional layers of the multilayered institutions of the global economy. Given the extraregional dependence of East Asia, however, regional economies did not have an incentive to replace global institutions with regional ones. Instead, they wanted more tools to complement global institutions in order to more effectively influence and reinforce those institutions.

ASEAN Plus Three, which consisted of the governments of ASEAN members plus China, Korea, and Japan, had its first informal leaders' meeting in December 1997. After the failure to create an Asian monetary fund, East Asian countries started to develop a network of currency swap agreements through the Chiang Mai Initiative.

ASEAN Plus Three could also have pursued an FTA that covered all of East Asia (East Asia Vision Group 2001), but it lacked the cohesiveness or the capacity to do so. As "economic logic favors preferential arrangements among larger, more inclusive groupings" (Scollay and Gilbert 2001, 150), with other things being equal, East Asian countries should ideally create an FTA to cover at least the entire region. However, many of the economies had difficulty liberalizing agriculture and other sensitive sectors.

Unlike forging an FTA for all of East Asia at once, step-by-step development through bilateral FTAs would help with the politically difficult adjustment required to liberalize sensitive items in each deal. The GATT Article 24 that applies to developed countries stipulates that an FTA has to cover "substantially all the trade" among its parties. Although there is no consensus about what constitutes "substantially all," precedents under the WTO suggest that an FTA should cover 80 to 90 percent of existing trade. An FTA could exert strong pressure to liberalize particularly sensitive items in a way that multilateral negotiations would not. This is a benefit of employing FTAs to complement multilateral trade liberalization, even though bilateral FTAs do not necessarily add up to an overall East Asian FTA, simply because it would require all the countries to drastically liberalize politically sensitive sectors all at once—not a realistic proposition in the short run.

In addition, it was unrealistic to assume that all East Asian economies could move at the same pace. There were large gaps in the stages of economic development and levels of government capacity to enforce trade agreements, and some economies were not even WTO members. Step-by-step strategies could provide a more focused approach to solving the diverse problems in different countries, which might apply to other members and potentially become models for larger forums. In fact, there would be ongoing feedback among various forums at bilateral, subregional, regional, cross-regional, and global levels: bilateral solutions could find broader applications, and new ideas discussed in larger forums might become legally binding agreements among like-minded economies.

Furthermore, there was no consensus in East Asia as to which economies should participate. Hong Kong and Taiwan, both important nodes in Asian production networks, are members of APEC but not of ASEAN Plus Three. There is no agreement as to which extraregional countries East Asia should have FTAs with, either. Some were exploring FTAs with such countries as Australia, New Zealand, and India. Although these countries are not (at least for now) tightly integrated in Asian production networks and therefore do not necessarily share the urgent need to reduce the various transaction costs of intra-industry trade, FTAs with them would help expand export opportunities for East Asian economies, as would FTAs with the United States and Latin American countries. Those more developed economies ready to conclude FTAs did not want to wait for an East Asian FTA to emerge and individually went ahead to take advantage of the opportunities open to them. This step-by-step process would allow flexibility over which other economies could strengthen economic relations with current members of ASEAN Plus Three and affect the pattern of interdependence and sense of community in the region. Thus, this process might expand the scope of "East Asia."

On the other hand, negotiating independent bilateral FTAs risks the proliferation of different rules of origin and other discrepancies, resulting in higher transaction costs. Many East Asian governments, however, are aware of the needs of production networks and have a strong incentive to avoid the so-called spaghetti bowl effect, hoping to eventually merge separately negotiated bilateral FTAs into a regional FTA with regional rules of origin and common rules.

Although some might argue that countries with large markets, such as Japan and China, would have more leverage in a bilateral rather than in a regional or multilateral context and thus should prefer bilateral routes, in reality neither country had a practical choice. Japan could not risk infringing the WTO rule. China was not ready for an FTA before its accession to the

WTO. When it became ready, not many countries were eager to conclude an FTA with it in the short run. In addition, size of market is just one of many factors affecting negotiation leverage. For example, a country that is excluded from an existing FTA would be more eager to conclude an FTA because it has a strong incentive to overcome the discrimination. The political dynamics of each bilateral FTA, however, are beyond the scope of this chapter.

Japan and Korea first triggered the trend toward bilateral FTAs. The two countries changed their long-standing policy of exclusive multilateralism, adopting a multitrack policy in which bilateral and regional preferential arrangements complemented the WTO. The Japan–Republic of Korea free trade agreement was conceived shortly after a historic summit meeting in 1998 between Korean president Kim Dae Jung and Japanese prime minister Obuchi Keizo (Munakata 2003b). It would create the largest bilateral free trade area in East Asia, including 170 million people with a combined GDP of $5 trillion, about three-fourths of the entire East Asian economy. An FTA between the only two Organisation for Economic Co-operation and Development members in Asia, with advanced rules commensurate with their economic level, could set a standard for economic integration in the region. The Korean side hesitated, however, fearing that the elimination of tariffs would increase its structural trade deficit vis-à-vis Japan. That fear is not unrealistic, since the average Korean tariff rate is higher than Japan's. Koreans are concerned that the Japan–Republic of Korea free trade agreement is not going to be a balanced deal. Antagonism regarding Japan's wartime atrocities has added to the Korean hesitation. Also, Japan was still dominated by single-minded dependence on the WTO and was unprepared to negotiate its first FTA. The two countries had government-affiliated think tanks jointly study the feasibility of a bilateral FTA. In the meantime, Korea chose Chile as its first FTA partner and launched negotiations in September 1999.

While Japan and Korea triggered the process, New Zealand and Singapore actually drove the move to bilateral FTAs in the region. New Zealand proposed an FTA in June 1999, and the two countries launched negotiations in September. Singapore, now ready to negotiate FTAs independently of ASEAN, proposed to Japan in December 1999 that the two countries should explore an FTA. Tokyo seized this opportunity to overcome its lingering hesitation and achieve a breakthrough in trade policy. It aimed to come up with an innovative economic arrangement that would not only eliminate tariffs but also include a wide variety of measures to reduce transaction costs between the two countries, potentially becoming a model for other FTAs (Munakata 2001). "An FTA with a free port" had to be innovative to be attractive in Tokyo. Singapore's policy of maintaining an internationally competitive business environment would also stimulate regulatory reform in Japan, and it turned out to be the ideal first FTA partner for Japan.

Japan's decision to negotiate an FTA with Singapore on October 22, 2000, had an energizing effect in and outside the region. Singapore explored the possibility of FTAs with the United States, Europe, China, and India. The United States and Singapore unexpectedly announced their intention to negotiate a bilateral FTA on November 16, 2000, at the APEC leaders' meeting. As Asian countries started to pursue FTAs, the U.S. "hub and spoke" approach ceased to be a common concern. Singapore's moves, while resented at first, stimulated other ASEAN members to explore FTAs, both collectively and individually, with other countries.

In summary, the decisive factor in the third period was defensive regionalism. At the same time, the contagion of the financial crisis brought home to East Asian countries the high degree of their interdependence. The freedom of experimenting with various forums turned the attention of East Asian governments to the substantive issues in each forum, further enhancing the role of intraregional economic interdependence.

Fourth Period: FTA Bandwagon

The fourth period is characterized by China's new confidence in the possibility of regional cooperation and the resulting intraregional competitive dynamics. Beijing had paid more attention to Asia since the early 1990s, as a way to secure a benign international environment that would allow China to focus on its domestic economic development. In addition, the positive experiences of the APEC processes helped China gradually overcome its long-held fear that multilateral frameworks could reduce its freedom and damage its interests (personal interview, Chinese official, October 2003).

In the wake of the Asian financial crisis, China became more confident and proactive, beginning the transition to the fourth period. In mid-1998, China succeeded in projecting an image as a responsible regional power by not devaluing the renminbi, albeit for its own interests (Segal 1998; Baker 1998). This episode further increased Beijing's confidence in its ability to positively shape the regional environment. It actively participated in the ASEAN Plus Three meetings, reversed its initial cautious attitude toward the Asian monetary fund proposal (Sakakibara 2000, 182–89), and supported the Chiang Mai Initiative at the ASEAN Plus Three finance ministers meeting. Furthermore, its accession to the WTO significantly heightened its sense of being a responsible great power.

From the late 1990s to early 2000, China's anxiety about its security environment spurred its efforts to improve relations with its neighbors. Sino-U.S. relations became tense in the aftermath of the bombing of the Chinese embassy in Belgrade in 1999. The Bush administration's initial policy of treating China as a strategic competitor further alarmed China and prompted it to take precautions against possible U.S. attempts to encircle and contain China (Fong 2003).

In the area of trade policy, China had warily watched its neighbors shifting their focus to FTAs just when it was preoccupied with the negotiations to accede to the WTO (Tsugami 2003, 210–13). At the same time, China perceived a heightened sense of anxiety among ASEAN economies about their economic future. Their developmental stages are close to China's, and their export structures overlap. An FTA with ASEAN would demonstrate China's willingness to let ASEAN gain from China's economic growth and help alleviate ASEAN's anxiety about China's rise. An FTA with ASEAN would be easier for China than one with more developed economies (Munakata 2003a) and could help China quickly catch up with the regional trend toward FTAs.

One month after Japan and Singapore announced the launch of FTA negotiations, China's premier, Zhu Rongji, proposed to have experts from ASEAN and China jointly explore the possibility of establishing a free trade area. Since China completed major negotiations for its accession to the WTO in 2000, it has become markedly more active in engaging in regional frameworks. Thus, China's proposal for an FTA with ASEAN marked the start of the period of FTA bandwagoning.

Since its proposal to ASEAN in November 2000, China has moved swiftly. In October 2001, China and ASEAN completed the joint feasibility study for an FTA, and in November, China persuaded ASEAN to establish an ASEAN-China free trade area within ten years. For most ASEAN members, China's exports present a competitive threat. Therefore, China's offer of "early harvest," to reduce certain agricultural tariffs early on, was important in getting ASEAN on board. In November 2002, China and ASEAN signed the Framework Agreement on ASEAN-China Economic Cooperation that would establish a free trade area by 2010 for the older ASEAN members and by 2015 for the newer members. The agreement covers the liberalization of trade in goods and services as well as investment. It also lists five priority sectors in which to strengthen economic cooperation: agriculture, information technology, human resources development, investment, and Mekong River basin development. In October 2003, beginning with Thailand, China started to implement the so-called early harvest measures to eliminate tariffs on some fruits and vegetables. It is not clear, at this point, how far China and Thailand are prepared to liberalize trade and investment or what specific measures they will take to reduce transaction costs through "economic cooperation."

In the meantime, Japan and Singapore concluded negotiations in October 2001. Although Japan's exclusion of most agricultural produce invited criticism from other countries, the agreement went beyond the usual terms of an FTA, including broad economic cooperation to reduce transaction costs and expand bilateral exchanges. Salient features of their agreement include mutual recognition of technical conformity assessment for electrical and electronic products and telecommunications equipment, customs cooperation to improve customs procedures through more extensive information technology use, legal recognition of certified digital signatures in both countries, mutual recognition of information technology skills certification, and facilitation of movement of business persons. The agreement between Japan and the Republic of Singapore for a New-Age Economic Partnership went into effect on November 30, 2002. Japan also started negotiations with Mexico in 2002, Korea in 2003, Malaysia, Thailand, and the Philippines in 2004, and Indonesia in 2005.

In January 2002, Japanese prime minister Koizumi Jun'ichiro visited ASEAN countries, signed the New-Age Economic Partnership Agreement with Singapore, and proposed an initiative for a Japan-ASEAN comprehensive economic partnership. It is widely perceived that the agreement to negotiate an FTA between China and ASEAN prompted Japan to move in the same direction (*People's Daily Online* 2003). In October 2003, Japan and ASEAN signed the Framework for Comprehensive Economic Partnership and began negotiations in 2005. On a bilateral level, Japan started negotiations with Malaysia, Thailand, and the Philippines in early 2004.

Washington also began to pay more attention to the region. China's rise, with its confident regional diplomacy, and Japan's stagnation indicated a potential shift in the regional balance of power. At the same time, a weakened ASEAN led to increased concern that it would become a hotbed of terrorism. In October 2002, President Bush announced the Enterprise for ASEAN Initiative (White House 2002). In May 2003, the U.S.-Singapore FTA was signed. In November 2003, Bush announced his intention to launch FTA negotiations with Thailand (White House 2003).

Bilateral FTAs provided Asian economies with effective measures to address specific problems without having to wait for a consensus in a larger group, where not all members share the same sense of urgency regarding particular problems. Previously, the forum came first and the substance was taken up only when it fitted the forum. Now, substance comes first and the forum is tailored to deal with it. Thus, multilayered approaches, where bilateral, regional, and global frameworks are developed in parallel, are now firmly in place in East Asia.

In this period, competitive dynamics has become an important factor. But more important is the factor of intraregional economic interdependence. So far, competitive dynamics have stimulated constructive responses and remained within a range that can accommodate and nurture that interdependence. At the same time, the rise of China, the availability of the WTO dispute settlement mechanism, and the availability of various alternatives including

FTAs, has substantially diminished defensive regionalism, although this motivation is still at work particularly in the area of financial cooperation. Intraregional competitive dynamics and defensive regionalism have not found a stable equilibrium, and the balance between them will change depending on how major powers interact.

The United States, Japan, and China in Regional Developments

Defensive regionalism, primary throughout the first three periods, significantly weakened in the fourth period. Intraregional economic interdependence consistently grew in importance. Competitive dynamics, which had been largely limited to interactions within ASEAN, emerged in the third period when bilateral FTAs became prevalent, becoming an important factor in the fourth period.

This concluding section deals with the question of how this evolutionary process of regionalism in turn affected the United States, Japan, and China and their influence on the shape of the regionalism in Asia.

The United States

The United States promoted globalization and prepared an environment conducive to regionalization in Asia. The U.S. market, its technology, and capital supported Asian export-oriented development.

The success of the U.S. strategy of promoting globalization, however, has ironically made it more difficult for the United States to continue its leadership role in trade liberalization (Destler 1995, 41–63). Especially since the 1970s, the U.S. economic structure has undergone a drastic change, exposing more U.S. producers and workers to foreign competition and the hardships of adjustment, which tend to be more conspicuous in the domestic political arena than are the thinly spread benefits from more open trade. In the 1980s, the relative decline of the U.S. position in the world economy, in addition to ballooning trade deficits (although the fundamental problem was not in trade but in macroeconomic imbalance), made free traders more vulnerable to protectionist pressure at home. The end of the cold war eliminated the glue among Western allies that had prevented trade frictions from jeopardizing their security cooperation, leading to U.S. congressional indifference to foreign policy issues. These developments all made it imperative for U.S. administrations to demonstrate substantial gains through improved market access overseas, in order to win domestic support for its leadership on trade liberalization. The strategic benefits of free trade in alleviating poverty and promoting political stability in developing economies, and the economic benefits of liberalization of its own markets in enhancing productivity and efficiency, have received much less attention in U.S. domestic politics.

The resulting narrow U.S. focus on market access in dealing with Asian economies, and the limited resources for Asian affairs, have often hampered the effectiveness and consistency of U.S. policy approaches toward Asia. When, in the late 1980s, Asia increasingly looked like an attractive future center of economic growth, the United States started to explore a multilateral institutional framework that would secure U.S. access to regional markets and provide meaningful leverage against the European Community. U.S. influence was decisive, and APEC became the primary forum for Asia. This success, however, was short-lived. The perceived narrow-minded focus of the United States on opening Asian markets for its domestic job creation, combined with its indifference to developmental concerns, its pursuit of regionalism in its own hemisphere, and its attempt to introduce tariff negotiations in APEC through EVSL, bred discontent among Asian economies with the U.S. leadership in APEC. The setback of EVSL, on the other hand, dealt a fatal blow to the enthusiasm for APEC remaining among the proliberalization private sector in the United States. The Asian financial crisis further dampened U.S. interest in the region, and the surge of defensive regionalism in its wake diminished U.S. influence on Asian regionalism.

In the fourth period, U.S. policy attention returned in response to competitive dynamics. Since the terrorist attacks on September 11, 2001, however, Asian countries perceive that the United States has been largely preoccupied with the war against terrorism and has paid less attention to the region than China has. Given its inability to consistently devote policy resources to local issues in Asia, its prevalent skepticism toward the efficacy of development assistance, and its occasional impatience with the gradual process of institutional change, it may be unrealistic to expect the United States to maintain constant attention on the entire region. Thus, the United States may have relatively less influence on the specific shape of the regional economic order in Asia.

It remains to be seen how evolving East Asian regionalism affects U.S. Asia policy and U.S. influence on Asia. The United States will remain the only superpower that has the ability to shape regional developments in areas that are critical to its national interests. The United States can also be instrumental through selective involvement in creating building blocks of regional arrangements that can serve as a model for advanced rules beyond the WTO and for reliable implementation on which to build larger institutions. Moreover, the United States seems more willing to pay attention to developmental concerns when it is serious about an FTA deal with developing countries (USTR 2003a, 2003b, 2003c). Similar willingness in dealing with Asia would strengthen U.S. influence on the process and shape of Asian regionalism.

Japan

The impact of Asian regionalism has been strongest and most profound on Japan. Japan spearheaded the regionalization process, contributed to the creation of APEC, and encouraged the role of ASEAN as a cohesive regional entity.

There is, however, a significant limitation to Japan's approach. Japan's external policy was constrained by its "dual structure" of competitive industries and protected and inefficient industries, with the former expected to earn national wealth to be distributed to the latter. T. J. Pempel argues in chapter 2 that this system resulted from "policy compromises" within the Liberal Democratic Party, between an urban, big business–bureaucrat coalition, and a rural, small business–farmer coalition. In the postwar era, this system helped develop domestic markets that nurtured domestic manufacturers. Increasingly, however, it also created a high-cost business environment. Now, the Japanese population is aging and shrinking, limiting the long-term prospects of domestic demand growth in addition to the immediate economic problems. High-performing industries, increasingly under competitive pressure, have started to shift their operations overseas, while inefficient industries remain at home, demanding protection and subsidies. The dual structure has become unsustainable, as costs of protecting the weak (which Pempel describes as "implicit guarantees that there will be no losers") have become prohibitive in a low-growth environment. At the same time, this structure prevents Japan from being responsive to its neighbors' requests to reduce trade barriers to Japan's sensitive items.

The Asian financial crisis had a large impact on the thinking of Japanese policymakers, prompting a recognition of the interdependence between Japan and the rest of Asia. Japan's deeper integration in Asia would revitalize its economy, provide more demand, help Asia recover, and let Japan capitalize on Asia's growth potential, creating a virtuous cycle. For this to occur, Japan would have to undergo structural reform. This thinking paved the way to using FTAs as a new vehicle of reform (Munakata 2001).[7] Thus, Japan started to pursue FTAs not only to improve the overseas business environment—in particular to reduce transaction costs in Asia and overcome discrimination caused by other FTAs—but also to promote domestic economic restructuring. Although nobody questions the efficacy of improving the overseas business environment, vested interests seeking to keep the protection system intact oppose the domestic restructuring purpose of the FTA. In response, the Japanese government has carefully chosen the countries with which to ne-

---

[7] It should be noted that this thinking is unique, especially when compared with the situation in the United States. It is widely perceived that trade barriers in the United States have been largely eliminated except for items with extreme political sensitivity that would not be easily overcome by an FTA.

gotiate FTAs, where perceived benefits were large enough to overcome the political resistance involved in each deal. Consequently, Japan agreed to eliminate or reduce many agricultural tariffs in the FTA negotiations with Mexico—a development that would have been unthinkable just a few years before.

At the same time, the Japanese economic system has not yet sufficiently adapted to this new competitive reality. In fact, it cannot change overnight. For a long time, Japan did not have adequate external markets in corporate resources. This deficiency has led to a shortage of general managers and professionals needed for corporate restructuring. The lack of well-functioning labor markets has led to a mismatch between the skills needed in new sectors and the skills of the unemployed, adding to public anxiety about rising unemployment. The Japanese political system, as Pempel elaborates in chapter 2, has also tended to reinforce the status quo. Uneven voting power in favor of rural areas, where a significant proportion of voters are employed in protected, subsidized sectors, in addition to well-organized vested interest groups, have helped politicians who resist structural reform to stay in power. Although there are signs of fundamental changes in the expectations and orientations of businesses, the general public, and the government, the inertia in economic, social, and political structures has made Japan's transformation all the more difficult and thus limited its ability to move decisively toward regionalism.

The new regional developments that Japan's nascent policy shift has helped set off, are, in turn, putting more pressure on Japan to complete its shift. Whether Japan will be able to play a more constructive role in the process of Asian regionalism eventually depends on whether and how fast it develops a political consensus to dismantle its dual structure.

China

The rise of China changed the regional landscape in two ways. First, its new role as a link in the production network contributed to the growth of intraregional trade. Second, China became an active player in promoting regionalism. The first element firmly positioned China as an indispensable member of regional economic frameworks in East Asia, reinforcing the second element.

China's advantage is that it is, for now, free from messy democratic processes and can make bold moves once there is a consensus among political elites. Although China is not free from political battles between proreform and antireform elements within elites, the voice of ordinary citizens can be reflected in its policy only if political elites decide to promote it in order to maintain domestic stability. For example, farmers, who are by far the majority of China's population but who lack political muscle, tend to receive much less attention than their weight in the population would warrant in China's decision to open agricultural markets in the process of its accession to the WTO. With this freedom, Beijing seems to be focused on a political agenda of reassuring ASEAN and enjoying the diplomatic goodwill that their FTA has brought about.

This approach, however, has its risks. China is still struggling to implement WTO rules in its vast territories, where local officials have varying levels of willingness and capacity to enforce rules and regulations. In this context, Ernst in chapter 7 notes an interesting contrast experienced by a Japanese businessman between the Japanese and Chinese ways of starting business: "It can be done" means an absolute commitment in Japan, but simply an eagerness to do business in China. Legally binding international agreements, however, carry a heavier weight than business communications preceding formal contracts. If China fails to faithfully implement FTAs, it will lose credibility with the business sector. Furthermore, Beijing's focus seems to be shifting from pursuing faster economic growth and technological progress to rectifying domestic gaps and achieving more equitable development. This shift in domestic policy focus could affect the pace of implementing existing agreements and taking new initiatives to accelerate the process of regional and global economic integration. Therefore, the question is: When will China start to align its external policies with its domestic capabilities and priorities?

With all these uncertainties, the market-driven regionalization processes and the politically directed attempts at creating regional institutions are mutually and interactively at work in East Asia, shaping regional developments while changing the domestic policy priorities of the major powers willing to engage the processes. How far they are willing to adjust their policies to the demands of building regional institutions will have an important bearing on their influence on the processes of regionalism. Moves toward East Asian regionalism have also been tempered by the nature of East Asian economies, their dependence on capital, technology, and markets from inside as well as outside the region, the presence of global institutions and mechanisms, and the difficulties in forging a strong ideational foundation for such an enterprise. The nature and relative weaknesses of contemporary regional institutions in East Asia are manifestations of the interactions of these competing forces.[8]

[8] I would like to thank one of the anonymous readers for Cornell University Press for helping me to formulate this concluding section.

III

THE END OF NATIONAL MODELS

7

Searching for a New Role in East Asian Regionalization: Japanese Production Networks in the Electronics Industry

DIETER ERNST

The electronics industry has been a trailblazer and test bed for East Asian regionalization—it dominates the region's international trade and investment, and it displays very high levels of integration into global production networks. Electronics has overtaken textiles as the region's main engine of growth, and governments compete to nurture this industry as a catalyst for industrial upgrading. An analysis of this industry can thus provide important insights into the forces that are remaking East Asia.

Japanese firms have played a critically important role in the region's electronics industry—they have been a major source of capital, components, and machinery, as well as business models and management techniques. However, in response to a persistent recession in this industry, the cards are now being reshuffled, giving rise to far-reaching adjustments in the region's trade and investment patterns, and in the development trajectories of its electronics industries. The traditional "flying geese" model of economic interactions between Japan and East Asia has clearly come to an end as a unifying force of regionalization (METI 2003; Ozawa 2003). But what new forces will shape East Asia's future regional development patterns?

Since the 1990s, U.S. corporations have consolidated their leadership in

The author gratefully acknowledges comments and suggestions from Peter Katzenstein, Takashi Shiraishi, Miles Kahler, Peter Gourevitch, T. J. Pempel, Derek Hall, Terutomo Ozawa, Hiroyuki Chuma, Kazufumi Tanaka, Mike Hobday, Peter Williamson, Barry Naughton, Denis Simon, Norio Tokumaru, Max von Zedtwitz, Richard Baker, Shen Xiaobai, and Lu Feng.

semiconductors and computers, creating new product, software, and service markets, for example, the Internet, e-business, advanced microprocessors, and operating systems for an increasing variety of digital devices (Ernst 2002a). Japanese electronics firms, on the other hand, have experienced a rapid erosion of their erstwhile leadership in consumer electronics and semiconductors, and they have failed to catch up with U.S. industry leaders in the above new product, software, and service markets.[1] The electronics industry thus appears to support the assessment of Stephen Roach (chief economist of Morgan Stanley) that "the world is more U.S.-centric now than it has ever been" (Roach 2003).

But does this imply that East Asia's electronics industry will be "Americanized"? And which role will Japanese firms play in this game? In this chapter I analyze one side of the equation. I explore how Japanese electronics firms are searching for new ways to transform their East Asian production networks (EAPNs) to cope with the new opportunities and challenges of a radically transformed East Asian regional economy. Far from withdrawing from East Asia, Japanese corporate capital in the electronics industry now critically depends on the region, not only as a global export production base but also as a major and increasingly sophisticated market for its products, services, and technology, and as a source of lower-cost knowledge workers.[2] To benefit from the growing importance of East Asia, Japanese electronics firms are searching for ways to expand and upgrade their regional production networks, with a particular focus on China.

The analytical challenge is to explain why Japanese firms are finding it difficult to make the necessary adjustments in the organization and management of their regional production networks. Accumulated weaknesses of the Japanese business model provide part of the explanation. However, equally important *exogenous* forces are at work. A central proposition of the chapter is that competition between distinct national business models is no longer the dominant determinant of East Asian regionalization. The dichotomy "Americanization versus Japanization" that has shaped the earlier literature is insufficient to capture what is really happening.

---

[1] While Japanese firms are leaders in next-generation digital consumer electronics, they are facing serious challenges from Taiwanese, Korean, Chinese, and U.S. companies (JETRO 2004, chap. 3).

[2] Data sources include the annual surveys of the Japan Bank for International Cooperation Institute (JBICI) on the overseas business operations of Japanese manufacturing companies; annual reports by the Ministry of Economics, Trade, and Industry (METI), Japan External Trade Organization (JETRO), and the Japan Electronics and Information Technology Industries Association (JEITA); the Nomura Research Institute (NRI); the Fujitsu Research Institute; the Japan Research Institute; the Japan Electronic Industry Yearbook (*Denpa Shinbun, Denshi Kogyo Nenkan*); and the *Yearbook of World Electronics Data;* and specialized newsletters, such as the *JETRO China Newsletter,* Nomura Research Institute Papers, *Oxford Analytica,* the *Interfax China IT & Telecom Weekly, Electronic Business, Electronics Engineering Times,* the *Semiconductor Reporter,* and CMPnet.Asia.

More important are fundamental transformations in the organization of international business that are especially pronounced in the electronics industry (Ernst 2005b): firms of diverse nationality compete and collaborate within multilayered global "networks of networks" of marketing, production, and innovation. This has forced Japanese firms into dense interaction with a multitude of firms from the United States as well as from East Asia's leading electronics exporting countries. Another critical *exogenous* force has been the rise of China as a global export production base; as a sophisticated growth market, especially for mobile communications and digital consumer devices; and as a new source of R & D and innovation (Ernst and Naughton 2005). Both forces combine to produce increasingly complex processes of regionalization. Economic interactions within the region, such as trade, investment, and competitive strategies, have moved beyond a "short causal" chain, where causes and effects are easy to disentangle and where it is possible to name names and to develop effective responses.[3] Identifying, monitoring, let alone "controlling" the transformational actors and mechanisms by nationality has become much more tricky.

This chapter introduces a few conceptual building blocks that we need to capture the interactions between international business organization and regionalization. It also describes the growing dependence of Japan's electronics industry on Asia; explores how Japanese electronics firms are searching for ways to expand and upgrade their regional production networks, with China as the main prize; and examines constraints to change. I highlight peculiar features of the Japanese network management model in East Asia that once may have reflected strength. Now these very same features have turned into systemic weaknesses, as they constrain the capacity of Japanese firms to cope with and shape East Asia's increasingly complex processes of regionalization. The chapter concludes with an illustrative example of how some Japanese electronics firms are seeking to turn around gradually their EAPNs, by developing strategic alliances with emerging new industry leaders in Asia, primarily from China.

Global Production Networks and Regionalization

"Regionalization" can be defined as the integration, across national borders but within a macroregion, of markets for goods, capital, services, knowledge, and labor. Barriers to integration continue to exist, of course, in different markets (especially for low-wage labor), so integration is far from perfect. But there is no doubt that a massive integration has taken place across East Asian borders that, only a short while ago, seemed to be impenetrable (Ng and Yeats 2003). This raises the question: Who are the "integrators"?

---

[3] See chapter 8 for an analysis of similar developments in renewable resource industries.

Research on East Asian regionalization has shown that, while states obviously play an important role in reshaping institutions and regulations, the dominant integrators have been corporations. Much of the literature has focused on the battle between "Japanization" and "Americanization" as the main drivers of regionalization. But there is little agreement on the precise features of business organization that differentiate the comparative capacities of Japanese and American firms to shape regionalization.

Unfortunately, there is very little theoretical work on this relationship; we still lack a unified theory of regionalization and international business organization. However, we can build on research that links theories of trade and FDI and theories of global production networks.[4] This research shows that corporate strategies, organization, and investment decisions shape trade patterns and the spatial division of labor of economic activities, as well as the transfer of technology and knowledge diffusion (Ernst and Guerrieri 1998). Corporations may also indirectly affect regionalization by lobbying states to change institutions and regulations. The driving force is competition (Ernst 2002a). In knowledge-intensive industries such as electronics, intense price competition needs to be combined with product differentiation, in a situation where continuous price wars erode profit margins. Of critical importance, however, is speed-to-market; getting the right product to the largest volume segment of the market right on time can provide huge profits. Being late can be a disaster and may even drive a firm out of business. The result has been an increasing uncertainty and volatility, and a destabilization of established market leadership positions.

No firm, not even a dominant market leader, can generate all the different capabilities internally that are necessary to cope with the requirements of global competition. Competitive success thus critically depends on "vertical specialization," a capacity to selectively source specialized capabilities *outside* the firm, which can range from simple contract assembly to quite sophisticated design capabilities. This requires a shift from individual to increasingly collective forms of organization, from the multidivisional (M-form) functional hierarchy (Chandler 1977) of "multinational corporations" to the networked global flagship model. Trade economists have recently discovered the importance of changes in the organization of international production as a determinant of trade patterns (for example, Cheng and Kierzkowski 2001; Feenstra 1998). Their work demonstrates that (1) production is increasingly "fragmented," with parts of the production process being scattered across a number of countries, hence increasing the percentage share of parts and

---

[4] Pioneering attempts to establish a unified analysis of FDI and international trade are the technology gap trade theory of Posner (1961) and the international product life cycle theory of Vernon (1966 and 1979). Other scholars have tried to link the theory of foreign direct investment to that of industrial organization of multinational enterprises (e.g., Dunning 1981; Ozawa 2000).

components in international trade; (2) that there is reintegration through global production networks (GPNs); and (3) that countries and regions that have been able to become a part of these network are the ones that have industrialized the fastest.

In this chapter I build on this work, but use a broader concept that emphasizes four characteristics of GPNs that influence regionalization (Ernst 2003, 2002b, 1997). First, *scope:* GPNs encompass all stages of the value chain, not only production but also sales, procurement, outsourcing, and R & D. Second, *asymmetry:* flagships exercise control over network resources and decision-making. Third, *knowledge diffusion:* the sharing of knowledge is the necessary glue that keeps these networks growing (Ernst and Kim 2002). Fourth, *information systems:* the increasing use of digital information systems to manage these networks enhances not only information exchange but also provides new opportunities for the sharing and joint creation of knowledge.

A Japanese EADN covers both intrafirm and interfirm transactions and forms of coordination; it links together the flagship's own subsidiaries, affiliates, and joint ventures with its subcontractors, suppliers, and service providers, as well as its partners in strategic alliances. A network flagship such as Hitachi or Sony breaks down the value chain into a variety of discrete functions and locates them wherever they can be carried out most effectively, where they improve the firm's access to resources, capabilities, and knowledge, and where they are needed to facilitate the penetration of important growth markets. It is important to emphasize that the chain of causation appears to work both ways; changes in the organization of Japanese EAPNs have led to changes in East Asia's trade patterns and investment allocation; those changes in turn give rise to further changes in the organization of the above networks.

Expanding and Upgrading Links with East Asia

Japan experienced a long-term decline in its share in global trade and FDI during the 1990s, the country's "lost decade." Its share in global exports fell to 7.6 percent in 2000, after peaking at 10.2 percent in 1986 (JETRO 2002, fig. V-3). In 1992, Japan's outward FDI stock was 12.4 percent of the world total, second only to the United States, but by 2000 it had fallen back to eighth, the same position it had occupied in 1980.[5] Moreover, after being the world's

---

[5] Ministry of Finance data, quoted in JETRO (2002, 25). Note however that Ministry of Finance data on FDI do not include the quite substantial amounts of reinvestments of Japanese subsidiaries in Asia that do not require a capital transfer from Japan to the region (e.g., Nakagane 2002, 55).

largest source of outward FDI flows in 1990, Japan dropped to seventh place in 2001.

Yet, since the turn of the century, a reversal of Japan's declining global presence has occurred, primarily driven by an expansion of trade and investment links with East Asia. From a peak of almost 22 percent in FY1997, the overseas production ratio (OPR)[6] of Japanese manufacturing firms had declined until FY 1999. Since then, there has been a steady increase to more than 24 percent in FY 2001, with projections of an increase to almost 32 percent in FY 2005 (JBICI 2003, 13). The electronics industry leads, with an estimated OPR in FY 2002 of almost 41 percent, up from 38 percent one year earlier. East Asia is the main destination of this expansion of overseas operations of Japanese corporate capital in the electronics industry. I will describe the growing dependence of Japan's electronics industry on Asia (excluding Japan), and explore how Japanese electronics firms are searching for ways to expand and upgrade their regional production networks, with a particular focus on China.

Growing Dependence on East Asia

Japan's electronics industry critically depends on East Asia. Over time, this dependency has deepened, and it also has become much more complex and multifaceted. Of primary importance has been the region's role as a global export production platform. Since the catalytic shock of the 1985 Plaza Accord, when the yen appreciation inflated Japan's production costs, Japanese firms have relocated manufacturing to locations in Asia with lower labor costs, first in Korea, Taiwan, Hong Kong, and Singapore, then in Malaysia, Thailand, Indonesia, and the Philippines. China's role as Japan's global low-cost export production base has substantially increased over the last decade. In FY 2002, almost two-thirds of the overseas manufacturing bases of Japanese manufacturing firms that have responded to the Japan Bank for International Cooperation Institute (JBICI) surveys were concentrated in East Asia, up from 60 percent in FY 2000 (JBICI 2003).[7]

Initially, the focus has been on consumer electronics and home appliances, as well as related components. Yet, over the last few years, there has been a substantial diversification in the product mix that Japanese firms produce in

---

[6] The "overseas production ratio" of a company is defined as (overseas production volume) / (overseas production volume + domestic production volume) in percent (JBICI 2003, note 8).

[7] In 2002, the greatest number of production bases (1,067) was in the ASEAN-4 countries (+16% from FY 2000). China was second with 890 Japanese manufacturing affiliates (+38% from FY 2000), followed by North America (752, +17%), and Asian NIEs (616, +16%). This indicates that China has experienced the largest increase in the number of Japanese manufacturing affiliates.

Asia, to include both hardware and software required for computing, communication, and industrial applications. At the same time, increasingly complex stages of production and overall supply chain management have gradually been shifted from Japan to other Asian locations. This upgrading is a response to the intensifying competition that Japanese electronics firms face both from above and from below.

From above, American electronics industry leaders have raced ahead in the most prized areas of technological innovation, as far as these can be measured by patent statistics. The U.S. "innovation score" more than doubled from 41 (in 1985) to almost 101 (in 2002), a rate far better than for any other country[8] (CHI/MIT 2003). In 2002, all fifteen leading companies with the best record on patent citations were based in the United States, with nine of them in the electronics industry. Japan has maintained its second place, with an increase in its "innovation score" from 15 to 33, but it is now trailing farther behind the United States. And European industry leaders both in telecommunications and consumer electronics have strengthened their market position by aggressively partnering with Asian companies, especially those from China.

From below, Japanese electronics firms are facing new competitors from six Asian countries (China, Korea, Taiwan, Singapore, Malaysia, and India) that have emerged as the new center of gravity in global electronics exports (Ernst 2004). China has now become the third largest exporter of electronics products (up from tenth in 2000), and the second largest importer (up from seventh in 2000). Taiwan ranks as the number one world market supplier for fourteen electronics products. This includes silicon foundry services (involving leading-edge wafer fabrication), with a 73 percent share in global production value; wireless local area networks; and digital audio-video equipment such as CD-ROMs and DVDs, with most of these devices being produced in China. Similar dominant world market positions exist for Korea (in computer memories, flat-panel displays and mobile phones), Singapore (storage devices, printers), and China (computers and peripherals and digital consumer devices) (Ernst 2005a). Furthermore, while India has failed to excel as a global manufacturing exporter, the country has firmly established itself as a global export production base for software and information services.

---

[8] The U.S. "innovation score" measures the number of patents granted by the U.S. Patent Office, multiplied by the so-called citation index that indicates the value of these patents. The citation index measures the frequency of citation of a particular patent. When the U.S. Patent Office publishes patents, each one includes a list of other patents from which it is derived. The more often a patent is cited, the more likely it is a pioneering patent, connected with important inventions and discoveries. An index of more than one indicates that patents are cited more often than would be expected for a specific group of technologies, while less than one indicates they are cited less often than expected.

An equally important aspect of Japan's growing dependence on East Asia are demand-side factors, that is, the growing sophistication of Asian markets for electronic products and services.[9] Gone are the days when Asia's protected markets were an easy dumping ground for low-end and mature products, locally produced by Japanese affiliates (the "mini-Matsushitas"). Procurement by Japanese subsidiaries in Asia has created a thriving market for Japanese exports of parts and components, as well as capital equipment (Ernst 2000). The development of rapidly growing electronics industries has further expanded the region's demand for such input imports. Over time, however, the procurement of Japanese subsidiaries and Asian firms has become less Japan-centered, substituting imports from Japan with purchases from within the region. Over the last decade, Japanese firms in Asia have substantially increased their localization of sales and procurement (METI 2002b, 10).

To some degree, this shift reflects the relocation of production by Japanese component suppliers to Asia, as part of an increasingly sophisticated division of labor within Japanese EAPNs (Ernst and Ravenhill 2000). One important result is that the sales of Asian subsidiaries now outpace Japan's exports to Asia: in FY 2000, Asian subsidiaries recorded sales of ¥364 billion, 1.7 times the value of Japan's exports to Asia (Takeuchi 2003, 13). An equally important cause for the regionalization of procurement by Japanese subsidiaries in Asia has been the emergence of highly competitive suppliers of manufacturing services in Korea, Taiwan, Hong Kong, Singapore, Malaysia, Thailand, the Philippines, and more recently China (Ernst 2005b).

In addition, Japanese electronics firms now belatedly realize the critical importance of Asia's thriving and increasingly sophisticated consumer markets. The contraction of Japan's domestic retail markets for home appliances, audio-video equipment, computing and communication devices provides a powerful incentive for developing aggressive market penetration strategies in the rest of Asia (JETRO 2003c, 19). In 2002, total consumer spending in East Asia was estimated to be $1,461 billion. China's share was almost 40 percent, up from 27.5 percent in 1991. The region's middle- and upper-class market, the primary target of global competition, is estimated to comprise around 140 million people, roughly 10 percent of East Asia's total population. The four newly industrializing economies, or NIEs (Singapore, Korea, Taiwan, and Hong Kong) dominate these high-end sophisticated consumer markets, but China, with almost 41 million high-end consumers, accounts for almost 30 percent of the region's higher income market.[10]

[9] With more than 40% of the overseas sales bases of Japanese manufacturing firms (in FY 2002), East Asia is well ahead of the EU and North America (JBICI 2003). The number of Japanese sales affiliates in Asia increased by 24% in the two years from FY 2000 to FY 2002, with the largest increase (+30%) in China (Takeuchi 2003, 2).

[10] There are of course huge geographic disparities. Beijing, the Yangtze delta around Shanghai,

Probably the most important change is the growing sophistication of China's markets for electronic products and services. China is now the world's largest market for telecommunications equipment (wired and wireless), the third largest market for semiconductors, and one of the largest and most sophisticated markets for digital consumer and computing devices. Major global market leaders count on a continuous rapid growth of the China market to reduce the negative impact of the persistent demand stagnation in global electronics markets. This is true for the telecommunications market where Japanese producers of infrastructure equipment (Fujitsu and NEC) and mobile phones (Matsushita, Sharp, Sanyo, Sony, Kyocera) are intensely competing as well as collaborating with global industry leaders (e.g., Motorola, Alcatel, Nokia, Cisco, Samsung, Siemens, Ericsson, and LG), and where all of them are competing for market share with emerging local firms, such as Huawei, ZTE, Datang, TCL, Haier, and Ningbo Bird. Global industry leaders are also eager to penetrate China's markets for computing and consumer devices and key components such as semiconductors.

Japanese electronics firms have not been particularly successful in penetrating these markets, and competition has become extremely intense. For the profitable high-end markets, main competitors are Korean (Samsung and LG) and European consumer electronics firms (Philips, Siemens), as well as U.S. computer companies (HP, Dell, Apple, and Gateway), which are now entering the digital consumer market with a vengeance. Competition is even more intense at the mid- and low-level market segments, where in addition to the already mentioned firms, Chinese firms and their Taiwanese partners play an increasingly important role. In practically all of these market segments across the region Japanese firms are on the defensive and are now belatedly trying to repair the damage of earlier inaction.

Priorities for Future Network Expansion and Upgrading

To benefit from the growing importance of East Asia, Japanese electronics firms are now searching for ways to expand and upgrade their EAPNs. The emphasis is on trying to fine-tune the division of labor between domestic and overseas production, and on reducing reliance on traditional "keiretsu-type" linkages with other Japanese firms. This shift in strategy is driven primarily by the need to expand market share in attractive Asian markets, especially in China and Korea, and to find scale economies, which are necessary to cope with the intense price competition from emerging new competitors within the region.

---

and the southern coastal provinces have all become leading growth markets, and in some cases even launch markets for digital consumer and mobile communication devices. But beyond these thriving high-end markets, persistent poverty keeps constricting effective demand.

This is a belated attempt by corporate headquarters to transfer to Asia basic changes in the Japanese business model. Of particular importance are attempts to move away from market-share expansion to profitability as the main measure of success, and attempts to strengthen vertical specialization, by outsourcing noncore activities. These changes in the Japanese business model have been debated at corporate headquarters since the mid-1990s. Yet the green light for implementing such changes in Asia was only given five years later, when the slowdown in the electronics industry gave rise to intensified competition and reduced profits.[11]

In 2003, Japanese manufacturing firms expected to pursue the following priorities in the expansion of their EAPNs (JBICI 2003, 28, 29). China stands out with a focus on expanding production (almost 73% out of 518 responses). ASEAN-4 has an equally high focus on expanding production (70% out of 341 responses).[12] But while in China this includes investment in new production lines, the focus in ASEAN-4 is almost exclusively on expanding and upgrading existing facilities. In NIEs, expansion of production plays a much less important role, with sales expansion being the dominant concern. In China, Japanese firms also assign a high priority to the expansion of sales functions (almost 60% of the respondents).

Particularly noteworthy is the low priority assigned by Japanese firms to an expansion of R & D in Asia. This contrasts with the approach of U.S. and European, as well as Korean and Taiwanese, companies, who are expanding R & D functions in their overseas affiliates in Asia (Choi 2003; Liu and Chen 2003). In Asia, the share of Japanese companies that intend to expand R & D hovers between 9 percent (for NIEs) to 13.5 percent (for China), compared to 19 percent for the European Union and almost 23 percent for North America. Japanese firms continue to neglect the huge potential of Asia as lower-cost sources of knowledge workers. Japanese firms, in their attempts to upgrade their Asian networks, still typically try to retain an unequal division of labor that keeps the development and production of leading-edge and high-value-added products and production stages in Japan. They also try to minimize possible leakages of technological knowledge. But their capacity to sustain this flying geese pattern of specialization has been critically weakened.

This provides yet another example of the slow pace of response of Japan's

---

[11] As Tachiki (1999) shows, it typically takes Japanese firms three to five years to translate a change in corporate business plans into decisions on the geographic location of resources and to mobilize organizational resources that are necessary to relocate overseas production. This reflects the strictly sequential procedure of corporate decision making in Japan: only after a systematic restructuring of the corporate business plan has occurred will management move on to a gradual implementation of changes in overseas operations.

[12] JBICI defines "ASEAN-4" to include Malaysia, Thailand, Indonesia, and the Philippines, while "NIEs" includes Singapore, Taiwan, and Korea.

major integrated electronics companies. In descending order of asset size, the industry leaders are Hitachi, Sony, Matsushita Electric, Toshiba, NEC, Fujitsu, Mitsubishi Electric, Sanyo, and Sharp. With massive overseas sales and extensive global production networks, these nine firms once embodied Japan's global leadership in the electronics industry. With a combined turnover of ¥46 trillion (ca. $380 billion), a total workforce of 1.4 million, hundreds of subsidiaries and thousands of component suppliers around the world, adjustments in strategy and organization only come about incrementally.

This is different for Japanese small- and medium-sized enterprises, most of them specialized suppliers of electronic components, who can respond much faster than the global Japanese flagship companies. These small- and medium-sized enterprises are the main drivers behind the current expansion of production into East Asia. For small- and medium-sized enterprises, this is a question of survival—smaller Japanese component suppliers are most directly affected by the increasing competition from Asian suppliers. In FY 2002, almost 88 percent of suppliers of electronics components were planning to expand their overseas production networks over the next three years, compared to less than 73 percent of final assemblers (most of them global flagships). And Japanese small- and medium-sized enterprises in the electronics industry have a record OPR of 45 percent, way above the average OPR for all industries, which is slightly below 32 percent (JBICI 2003, 67).

The rapid internationalization of Japan's domestic supplier base in the electronics industry indicates that the widely feared "hollowing out"[13] has hit smaller specialized suppliers especially hard. This is borne out by the finding of the FY 2002 JBICI survey (2003, 16) that, compared to earlier surveys, fewer companies in the electronics industry intend to invest in an upgrading of domestic operations. Japanese electronics firms may thus lose one of their major traditional strengths, a vibrant and flexible domestic base of supplier industries.[14]

Larger global players on the other hand are under tremendous pressure to combine the expansion of production in Asia with a vigorous upgrading of their domestic production and innovation systems. Laying off workers in Japan is costly, as retrenched workers must be adequately compensated to en-

---

[13] "Hollowing out" stands for a decline in the manufacturing sector's contribution to economic activity (e.g., output or employment) in the home economy in response to increases in FDI outflows.

[14] Yoshihide Ishiyama's interesting study ("Is Japan Hollowing Out?"), published in 1999, was apparently too optimistic. He argues (Ishiyama 1999, 242) that "'hollowing out' . . . should not be a concern for Japan . . . [as] . . . Japan's manufacturing industry seems to be much more resilient than that of other countries. . . . After a short while, Japan's manufacturing corporations manage to increase efficiency in producing existing products, upgrading products, or moving to new product lines to defend turf against imports and sustain export revenue." Since then, this belief in Japan's invincibility has been thoroughly weakened.

able companies to maintain their reputations as good employers. This implies that wages are a de facto component of fixed costs. To sustain jobs especially for expensive knowledge workers, large Japanese firms attempt to sustain an unequal division of labor with Asia. They attempt to keep basic and applied research at home, plus "design work which promotes added-value, and basic programming development," while product and system customization plus process adaptation are developed in major overseas markets such as the Asian NIEs and China (JBICI 2003, 21).

Constraints to Change: Systemic Weaknesses

To establish why Japanese electronics firms find it difficult to implement the above priorities for future network expansion and upgrading, I highlight five peculiar features of the Japanese network management model in East Asia that once may have reflected strength but now have turned into systemic weaknesses: persistent diversity of organization; dispersed location driven by risk minimization; Japan-centered sales destination and a neglect of local market characteristics; a limited capacity to tap the creativity of non-Japanese skilled workers, engineers, and managers; and a reluctance to outsource R & D.

Partial Convergence and Persistent Diversity

Responding to the resurgence of the U.S. electronics industry during the New Economy boom, both the leading global Japanese flagship companies and smaller companies such as Kyocera have attempted to emulate what they perceived to be successful strategies by their American counterparts. Imitation has been an important force of change. Yet, imitation has not transformed Japanese companies and their EAPNs into clones of their American benchmark models. Instead, it has generated "a complex process of hybridization where partial convergence coexists with persistent diversity" (Ernst and Ravenhill 2000, 242).[15]

---

[15] The debate about whether there are differences between Japanese and U.S. FDI has a long history. Over time, the focus of analysis has shifted from trade impacts (e.g., Kojima 1978, 1986), transfer of technology, and the importance of relative factor endowments (Ozawa 1979; Urata 1999) to differences in the ways Japanese and American firms have organized their international business operations, and how these differences affect transaction costs, learning, and knowledge diffusion (e.g., Westney 1999a; Fruin 1997). By the late 1990s, a growing literature was addressing how these issues affected Japanese and U.S. production networks in Asia (e.g., Encarnation 1999; Hatch and Yamamura 1996; Ernst and Ravenhill 2000; Ernst 1997, 2000). Important differences have been identified in seven areas: geographic dispersion, product mix, localization of management, sourcing of components and capital goods, replication of domestic production networks, impact on trade, and distribution of R & D activities.

Table 7.1. Japan's integration into the global economy, 2000

	Japan (%, $billions)	United States (%, $billions)	Germany (%, $billions)
Balance of Overseas Direct Investment/GDP	5.9	25.0	22.7
Overseas Production Ratio	14.3	30.7	46.8
Net Direct Production Ratio	4.9	103.2	4.6
Income Received	8.2	149.3	16.8
Income Paid	2.6	68.0	9.6
License Royalties, etc. Received	10.2	38.0	2.8
License Royalties, etc. Paid	11.0	16.1	5.5
Net Direct Investment Income/GDP	0.1	0.8	0.4
Net Direct Investment Income/Investment Balance	3.0	6.0	4.0
Export Reliance	9.7	7.8	26.3
Import Reliance	7.2	12.4	26.3
Balance of Inward Direct Investment/GDP	1.1	27.7	23.6

Source: Takeuchi 2003.
Note: The figures are for 2000, except for the overseas production ratio for the United States, which refers to 1999.

Convergence occurred in the mix of products that are produced in Asia. By the mid-1990s, Japanese firms had joined their U.S. counterparts in moving a substantial portion of personal computer production to the region. Japanese firms have also jumped onto the bandwagon of OEM (original equipment manufacturing) contracts that provided substantial competitive advantages to U.S. computer companies.[16] Similarly, U.S. firms were the first to take advantage of the growing concentrations of expertise in various areas of electronics production in East Asia by transferring increasing responsibility for engineering and electronic design to subsidiaries (Ernst 2004). Again, this has proved to be a cost-effective strategy that some Japanese firms were beginning to emulate starting in the mid-1990s. The new responsibilities devolved to Japanese subsidiaries have inevitably required changes in management practices that have brought them closer to their American counterparts (Ernst 2000).

Yet, important differences persist in the organization of Japanese EAPNs. An important reason for this persistent diversity is that Japan continues to lag behind the United States in its integration into the global economy (table 7.1). This truncated integration into the global economy constrains any convergence of Japanese networks with the U.S. model. As long as Japan continues to trail behind in its overseas production ratios and especially in its net direct investment income, Japanese firms will remain under pressure to min-

---

[16] During the early 1980s, when the U.S. dollar appreciated rapidly, cash-strapped American firms were the first to experiment with new forms of international production outsourcing (Ernst 1997).

imize risks by centralizing management control in the parent company, and by relying heavily on the parent and other long-standing partners for the supply of capital goods and components.

Dispersed Location

Until the mid-1980s, affiliates of Japanese electronics firms were more geographically dispersed across Asia than U.S. ones, due to their primary focus on protected local markets. Once the focus shifted to export-platform production, locational patterns converged: both Japanese and U.S. electronics firms invested heavily in megaplants in a few industrial sites in Malaysia, Taiwan, Singapore, and Thailand. Since the turn of the new century, attempts to be more selective have gained momentum. Japanese firms are now attempting to gain scale economies through consolidation of investment in China and to catch up with global competitors in the penetration of the China market.

A huge investment gap remains in the China market between U.S., European, and Korean companies, on the one hand, and Japanese companies, on the other. The first group has focused on consolidating much of its global production in China, serving both the Chinese and global markets, and hence maximizing both economies of scale and scope. In contrast, as a share of Japan's accumulated stock of FDI, China still lags substantially behind Asian NIEs and ASEAN-4 (table 7.2).

In China, Japanese electronics firms have invested in production much earlier than U.S., European, and Korean companies, but they were constrained, because the Chinese government did not allow foreign firms to invest in the final-product manufacturing of electronics products except for a few export-oriented joint ventures, primarily by Hitachi and Sanyo (Marukawa 2002, 184–87).[17] This is why, during the "China fever" between 1991 and 1995, Japanese electronics firms in China concentrated on the production of key components for the consumer electronics industry. By providing key components such as cathode ray tubes, compressors, and integrated circuits to Chinese set makers, and by assisting their integrated circuit design, Japanese firms supported the development of technological capabilities by Chinese firms that are now industry leaders, such as Haier, Konka, TCL, and others.

Japanese electronics firms, however, were unable to enjoy first-comers' advantages, such as Shanghai Volkswagen did for cars, and they failed to establish strong positions in China's final-product markets. This is true even for consumer electronics, a market that Japanese firms dominate in Southeast

---

[17] Until 1994, the domestic market was reserved for Chinese state-owned enterprises and virtually closed to foreign companies.

Table 7.2. Japanese foreign direct investment stock, by destination, 2002

NIEs[a]	$24.9 billion
ASEAN–4[b]	$18.78 billion
China	$12.48 billion

Source: Compiled for JETRO 2003.
[a]Singapore, Taiwan, Korea.
[b]Malaysia, Thailand, Indonesia, Philippines.

Asia. It thus made perfect economic sense for Japanese firms to sustain a dual production base both in Southeast Asia and in China. Today, this dispersion of production networks across Asia has become a major disadvantage, as it prevents Japanese firms from reaping cost-reducing scale economies in China.

Attempts to shift the center of gravity of Japanese EAPNs from ASEAN to China are constrained by a deeply entrenched history of Japanese management trying to shelter the company from risks and uncertainties (Tachiki 1999, 186).[18] Japanese firms are concerned that once they move most of their investment to China, their profitability will suffer, as they become unduly dependent on an array of perceived disadvantages and risks of investing in China. A major concern is that the legal framework and the tax system are opaque, and that both are prone to frequent, sudden, and unpredictable changes. Equally important are concerns about the absence of effective intellectual property rights protection, difficulties in raising local investment funds, and delays in the collection of account receivables, while Japanese firms are requested to settle accounts immediately. Japanese electronics firms are also concerned about an industry structure that gives rise to "excessive" competition and periodic overheating, and a tendency to shirk WTO regulations and to introduce hidden nontariff barriers (JBICI 2003, 34).

A fourth major area of concern is the availability of local managers and engineers and labor relations. Japanese electronics firms are concerned that the rising cost of managers and engineers in China may soon reduce the cost advantage relative to other locations in Asia.[19] Frequent complaints include high employee turnover, a low level of basic factory skills, and conflicts about wage level gaps between Japanese staff and Chinese workers. Because of these perceived difficulties and risks, Japanese electronics firms typically are very

[18] A typical example is Sony's "two-plant policy" that tries to avoid, at almost any cost, being dependent on only one centralized plant for a particular macroregion (Form 20 F report 2003).
[19] Japanese subsidiaries in China report that "in order . . . not to lose skilled managerial and technical personnel to other companies, we are paying them like we would Japanese employees. We are also giving favorable treatment for transportation and housing" (JBICI 2003, 39, 43).

reluctant to move from dispersed Asian production networks to concentrated networks within China. Risk minimization, in other words, limits the pursuit of vertical specialization, and this sets Japanese companies apart from their American and European counterparts.

But there are signs of a possible reversal: Japanese FDI into China, which had stagnated in value since FY 1995, increased again for the first time in FY 2000 (JETRO 2002b, 35).[20] Since then, Japanese FDI inflows into China have accelerated, rising almost 60 percent in 2001, to $4.6 billion, the highest level to that point. And during the first six months of 2002, Japanese firms invested an additional $3.15 billion (JBICI 2003).[21] Like the first China fever in 1992, the appreciation of the yen has been a powerful catalyst. However, there are now additional attractions, such as substantial improvements in infrastructure and logistics, at least in China's three main growth poles; the signaling effect of China's WTO accession; the emergence of support industry clusters; and vast improvements in the quality of human resources, especially China's seven hundred thousand annual science and engineering graduates.

Sales Neglect of Asian Markets

A third persistent difference can be found in the contrasting sales destination of Japanese and American EAPNs (Takeuchi 2001). While Japanese electronics companies have moved from sales to local markets to third country exports, and now to reverse importing into Japan, U.S. companies have moved in the opposite direction: from a primary focus on reverse imports into the United States to an increasing emphasis on sales in Asia. Throughout the 1990s, a defining characteristic of Japanese EAPNs in the electronics industry has been the rapid rise of reverse imports into Japan—more than 60 percent of Japan's imports from Asia are imports from Japanese subsidiaries (METI 2002b).

By the turn of the century, Asia replaced the United States as the main

[20] In the ASEAN region, Japanese firms over the last few years have concentrated primarily on financial consolidation and on the rationalization of supply chains and distribution channels. There have also been attempts to upgrade existing subsidiaries toward flexible mass production of products that, while no longer competitive in Japan, are considered to be too risky to transfer to China because of quality or intellectual property protection concerns. Overall, however, Japanese FDI in the ASEAN region is unlikely to expand: a "wait-and-see" approach is combined with selective upgrading of some major operations.

[21] Examples of this renewed inflow of Japanese FDI include NEC's decision to shift 70% of its cell phone production to China; Sanyo's decision to concentrate all air conditioner production in China; Canon's $80 million investment in Suzhou, producing copiers; Sony's investments in new notebook computer production lines; Toshiba's decision to build a very large production line for laptops in Hangzhou, and to transfer a substantial part of its digital TV set production; and Matsushita's $26 million investments in two new plants that produce semiconductors for homes appliances.

source of Japanese imports for computers, semiconductors, and electronic components. For semiconductors, Japan's import dependence ratio[22] grew rapidly, from below 20 percent in 1991 to around 50 percent in 1999. This was primarily due to foundry contracts and contract manufacturing arrangements for semiconductors, primarily with Taiwanese and Singaporean firms. By 2000, Asia accounted for over 60 percent of Japan's semiconductor imports, while the share from the United States had fallen to around 30 percent. This has resulted in a dramatic reversal of Japan's trade balance with Asia in the electronics industry, from a surplus to a deficit.

The Japan-centered sales destination has resulted in another major weakness of Japanese EAPNs: a lack of aggressive strategic marketing to address the specific requirements of East Asian markets (e.g., Meyer-Ohle and Hirasawa 2000). Japanese firms are on the defensive in practically all important electronic market segments across Asia, and they are now belatedly searching for ways to repair the damage of earlier inaction. Throughout Asia, and especially in China, Japanese electronics firms have failed to develop and exploit unique market positions. In consumer electronics, for instance, Japanese majors like Sony and Matsushita have been caught in price wars with the dominant local players, while in the high-end markets they are lagging behind Korean and European set makers, such as Samsung, LG, and Philips. And for computing and communication devices, Japanese firms seem to be in a bind. On the one hand they have difficulties advancing into the new product, software, and service markets developed by U.S. leaders, for example, the Internet, e-business, advanced microprocessors, and operating systems for an increasing variety of digital devices. On the other hand, for price-sensitive devices, such as laptops and mobile phones, Japanese firms are being squeezed by global brand leaders from the United States, Europe, and Korea, which are outsourcing manufacturing and design to low-cost suppliers of EMS (electronic manufacturing service) and ODM (original-design manufacturing) services. The Japanese are also being squeezed by Chinese set makers that can gain access to the latest product technology, say for smart phones, by licensing reference designs and so-called silicon intellectual properties, the building blocks that facilitate system-on-chip design (Ernst 2005a).

In China specifically, Japanese electronics firms need to differentiate themselves from their increasingly important Asian (primarily Korean and Chinese) competitors. Debates on how to improve their market position emphasize that it is necessary to "maintain non-price competitiveness in areas where differentiation is possible in terms of technology and know-how" (Konomoto 2002, 8). But accomplishing this will not be an easy task. Take China's mobile communications market, which has experienced exponential

---

[22] Import dependence = imports/(production − exports + imports).

growth, tripling in value between 1998 and 2002. Reflecting China's WTO membership obligations, foreign companies can establish joint ventures in China as of January 2003, for mobile phones, data communications, fixed telephones, and international telephone services. Furthermore, China's government is expected to introduce 3G mobile phone service during 2005.

To succeed in China's telecommunications market, global companies must be willing to share their accumulated experience in providing "integrated solutions" for complex technology systems. According to Davies et al. (2001, 5), "integrated solutions" encompass four sets of capabilities: (1) system integration: designing and integrating components and subsystems into a system; (2) operational services: maintaining, financing, renovating, and operating systems through the life cycle; (3) business consulting: understanding a customer's business and offering advice and solutions that address a customer's specific needs; and (4) finance: providing a customer with help in purchasing new capital-intensive systems and in managing a customer's installed base of capital assets. By and large, U.S. and European electronics firms have sophisticated and proven strategies in place that can provide these four critical support services.

Japanese firms (both equipment vendors and service providers) lag well behind their rivals from the United States and Europe in the penetration of China's communications markets. For instance, NEC and Matsushita Communications Industrial established a joint venture to develop 3G mobile handsets at the end of 2001. But as this venture was about to become operational during 2003, price competition had already drastically increased for mobile handsets. Intense price competition is driven primarily by purely Chinese manufacturers such as Ningbo Bird, TCL, Legend, and others that can provide low-cost handsets, based on key components and reference designs that they have licensed from global platform leaders such as Ericsson, Texas Instruments, and Philips. In short, Japanese firms may have again missed the opportunity to reap first-mover windfall profits.

There are several reasons why Japanese firms have made little headway in penetrating China's emerging "systems solutions" markets. Probably of greatest importance are constraints imposed by the Japanese production system that prevent Japanese electronics firms from sharing "integrated solutions" capabilities. As convincingly demonstrated by Yoshihara (2000, 67–68), Japanese parent companies typically insist on an (almost) exact replication of plant layout, quality control, and management routines in overseas subsidiaries, and they exercise tight control over capabilities required for "integrated solutions." This unwillingness to share the basic ingredients of the Japanese production system with outsiders has become a major stumbling block for Japanese penetration strategies into the China market.

Human Resources Management

Human resources management (HRM) used to be considered a major advantage of the Japanese business model (e.g., Dore 1986; Aoki 1988; Nonaka and Takeuchi 1995; Fruin 1997). Somewhat ironically, it has now become an important weakness. No other factor arguably constrains Japanese electronics firms in East Asia more than their very limited capacity to recruit, develop, and benefit from non-Japanese skilled workers, engineers, and managers. In China, for instance, European and American firms put enormous energy and money into training Chinese staff and promoting them on the corporate ladder. Japanese companies have instead bred "China experts"—Japanese fluent in Chinese who have studied Chinese business practice and behavior. These Japanese managers maintain a firm grip on the business and keep their Chinese colleagues at a distance.

Typically, Japanese companies manage their Asian subsidiaries in a top-down, bureaucratic way. The main objective is to make sure that the subsidiary responds faithfully to orders from Japan, which requires taskmaster managers. Existing organizational structures and incentives do not help to breed initiative and innovation. Such a top-down HRM approach worked as long as the main objective was to exploit low labor costs. Typically, Asian subsidiaries produced lower-end, commodity-type products to a given design, and they provided a narrower range of products and services than in Japan. As a result, it was relatively easy for Japanese expatriate managers to convey the wishes of headquarters' management to the shop floor. The main task was to achieve results, and there was not much need to listen to local subordinates. This system provides very little flexibility, however: without the Japanese expatriates, the subsidiaries cannot function. As Japanese managers make most decisions among themselves, they "often find themselves making decisions based on hearsay (e.g., about what strategies rivals may have adopted) and guesses (e.g., about what customers may be thinking)" (Konomoto 2000, 9).[23]

I experienced a vivid example of this system during an interview in November 2002 with the general manager of a subsidiary of one of the largest Japanese electronics conglomerates in China. As he spoke only Japanese, he brought along two interpreters, one to translate between Japanese and English, to communicate with me, and the other to communicate with his six

---

[23] This can have disastrous effects. For instance, Sony's critically important release of its PlayStation 2 game console in China was delayed by an embarrassing miscommunication with the Chinese government. Although the Chinese Ministry of Culture classifies the PS2 as a gaming machine, Sony registered it as an electronics product, and hence did not get the required approval in time for the 2003 Christmas season. It took Sony a few weeks to correct its mistake (*Interfax China IT & Telecom Weekly*, January 31, 2004, p. 3)

Chinese middle managers (representing the main functions of the subsidiary, such as sales, production, quality control, R & D, procurement). Under these conditions, communication was not easy and required a quite extraordinary amount of concentration on all sides. Fortunately enough, the Japanese general manager was mild mannered and had a good sense of humor. But what was supposed to be a standard hour and a half interview required almost three hours. Even then, we had not achieved what we wanted to discuss, but all participants agreed to end the interview due to sheer exhaustion.

Such communication barriers are ever present in Japanese subsidiaries in Asia: "The cultural and linguistic gap between expatriate Japanese managers and local employees has obscured the latter's true feelings from the former" (Konomoto 2000, 10), giving rise to misunderstandings and mutual recriminations. This has had a negative impact on local staff morale. In addition, obscure selection criteria for choosing local senior managers, and persistent glass ceilings for non-Japanese managers, de-motivate local employees: "Veteran employees arrange with each other to do the minimum amount of work necessary and wait for instructions rather than volunteer suggestions" (Konomoto 2000, 6). Japanese subsidiaries are especially weak in motivating higher-skilled local employees with scarce skills: "The greater the educational qualifications of employees . . . , the more they tended to be dissatisfied with the company's merit orientation" (Konomoto 2000, 6). Unsurprisingly, such employees tend to search for quick financial gains, especially in the highly competitive skilled labor markets of China.

An important reason for these communication barriers is that headquarters management in Japan fails to examine the motivations of local managers and engineers, which shape the corporate culture of Japanese subsidiaries. This gives rise to a vicious circle. Because of an unwillingness to promote local managers to top positions and because of the operation of a seniority system that inhibits rapid promotion, Japanese companies have found it difficult to recruit and retain quality managers and engineers in their Asian subsidiaries. Japanese managers typically argue that they cannot feel confident about increasing the role of local management "because the skill level of locally recruited managers is low" (JBICI 2001, 68). They continue to have great difficulties in Asia in recruiting top technical talents and local managers. Linguistic barriers are one important reason: the capacity to speak Japanese is often a prerequisite for hiring local managers, but Asian managers prefer to learn English.[24]

---

[24] For local employees, knowledge of Japanese can be a double-edged sword. On the one hand, it might foster their chances to move up the carrier ladder, even if other skills are missing. On the other hand, these local employees tend to be used as troubleshooters and frequently get caught in the middle of conflicts between shop floor workers and senior Japanese managers, who often cannot communicate directly. As a result, they find it difficult to concentrate on improving

Another reason is the negative image of Japanese firms as employers of skilled labor. Surveys have shown that most Asian managers consider working conditions and promotion opportunities in U.S. subsidiaries to be far more favorable, placing Japanese subsidiaries at a competitive disadvantage. The rapid expansion of the electronics industry in Asia has offered high-caliber personnel the opportunity to change employers. Extensive job-hopping is the name of the game, a phenomenon that Japanese corporations have found alien.

To address this problem, Japanese electronics firms have adopted a strategy of in-house training of their engineers. Based on a careful selection process, an affiliate in Asia develops a pool of highly motivated operators who are then trained over a period of five to seven years to become (sometimes unlicensed) engineers. In this manner, engineering skills are made firm-specific, reducing the likelihood of job-hopping behavior.[25] The disadvantage, however, is that this requires a lot of time. Most important, this reliance on internal recruitment gives rise to an increasingly serious failure to compete for the best local management and engineering talents across the region, who could provide new ideas and a fresh commitment to upgrade Japanese EAPNs.

Japanese electronics firms recognize that they must drastically change their human resources management practices in East Asia. They are searching for ways to catch up with more open, flexible, and decentralized HRM approaches of global industry leaders, including those of Korean and Taiwanese competitors. Japanese firms know that without such changes in HRM, "any competition strategy they have will prove ineffective" (Konomoto 2000, 1). After years of hesitation, Japanese firms are now eager to tap into East Asia's huge pool of lower-cost managers and engineers to facilitate and accelerate decision making, and to cope with the frantic pace of change in Asian business practices, values, and ways of thinking (JETRO 2003c, 33).

Necessary changes in HRM include the introduction of transparent performance evaluation criteria, adapted to local routines and labor market regulations, and career perspectives that match those of competing U.S., European, and Asian firms. Above all, local staff needs to become an integral part of the decision-making process and of the search for solutions to problems. Furthermore, local managers need to be groomed for and transferred to global positions, like Motorola does, for instance, when it sends the general manager of its Penang subsidiary to manage its newly established Chinese facilities.[26] This high interfirm and geographic mobility of local senior man-

---

their specialist skills, while at the same time becoming the objects of jealousy from their local coworkers.

[25] Information provided by Dennis Tachiki.

[26] Incidentally, this general manager, P. Y. Lai, used to head Intel's Penang facility in 1992 when I interviewed him in that position, which indicates the breadth of his exposure to leading-edge management practices by U.S. global industry leaders.

agers that work for U.S. global network flagships contrasts with the Japanese approach of promoting the intrafirm transfer of (overwhelmingly) Japanese managers.

R & D Management

Before the mid-1990s, Japanese corporations undertook little R & D in their East Asian subsidiaries. This contrasts with U.S. subsidiaries whose parent companies increasingly delegated responsibility for product design and development to them, in some instances not only for local but for global markets. By the turn of the century, R & D continued to play a limited role in the EAPNs of Japanese firms, compared to those of North America and the European Union. But as East Asian customers become increasingly demanding, Japanese firms can no longer rely on products designed in Japan to penetrate Asian markets. Instead, localization of design and engineering is necessary to customize products and services and to accelerate speed of response to changes in demand. Successful market penetration in East Asia thus requires a break with established patterns in R & D management.

Yet we have seen that Japanese firms continue to assign a low priority to an expansion of R & D in East Asia. This reflects a defensive bias of Japanese R & D management: intellectual property rights protection and restrictions on royalty payments are the predominant concern. This is in stark contrast to R & D management in American electronics companies where value creation through aggressive commercialization of a company's intellectual property rights now has become the top priority. Leading competitors in the United States, Europe, and Korea have aggressively moved ahead with R & D outsourcing to tap into the region's vast lower-cost pool of human resources and specialized skills. Japanese firms thus need to complement intellectual property rights protection with a consistent strategy of relocating more R & D to major new clusters in East Asia (e.g., Walsh 2003).

However, after a long period of being reluctant to do so, Japanese firms are finally investing in R & D centers, both in China and Southeast Asia, and the focus is shifting from product customization and process adjustment to chip design and software services.[27] However, retaining control over core production technologies remains a dominant concern, reflecting fears that Japan's competitiveness might be eroded by production technologies leaking over-

---

[27] The number of Japanese R & D affiliates in the region covered by the JBICI surveys has increased by 102%, from thirty-nine (in FY 2000) to seventy-nine (in FY 2002). Yet, this compares with ninety-two R & D affiliates in North America and seventy in the European Union (2002). China again has experienced the fastest growth: the number of Japanese R & D affiliates there increased by 115%, from thirteen to twenty-eight.

seas (JETRO 2003c, 44).[28] This reluctance to penetrate aggressively Asia's emerging technology markets runs counter to important long-term interests of Japanese electronics firms. As Takeuchi (2003, 17) demonstrates, Japanese firms need to increase their revenues from both FDI and technology licensing, in order to compensate for declining export revenues. Some Japanese industry leaders have developed robust leadership positions in key technologies such as system-on-chip design, liquid crystal and plasma displays, and nanotechnology.[29] This should help them to bear the risks of relocating some parts of R & D to East Asia.

Hybridization—Partnering with Asian Companies

Japanese electronics firms are now searching for ways to readjust their production, distribution, and innovation networks to cope with the opportunities and challenges resulting from the increasingly complex regionalization in a radically changed East Asia. This constitutes a fundamental change in Japanese corporate strategy and organization. At long last, Japanese electronics firms appear ready to accept that they are no longer capable of imposing an unequal flying geese division of labor on East Asia. Equally important, the belief in the innate superiority of the Japanese business model has become an endangered species—Japanese electronics firms are all trying to emulate successful features not only of American and European rivals but also of leading Korean, Taiwanese, and Chinese firms. For the first time, Japanese electronics firms are now also using successful Asian firms, such as Samsung, LG, Acer (BenQ), Hon Hai, Haier, and TCL as benchmark examples to reformulate their regional networking strategies. And they are searching for ways to develop strategic partnerships with emerging new industry leaders in Asia, most prominently with Chinese companies.

Some Japanese firms are belatedly following the partnering strategies pio-

---

[28] A unifying theme of current Japanese R & D strategies that shows up in many annual reports and strategy papers is the concept of "black box" technologies. Matsushita defines them as technologies "that cannot be easily imitated by competitors because they are (1) protected under intellectual property rights, such as patents; (2) made of complex materials, processes, and know-how that cannot be copied; or (3) made using unique production methods, systems or control technologies "(Matsushita Annual Report 2003, 7). And Sharp, one of the most innovative Japanese electronics companies, believes that protecting technologies through patents alone is insufficient, and that the key to success is to maintain exclusive control of manufacturing technologies by "concealing them more assiduously than product technologies" (JETRO 2003, 44).

[29] For instance, NEC, the leader in R & D among the nine major Japanese electronics corporations, is a world leader in nanotechnology research, having invented the carbon nanotube that will be the basis for extremely lightweight computer display screens and miniscule and orders-of-magnitude more efficient semiconductors.

neered by such global industry leaders as Motorola, Intel, IBM, Cisco, Alcatel, Philips, Siemens, Infineon, as well as Korea's Big Four (Samsung, LG, SK Telecom, and KT), Singapore's Temasek, and Taiwan's industry leaders.[30] Particularly instructive is a partnership between Sanyo and Haier (announced in January 2002) that shows signs of a radical break with the tradition of unequal ("vertical") forms of collaboration, where the Japanese partner dominates, to a "horizontal" relationship among equals. As the first attempt by a major Japanese electronics company to establish a comprehensive business alliance with a Chinese industry leader, the Sanyo-Haier agreement has been hailed by METI as the new "standard for Japan-China business relationships. . . . Rather than antagonizing Chinese players, Japanese businesses should team up with them to share profits in mutual markets."[31] But this agreement has also encountered "an enormous number of protests from various sides,"[32] indicating the still substantial resistance of Japanese firms to changes in their China strategies.

The Sanyo-Haier agreement has four components: (1) sales of Sanyo products in China under Sanyo and Haier brand names through Haier's distribution network; (2) sales of Haier products in Japan through a joint venture in Japan, with Sanyo owing 60 percent and Haier 40 percent; (3) a new Sanyo factory to be built next to Haier's huge refrigerator factory in Tsingtao, to supply Haier with Sanyo's leading-edge compressors; and, most important, (4) technological collaboration across a broad range of key components.

For Sanyo, important benefits include privileged access to Haier's vast sales network in China, the largest of any electronics company.[33] Additional attractions are Haier's market leadership across a broad product portfolio;[34] Haier's state-of-the-art production system; and, most important, a highly motivated and well-trained workforce (with a high share of engineers and managers trained in the United States) that is exposed to strictly enforced performance-based evaluation and incentives. Sanyo's CEO, Satoshi Iue (the son of the company's founder), was greatly impressed during an earlier visit to a massive Haier Group plant that is four times larger than his company's largest factory.[35] He was particularly impressed by Haier's ability to purchase

---

[30] Although large Taiwanese firms such as Hon Hai, Acer, and Mitac are constrained by government regulations, they have been highly innovative in developing indirect and informal partnerships with Chinese firms.

[31] "Sanyo–Haier Group Alliance Offers Lucrative Foothold," *Nikkei Weekly*, January 15, 2002.

[32] "China Alliance Brings Opportunity, Problems," *Yomiuri Shimbun*, September 23, 2002.

[33] Haier's sales network consists of forty-two subsidiaries, nine thousand sales locations, and almost twelve thousand service locations.

[34] In addition to refrigerators, home air conditioners, washing machines, and vacuum cleaners, in which Haier is the market leader, the company also has moved aggressively into higher value-added digital consumer and communication devices.

[35] *Asahi Shimbun* 2002a. "Deal Sees Sanyo, Haier as Equals," January 10, 2002.

the sort of expensive, leading-edge machinery (primarily from European suppliers) that is beyond the reach of Japanese manufacturers, due to their financial difficulties.[36]

For Haier, in turn, the main attraction has been Sanyo's willingness to sell and support its products in the Japanese market, a first in the notoriously closed Japanese market. Haier understands that it will take time to overcome the resistance of Japanese customers, because of the persistent "low quality" image of Chinese products. But it expects to use Sanyo's decision to support its products in the famously difficult Japanese market to enhance its brand recognition in other markets, including the increasingly demanding Chinese market. Although several leading Japanese firms had been courting Haier, it appears that no other company was willing to follow Sanyo's offer of a comprehensive business alliance that includes broad-based technological cooperation.

Arguably the most interesting development is a new sense of urgency on the part of Sanyo managers to make a serious effort to overcome communication problems with their Chinese counterparts, and to adjust to modern Chinese business practices. Symptomatic is the approach taken by the thirty-five-year-old president of the Sanyo-Haier joint venture.[37] He admits that this comprehensive business alliance is "a new type of project that Sanyo has no experience with. Dealing with the Chinese style of business creates problems I've never faced before, but . . . I am comfortable with it and enjoy this challenge." To illustrate this, he told the following story:

> The Chinese way of starting business is to take orders regardless of their capabilities to fill the orders at the time. When they are asked to do something, the Chinese normally respond by saying, "It can be done." This means an absolute commitment in Japan, but in China it is used to express one's eagerness to do business. . . . In such a situation, the Japanese would respond by saying, "We'll take it back to our office to determine whether we can accept the job." In the beginning, we trusted our Chinese counterpart's words and began doing our part. After a while, we found out our partner could not live up to its part of the agreement. *That was our mistake—we should have been aware it was the Chinese way of getting orders, and we shouldn't have taken their first response as a full commitment. . . . I have finally come to understand that they are not malicious. . . . I* admire the eagerness and aggressiveness of the Chinese toward business. The Japanese tend to be too humble and uncertain when doing business. The Chi-

---

[36] Machine-tool orders placed with Japanese firms totaled ¥790 billion in 2001, down 19% from a year earlier. As recently as 1997, this figure exceeded ¥1 trillion (METI figures, quoted in *Asahi Shimbun* 2002b. "Machine Tools: A Shrinking Domestic Market," February 6, 2002).

[37] Toshiaki Iue, president of the Sanyo-Haier joint venture and son of Sanyo's CEO, as quoted in "China Alliance Brings Opportunity, Problems," *Yomiuri Shimbun*, September 23, 2002.

nese are more determined, and I think that has led to their recent economic growth. (emphasis added)

This chapter has demonstrated that, far from withdrawing from East Asia, Japanese corporate capital in the electronics industry now critically depends on the region, not only as a global export production base but also as a major and increasingly sophisticated market for its products, services, and technology, and as a source of lower-cost knowledge workers. This explains why Japanese electronics firms are searching for ways to expand and upgrade their regional distribution, production, and R & D networks, with a particular focus on China. These networks will continue to affect Asian regionalization patterns, but their impact will now differ from earlier periods. I have shown, for instance, that Japan's trade links with Asia have shifted from surplus to deficit, and that important changes have occurred in the composition of traded products. Japanese firms continue to be a major source of components and machinery. They also continue to play an important role as providers of shop-floor management techniques for Asian suppliers (e.g., quality control and supply chain management). But in many other areas of management, Japanese firms now play second fiddle.

We have seen that Japanese firms are finding it difficult to make the adjustments in organization and management that are necessary to expand and upgrade their regional networks. I have highlighted five peculiar features of the Japanese network management model in East Asia that once may have been strengths but now have turned into systemic weaknesses: persistent diversity of organization; dispersed location driven by risk minimization; Japan-centered sales destination and a neglect of local market characteristics; a limited capacity to tap the creativity of non-Japanese skilled workers, engineers, and managers; and a reluctance to outsource R & D.

I have also identified equally important *exogenous* forces. In the electronics industry, firms of diverse nationality compete and collaborate within multi-layered global "networks of networks" of marketing, production, and innovation. This has forced Japanese firms into dense interaction with a multitude of firms from the United States as well as from East Asia's leading electronics exporting countries. A second critical exogenous force has been the rise of China as a global export production base, as a sophisticated growth market, especially for mobile communications and digital consumer devices, and as a new source of R & D and innovation. Both forces have produced increasingly complex processes of regionalization. And they are both unlikely to fade away. Increasingly, global networks are being extended beyond manufacturing into the production of knowledge-intensive services, such as software, information services, engineering, product development, and research (Ernst 2005a), creating ever more fine-grained patterns of East Asian specialization. And while periodic hard or soft landings may slow down China's growth, the country is unlikely to lose its role as an engine of regionalization (Ernst, Guerrieri, and Iammarino 2005).

To cope with the new challenges they are facing in a radically changing East Asia, Japanese firms are now beginning to emulate successful features of Korean, Taiwanese, and Chinese business models. Belatedly, some Japanese firms are now attempting to develop more equal partnerships with emerging new industry leaders in Asia, primarily from Greater China. This outlier behavior may act as a powerful catalyst for change. The key to successful alliances with Asian partners is hybridization of business organization beyond national models, where Japanese firms adopt successful features of East Asian firms. In this sense, Asianization of production networks may be in the process of superseding in the longer run the battle between Japanization and Americanization.

8

Regional Shrimp, Global Trees, Chinese Vegetables: The Environment in Japan–East Asia Relations

DEREK HALL

It was inevitable that the death of the Showa Emperor should have occasioned a deluge of reflection on Japan's place in the modern world. Hirohito's reign, which began in 1926, covered a staggering range of experience in Japan, and his death came just as the country seemed, finally, to have "caught up" with the West and to be making a play for regional or even global hegemony. That the end of the Showa era became a locus for debate over Japan's past and future is thus no surprise. It is perhaps more remarkable that it destabilized the global shrimp trade. In the period between Hirohito's collapse in September 1988 and his funeral in February of the following year—five and a half months that "were lived with particular intensity by most Japanese" (Field 1991, xv)—Japan's entertainment industry went into a profound slump. With luxuries inappropriate during a period of national mourning, shrimp consumption fell off sharply. The consequent crash in prices made itself felt across the vast swaths of coastal Southeast Asia that had, over the previous five years, been converted into shrimp ponds to feed Japanese demand, which was pumped up on *endaka* (high yen) and *baburu* (the bubble). Hirohito's death

For their very helpful comments and suggestions, I would like to thank the editors; the other participants in the Kyoto and Honolulu workshops, particularly Dieter Ernst, Peter Gourevitch, and Miles Kahler; an anonymous reviewer for Cornell University Press; participants in the 2003 annual meeting of the German Association for Social Science Research on Japan at Tutzing, Germany, especially Verena Blechinger and Klaus Vollmer; and Paul Gellert and Eric Helleiner. All errors are my own.

not only drew the curtain on the Showa era; it also marked the end of the golden age of Southeast Asian shrimp farming.

This episode provides a useful window onto the transformations in Southeast Asian environments brought about by bubble-era Japanese demand. In the late 1980s, even more than today, intensive shrimp farming was a risky, gold rush–style endeavor—a "prawndike" (*Business World* 1996)—with severe environmental consequences. It was bad enough that large areas of environmentally critical mangrove swamps were cleared to make way for this boom crop (Menasveta 1997), but insult was added to injury when production in the new ponds was abandoned after a few short years as a result of the disease and pollution problems that shrimp farms caused themselves (Skladany and Harris 1995). This sense of out-of-control Japanese demand wreaking havoc on Southeast Asian environments was repeated in other sectors, such as the eucalyptus plantations being planned in hopes of exporting wood chips to Japan, and the resort developments that razed hills and used vast amounts of chemicals and fresh water to lure Japanese tourists with weekends of cheap golf.

In this chapter I seek to use the insights that can be gleaned from these and other sectors to examine the place of natural resources and environmental change in the restructuring of Japan's relations with Asia. This question may be approached from a number of directions. Most straightforwardly, Japan-oriented shrimp farming, tree plantations, and tourism in Southeast Asia during the late 1980s expanded the role of "resource hinterland" for Japan that American postwar planners assigned the region in the wake of World War II and the Communist revolution in China (Borden 1984; Cumings 1987). The resource needs of the Japanese political economy, whether for food, fiber, fuel, or minerals, far outstrip the capacities of the archipelago. Providing for these needs has been a constant challenge for the Japanese (Ciccantell and Bunker 2002), and has, historically, implied a deepening engagement with Southeast Asia by Japanese firms and the state, as well as a growing regional orientation toward the Japanese market.

Shrimp, eucalyptus, and golf have also, however, required the reorganization of Southeast Asian ecosystems, with significant consequences for the people who depend on them, who in many cases were relocated by force to allow Japan-oriented production to take place. There is an extensive literature on the environmental damage done outside of Japan by the Japanese political economy, that is, on Japan's "shadow ecology."[1] In his study of Japan's timber trade with Southeast Asia, Peter Dauvergne defines "shadow ecology" as "the aggregate environmental impact on resources outside its territory of govern-

---

[1] This term originates in MacNeill, Winsemius, and Yakushiji 1991; for an early application to Japan, see Maull 1991.

ment practices, especially official development assistance (ODA); corporate conduct, investment and technology transfers; and trade, including consumption, export and consumer prices, and import tariffs" (Dauvergne 1997, 2–3). Examples include the impact of Japanese consumption on global fisheries and the deforestation caused by Japan's appetite for wood. Here again, the countries of Southeast Asia, and especially Indonesia, Malaysia, the Philippines, and Thailand, have been at the heart of the most contentious issues surrounding Japan's shadow ecology. The interaction between regionalization and the related concepts of "resource hinterland" and "shadow ecology" has involved increasing participation by Japan in Asian production, increasing orientation toward the Japanese market by regional states and firms, and the accompanying transformations of local social and ecological relations.

Japan's environmental impact in Asia inspired a great deal of intellectual effort by activists, academics, and policymakers in the years around 1990. Almost fifteen years after Hirohito's death, however, the events of the bubble era continue to frame our understanding of Japan's Asian shadow ecology. This is true despite the dramatic changes that have taken place since the bubble. Most obviously, after more than a decade of economic stagnation the Japanese are much more likely to be berated on the world stage for not consuming enough than for consuming too much. The domestic Japanese economy has seen wide-ranging restructuring, and regional trade patterns have been profoundly altered by globalization, U.S.-led trade liberalization, and economic growth and agro-industrialization in Asia. Perhaps most strikingly, China, which barely makes an appearance in the literature on Japan's shadow ecology, has dramatically increased its share of Japan's trade in a number of resource-intensive sectors. Conceptions of the relationship between natural resources, environment, and regionalization, however, remain rooted in the era of the bubble and the first flush of endaka. The major aim of this chapter is to update this literature. Its main finding is that, with respect to renewable resources at any rate, Japan's need for an overseas shadow ecology has not led to a continued deepening of relations with Southeast Asia. Rather, Japan's shadow ecology has become more global, on the one hand, and more focused on China, on the other. I also argue that transformations in the organization of imports of renewable resources may mean that Japan's environmental impact on Asia may simultaneously be becoming greater and more difficult to perceive.

The concepts of resource hinterland and shadow ecology represent, then, two directions from which the interactions between environment, natural resources, and regionalization in Japan-Asia relations may be approached. The third perspective that I use draws on a growing interdisciplinary body of research on political ecology. This work has made the case that a proper social-scientific understanding of nature must go beyond simply examining the consequences of human actions for the environment. Rather, it must fully incorporate nature as an active force that shapes human behavior. The final section takes up this perspective to add a new "actor" to our understanding of regionalization in Asia, arguing that environmental change itself has implications for the spatial contours and organization of Japan's shadow ecology. In sectors such as shrimp farming and the timber trade, the environment has impacts on regional production and trade that are not ontologically reducible to the human actions and structures that are the focus of political economy.

I trace the changes in Japan's Asian resource hinterland, shadow ecology, and international political ecology since 1990 across a number of spatial scales—Japanese and Asian, local, national, regional and global. Given the scope of this task, I will limit my attention to Japan's imports of renewable resources (both raw and processed), that is, to the agricultural, fisheries, and wood-products sectors. I do not address the environmental aspects of Japanese and Japan-oriented industrial production in Asia, or of Japan's imports of such nonrenewable resources as oil and minerals. I have chosen these sectors for a number of reasons, including the availability of information (which, while limited, is more extensive than is data on the environmental impact of Japan's manufacturing FDI); the rapidity of spatial and organizational change; the possibility that environmental limits are close to being exceeded in some of these sectors; and the centrality of these sectors to the politics of Japan's shadow ecology. It is my hope that this focus will complement Stephen Bunker and Paul Ciccantell's ongoing research on Japan's nonrenewable resource imports (Bunker and Ciccantell 1995; Ciccantell and Bunker 2002).[2]

The analysis of Japan's Asian resource hinterland and shadow ecology begins with a brief overview of macrolevel trends in Japan's renewable resource

[2] The chapter also gives short shrift to three other forms of interaction between regionalization and the environment in Asia. The first of these is the way outrage over the destruction of the Southeast Asian environment for the benefit of Japanese consumers helped to promote networking efforts by Asian NGOs during the late 1980s and early 1990s (Asudei Nihon 1992; Nihon Bengoshi Rengokai 1991). Important regional links were formed around the issue of tropical timber, for instance, and opposition to Japanese golf tourism spawned GNAGA, the Global Network for Anti–Golf Course Action. Much of the motivation for regional networking against golf on the Japanese side was the concern that the success of anti-golf movements in Japan was pushing the export of a new kind of polluting industry to Asia (Paxton 1992, 22). Although I will not focus on these networks, I give them brief consideration in the conclusion. Second, and perhaps ironically, the Japanese government and some academics came to see Japan's experience of environmental catastrophe and cleanup during the 1970s as constituting an important model (often explicitly framed in "flying geese" terms) for Asian countries, and took steps to regionalize Japanese environmental policies, in part through environmental development assistance (Government of Japan 1991; Ueta 1995; Dauvergne 2001; Hall 2001). Finally, this period saw the beginnings of serious efforts at regional coordination and institution-building around environmental issues (Drifte 2003; Elliott 2003; Rozman 2001). All three of these questions would need to be considered in a fuller examination of the role of the environment in Japan-Asia relations.

imports since the early 1990s, and identifies four main explanations for these trends. First, domestic changes in Japan, notably shifts in consumption patterns and in retail, have altered Japanese demand for renewable-resource-intensive products. Second, I examine the impact of the interaction of trade and investment liberalization and Asian agro-industrialization on the ability of Asian countries to respond to this demand. Third, I discuss the dramatic rise of China as an exporter of renewable-resource-intensive products to Japan, with a particular focus on fresh and frozen vegetables and on wood products. Each of these sections highlights the important actors involved in these changes—states, firms, NGOs, consumers, and local people. Each also shows that while the processes of globalization, regionalization, Americanization, and Japanization highlighted in Peter Katzenstein's introduction are at work in reshaping Japan's shadow ecology, they are (as he notes) very difficult to disentangle. The final section takes up the themes of political ecology with respect to shrimp and timber, and of China's rapidly growing export-oriented organic vegetable production.

Macro Patterns in Japan's Renewable-Resource-Intensive Imports

Because most research on Japan's Asian shadow ecology took place in the late 1980s and early 1990s, the literature portrays Japan both as a large economy and as a rapidly growing one. The first of these characterizations is obviously still true, and Japanese demand continues to play a major role in any number of resource-intensive sectors in Asia, even as exploding Chinese demand bulks ever larger in shaping regional trade (Goodman 2004; Rohter 2004). The second, though, no longer applies: Japan's economy barely grew during the 1990s. Slow growth cannot be assumed, however, to translate directly into slowed consumption of, or imports of, particular products. Indeed, economic stagnation has in certain ways been an impetus to *increased* imports of resource-intensive products.

Japan's renewable-resource imports have long been characterized by a mix of spatial strategies, with some commodities sourced mainly from Asia while others are imported from around the globe. Japan's tropical timber, for instance, has mostly come from Southeast Asia (with Philippine production giving way to imports from Indonesia, Malaysia, and Papua New Guinea), while the United States and Canada have provided most temperate region wood. Japan's fish imports, and the activities of Japan's fishing industry, have been truly global, while imports of farmed shrimp have come primarily from a closely integrated aquaculture sector in Southeast Asia. When significant meat imports began in the 1980s, they came mostly from the United States and Australia, and the incipient trade in fresh and frozen vegetables involved primarily the United States and Taiwan. During the 1990s, some aspects of this import structure remained remarkably stable (whether in terms of quantities or of trade partners) while others saw dramatic change. Over a decade of economic stagnation, Japan's imports of wood products increased 7 percent (in dollar terms),[3] fish 33 percent, meat 60 percent, and vegetable imports roughly doubled.[4] The regional breakdown of Japan's food imports showed an increasing dependence on Asia. However, as of 2000, the first, third, and fourth-largest sources of Japan's $46 billion in food imports were non-Asian: the United States ($12.3 billion), Australia ($3.2 billion), and Canada ($2.6 billion). China placed second, with $6 billion, Thailand fifth ($2.3 billion) and South Korea sixth ($1.8 billion). China's meteoric rise as a food supplier to Japan is graphically illustrated in figure 8.1.

In the following paragraphs, I will examine changes in Japan's imports of a number of products that have been shown to have serious environmental impacts. In the seemingly quiescent wood products sector, slow import growth masks very significant changes. First, Japan's imports of primary tropical timber products[5] dropped precipitously. Most notable is the change in tropical log imports, the product category that was at the center of attacks on Japan's timber imports in the 1980s (Nectoux and Kuroda 1990). Japan's 1991 imports of 10 million cubic meters of tropical logs were already well down from the peaks of the 1970s, but by 2002 the figure had fallen more than 80 percent to 1.67 million cubic meters. Indeed, Japan has dropped to third place in world imports of tropical logs behind China and Taiwan. Tropical plywood has substituted for some log imports since first Indonesia (in 1985) and then Sabah (1993) banned log exports, but this trade has not grown enough to fully compensate.[6] Rather, temperate region logs and new products are picking up the slack.

Second, there were major changes in the geography of Japan's timber trade. Figure 8.2 gives only a highly aggregated sense of current developments, but emphasizes the fall in the share of the United States in Japan's

---

[3] Expressing these figures in dollar terms has certain fundamental drawbacks, not only because of fluctuations in currency values but also because environmental degradation is more likely to be related to the bulk of the commodity extracted than it is to its dollar value. However, few statistical organizations keep records for such aggregated categories as "fish" by weight. Changes over time in the kinds of fish, wood, and food products imported can mean that the trajectories of the value and tonnage of goods imported can diverge widely: a shift, for instance, from imports of feed grain for cattle to imports of beef will increase the dollar value of food imports while reducing the weight.

[4] Unless otherwise noted, commodity trade statistics cited in this chapter are taken from the UN's Commodity Trade Statistics, available at http://unstats.un.org/unsd/comtrade/.

[5] That is, logs, sawn wood, veneer, and plywood from International Tropical Timber Organization producer countries, with the preponderance coming from Indonesia and Malaysia.

[6] All figures from International Tropical Timber Organization, *Annual Review*, various issues.

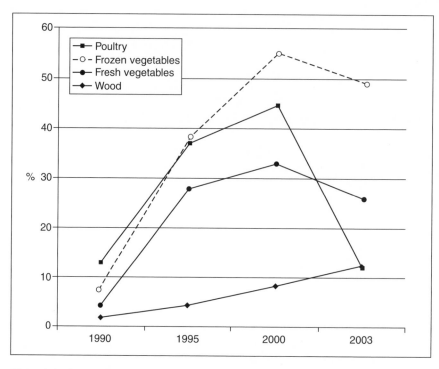

Figure 8.1. China's share of Japan's imports of selected commodities, 1990–2003. Note: Based on value in dollars. *Source:* UN Commodity Trade Statistics.

wood imports (from 35% in 1990 to 9.4% in 2003) and the equally rapid rise of China (from 2% to 12%). Over this period, the share of the United States, Canada, Indonesia, and Malaysia in Japan's wood imports fell from 76 percent to 45 percent. Third, Japan's imports of secondary-processed wood products, which consist mostly of furniture, have increased sharply. Japan's imports have mirrored broader global trends, which have seen international trade in tropical secondary-processed wood products rise from 17 percent of the primary products trade by value in 1991 to 71 percent in 2000 (ITTO 2002, 32).

Changes in the sources of Japan's fish imports are somewhat difficult to parse, as the fleets of the exporting country may have caught the fish well beyond their national waters (the same applies to Japan's "domestic" catch).[7] Farmed shrimp imports generally do originate in the exporting country, how-

---

[7] A dramatic visual representation of the postwar global extension of Japan's pelagic longline fishery, and of the declining catch per unit effort as stock after stock was fished out, can be found at http://fish.dal.ca/~myers/Myers_Supplementary2.pdf. See also Bestor 2001.

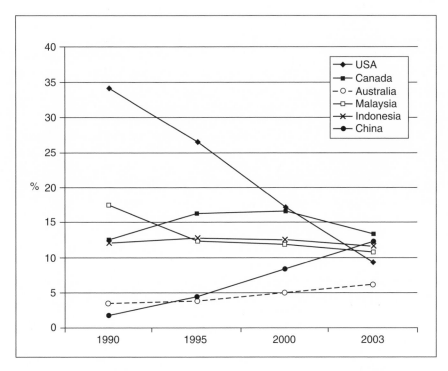

Figure 8.2. Share of Japan's imports of wood and articles of wood, 1990–2003. Note: Based on value in dollars. *Source:* UN Commodity Trade Statistics.

ever, and shrimp has been one of Japan's most important food imports for some time. Imports boomed in the late 1980s, peaked in 1994, and fell back to 1987 levels by 1999 (Ryuken Research 2002). Consumption has been hit by hard times in the entertainment industry, by cutbacks in corporate New Year's parties (where shrimp is a common offering), and by a renewed preference for wild-caught shrimp. This fall in Japanese demand has caused serious problems for shrimp farmers in Asia, who have been looking elsewhere for new markets (Webb 2001). The sources of Japan's farmed shrimp imports changed significantly during the 1990s, but remained primarily Asian.

Trends in meat imports have varied by commodity. Beef imports saw little change during the 1990s, whether by value (up 21%) or by import partner (with the United States and Australia continuing to account for 95% of imports). Pork imports, by contrast, doubled during the 1990s, reaching $3.38 billion in 2001. The most striking development was the rise and fall of Taiwan. Taiwan's share took off around 1990, peaked in 1996 at roughly twice the level of any other exporter (at 250,000 tons), and then dropped to zero when imports were banned after the March 1997 outbreak of foot-and-mouth disease (Wang 2000, 122). In 2003, Denmark, the United States, and Canada accounted for 84 percent of Japan's imports. Chicken imports, finally, rose 45 percent during the 1990s, with Thailand and then China seeing rapid growth as suppliers. The two countries made up two-thirds of Japan's imports at decade's end. In terms of import sources, then, virtually all of Japan's beef and pork comes from non-Asian developed countries, while chicken comes largely from China and Thailand (and also the United States).

Fresh and frozen vegetables are one of the newest elements of Japan's food import profile. Export-oriented vegetable production has been a central part of agricultural restructuring in many developing countries over the last twenty years, bringing with it significant environmental consequences, and Japanese demand has helped to drive this process in Asia (McMichael 2000). Indeed, vegetables have recapitulated the slightly earlier tale of meat imports, as Japan has moved very quickly from being almost self-sufficient to substantial import dependence (imports were 5% of national consumption in 1984 and 15% in 1995: [Fujishima 1997, 19–20]). Citing figures that try to incorporate the original weight of the vegetables used in processed products, Fujishima Hiroji (1997, 18) has estimated that Japan imported the equivalent of 3.42 million tons of vegetables in 1995, up from 1 million in 1984. Vegetable imports have also become much more diverse, as the initial dominance of onions gave way to large-scale imports of *kabocha* (squash), broccoli, garlic, carrots, tomatoes, eggplant, and so on (Fujishima 1997, 28–29). China dominates Japan's vegetable trade (fig. 8.1).

These figures allow us to update the periodization of Japan's agricultural trade developed by Philip McMichael for the period up to the early 1990s (McMichael 2000). At the most general level, McMichael presents the history of Japan's postwar agricultural trade as the shift from a U.S.-centered, bilaterally managed import regime with significant public involvement to a multilateral, regionalized system organized primarily by transnational corporations. McMichael lays out three major stages in the evolution of the postwar regime. In the 1950s, the central component of Japan's food imports was wheat from the United States, which substituted for consumption of protected, more expensive Japanese rice. From the early 1960s, liberalization encouraged a shift to imports of feed grains (corn and soybeans), which were fed to Japanese livestock to produce meat. Beginning in the 1980s, however, feed grain imports stagnated as trade liberalization and FDI facilitated a shift away from Japanese meat production to large-scale imports of beef, chicken, and pork. More generally, the 1980s saw, in McMichael's words, "a palpable shift away from the standard, low-value bulk goods associated with the postwar food regime to high-value food products associated with the proliferation of 'nontraditional exports'" (416). These new products were symbolized by imports of meat, farmed shrimp, and fresh fruits and vegetables. Similar dynamics were at work in the wood-products sector, with furniture imports rising at the expense of those of primary timber.

McMichael's arguments have largely been confirmed by developments since the early 1990s, though there have been some changes. Feed grain imports have indeed remained flat, while imports of meat (especially pork and chicken) have increased. The rise of nontraditional imports that McMichael stressed has continued, as have imports of processed food. McMichael's argument that newly agro-industrializing countries (NAICs) such as Thailand, Taiwan, Mexico, and Brazil are providing increasing amounts of Japan's meat imports (413) has received more mixed support, with Australia and the United States still dominating the beef trade and Taiwan being knocked out of pork exports. More broadly, Japan does not seem to be making any dramatic moves to intensify its dependence on the Southeast Asian "agro-export zone" on which McMichael focuses attention. Rather, the major development since McMichael's data ends is the sudden emergence of China as Japan's second-largest food supplier.

Changes in Japan: Consumption, Retail, and Sourcing Strategies

In accounting for these dynamics, I will begin with consumption in Japan, work backward through import pathways and East Asian agro-industrialization, and finally arrive at the point of production and environmental transformation in Asia. I will focus mostly on food, and comment occasionally on wood products. Three interrelated changes in food consumption and retailing have helped to restructure Japan's food imports. The first of these seems contradictory at first glance: the post-bubble decade witnessed a heightened concern for both price and quality among Japanese consumers. Growing pressures on pocketbooks in a time of economic stagnation has led to vigorous price competition (*kakaku hakai,* or "price destruction") in food retailing, and the rapid expansion of low-cost retailers. Simultaneously, however, a series of food-quality scares (such as the Snow Brand milk scandal and the discovery of BSE—mad cow disease—in a Japanese cow, both in 2001), as well as more general concerns over food safety, genetically modified organisms (GMOs), and agricultural chemicals, have pushed retailers to respond to consumers' concerns over food safety (Bestor 2004, 144–47). "Organic" and "GMO-free" labels have played a major role in this push. Somewhat ironically, anxiety over food safety, much of which has been sparked by domestic scandals, has led retailers to market food as "100% domestic" to take advantage of the assumption that food grown in Japan is safer than imports. This interest in quality has encompassed questions of taste as well as safety, and has played an important role in keeping demand for wild-caught shrimp afloat even while consumption of farmed shrimp has dropped. In their 1997 study of the development of food market channels in Japan, Heilbron and Larkin argued that these heightened concerns for price and quality correspond to two different periods, with the early 1990s being the main era of *kakaku hakai* and the mid-1990s seeing a backlash against cheaper, imported foods and a strong shift of consumer preferences "in favor of domestic high quality produce in which the powerful Japanese food corporations excel" (Heilbron and Larkin 1997, x). However, both trends seem to be enduring aspects of the restructuring of Japanese food retailing, with price consciousness working to encourage food imports, while quality-consciousness inhibits them.

Japan's food imports have also been affected by the continued Americanization of consumption. This trend is far from new and has its postwar roots in increasing consumption of wheat starting in the 1950s, meat beginning in the 1960s, and the introduction in the 1970s of American fast food chains. The major recent innovations have arisen from the spread of supermarkets and convenience stores, in part as a consequence of liberalized retail store laws. These changes have been intimately tied to imports of certain kinds of food, particularly frozen vegetables and semiprocessed or processed, ready-to-eat products. The shift toward individuals buying their own meal at the *konbini* (convenience store) on the way home and eating alone rather than with other family members is driving the popularity of ready-to-eat meals, and has been decried in Japan as heralding family breakdown and atomized Americanized lifestyle patterns. The extent to which such changes in consumption represent the adoption of a specifically American lifestyle rather than reflecting enduring local diversity are, of course, open to debate. This point is made cogently in the book *Golden Arches East,* which shows that the meanings attributed to eating at McDonald's, and the ways in which people make use of the restaurant, vary widely across Asia (Watson 1998). I will simply emphasize here that these changes are consequences of technologies and styles of food consumption that originated in the United States and are intimately connected with images of American affluence.

Price competition and retail innovations have also affected the ways that agricultural products are imported into Japan. Heilbron and Larkin argue that the early years of endaka did not bring about any major structural changes in food imports, but rather saw a more straightforward increase in volume. Significant restructuring began in the early 1990s as discount stores and other retailers began sourcing directly from overseas producers and reducing their reliance on the byzantine Japanese food distribution sector (Heilbron and Larkin 1997, 23). As with the increased price sensitivity of Japanese consumers in the early 1990s, there seems to have been a two-part movement of retailers experimenting with more direct import pathways in the early parts of the decade and then retreating; certainly the *sogo shosha* (general trading companies) remain central to Japan's food imports (Heilbron and Larkin 1997, 18, 84). The key point, however, is that the price pressure these arrangements have brought to bear on the distribution system has forced domestic distributors to rationalize and has thus contributed to lower prices, and increased volumes, of imported food.

On the Japanese side, then, the key actors at work in restructuring and stimulating food imports seem to be consumers and firms (though not always multinational corporations). The Japanese state's attitude to these changes is difficult to determine. In their recent survey of Japan's nonrenewable-resource imports, Ciccantell and Bunker continue to see close relations between cartelized importers and the state, particularly METI (Ciccantell and Bunker 2002). Although much work remains to be done on this question, it does appear that in Japan's agricultural trade, at any rate, the role of the state in organizing imports relative to that of firms has fallen significantly over the last fifteen to twenty years. Paul Gellert has made a similar argument with respect to Japan's tropical plywood imports from Indonesia. After Indonesia banned log exports in 1985, plywood manufacturers (under the leadership of Suharto crony Bob Hasan) formed Apkindo, an association that took control of prices and production. Apkindo forged an alliance with the small Japanese trading company Kanmatsu Shoji to create Nippindo, a new trading house with exclusive rights to all Indonesian plywood exported to Japan. Remarkably enough, this alliance with a renegade trading company allowed Apkindo to grab control of much of Japan's plywood trade from the *sogo shosha*. Despite a significant reallocation of rents from Japan to Indonesia, the Japanese state declined to interfere. As Gellert concludes, "Unlike in the strategic mineral sectors that Bunker and Ciccantell analyzed, there is little, if any, evidence of Japanese state interference in the (domestic) access strategies of the Japanese trading houses" (Gellert 2003, 74).

Liberalization and Agro-Industrialization in Asia

Changes in Japanese consumption preferences will, of course, have little impact on Japan-Asia trade if Asian countries cannot respond to them. Central to the ability of Asian producers to respond has been the rapid spread and deepening of agro-industrialization. This process has seen certain developing countries, in the context of regional and global liberalization and under the impetus of supportive government policy and FDI from agribusinesses, shifting away from exports of traditional bulk commodities (such as sugar, coffee, and rice) and toward higher-value-added products like shrimp, fresh vegetables, canned goods, and processed foods. Thailand, which has excelled in export-oriented production of farmed shrimp, broiler chickens, canned tuna, and other nontraditional exports, has become the paradigmatic example of an NAIC. The ability of Japanese firms to increase imports of higher-value-added food products has been strongly related to Asian agro-industrialization.

Asian countries have been drawn ever more firmly into the U.S.-centered, rules-based international trade regime through GATT and WTO negotiations (McMichael 2000). The implications of the spread in Asia of the "new constitutionalism" (Gill 1992) have been particularly important in agriculture. On the import side, Japanese agricultural trade has seen a number of liberalizing initiatives since the mid-1980s. Continued protectionism in the politically important rice sector makes it easy to forget the liberalization that has taken place with respect to, for instance, meat and vegetables. Harmonization of health and quality standards has also been an important driver of Japan's imports (Yano 2000, 56–60). For instance, food must now be labeled by best-before date rather than by date of manufacture, a move that is meant to level the playing field for imports that take some time to reach Japan. In Asia, and particularly in China, increasingly liberal trade in agriculture has profoundly affected the mix of products sold to Japan as production and trade come more closely to mirror comparative advantage (Bhattasali and Kawai 2002).

Firms (both Asian and non-Asian) have taken advantage of trade and investment liberalization to dramatically increase their FDI in agriculture, setting up production across Asia to capture both domestic and export markets. Just how FDI has worked, however, is less straightforward. Bill Pritchard (2000, 246) argues that

> despite wide acceptance of the proposition that agro-food transnational corporations (TNCs)—particularly from the West—are pivotal players in the emergent regulatory structures of the East Asian agro-food system, there has been little explicit concern to account theoretically or empirically for their prevailing socio-spatial practices and strategies.

In trying to sketch what is known, I will begin with FDI from Japan, which first took off in the late 1980s under the influence of endaka. A notable characteristic of these early years was the number of large-scale investments in beef feedlots in the United States and Australia (Lawrence and Vanclay 1994). In the 1990s, however, Asia has been the main target. A further shift has been evident within FDI to Asia: until the 1990s, the main recipients were Korea, Taiwan, Thailand, and Singapore, but in the 1990s China became the key country (Mitoro 2000, 14–16). The main aims of FDI to Asia are securing low labor and materials costs. FDI has been a critical mechanism for the transfer of technical standards, technology (including freezer technology), and crop varieties to Asian production sites (Fujishima 1997, 30–34). It has also helped to transmit Japanese consumer preferences to Asia, as Asian firms have often had difficulty in producing precisely the kind of food that will sell in Japan. This last form of Japanization does not necessarily have wider implications for Asian agriculture.

This FDI has been carried out by a variety of firms. The *sogo shosha* have accounted for a good deal, setting up overseas production for the purpose of exporting to Japan; specialist food traders have done the same (Heilbron and Larkin 1997, 32). A recent report by the Economic Research Service of the U.S. Department of Agriculture notes that, with respect to the vegetable trade, "China substantially attracted foreign investment especially from Japanese trading companies, which provided the seeds, spores, and techniques of production and packing, and imported the harvest for Japanese retailers" (Huang 2002, 4–5). However, much of Japan's FDI in China has been carried out by small- and medium-sized processing companies, sometimes alone, sometimes in conjunction with the *sogo shosha* (Mitoro 2000, 21–22). Interestingly, in China, Japanese FDI in sectors oriented to reexport to Japan (mostly frozen foods, fish products, and vegetable processing) involves smaller projects than do investments aimed at the domestic market. FDI by small- and medium-sized companies has also characterized Japan's involvement in shrimp processing in Indonesia (Suzuki 1997).

Even less clear is the role that non-Japanese FDI has played in Japan's agricultural trade. The report by Heilbron and Larkin was written as part of an Australian government effort to understand why the country was having little success in penetrating the Japanese food market, in particular with respect to higher-value-added products. One thus detects a hint of sour grapes in their statement that

> it is no coincidence . . . that the main burst of import penetration and the period of intense off-shore investment in food production and food processing took place together in the early part of the 1990s: this was Japanese money, sourcing "Japanese" product for the Japanese market—something which foreign producers, on their own, seem to have great difficulty with. (Heilbron and Larkin 1997, 33)

Huang, on the other hand, sees Taiwanese FDI as critical to the development of China's vegetable export trade with Japan. She writes that "the exodus of Taiwan's frozen food manufacturers to China, like many of Taiwan's other manufacturing industries, was the main cause for Taiwan's drastic decline in its market share of Japan's frozen vegetable imports, while it boosted China's presence in Japan in the 1990s." Investment by Chinese, Taiwanese, and Japanese capital, in the context of GATT/WTO–driven liberalization, has allowed China to vault past other NAICs in a wide variety of sectors.

Technology transfer through Japanese and non-Japanese FDI, domestic innovation, and government policy have together given rise to the increasing level of processing and sophistication visible in Asian food exports to Japan. These processes have in turn contributed to expanding the range of Japan's shadow ecology through the environmental damage done by export-oriented vegetable production and food processing. Much research remains to be done before we can be confident about the specific ways in which Asian production has changed in response to Japanese consumption patterns. We might note, however, that in the cases of vegetable production and food processing, and in the case of Chinese production of secondary-processed wood products, the overlap of Japanese, Chinese, American, and other Asian production networks in the region that Katzenstein highlights in the introduction is very much in evidence. Further, what looks like Americanization in Japan can look very different from an Asian perspective. The rise of preprepared frozen foods purchased at convenience stores and supermarkets may look, in Japan, like the Americanization of consumption patterns. But there is nothing particularly "American" about the production in Thailand, by Japanese firms, using Japanese technology, and for Japanese tastes, of the frozen deep-fried octopus balls (*takoyaki*) sold in Japan's convenience stores. We thus discover here that the end result of this form of Americanization is the regionalized production of food that no red-blooded American would consider eating.

The Rise of China

Japan's Southeast Asian "agro-export zone" faces a very serious threat from China. Indeed, during the 1990s much of the growth in renewable-resource-intensive exports to Japan that was predicted for Southeast Asia took place in China instead. The trajectory sketched in the discussion of export-oriented vegetable production has been repeated in sector after sector, from poultry to furniture. It is striking, for instance, that despite Thailand's much-vaunted status as a NAIC, the support that the government and Thai multinational corporations have provided for vegetable production, and the country's centrality to discussions of Japan's Southeast Asian resource hinterland, Japan's vegetable imports from Thailand actually fell during the 1990s. During the same period, Japan's overall vegetable imports doubled and imports from China rose by nearly 350 percent.

Thus, while the role China played in McMichael's map of regionalized agriculture in Asia was mostly that of a food importer (and chicken exporter), the country is also emerging as an export-oriented NAIC that is now the second-largest food exporter to Japan after the United States. The rapid expansion of China's renewable-resource-intensive exports to Japan is obviously rooted in a wide range of factors, including the agricultural revolution that has taken place since 1978 (Zhou 1996), trade liberalization, FDI, and government support. China's new role in the Asian wood-products trade provides an excellent example of the way these and other factors have allowed a rapid reorganization of long-standing patterns of regional trade and production. Japan's dominance of the Asian tropical timber trade, a basic feature of that trade since the 1950s, has recently come to an end, with China emerging as the largest importer of tropical logs and sawn wood in the world. Log imports have been driven by rapid economic growth and by government policies aimed at increasing plywood production (which quadrupled in the five years before 2002), reducing reliance on imports, and developing a plywood export trade (ITTO 2002, 21–22). China has been importing both tropical and temperate logs (with Siberia an important source of the latter) in order to fuel this production. The speed of China's rise (and Japan's fall) may be gauged from the fact that, while China first passed Japan as an importer of logs from all sources in 2001, its 2003 imports were double Japan's (ITTO 2004, appendix 1, table 1-1-a).

China is not merely replacing Japan as the main log importer in Asia. It is also using those logs to export both primary and secondary-processed wood products to Japan. This reexport helps to explain the striking fact noted earlier that China now exports more wood products (by value) to Japan than does the United States. For instance, China now exports a small but growing amount of tropical plywood to Japan (ITTO 2002, table 2-4, p. 146). In 2000, China overtook Thailand as Japan's largest furniture supplier, and in 2003 it passed Italy to become the world's largest exporter of secondary-processed wood products (ITTO 2004, viii). China's export-oriented furniture industry has been developed by joint ventures between Chinese companies and firms from the United States, Taiwan, Singapore, and other parts of Asia. FDI attracted by low wages and supportive government policy has transformed Guangdong into "the largest furniture production and export base in the Asia-Pacific region" (ITTO 2002, 34, 36). Japan's wood-products trade has thus come a long way since the days when imports of unprocessed logs dominated. One result is that the true source of the wood in the products Japanese consumers buy is becoming harder to discern; similarly, it is less obvious to the people at the point of timber extraction where the trees being harvested will end up.

It is important not to overestimate the importance of these developments for the overall state of the environment in China. Gaining even a vague sense of the environmental impacts of export-oriented vegetable production in China, for instance, is virtually impossible because of lack of information. It is unlikely that it will be possible to separate out the impacts of vegetables grown for Japan from that of those grown for the domestic market, which is far larger than the export trade in any case. Although the environmental effects of agro-industrialization cannot be predicted a priori (Barrett, Barbier, and Reardon, 2001), evidence from Brazilian agriculture has shown a troubling pattern in which pesticide use, which has doubled over the last decade, is concentrated in areas dependent on export-oriented cash crops and with higher numbers of large farms (Dasgupta, Mamingi, and Meisner 2001, cited in Barrett, Barbier, and Reardon 2001, 422). The authors of the study note that much chemical use is driven by the desire to produce flawless produce for consumers with high sensitivity to food appearance, and the Japanese market is notorious on this score. Evidence from Chinese vegetable farming also shows significant environmental problems (Veeck and Wang 2000). The agro-industrial and food processing sectors tend to be among the dirtiest in developing countries (Barrett, Barbier, and Reardon 2001, 425); on the other hand, FDI by Japanese firms using more up-to-date technology and trying to meet Japanese import standards may mitigate the sector's environmental impact. It is clear, however, that an increasing amount of the environmental damage done outside of Japan by Japanese consumption is taking place in China.

Regional Political Ecology

A complex mix of forces operating in Japan and Asia has reshaped the organization and spatial distribution of Japan's renewable-resource-intensive imports over the 1990s. The forces at work are not limited, however, to the realms of consumption decisions and the political economy. The dynamics of Japan's shadow ecology, and thus of regionalization and engagement with Asia, have also been deeply affected by the local-level environmental change brought about by production for Japanese markets, and by the ways in which local people, firms, NGOs, and states have responded to this change. Recognition of these forces points to the need for the development of an "international political ecology" that analyzes the ways in which the characteristic environmental problems of different sectors shape regionalization through their effects on the sustainability of production. A key part of this project is the insistence that nature plays an active role (Goodman 2001) in regionalization that is not reducible to human action.

Unfortunately, variations in the amount of data available by sector and country make it difficult to gain an overall sense of this question. In Taiwan, for instance, the effluent and water problems caused by pork production were serious enough that the government made an effort to restrict export-oriented production and reorient the sector to self-sufficiency, although agricultural capital was able to beat this back. In a comprehensive survey of the sector, Wang predicts that environmental problems and regulation, particularly in relation to water use, are likely to damage the competitiveness of Taiwanese production, and exports to Japan were shut down completely by the outbreak of foot-and-mouth disease (Wang 2000, 131). It is difficult, however, to say much more than this.

Two critical sectors for which more information is available (for Southeast Asia, at any rate) are shrimp farming and timber. Although Japan has been a major shrimp importer since the 1960s, the country began to import large amounts of farmed shrimp only about twenty years ago. Southeast Asia provided the preponderance of Japan's farmed imports during the initial boom and continues to do so today. Within Southeast Asia, however, the location of shrimp production has shifted rapidly both between and within countries, often following a pattern that Skladany and Harris (1995) call "slash-and-burn aquaculture." Taiwan experienced the first and most spectacular boom and bust. The main exporters to Japan in the years after Taiwan's crash, Indonesia, Thailand, and the Philippines, followed widely divergent paths during the 1990s (Hall 2004b). Indonesian exports to Japan have kept relatively steady (though production has moved away from Java to Sumatra, Sulawesi, Kalimantan, and other outer islands), while Thailand has shifted toward the U.S. market and processed exports to Japan. In the Philippines production has collapsed, particularly in the erstwhile boom area of Negros. India and Vietnam are Japan's up-and-coming sources, and China has also returned to farmed shrimp exports after a twenty-year hiatus.

Much of the explanation for these rapid shifts in location can be found in the environmental problems that have plagued intensive shrimp farming across the world, most of which relate to water management. The need to mix large amounts of fresh and salt water to provide a suitable growing environment means that farms often put severe strains on local fresh water supplies while also salinating them. More seriously from the point of view of production, difficulties in managing effluent have led to diseases spreading rapidly from farm to farm and wiping out harvests. Approaches to, and success in, managing these problems have differed by country and by locality. It is abundantly clear, however, that the environmental problems of shrimp farming have shaped the regional contours of the sector, whether in terms of where production takes place or of discouraging early Japanese attempts to get directly involved in production.

Japan's imports of tropical timber have long been highly regionalized, and indeed played a major role in the return of Japanese capital to Southeast Asia after World War II. The political alliances made between Japanese firms and state and patron-client networks in Southeast Asia were an important part of region-formation and were supported by Japanese official development assistance (Dauvergne 1997). Tropical timber imports thus represent, with shrimp, one of the clearest examples of the Southeast Asian resource hinterland model, and Indonesia and Malaysia still account for most of Japan's imports of primary tropical timber products, though Papua New Guinea and several African states now play important roles. The environmental damage done by decades of intensive logging for Japanese markets does not need to be rehearsed here (Dauvergne 1997; Nectoux and Kuroda 1990). More important for our purposes is the way in which resource depletion has pushed the Japanese to keep changing their sources of supply. For decades these shifts went on primarily within Southeast Asia, as the most economically attractive tree stands were logged out in the Philippines, Indonesia, and Sarawak and Sabah. More recently, however, Japanese firms have begun to look further afield for raw materials and to substitute different kinds of wood, whether from temperate forests or industrial tree plantations. The Japanese plywood industry is substituting softwoods for hardwoods (with larch, imported from Russia, now a preferred species) and developing new product types, as well as establishing joint ventures in producer countries in order to reduce costs (ITTO 2002, 12, 21).

These problems of resource depletion have long been recognized by key wood-consuming industries in Japan, and they have planned their responses accordingly (Hall 2002). Japan's paper industry, for instance, realized in the 1980s that increased regulation of logging (particularly in the United States and Canada) and the exhaustion of tree stands in traditional trade partners in Southeast Asia would require them to adopt new sourcing strategies. The primary strategy adopted was FDI in overseas industrial tree plantations where fast-growing species could be harvested for wood chips. As Morimoto Taiji argued in 1993:

> In order for our country's paper industry to continue consistently producing paper . . . it has become vital for us to reduce our dependence on wood products from natural forests and to attempt to shift to resources that can be more freely utilized over the long term—concretely, forests that we ourselves plant and manage, or so-called raised resources. (Morimoto 1993; my translation)

In the early 1970s, a public-private organization called the Nanpo Zorin Kyokai (Southern Afforestation Association) identified Southeast Asia as the most promising future area for industrial tree plantations, and began running experimental plantations in the region. Southeast Asia was also the focus of initial interest when Japan's paper industry began a wholehearted turn toward overseas plantation forestry. Starting in 1989, Japanese companies began setting up plantations overseas as the paper industry announced a commitment to source one-third of its wood chip consumption from foreign plantations by 2010. By 2000, Japanese companies had established 257,600 hectares of tree plantations abroad. However, only one of these projects was located in Southeast Asia (Vietnam); new projects were concentrated in Australia (13), Chile (3), and New Zealand (2). Early efforts to develop plantations in Southeast Asia were quickly scuttled by conflicts over land and resource access and by environmental degradation, and these conflicts played a key role in moving Japan's tree plantations away from the classic Southeast Asian "hinterland" and toward Australia. The move away from a Southeast Asia–focused and toward a self-consciously global approach to tree plantation siting was explicitly flagged in 1998 when the Southern Afforestation Association was reorganized into the Kaigai Sangyo Shokurin Senta (Japan Overseas Plantation Center). These issues have thus had very direct impacts on the extent to which Japan's shadow ecology is regionalized. They have also meant that Japanese participation in key patron-client networks around the extraction of timber has dropped significantly in one Southeast Asian country after another.

Analysis of a third important case, the impact of Chinese export-oriented vegetable production for the Japanese market, must remain speculative at this stage. I have sketched one possible outcome of Japan's rapidly growing demand for imported vegetables—intensifying environmental damage in China. Another possibility, however, is that Japanese concern over the environmental implications of industrial agriculture in Japan will stimulate imports of organic vegetables from China, or from Asia more broadly. Organic food exports from developing countries have increased rapidly in recent years and are estimated to be worth $500 million globally (Barrett, Browne et al. 2002). Export-oriented organic agriculture has been expanding in China at a blistering pace, with the area certified by the Green Food Development Center, one of two state certification agencies, passing two million hectares by the end of 1997 (Thiers 2002, 365). Given strong consumer interest in organic foods in Japan, rising production in China, and the already well-established trade in fresh and frozen vegetables between the two countries, organic food seems to hold out the promise of consumer concern in Japan driving a less environmentally destructive form of agricultural regionalization. Indeed, some Japanese companies are already involved in contract-farming and importing organic food from China (FAS Online 2001; Thiers 2002, 368).

Paul Thiers's fascinating analysis of the dynamics of organic certification and marketing in China, however, suggests that significant problems will have to be overcome. Organic farming has emerged in China not as a grassroots movement but rather as a developmental project pushed by "fragments" of the state interested in organic food as a source of revenue. The two state certifying agencies have major interests in the marketing of organic produce, and hence they are far from being independent third-party regulators. In part for this reason, their certification of food as organic is not recognized in most international markets. Peculiarly enough, then, while Chinese "organic" agriculture has developed as a state-backed project aimed at capturing international markets, the very nature of the organizations that have promoted it limit China's overseas sales. Thiers argues further that the various contradictions of the system (including the often coercive measures state "fragments" use to force farmers to grow "organic" crops) may well mean that China's "organic" farming is actually causing a significant amount of environmental damage. On the Japanese side, meanwhile, Chinese vegetables are more closely associated with a series of export bans on products such as spinach because they contain excessive pesticide revenues.

Regionalization, Environment, Globalization

This analysis of the environmental aspects of Japan-Asia relations has differed significantly from the predominant approach in the literature on environment and international political economy in Asia. I have largely passed over the explicit efforts that states have made to address environmental questions (for instance, through environmental development assistance[8] and the building of international institutions) in favor of a study of the less coordinated, less state-centric, and (in James Scott's terms) more "polyp-like" activities that have helped to shape Japan's shadow ecology (Scott 1985). Although states (particularly Japan's) have played a central role in helping to structure these latter processes, their role in doing so has generally been an unintentional one; that is, the relevant policies have not been framed with the environmental consequences of Japan's relations with Asia in mind, but for other purposes. The environmental implications of Japan-oriented production in Asia are rarely the subject of high-level government concern, on the part of the Japanese government or, a fortiori, of the American. While the Japan Environment Agency has highlighted the environmental consequences of Asian production for Japanese markets in various publications (Hall 2001), the ministries that actually control Japan's environmental development assistance to Asia are less likely to stress this perspective. Official development as-

---

[8] Japan's environmental development assistance has been a significant and rising part of Japan's overall development aid since the country's diplomats developed the idea of the "environmental superpower" around the time of the Earth Summit in Rio in 1992, and the country has devoted substantial funds to environmental projects in Asia. Environmental aid has, for instance, been a growing part of Japan's official development assistance to China (Pharr and Wan 1998; Inada 2002). For the most part, however, Japan's environmental development assistance is not directed explicitly toward the sectors outlined in the first part of this chapter or to repairing the damage done by Japan in the region (though see Noikorn 2000).

sistance tends not to be directed to the issues highlighted here, stressing rather technology transfer and Japan's role as a potential environmental role model for Asia. However, ongoing debates in Japan over food security (the nation produces less than 50% of the calories its citizens consume) make it difficult to believe that the government is indifferent to this import structure.

The evidence presented here largely supports Philip McMichael's contention that regional agricultural trade is increasingly organized not by states but by firms and their supply chains (McMichael 2000). The timber case, in particular, shows that local people and NGOs have played a major role in shaping regionalization. The actors in this story, then, are firms and local people as much as states, and it is also necessary to consider the environment itself as an "actor." Given the scope of the questions under discussion, it is no surprise that the range of causal mechanisms in play is also large. While bargaining and coercion play important roles, perhaps the most important mechanisms in the story are, to use Katzenstein's terminology in the introduction, transformational (micro–macro) ones. Whether in terms of the aggregation of Japanese consumer preferences shaping demand for Asian production, or of the ways in which small-scale environmental changes across coastal Southeast Asia have come together to shape the organization of shrimp farming, regionalization cannot be understood outside of its local manifestations (Bernard 1996). Finally, at least two aspects of the multifaceted process of Americanization stand out. On the more active side, trade liberalization under the impetus of a U.S.-led WTO regime is helping to reorganize the way that agricultural production and environmental burdens are distributed in Asia. At a less immediately obvious level, changes in consumer preferences in Japan that can be construed as an Americanizing—or, at least, a globalizing—of taste and eating habits have also helped to propel this process, though with consequences in Asia that often seem far from Americanizing.

All of these processes have contributed to a significant increase in the complexity of Japan's shadow ecology in renewable-resource-intensive products during the 1990s. In past studies of Japan's tropical log, beef, or shrimp imports, it has generally been possible to draw a fairly straight line—a short causal chain (Keck and Sikkink 1998)—from environmental damage at the point of production to imports to Japan. Many of the trends discussed here, however, seriously complicate this project (which was never simple to begin with). The case of timber being imported to China from around the world before being reexported to Japan as furniture, or the indications that some of the shrimp being processed in Thailand for export to Japan originate from other countries (Jinakul 2003), are examples. Perhaps the most striking aspect of these trends is the way in which Japan's agricultural and resource imports, pushed as they have been by the actors and mechanisms discussed earlier, are increasingly coming to resemble electronics and other global industries in embodying elements from a variety of production sites in different countries that have been brought together for assembly before export.

Overall, then, stagnant economic growth has not translated into any straightforward stagnation in imports of renewable-resource-intensive products into Japan. In some cases, such as fish, vegetables, and pork, imports have increased significantly. In others, such as timber, a fall in certain product categories (such as tropical logs) has been offset by heightened imports of other forms of wood. In all of these sectors, the movement of processing from Japan to Asia has meant that the environmental impacts of that sector have been shifted to Asia as well. In none of these cases is it possible to simply assume that higher imports necessarily mean more environmental damage overseas: improvements in technology and in practice can offset the increase in quality. Gaining a sense of Japan's shadow ecology means detailed, careful work to trace the origins of imports and their environmental consequences, and it is precisely this work that is made more difficult by the heightened complexity of regional production and trade.

This new complexity may also be affecting regional NGO organizing. Concern over Japan's shadow ecology has brought together activists across the region for decades, beginning with simultaneous 1973 demonstrations in Bangkok and Tokyo against Asahi Kasei's mercury dumping in Thailand (Hirayama 1974), and continuing on through regional networking campaigns around tropical timber and golf tourism in the 1980s and 1990s. To the extent that the environmental burden of Japanese production becomes more diffuse, however, it seems likely that NGO organizers will lack the easily publicizable targets of the past. Regional NGOs are also likely to have more difficulty organizing campaigns in China than they did even in authoritarian Southeast Asia. It is thus possible that globalization, Americanization, Asian agro-industrialization, and the various other forces discussed here are bringing about a situation in which Japan's shadow ecology will be weighing more heavily in Asia, while also becoming less contentious.

9

A Narrow Place to Cross Swords:
Soft Power and the Politics of Japanese
Popular Culture in East Asia

DAVID LEHENY

Five of the most prominent American movies of 2003—Sofia Coppola's Os-
car-winning *Lost in Translation,* the two anime-influenced *Matrix* sequels,
Quentin Tarantino's nearly fetishistic *Kill Bill,* and the Tom Cruise vehicle *The
Last Samurai*—starkly display the weight of Japanese cultural influences in
Hollywood. Even so, there may be no better symbol of Japan's ostentatiously
transnational popular culture than Kitano Takeshi's film *Zatoichi.* Based on a
beloved film series (though one not often seen outside Japan), Kitano's version follows the blind masseur/swordsman as he cleans up a town dominated
by a shadowy group of criminals. Clearly aiming at wide audiences both in Japan and overseas, Kitano crowds his movie with a cacophony of cultural references. There are the obvious similarities to the Zatoichi tradition, such as a
plot that refers to the inescapability of memory and the desire for revenge.
But there are also digitally enhanced sword-fighting sequences, Zatoichi's in-
explicably blond hair, and finally a noted tap-dancing sequence led by a Japanese troupe, the Stripes, and set to a hip-hop–inflected score. Immensely
(and sometimes desperately) entertaining, *Zatoichi* captured major awards at
the Venice and Toronto film festivals and made a splash at art-house cinemas
in the United States.

The growing global popularity of Japan's culture and entertainment industries is an undeniable and yet ambiguous fact. Its interpretation in Japanese political circles owes at least as much to observers' reliance on durable
ideas about Japan's role in Asia and their efforts to come to grips with a messy

and uncomfortable social reality at home as it does to their instrumental policy goals. I will problematize reports of Japan's imminent cultural hegemony as well as the intellectual discourses that have allowed policymakers to connect popular culture to political power. The term most frequently used in both English- and Japanese-language accounts of the phenomenon has been "soft power." Similarities in the term's deployment across national contexts suggest that soft power has become a way for observers to cope emotionally and intellectually with national decline by believing that virtues they see in their own nation are validated overseas, and that they become power resources in their own right. Japanese interest in pop culture and soft power reflects in part the international popularity of the film *Spirited Away,* PlayStation 2, and pop star Hamasaki Ayumi. But it also highlights fears over how a country beset by rapid social transformation and economic malaise can maintain a powerful role in a changing Asia.

I trace the evolution of policy debates about the regional importance of Japanese popular culture from five vantage points. First, I discuss some of the strong areas of Japanese popular culture, such as anime and video games, and the myriad other entertainment industry sources in the Asia Pacific region, including the United States and China. Second, I examine how an earlier wave of American scholars and policy experts sought to conceptualize how the cultural strength of U.S. entertainment industries mitigated more general fears of national decline, culminating in the stipulation of American "soft power." Third, I trace recent Japanese efforts to theorize about the role of the country's popular culture, which reconfigure soft power to account for both Japan's rapid social changes and its putatively long-term relationship to modernizing Asia. Fourth, I detail the ways in which the discursive link between popular culture and soft power appears to have affected policy choices in contemporary Japan. Finally, I reexamine the meanings that people attach to Japanese popular culture in Asia, arguing that audiences in Asia do not see Japan in its cultural products as much as they see their own futures. This is partly what Japanese policymakers have in mind for soft power, but it is probably less instrumentally useful than it appears.

Japanese Popular Culture in Asia

How influential has Japanese popular culture become internationally? Because of the diversity of the industries involved—music, magazines, films, broadcast television, video games, cellular phone content, to name but a few—no one has yet compiled a comprehensive statistical account, let alone provided a compelling way to disentangle Japanese cultural products from the many transnational flows emanating from other Asian nations, the United

States, and even Europe. Even the Japanese government has thus far been stymied in its efforts to determine precisely how large the trade in cultural goods has become. As a consequence, the information available is primarily illustrative and anecdotal, and usually slanted in a direction designed either to indicate that "cool" Japan dominates Asia or that "passé" Japan has already been eclipsed by other sources of cultural power in the region.

Popular music, for example, has been one arena in which Japanese artists clearly gained ground during the 1990s. Although the popular Japanese acts in the United States and Europe were usually alternative groups such as Shonen Knife, which had devoted cult but not mass followings in Japan, Asian markets rapidly embraced J-Pop singers. In 1996, the trio Dreams Come True sold one hundred thousand copies of its album *Love Unlimited* in Taiwan, where, as in South Korea, Japanese popular music had faced legal restrictions for decades (Burpee 1997). In 1998, Singapore licensed a new FM station dedicated to J-Pop (though mainly aimed at the city-state's Japanese expatriates), and by 2000 the girl-group Puffy (known in the U.S. market as Puffy Ami-Yumi, due to copyright concerns involving rap impresario Sean "Puffy" Combs) had sold two hundred thousand albums in Asia (McClure 2000). Already extremely successful in Taiwan and somewhat so in Hong Kong, the Japanese music industry was clearly delighted in 2000 when the South Korean government lifted a restriction against the sale of Japanese pop there, provided that the lyrics were not in Japanese (Kim 2000), which presaged further liberalizing moves in 2003 (*Yomiuri Shimbun* 2003b). Yet at least some music industry experts believe that Korean popular music—which more seamlessly blends hip-hop influences and relies on authentically multilingual band members—might have already overtaken J-Pop in Asia (Yoon 2001).

Japanese video games have faced mixed success in the Asia Pacific region. Although Nintendo has become the world video game champion, originally riding arcade games such as Super Mario Brothers to success, it has faced intense competition in the crucially important home video console market. The Sony PlayStation and PlayStation 2 perform far ahead of competing console lines (like the Gamecube and Microsoft's X-Box, America's main entry in the market), but they have been limited in Asia because of the probability of software piracy (Mollman 2001a). The money in video games usually comes not from the consoles—often sold at a loss—but from specific software lines or game franchises (Mollman 2001b), and so the threat of license and copyright violation is especially daunting to a fast-moving industry working on razor-thin profit margins. Moreover, video game software is far from exclusively Japanese, with U.S. firms such as Electronic Arts and Activision and even European firms such as France's Ubivision playing important roles. Even where the hardware is available, the threat of software piracy is large enough to have limited software distribution, so that sales in Thailand, Malaysia, Singapore, Hong Kong, and Taiwan have been quite limited (Dejitaru Kontentsu Kyokai 2003). Moreover, the main console games cost roughly $50, which limits the appeal of Japan's leading console systems in most Asian nations, privileging less expensive online gaming in which Japan competes with software developers elsewhere.[1]

At times, Japan's live-action television programs have been extraordinarily popular in Asia. Japanese television dramas have played to large audiences in Southeast Asia, particularly in Singapore and Thailand, but they have left an especially large impression on China, Taiwan, and Hong Kong. Particularly in the mid-1990s, Japan's limited-run dramas—usually ten to twelve episodes, unlike American programs, which generally go off the air only after wearing out their welcome—impressed Asian viewers with their high production values, the accessible beauty of their young casts, and the putative realism of the narratives (Iwabuchi 2002, 135–57).

But the undoubted champion in Japan's pop culture team around the world, especially in Asia, has been anime. Although American animated films continue to dominate the U.S. box office, television revenues in the United States and around the Pacific Rim paint a strikingly different picture. With *Pokemon, Sailor Moon, Dragon Ball Z,* and *Digimon,* Japanese animation creators have achieved extraordinary global success in part because of their ability to indigenize their programs for local markets. By some estimates, Japan is the source of 60 percent of the world's animated television programming. Moreover, annual sales of anime-related licensed goods such as action figures and trading cards are estimated at $17 billion (*Focus Japan* 2003). Although anime are extraordinarily popular throughout Asia, licensed-good sales appear to be especially heavy in the United States and Japan. For Bandai, one of the leading licensed-good manufacturers, "our business activities in Asia center on the production of toys in Hong Kong, Thailand and elsewhere. . . . [These products are] destined for the parent company in Japan and overseas sales subsidiaries" (Bandai Group 2002). Of course, on the streets of Shanghai or Hong Kong one can easily buy dolls and action figures modeled after Japanese anime characters, but these unlicensed goods result in no proceeds for Bandai and the other Japanese firms.

The changing composition of the casts and crews of films may be the best symbol of newly integrated entertainment markets in the Asia Pacific. The primacy of Chinese films in the region, especially with the long-term success of such stars as Jackie Chan and Andy Lau, will likely keep the industry centered

---

[1] See the comments by Capcom president Tsujimoto Kenzo, in "Kontentsu Sangyo Kokusai Senryaku Kenkyukai (Dai 1 Kai) Gijiroku" (Minutes of the First Meeting of the Content Industry International Strategy Research Group), April 2003, pp. 5–7. Available in pdf format from the METI website, http://www.meti.go.jp.

in Hong Kong, but Japanese and Korean firms too have clearly seen the possibilities afforded by joint productions featuring multinational casts. Director Wong Kar-Wai's use of half-Japanese, half-Taiwanese Kaneshiro Takeshi in his *Chungking Express* and *Fallen Angels* certainly improved their marketability in Tokyo, especially with moments such as the *Chungking Express* scene in which the multilingual charmer attempts to seduce a woman by using two Chinese dialects, Japanese, and English. Wong's 2004 science fiction film *2046* includes a performance by Japanese superstar Kimura Takuya, alongside such pan-Asian superstars as Tony Leung and Zhang Ziyi. Kimura's bandmate from the group SMAP, Kusanagi Tsuyoshi, learned Korean to break into the Korean television and film market, and now appears in a Korean-language Japanese film, *Hotel Venus,* based on his popular television program *Chonan Kan* (Kunikawa 2004). And the Korean action film *2009 Lost Memories* posits an alternate world in which Japan completely dominates Asia, but even in this brazenly nationalistic film we see Japanese star Nakamura Toru as one of the film's leads, which has been a crucial marketing element for Tokyo theaters. Here, straightforward box office considerations have pushed directors to reach across borders to attract recognizable talent, producers to find acceptable cross-border themes, and stars to learn new languages to help them stay on top.

Within Japan, the widely acknowledged zenith of the country's pop culture success overseas has been the 2002 Academy Award for best animated film for Miyazaki Hayao's *Spirited Away* (*Sen to Chihiro no Kamikakushi*), itself the most successful film in Japanese box-office history. It earned $150 million in Japan, beating the record previously held by *Titanic* (*BBC Online* 2002). It had reasonably successful runs in Asia, especially with over one million tickets sold in South Korea (Kyodo News Service 2002), and ultimately earned over $260 million in global ticket sales. Even more widely reported in Japan, however, was the film's extraordinary critical acclaim, symbolized by the Academy Award. Even so, in the United States, its $10 million in revenues was easily outdistanced by those of its competitors for the Oscar: *Ice Age* ($65 million) and *Lilo & Stitch* ($145 million).[2] Of course, box office receipts and television ratings do not necessarily tell us much about influence in popular culture. After all, many popular Japanese dramas and other commodities are popular as black-market, pirated discs (Nakano 2002), suggesting that the measurements themselves may be wildly imprecise. Pop culture markets, moreover, are extraordinarily ineffective at measuring the effect, let alone the quality, of a given creative effort.

My point here is simply that Japan is extremely important, though certainly

[2] Comparative international and U.S. box office data supplied by the website Box Office Mojo, at http://www.boxofficemojo.com.

not hegemonic, in Asian popular culture, at least as far as the conflicting data allow one to determine. But one might be forgiven for reading a great deal into the success of anime, video games, and J-Pop. Significantly, their popularity has been noted at a time when Japanese seemingly have little else to cheer about. As T. J. Pempel points out in chapter 2, political and economic stagnation continue to unnerve Japanese observers, who may be even more dismayed by the radical social changes seemingly eating away at the country's institutions, as William W. Kelly and Merry I. White suggest in chapter 3. If Japanese entertainment industries really are remaking Asia and the world, they would represent a ray of hope in an otherwise bleak landscape of national malaise. Japan's overall cultural weight is open to debate, though Japanese excitement about it is understandable.

"Soft Power" as an Idea

The debate is especially open if one connects, as some observers have, cultural weight to political power. A similar question appeared in American political discourse nearly twenty years ago, though it is actually unintelligible without remembering Japan's global role in the 1980s. Although in the 1980s the United States was still locked in the cold war with the Soviet Union, Gorbachev's fledgling reform efforts, the triumphalism of the Reagan years, and the weight of the United States in global markets left little doubt about America's status as the only contender likely to remain standing. And yet a growing chorus of academic voices, building partly from the work of Charles Kindleberger (1973), began to examine how the behavior of the United States as a global hegemon would inexorably empower new rivals and ultimately lead to its decline. In this line of thought, hegemons would be unable to maintain control because their provision of public goods, such as a free trade regime and stable security relations, would allow smaller powers to benefit disproportionately from the system and thereby free ride their way to long-term economic success.[3]

Popularized by historian Paul Kennedy (1988), "hegemonic stability theory" underscored growing skepticism among American researchers regarding the long-term ability of the United States to dominate the global system. Richard Rosecrance (1986) focused especially on the rise of West Germany and Japan, two "trading states" whose emphasis on neomercantilist economic policies and disdain for heavy military expenditures would likely allow them to rival and perhaps replace military superpowers such as the United States. Indeed, with the end of the cold war, the costly reunification of Germany, and

---

[3] For a superb summary, see Gilpin 2001. For critiques, see Snidal (1985) and Strange (1987).

the then still underestimated effects of the Japanese bubble economy, it increasingly seemed to American political and academic observers that Japan would likely be judged as the winner of the cold war.

And yet to some, the proposition that Japan would replace the United States somehow *felt* wrong. In the absence of clear evidence regarding what would likely happen in the following ten years, several American scholars emphasized that Japan, whatever its successes, was not America, at least not in terms of its global cultural weight. Though not addressing Japan directly, Bruce Russett (1985) argued that American popular culture—the global role of blue jeans, rock and roll, and the like—provided the United States with power resources that were indistinct and yet very real. Significantly, Russett left this suggestion to the end of an otherwise carefully substantiated article, ultimately indicating that although it is impossible to quantify, there is something else out there, some relevant aspect of global power other than those that political scientists normally emphasize.

Joseph Nye, in his ominously titled 1991 book *Bound to Lead,* defined this type of resource as "soft power," or the power to persuade rather than the power to coerce. For Nye, the term referred not only to the United States but to the nature of power in a radically changing global system. Soft power would be a driving force in the future, and for the time being only the United States had it in abundance. For Nye, part of this appeal derives from American cultural and commercial influences overseas, especially when they in some way encode American values of democracy, liberalism, tolerance, and the like. Nye specifically argued that Japan will not be able to compete with U.S. power because it, unlike the United States, accepts few immigrants, an important feature of U.S. power that not only convinces outsiders of America's good intentions but also allows easier cross-border pooling of ideas, good will, and common sense.

Little noticed in the critical response to Nye was the extraordinary level of coincidence between the ways *Bound to Lead*'s other countries and educated American liberals view the United States and American values. And so freedom, liberalism, openness, and tolerance of other cultures become the sources of America's "soft power"; they are the reasons that others like the United States, and, conveniently enough, also the aspects of which Nye and his readers are most proud. Indeed, although the books aim in different directions and support quite divergent political agendas, Nye's view of American "soft power" bears more than a passing similarity to Francis Fukuyama's oft-noted *The End of History.* Although Fukuyama aimed primarily at developing a theoretical argument about liberal democracy's triumph over communism and fascism, his book has been used to provide a more hard-edged, conservative version of the universally desirable values Nye recognizes in his own nation. Where Nye argued that these would earn friends for the United

States and its values, Fukuyama maintained that time has run out for alternative ways of understanding the role of the state: to quote the anime-influenced film *The Matrix*, "It is the sound of inevitability."

To be fair, Nye's more recent refinements of his "soft power" claims focus on the need for multilateralism in U.S. foreign policy, and he has downplayed the role of cultural influence (Nye 2002, 2003). But this is a different debate held at a different time. American "hard power" seems, at least as of this writing, beyond any dispute, and so there is little reason to focus on the cultural component of superpower status. Nye now argues that America cannot achieve long-term security by alienating all of its allies, a claim that certainly resembles his earlier point about the changing nature of power in the post–cold war system. But the argument has teeth for different reasons than before. Soft power is no longer the compensation for a country with diminished hard power resources; it instead reflects responsible governance for a country that should be thinking in the long term. As such, this seems less like an argument for the strength of American cultural and political institutions and more like a plea for humility.

The New Attention to Japanese Popular Culture

Until recently, most of the theorizing about Japanese popular culture and entertainment came from researchers concerned with Japanese leisure practices that might shed light on everyday structures regarding gender, class, sexuality, and power (see, e.g., Robertson 1998; Martinez 1998; Linhart and Früstück 1998). Japanese intellectuals and opinion magazines began to focus more assiduously on the spread of the country's popular culture in the 1990s. At the height of the Power Rangers craze, a 1994 issue of *Gaiko Foramu* (Diplomatic Forum), published by the Ministry of Foreign Affairs, included an article on the increasing popularity of Japanese popular culture and the country's place as a leader of a "new Asian civilization" (Iwabuchi 2002, 70). In a 1997 article, Saya Shiraishi (1997) examined the cultural meanings of the popular anime *Doraemon*, which was shown throughout Southeast Asia. And in a special collection on Japanese culture in a globalizing era, the left-leaning opinion monthly *Sekai* included studies of Japan's consumer society and its effects on artistic creativity (Tsujii 1998), Japanese cultural products and their indigenization by Asian consumers (Iwabuchi 1998), and Chinese audiences' use of Japanese television programs and magazines to learn about life outside of China (Cho 1998). In these articles, the focus is not on Japanese influence per se, but rather on patterns of globalization that alter both the efforts of artists and the experiences of the audiences.

The *Sekai* issue, however, also includes a fascinating and instructive conversation between commentator Shin Sugok, a third-generation Korean-Japanese woman, and musician Kina Shoukichi, who is sometimes described to English-speaking audiences as an Okinawan Bob Marley because of his musical talent, his political messages, and his ability to blend popular music with "authentic" sounds from an exotic island. Covering gender relations, ethnic conflict, sexual fetishes for mothers (*mazakon*) and young girls (*rorikon*, though they do not use the term), Kina and Shin address the possibility that Japan's post-bubble economic funk will open up space for new diversity, creativity, and openness. Shin in particular stresses that the collapse of traditional authority structures in the post-bubble era may open up space for alternative voices (perhaps including those of the "singles, slackers, and strangers" that Kelly and White describe in chapter 3) that have implicitly been left out of traditional discourses about what Japanese culture is (Kina and Shin 1998, esp. 123–25).

Though expressing this in terms harsher than many subsequent commentators would use, Shin nicely captures a developing sense among scholars and observers that Japanese popular culture has become exciting, fast-paced, and active, specifically because the obliteration of "traditional" structures has somehow opened the floodgates for pent-up creative urges. And yet the main consumers of these urges were, until recently, the least likely heroes for Japan: the *otaku* (creepily obsessed anime or manga fans). Journalist Nakamori Akio is credited with coining the term, which generally refers to hard-core anime and manga fans with few social skills and even fewer prospects. In 1989, the term took on a sinister new meaning with the arrest of child molester and murderer Miyazaki Tsutomu in Kobe, who owned a vast number of pornographic comics and videos (Kinsella 1998, 308–10). The term, however, has become more widespread, losing some of its stigma along the way (Nakamori and Miyadai 1999). There is some overlap between the otaku and the slackers of chapter 3, though the distinction is important. Most part-time workers are not obsessive otaku, though some may be aspiring manga artists or spend countless hours playing video games. Similarly, many otaku have full-time jobs, though one might not want one in the next cubicle.

By all accounts, Japan's current cultural vitality is unimaginable without the otaku, the term's pejorative connotations notwithstanding. Perhaps the most important spokesperson for the contemporary aesthetic that fuels Japanese popular culture, the painter Murakami Takashi, allies himself deliberately with the otaku. Building an artistic movement based on his "superflat" conception, Murakami argues that Japanese art is simultaneously two-dimensional and lacking in perspective, similar to traditional Japanese visual traditions (flat), and also compressed, crowded, devoid of meaning (superflat). Murakami's sculptures reflect this view, with caricatured versions of Japanese pop culture icons, and his own otaku-staffed studio blurs the line between high art and commercialized icons (Darling 2001). Just as he appears to be critical of an overly commercialized society that compresses meaning through the proliferation of mass-produced junk, he also embraces the contemporary aesthetic that it generates. The superflat conception is important not because it is in any sense self-evidently true but because it is a kind of unifying theme among many in Japan's contemporary arts business.[4]

The Japan depicted in these accounts is a dissonant, postmodern mess, yet all the more appealing for it. Shin's view of the breakdown of traditional authority implicitly lies at the center because of the self-conscious way in which marginalized groups—otaku, ostentatiously self-sexualized schoolgirls, foreigners—play a role. To an extent, of course, this general proposition dramatically overstates the shift in power, just as earlier views of orderly, white-collar Japan badly missed how marginalized groups handled life in a society that ideally would not have them. But this celebration of Japan's seemingly anarchic popular culture appears to be possible only because of something topsy-turvy in contemporary Japan. The losers are now winning, and they are changing Japan along the way.

It was into this environment that U.S. journalist Douglas McGray stepped in 2001, working on a grant from the Japan Society. As a researcher in Tokyo, McGray spent time with the popular arts community, interviewing key figures (including Yamaguchi Yuko, designer of Sanrio's Hello Kitty) and trying to understand how conservative, stodgy, and ultimately depressed Japan was responsible for vibrant and popular culture products embraced by consumers around Asia. Often overstating the extent of Japan's domination of Asian markets (after all, the success of one or two singers in Taiwan does not make for a regional J-Pop boom, particularly when compared to K-Pop's success), McGray argued in *Foreign Policy* that Japan was likely to remain powerful and important because it was a lifestyle leader, able to generate consumption and social patterns elsewhere because of its local artistic creativity. In his famous formulation, Japan would achieve a kind of soft power because of its "Gross National Cool" (McGray 2002).

Clearly aiming to capture an eye-catching trend while appealing to its Japanese readers, *Time* magazine published a special issue of its Asian edition with the cover "Cool Japan." Referring frequently to McGray's thesis about post-bubble Japan's position as the cultural touchstone for the rest of Asia, *Time*'s feature story emphasized that Japan's facility in popular culture would be part of a larger shift toward service industries, thereby offsetting the hol-

---

[4] In addition to Murakami's own book *Superflat*, see, e.g., Yamaguchi (1999) and Nagae (2003). Yamaguchi's book (in Japanese, English title notwithstanding) is especially effective as a cacophonous visual accompaniment to her central point about the horrid beauty of modern Tokyo: everything is trash, everything is equal, everything is part of the mix.

lowing out of Japan's manufacturing base and some of its less competitive sectors (Frederick 2003). In shorter pieces, *Time*'s writers provided glowing vignettes and studies of the creative forces behind Japan's transition, from construction magnate Mori Minoru to filmmaker Kore-eda Hirokazu to Finance Minister Takenaka Heizo. Collectively, the *Time* articles address Japanese changes, making punk bands, anime, skyscrapers, and neoliberal economics part of the same general trend toward Japanese rejuvenation. And all of it is "cool."

Although Japanese scholars of international relations doubtless knew of "soft power" shortly after Nye coined the term, few used it with regard to Japan until McGray's article appeared. Only the United States, in most eyes, had soft power. In 2001, before becoming finance minister, Takenaka—then a professor at Keio University—edited a volume on the possible development of soft power for Japan. Takenaka's introduction deals with soft power cautiously, arguing that, for historical and linguistic reasons, the United States has soft power resources that will likely remain elusive for Japan. But he also suggests that Japanese economic reform can pave the way toward a more vibrant economy that will once again shape other countries' plans and expectations (Takenaka 2001a, 2001b). Other authors in the collection address more straightforwardly the issue of popular culture and soft power. Kamiya Matake (2001) of National Defense University takes seriously Nye's judgment regarding the importance of shared values, and not just the spread of American commodities; he argues that *Pokemon* and other Japanese anime exports will not lead to greater soft power. Instead, he locates Japan's likely soft power in its ability to reform its economy and then take a more active and open role in global politics. The renowned anthropologist Aoki Tamotsu (2001) writes nearly with despair about the uselessness of pop culture in promoting soft power; even though European children watch *Pokemon,* Japanese studies centers are shrinking, and Japan seems not to be in vogue as a topic or a country.

And so the popularization of the term owes far more to McGray than to Takenaka and colleagues, partly because of McGray's cleverness with his "Gross National Cool" phrasing but largely because he was American. Indeed, vocal approval from Americans seems to have been extraordinarily important to Japanese discussions of the role of Japanese popular culture, far beyond any measurable economic impact. The *Spirited Away* phenomenon—which coincided with McGray's piece—captures this perfectly. Although the movie's U.S. and even global box office receipts were actually modest, its Academy Award victory has been used in Japanese policy discourse to suggest that Japan has arrived. Combined with the staggering popularity of *Pokemon* and other anime in the West, Miyazaki's film generated growing interest in Japanese policy circles. Indeed, the Digital Contents White Paper (*Dejitaru Kontentsu Hakusho*), an annual report published by the Ministry of Economy,

Trade, and Industry (METI)-affiliated Dejitaru Kontentsu Kyokai, uses *Spirited Away*'s transnational success as the first and most important example of the changing appreciation for Japanese popular culture (Dejitaru Kontentsu Kyokai 2003, 24–25). And Gross National Cool captured the Japanese elite's imagination in a way that few other recent American articles have. In November 2003, Japan's leading business newspaper, the *Nikkei Shimbun,* co-sponsored a symposium, featuring McGray, on "Cool Japan: Japan's Cultural Power."

As *Time*'s special issue notes, the term "Gross National Cool" is known to virtually every bureaucrat in Japan, with "soft power" usually accompanying their comments. In 2003, *Gaiko Foramu,* run by the Ministry of Foreign Affairs (MOFA), produced a special issue with nearly a dozen articles focusing on the theme of Japanese soft power and the country's popular culture success overseas. Four of the articles were essentially short testimonials by anime- or J-Pop–loving professionals in Thailand, China, Russia, and Australia, and with one longer one by the Guatemalan ambassador to Japan, who enthusiastically discussed the enduring popularity of Akira Kurosawa films.[5] And in May 2003, *Chuo Koron,* a leading mainstream opinion journal, had a special issue on the same general topic, including a translation of McGray's article, a new piece by Keio University law professor Tadokoro Masayuki about Japan's "soft power" (Tadokoro 2003), and a conversation between American scholar Susan Napier and anime director Okada Toshio described as a "showdown between Japanese and American anime otaku" (*nichibei otaku taiketsu*) (Napier and Okada 2003).

The use of the word *otaku* to describe the authors in a leading journal is instructive, in that it signals that the marginalized have entered the mainstream. The *Chuo Koron* and *Gaiko Foramu* issues share something with *Time*'s special coverage: an understanding that "cool" Japan has emerged from the rapid and often disorienting social changes that many middle-aged Japanese believe have been unleashed on them. And they provide reassurance about what these changes will mean. The articles paint a picture of a Japan in transition, though marked by important cultural legacies from the past. "Uncool Japan"—presumably the Japan of lifetime employment, examination hell, rigid gender differentiation, and obsessive deference to authority—would have been unable to have this kind of cultural effect on the rest of Asia, because it simply could not have produced this kind of vibrant, diverse, and yet distinctive entertainment environment. In this view, Japan has experienced a phoenix-like rebirth from the self-inflicted wounds of rapid modernization; combined with its unique traditional culture, this has generated a new cultural milieu that is simultaneously viewed as surprising and yet somehow in-

---

[5] *Gaiko Foramu* 174 (January 2003), especially the international vignettes from pp. 30–45.

evitable. But the hope goes even further: because the world—particularly Asia Pacific—is catching on, with even the Americans rejecting their own mass-produced pop culture in favor of Japan's zanier alternatives, Japan stands to benefit politically, provided that it can figure out how to make the most of an auspicious moment.

The appeal of soft power is understandable—and very broad. For Japanese liberals, soft power represents a way for nonmilitary Japan to have an effect on global politics. Tsujimoto Kiyomi, the now-disgraced former policy chief of the Social Democratic Party, emphasized that Japan's security policy should begin with a downgrading of the Defense Agency's role and shift from hard power to soft power, primarily expressed through economic assistance.[6] For mainstream or more conservative observers, soft power can help Japan be seen as more "trustworthy," meaning that the global spread of Japanese popular culture can increase international friendship and trust. In this framework, soft power and support for the arts become a component of public diplomacy, thereby helping Japan make more effective use of its hard power (Takashina, Fukukawa, and Fujii 2003, esp. comments by Fujii, 20, and Takashina, 22). Indeed, Japan's recent expansion of its global security role in support of U.S. military activities in Afghanistan and Iraq would have been impossible without government efforts to build trust with its Asian neighbors (Midford 2003).[7] Because of its impressive elasticity, soft power appeals equally, though very differently, to Japanese policy- and lawmakers of virtually all stripes.[8] Moreover, soft power may represent to concerned Japanese what it did to concerned Americans—that reports of their country's demise are premature.

This means that Gross National Cool and soft power are almost certainly going to be politically consequential, though perhaps not in the way that the terms' users might suppose. If we think of soft power not as a category of power resources but rather as an idea—a component of a cultural and ideographical structure of governance—it can affect Japanese policy even if Japan does not really have soft power. Of course, whether Japan has soft power or not is almost certainly impossible to tell, and is not in itself germane to policy. After all, the term "soft power" became popular in the United States not

---

[6] Tsujimoto's Web page now focuses on her apologies for the financial scandal that toppled her from office and may land her in prison. Older pages for her policy positions, however, still exist. See http://www.kiyomi.gr.jp/seisaku/, accessed October 27, 2003.

[7] The Liberal Democratic Party's 2003 campaign "Reform Declaration" (*kaikaku sengen*) makes this connection explicit. See http://www.jimin.jp.

[8] Indeed, one can easily find references to "soft power" in the Web pages of the New Komeito, http://www.komei.or.jp/policy/detail/5–1.htm; the Democratic Party's Hatoyama Yukio, http://www.hatoyama.gr.jp/cont09/cont08.html; and the long version of the Liberal Democratic Party's 2003 "policy manifesto," available at lower house member Kosugi Takashi's Web page, http://www.threeweb.ad.jp/~takosugi/manifesto/. All sites accessed October 27, 2003.

only because of Nye's writings and his important position in international relations theory but also because it sat well with Americans' views of themselves. Because American culture and values are constitutive of Americans, it is practically impossible for Americans to determine effectively whether their values are really shared or not. The same is likely true for Japanese.

One of my favorite things about living in Japan is my daily ability to chat with Japanese friends, colleagues, and acquaintances about life here and overseas. Aside from being good practice for my Japanese, it also affords me the opportunity to try to understand the world as Japanese see it—phenomenology on the cheap. There is, of course, a certain amount of temporary intellectual dishonesty involved; during the time I speak with a Japanese person about some issue, I am likely to take that person's views as somehow representative of a larger community: Japanese women, Japanese conservatives, or, in moments of complete laziness, all Japanese. But when we speak about the United States, and my counterpart says something with which I disagree, my tendency is not to accept the comment as possibly valid or representative of something useful or important; it is quite simply wrong, because I as an American understand my country, and she or he as a Japanese does not. Of course, as a researcher, I try to fight this foolish impulse, but its existence speaks to a larger concern: other countries' (or, rather, people's) views of one's own country have no independent merit except insofar as they correspond to something we believe. This means that when we speak about how other countries see us, we are almost certainly talking about how we see ourselves, and using other nations as a kind of mirror to express our own pride, insecurity, anger, or sadness. Americans are probably the worst judges of our own soft power, because we cannot separate our cultural effects elsewhere from our own deeply ingrained views of ourselves.

For this reason, the rapid increase in attention in Japan to soft power and Japan's cultural weight elsewhere probably has less value as a tool for evaluating Japan's regional importance than it does as a heuristic device for grasping how Japanese policymakers now see their regional role. And the motifs I have discussed—contemporary Japan's rise from the ashes of economic recession, the continuity between rebellious Japan's pop culture and earlier cultural traditions, and the political weight afforded by the wide acceptance of Japanese entertainment icons—figure prominently in contemporary understandings of Japanese soft power. Whether one wants a nonmilitary and generous Japan or an assertive yet trusted Japan, the prescription is similar: Japan needs to support the spread of its popular culture overseas in order for other countries to see what today's Japan really is. It is a changed country, a country of originality and even individuality, a country that remembers its traditions even as it boldly meets the challenges of modernity. It is a country that would not hurt a fly.

Policy Outcomes: Culture as "Content" and Power

As a policy idea, improving soft power through cultural promotion has empowered certain policy organizations to take steps they otherwise might not have, and it has also introduced a new potential criterion for evaluating policy success. This is not to say that it has been solely or even primarily responsible for creating new policies; instead, it has offered new opportunities and rationales for engaging in initiatives that policymakers already intended to pursue. After all, government strategies for cultural exchange, information technologies, and tourism hardly began with McGray's article. As early as 1995, the Culture Agency (Bunkacho) created a working group on multimedia, and then subsequently produced a 1997 report on "new media arts" for the twenty-first century (Uehara 2003). But the sudden excitement about Japan's Gross National Cool has provided options for state engagement with recreation and entertainment industries, in some ways allowing administrators to put dislocating (and even frightening) forms of social and economic change to national purpose.

This would hardly be the first time. In the 1980s, with the rapid increase in the value of the yen and subsequent decrease in the cost of overseas tours, administrators in the Ministry of Transport (now a component of the Ministry of Land, Infrastructure, and Transport) projected that Japanese outbound tourism would likely double in only a few years. In some ways, this might have been a terribly undesirable turn of events. After all, the increase in outbound tourism clearly came at some expense to the domestic tourism market, over which the ministry had jurisdiction; Hawaii's gain would be Ishikawa Prefecture's loss. The demographics were also worrisome; with Japanese business and family travel increasing only marginally, much of the outbound travel action came from groups of women—most disconcertingly, unmarried women—traveling overseas. In spite of occasional public outcry about the threat of AIDS and the rumor that Japanese women were traveling to Bali for sex, clever Tourism Bureau members recognized that this change in leisure patterns could just as easily be interpreted as Japan's willingness to redistribute the economic gains from its massive trade surplus, thus promoting international understanding, economic fairness, and open borders all at the same time. They therefore created, in 1986, the Ten Million Program, which "aimed" at doubling Japanese outbound tourism, to levels that the administrators assumed it would hit with or without their encouragement. By doing so, they were able to justify greater access for their ministry to the national budget and the establishment of new institutions over which they had jurisdiction, two common goals of Japanese policy organizations (Leheny 2003, 133–73).

The Gross National Cool and soft power initiatives share with the Ten Million Program an eagerness to embrace social change, put it to national use, and support existing policy priorities. Clearly, I do not mean to suggest that Japanese ministries are incapable of change any more than I would argue that the collapse of the bubble acted as a light switch, automatically changing Japan from an economic dynamo to a bedridden victim. But institutions are important specifically because they define what people take for granted, and therefore how they will understand new information, their environment, and their goals.[9] Derek Hall (2004a) has argued that the large-scale drive toward economic "liberalization" in Japan is not in fact a retreat from institutionalized economic nationalism; instead, liberalization is defended and apparently understood in nationalist terms. Similarly, government officials now working with popular culture and "digital contents" are trying to do what they have always done: to promote the development of industrial forces that can serve national goals.

Tourism once again provides an excellent example. Partly as an effort to demonstrate his support for local regions badly hurt by Japan's economic recession, Prime Minister Koizumi in 2002 announced the establishment of the Tourism Policy Advisory Council. The goal of the group was to develop new ideas for attracting foreign tourists to Japan, policies that would likely be attractive to Ministry of Land, Infrastructure, and Transport Tourism Bureau members aiming to maintain budgetary interest in their management of the nation's recreational travel infrastructure. Of course, with the continued high cost of travel to Japan, terrorism-related reductions in international air travel, and occasional Asian shocks such as the SARS (severe acute respiratory syndrome) crisis, the council almost certainly recognized that a rapid or even medium-term increase in tourism to Japan was extraordinarily unlikely. And so their final report emphasizes not the economic returns to Japan of tourism but rather the political returns of increased exchange. Indeed, it explicitly links cultural exchange, soft power, and the creation of "cultural security" (*bunka anzen hosho*). It also cites McGray to point out that Japan's Gross National Cool is now part of the country's appeal (Kanko Rikoku Kondankai 2003; see also Awata 2003).

Similarly, the Ministry of Foreign Affairs has also begun to incorporate soft power into its lingo, though it is careful about any suggestion that Japan is trying to exercise power over its neighbors. In a speech to the Vancouver Board of Trade, Foreign Minister Kawaguchi Yoriko (2002) emphasized that Canada and Japan both share an idea of soft power, in that they prefer to exercise their international authority through peaceful means. And the Japan Foun-

---

[9] This is how I read Jepperson's definition of institutions, which holds that they are "socially constructed, routine-reproduced (*ceteris paribus*), program or rule systems. They operate as relative fixtures of constraining environments and are accompanied by taken-for-granted accounts." See Jepperson 2001.

dation, previously administered by and still related to MOFA, stresses the importance of cultural and educational exchange programs for Japan's diplomacy, stressing that these contribute to the nation's soft power. This language nearly supplants earlier emphases on "mutual understanding." Citing McGray, the Japan Foundation refers to "Gross National Cool" and suggests that Japan's cultivation of its cultural resources can improve its "national image" and thereby strengthen its global hand. The report focuses heavily on the role that soft power plays in a changing world, culminating in recommendations for MOFA and Japan Foundation activity, which are largely consistent with existing priorities (Kokusai Koryu Kenkyukai 2003). That the goals are largely economic can perhaps best be seen in the January 2003 issue of MOFA's *Gaiko Foramu*, which carries the slogan "'Nihon Burando': Kokka no Miryoku o Kangaeru" ("Brand Japan": Considering the Appeal of the Nation).[10]

Japan's economic policymakers have seized on soft power as a crucial wedge for funding and supporting their efforts to promote Japan's "content industries," a term that refers largely to online content. With the Internet revolution, virtually any cultural product—film, piece of music, artwork, and so forth—can be digitized and transmitted globally. Because the money in information technology now appears to lie largely in the content itself, and not necessarily in the infrastructure used to transmit it, there can be significant rewards for firms, individual artists, and perhaps even governments able to sell people what they want, or perhaps influence what they want. The old Ministry of Posts and Telecommunications[11] began to commission reports on information technologies in 1995, as did its research affiliate, the Posts and Telecommunications Research Institute (Uehara 2003, 2). Although these focused primarily on the types of infrastructure involved, they presaged an era in which the government would start to consider the importance of government intervention in the content and not just existence of information.

Alongside the Ministry of Public Management, Home Affairs, and Posts and Telecommunications, the organization most responsible for conceptualizing Gross National Cool is the Ministry of Economics, Trade, and Industry. Although long dominated by an interest in manufacturing industries, METI has more recently devoted considerable attention to information industries. To some degree, the ministry's interest in defining virtually all artistic work as "content" involves a bit of historical revisionism; the METI-affiliated Digi-

---

[10] This is an unusual translation of *kokka,* which normally refers to the "state" rather than the nation. I have chosen (temporarily) to go with the less inflammatory version, "nation," though I am open to suggestions.

[11] It has since been merged with the former Ministry of Home Affairs to become Somusho, which literally translates as the General Affairs Ministry, but is officially known in English as the Ministry of Public Management, Home Affairs, and Posts and Telecommunications.

tal Content Association now includes a timeline of digital content that traces
the development of film in the late 19th century, music recordings in the
1920s, and the like (Dejitaru Kontentsu Kyokai 2003, 158–61). Especially
since 2002, METI has taken an impressively ambitious approach to the issue,
establishing study groups on comprehensive and specific aspects of media
content governance, all aimed at generating recommendations on how the
ministry can help generate long-term creativity in Japan, protect Japanese intellectual property rights in Asia, cross-fertilize different media industries,[12]
and the like. METI aims at ensuring that Japanese content creators and providers—anime, J-Pop, film studios, game developers, toy producers, and
virtually any other entertainment industry capable of catching global attention—remain competitive over the long term. To that end, its study groups
inquire widely about the nature of entertainment after the Internet revolution. METI benefits from the increased public visibility of Cool Japan through
generous budgeting of its training and coordination programs, which are
meant to help those artistic and creative endeavors judged likely to be globally competitive over the long term.[13]

Even more remarkable than METI's ambition, however, is the broad governmental acceptance of the Gross National Cool core: Japan has become hip
and fashionable specifically because it has changed into something different.
And so the Digital Content Working Group, part of a government advisory
council, asks about what kinds of firms will be needed in the future: large entertainment firms capable of professionally capturing the global market, or
small firms of near-amateurs who have ideas that rapidly catch fire? Will the
market be driven by hip trendsetters or by the reclusive otaku whose obses-
siveness speaks to a particular character's or program's appeal? Should the
government be focused on necessity (*pan*, or bread) or on the entertainment
of its citizens (*sakasu*, or circuses)?[14] In other words, the uncomfortable social changes (e.g., otaku empowerment) have now become central to Japan's
economic resurgence, to its national cool. And so the question becomes how
government industrial policy, very nearly the perfect symbol of pre–Cool Japan to many observers, can harness the power of developments attributed
largely to a Japan in which ministries no longer call the shots.

Japan is far from the only country in which those in power seek to co-opt
the appeal of marginalized or self-marginalizing figures. After all, in its public celebration of social change that its owners would likely have opposed, the

[12] See once again Tsujimoto Kenzo's comments in the "Kontentsu Sangyo Kokusai Senryaku
Kenkyukai (Dai 1 Kai) Gijiroku," pp. 5–7.

[13] Interview, October 30, 2003.

[14] These questions appear in the general working group document "Dejitaru Kontentsu WG no
Kento Jokyo" (Investigative Conditions for the Digital Content Working Group), produced by the
Joho Tsushin Sofuto Kondankai (Information Transmission and Software Discussion Council).

Nikkei Shimbun's 2003 ad campaign—"Onna wa kawatta. Otoko wa dou da?" (Women have changed. Now how about men?)—is no more ghastly than is U.S. corporate sponsorship of successive Woodstock monstrosities. But this is not a corporation acting as the disinterested face of global capitalism, using whatever icons it can appropriate to sell newspapers or soda to middle-aged consumers trying desperately to deny their surrender to "the system." Instead, state actors seem to accept that the creative forces they now seek to employ can exist only in a system that does not aim to control or use them. Cool Japan exists because Uncool Japan collapsed; now Cool Japan needs to show that it is, after all, still Japan.

What Kind of Power?

This leaves open the question of how Japanese popular culture will ultimately matter in Asia, even if one starts from the assumption that its entertainment industries will continue to grow and even dominate. In one possible view, consumers watching Japanese video games, listening to J-Pop songs, or displaying a poster of pop star Matsuura Aya on their walls are cogs in the "culture industry" (see, e.g., Adorno 1991). The spread of Japanese convenience stores or fast-food chains like Hoka-Hoka Bento in Indonesia (*Mainichi Shimbun* 2004) prove nothing more than do the ubiquitous Kentucky Fried Chicken shops in the region. These examples represent little other than the ability of Japanese firms to sell their mass-produced icons and ditties to an increasingly and depressingly global market. This might be good for Japanese firms and, if properly managed, for the overall Japanese economy, but its political benefits for Japan are likely negligible.

For many in the Japanese government, this would clearly be insufficient. As Iwabuchi (2002, 33–35) notes, Japanese popular culture overseas often carries a *mukokuseki* quality, meaning that its national origin cannot easily be determined. With anime characters, stories, names, and titles being designed for transnational audiences, Japaneseness has somehow been bled out of them. Iwabuchi, however, notes that in addition to the way in which mukokuseki actually becomes a signifier of Japanese origin, there are a number of Japanese entertainment products—bands, television dramas, and so forth—that have a clear Japanese "odor." Obviously aiming to link the products and the country that produces them, Japanese policymakers, particularly in MOFA, have promoted the idea of Nihon Burando or the Japan Brand. The goal here is to improve public diplomacy by making other people more aware of Japan's contributions to global culture, design, and entertainment.[15] Un-

---

[15] See the articles in the January 2003 *Gaiko Foramu* special issue on "Nihon Burando."

less people overseas know that Japanese created *Sailor Moon*, how can it confer soft power on the Japanese government?

Iwabuchi, though trying to show that Japanese popular culture has become part of a fragmented process of globalization, concedes that in certain cases Taiwanese audiences, for example, have consciously identified themselves more closely with Japanese dramas and films than they have with Hollywood fare, which seems both more fantastic and more foreign (Iwabuchi 2002, 139–57). Using interviews with Chinese audiences in five cities, Nakano Yoshiko and Wu Yongmei (2003) make a similar finding. Yet they too reject the notion that this is the result of some kind of simple and unproblematic "cultural proximity," to use Iwabuchi's language. Instead, Nakano and Wu argue, this fascination arises from the yearnings of the new bourgeois classes in China for a wealthier and more open lifestyle just around the corner. In this view, Japan acts as a combination crystal ball and mirror: it is one version of the future that the modernizing economies of Asia hope to achieve.

Well before Japan became the pop culture maverick that it purportedly is, it already served as a kind of cultural touchstone for its neighbors in Asia. Indeed, for many in 1960s Taiwan, South Korea, and elsewhere, Japan's technological achievements served as representatives of what they might themselves enjoy in their lifetimes if they worked hard enough and had enough good fortune. Set in 1962 Hong Kong, Wong Kar-Wai's masterpiece *In the Mood for Love* brilliantly evokes his characters' class positions, as well as the setting of his story, through clever references to the commodities they can purchase. When Mrs. Chan's husband returns from a business trip to Japan with an automatic rice cooker, it immediately becomes the talk of the apartment building, not because it is Japanese and exotic, but rather because it is convenient and modern. Japan is ahead, and it serves as a symbol of what other Asians, even the Shanghainese community in Hong Kong, might accomplish.[16] Many Japanese products overseas—whether they are Matsushita rice cookers in 1960s Taiwan or the TV series *Tokyo Love Story* in 1990s China—gain at least part and perhaps most of their meaning from their representation of modernity.

In the 1960s and 1970s, Japanese too looked abroad to find relevant examples of how their lifestyles might improve, though their models came primarily from the United States and Western Europe. To a degree, this tendency became a target of government policy as well. In a methodological discussion in their massive 1974 report entitled *Yoka Soran* (Overview of Leisure), published by the MITI (METI's predecessor) Leisure Development Office, advisory committee members explained that their research on appropriate leisure and lifestyle changes included a number of comparative case studies,

---

[16] I thank Nakano Yoshiko for making this point in correspondence.

but that only the ones from advanced industrial nations (Western Europe and North America) would be relevant:

> The various subcommittees focused on fifteen countries from North America, Western Europe, the Communist countries, and four other regions. But if one examines the structure of leisure in these different countries, one sees great diversity from the advanced countries that have already entered an era of a new leisure civilization [*atarashii yoka bunmei no jidai*] to the lesser developed countries that still have no fixed understanding of what "leisure" means. (Tsusho Sangyosho Yoka Kaihatsushitsu 1974, 315)

This report, one of two major MITI-sponsored leisure studies at the time, became the intellectual cornerstone of government policies designed specifically to align Japanese recreation and entertainment industries with those of the United States and Europe.

This tendency to see the future through the current conditions of other nations continued well into the 1990s. The Leisure Development Center, a special foundation funded by MITI to provide policy-relevant research on recreation-related industries, used a combination of domestic research surveys and comparative studies to provide the necessary information on Japan's best approach. When I asked one official why the researchers focused on the United States and Europe rather than on, for example, Korea, Zimbabwe, or Brazil, he seemed stunned by the question and responded (very slowly, probably because he believed at this point that I had asked my question incorrectly or that I simply was not very bright), "because those are the advanced industrial nations." There was simply no alternative. The Western nations were valuable examples not because one liked or trusted them but rather because they were ahead (Leheny 2003, 15, 179–80).

For some, the idea that Japanese popular culture represents modernity to Asia would be highly attractive to Japanese policymakers. In one line of argument, Japan would be an especially appealing country for many around the globe, particularly in Asia, specifically because it has successfully negotiated between the demands of economic and political liberalization, on the one hand, and the maintenance of a distinctive culture, on the other (Takashina, Fukukawa, and Fujii 2003, esp. Fujii, 23). If countries aspire to be like Japan, perhaps that confers a kind of soft power—an ability to persuade rather than coerce.

But the benefits are unclear. As Benedict Anderson (1991) has noted, nations write their histories in ways that reflect their exposure to established narratives of development. It therefore becomes important, for example, for Thailand and Jamaica to have "their" own French Revolutions, because a country's history requires some sort of cataclysmic break from the past (Anderson 1991, esp. chap. 5). The French Revolution looms large in the world's national imaginations, but it is unclear how the French government benefits from its metonymical spot as the place where lightning struck first. Japan's pop culture policy specialists seem focused on how creative, rambunctious, and proudly engaged post-bubble Japan can influence the rest of the world, but they might do well to ask how "the world" influenced Japan's lifestyle policy shifts only a quarter century ago. The relevant sources from that era suggest that Western Europe and especially the United States provided Japan with a crucial guidepost for how the country would need to develop, but there is neither gratitude nor admiration expressed in these documents. Instead, there is simple acceptance that this is the way things will be. To be sure, the United States likely benefited from this ambivalent relationship in a number of ways, but it is unclear that U.S. leaders understood or even could have understood how to use it.

Through Being Cool

Can Japanese leaders learn how to harness their symbolic place as a lifestyle leader in Asia? The evidence thus far is not encouraging, though not because of any failure on the part of Japan's entertainment or culture industries. Instead, like those Americans who deploy the term "soft power," Japanese policymakers are likely to be preoccupied by their deeply held views of their nation's values and its proper global role; they are rather less likely to see their nation as outsiders do. Because of concerns in both countries over national decline, there should be little wonder that first Americans and now Japanese have been so quick to embrace the soft power idea, given its reliance on appealing images of each nation. Soft power contains a special charm for Japanese elites because of their country's mixed, ambiguous relationship with Asia Pacific. In one variant, it represents a peaceful Japan that can encourage other nations to become wealthy and wise through Japan's own example and its generosity. In another, it offers the opportunity to convince other people that Japan's development as a normal country, with a normal military, is not to be feared, because this is a nation that has only the best of intentions. If people just get to know the Japanese—through their songs, their television hits, their anime—they will realize that they are kind and decent, creative and curious, and not to be feared. But no policymakers seem ready to concede that the images being transmitted are of a prosperous imagined future for Japan's neighbors, not Japanese values of transparent and immediately accessible meaning.

And so, perhaps what is most remarkable about the sudden interest in Japanese pop culture's political role in Asia is what it reveals about how the Japanese government views the region and itself. From this rarefied perspective, the rest of Asia, like Japan, struggles to maintain traditional identities in the face of modernization, and so soft power both emanates from and employs Japan's special position as a non-Western country that has successfully developed both politically and economically. In this logic, part of Japan's bumpy ride to modernization has been the post-bubble collapse of traditional authority structures, and the flowering of creative talents too long suppressed by the country's social stagnation. And so now, as in the past, it is the government's job to make sure that these talents are successfully developed, harnessed, and turned to the nation's advantage. I do not mean to argue that government strategies for promoting "digital contents" will fail as industrial policy. Instead, I simply suggest that the discourses surrounding the confounding and ambiguous place of transnational cultural flows provide clues about official intentions and prevailing political trends. These too may be important, and may become especially so through state efforts to utilize current popular trends.

But I do not envy those trying to disentangle the Gordian knot of transnational cultural flows—trying to determine what is Japanese, American, Korean, or Chinese—particularly if their political success depends on their somehow getting it right. Roughly thirty minutes into Kitano's film, Zatoichi faces off against a ronin in the middle of a tiny restaurant. Because the ronin, like Zatoichi, is a brilliant and fearless swordsman, their extended battle would be a messy and unsatisfying affair in such a cramped room. Zatoichi blocks the ronin and quietly says, "Konna semai tokoro de katana o sonna fu ni tsukanja dame da yo" (You shouldn't brandish your sword in a narrow space like this). With a narrow space like the Asia Pacific, and an especially large number of swords, it might be impossible to tell whose is whose.

IV

NEW SOCIAL FORCES IN EAST ASIA

10

The Third Wave: Southeast Asia and Middle-Class Formation in the Making of a Region

TAKASHI SHIRAISHI

The process of region-making in East Asia can no longer be analyzed in terms of the "flying geese" model of interaction between Japan and Asia, which is based on a Japan-centered regional economy sustained by Japanese finance, a Japanese mode of development, and Japanese production networks. Regionalization instead entails complex and dynamic interactions between and among governmental and nongovernmental actors and results in a hybrid East Asia.

This concluding chapter examines the social bases of regionalization and regionalism by looking at the formation of middle classes in East Asia. Successive waves of regional economic development, powered by developmental states and national and transnational capitalism, have nurtured sizeable middle classes that have a lot in common in their professional lives and their lifestyles, in fashion, leisure, and entertainment, in their aspirations and dreams. They are the main engine of hybridization. Although the national significance of the middle classes varies according to where they are placed in different political and social structures—that is, they occupy different positions in their respective societies as well as in relation to their nation-states—their regional significance is without doubt because they constitute the expanding regional consumer market. The kind of life they espouse and live carries social and environmental costs. Their survival and expansion as a class are largely dependent on the economic performance of their respective coun-

I thank Caroline Sy Hau, my partner, for her careful reading and commenting on this chapter.

tries; their countries' failure in economic development may render them vulnerable to political and social crises. At the same time, the regional market of which the middle classes are the main consumers mediates new forms of national and regional identities that can potentially advance regional integration.

In the first section of this chapter I address the issues raised in previous chapters concerning the role of mutually overlapping and reacting spheres of states, markets, and societies in the region-making process. The second and third sections locate the rise of Southeast Asian middle classes in a longer historical and larger regional perspective by arguing that these middle classes represent the "third wave" of class formation following that in Japan and then in South Korea and Taiwan. The next three sections discuss four political and social structures—represented by Thailand, Malaysia, Indonesia, and the Philippines—in which Southeast Asian middle classes are placed. The final section explores the implications of middle-class East Asia for region making.

States, Markets, Societies

This book has examined the ways in which Japan engages with East Asia in three mutually overlapping and reacting spheres: states, markets, and societies.

In the realm of states, the United States has remained hegemonic, casting a long shadow over the regional architecture. This is especially evident in security, and to a lesser extent in finance and trade. Three of the chapters in this book address the question of what kinds of constraints and spaces for maneuver structure Japan's security, finance, and trade policies under the condition of Japan's political stasis, while another chapter examines Japan's political stasis itself.

Richard Friman and others in chapter 4 argue that Japan's security policy can best be understood in terms of continuity. Its security stance is that of a state committed to the broad protection of a society accustomed to domestic safety and order. The limited shifts in its external military policy show the government's sensitivity to its international environment, above all the military security concerns of the United States, while the slower pace of change in government policies on transnational concerns such as drugs, immigration, and counterterrorism display the maintenance of basic state-society agreements over how the government is supposed to protect the Japanese. Natasha Hamilton-Hart in chapter 5 shows that Japan's international and regional finance policy can best be understood as discontinuity in continuity. She argues that the 1997–98 crisis marked an important break with trends in the preceding decade, but the discontinuity is neither a reversal of Japanization nor a shift toward exclusive regionalism in finance. The foundations for a formal regional architecture for managing finance are now in place, but they remain linked to the U.S.-led global finance structure. There is, however, no clear and uncontested trajectory along which they will develop. In chapter 6, Naoko Munakata shows that Japan's trade policy is characterized by discontinuity. She argues that Japan has adopted a multitrack trade policy where bilateral and regional preferential arrangements complement the WTO and that the Japan-Singaporean Economic Partnership Agreement marked a clear departure from Japan's long-standing policy of exclusive multilateralism. The change took place because Japan had become more deeply embedded economically in East Asia in the post–Plaza Accord era and because there is an institutional complementarity between Japan's domestic structural reform and deeper integration with the rest of Asia.

In each of the above cases, Japan's political stasis as analyzed by T. J. Pempel in chapter 2 is a major explanatory factor, while U.S. hegemony looms large and makes itself felt differently. In security, Japan's political stasis combined with U.S. centrality in Asian security ensures continuity. Japanese policymakers adapt to a changing external environment as defined by the United States within the political constraints of Japanese domestic institutions and norms, though Friman et al. underline the potential importance of rapid social changes in Japan. In finance, the United States has set the limits within which Japan has worked to create the foundations for a regional financial structure (hence discontinuity in continuity) and vetoed an Asian monetary fund. As Hamilton-Hart notes, any future reshuffling of influence between region-making and the U.S.-led global financial regime would depend on Japan's financial structure returning to health and on developing an infrastructure of information, analysis, and formal interstate coordination to deploy Asia's currency reserves and regional liquidity arrangements for region-making. And Munakata notes that in the absence of systematic U.S. intervention in regional trade, Japan has embarked on constructing bilateral and regional preferential trade arrangements with free trade agreements and economic partnership agreements (EPAs) as its instrument. This explains the discontinuity, but the ultimate success of FTAs and EPAs depends on how far the new arrangements can go in dismantling Japan's dual structure and restructuring its internationally uncompetitive, protected, inefficient industries when its political system is in stasis.

Japan's political stasis, however, does not mean that nothing has been happening there. As Pempel notes, changes now taking place, including corporate restructurings, the financial Big Bang, generational change in the political class, social changes that undermine the very foundation of the family, and the breaking of the social contract, may eventually lead to a substantial overhaul of an extensive and deeply entrenched set of policies, procedures, and institutions. But many of these changes take a long time to play out politically, and in the meantime the general trends in regional security, finance, and trade will most likely stay as discussed in the chapters.

In the realm of markets, Dieter Ernst shows in chapter 7 that Japanese corporate capital in the electronics industry is attempting to restructure, expand, and upgrade its Asian production networks—accelerating manufacturing FDI in China, while maintaining operations in Southeast Asia and rationalizing their overlapping networks—and thus it continues to affect Asian regionalization patterns. He also argues that despite attempts to replicate the American model, Japanese firms will still end up with very different forms of network organization in East Asia and may build strategic alliances with emerging new industry leaders in East Asia, above all in Greater China and Korea, and use these alliances as a catalyst for domestic upgrading and breakthrough innovations. In chapter 8, Derek Hall shows that with the emergence of Japan as a consumption superpower, Japanese consumption patterns, rather than investment decisions, have come to have far more important implications for ecologies outside Japan. Japan's economic stagnation (and declining purchasing power) and changing Japanese lifestyles (including the Americanization of food consumption) have led to the rising consumption of processed and semiprocessed food, the development of agro-industry, and the creation of Japan's shadow ecology, which is less Southeast Asia–centered and more China-centered and global, and which is less contentious but equally as devastating ecologically as the old.

Finally in the realm of societies, William W. Kelly and Merry I. White in chapter 3 identify neuralgic points in the Japanese social body in which social and institutional reorganization is taking place. Looking specifically at students, young workers, women, the elderly, and non-Japanese permanent residents and ethnic Japanese returned migrants, they demonstrate that disparate, parallel, and personal actions are rubbing against and unraveling the skein of ideologies and institutions, above all the ideology and institution of the family in Japan. David Leheny in chapter 9 documents the success story of the export of Japanese cultural products. Although the Japanese government has attempted to capitalize on this success as evidence of Japan's "soft power," Leheny underscores the fact that the success story is less about self-evident soft power than about the manifold ways in which Asian consumers appropriate these products as part of their middle-class aspirations.

Two implications can be drawn from all the chapters in the book. First, Japan no longer dominates the regionalization process in East Asia. It is no longer possible to understand region-making as the mere extension of a single national model. The Japanese government's freedom of action is largely circumscribed by the primacy of the U.S. security agenda and its neoliberal policies, and by Japan's own internal structural constraints and domestic politics. Moreover, China's emergence as the world's manufacturing powerhouse as well as its political initiatives toward region-making—for example, the FTAs with ASEAN and proposed FTAs with Japan and South Korea—further complicates Japan's attempts to exercise national leadership in regional affairs as seen in the Chiang Mai and economic partnership initiatives. Indeed, the issue can no longer be framed by the concept of leadership, whether that of Japan or that of China.

Second, and more important, regional economic development in the 1980s and 1990s, significantly driven by Japanese, South Korean, Taiwanese, and "overseas Chinese" FDIs, has changed East Asia in a fundamental way. Economic development has laid the social foundations for new types of national politics, emerging consumer markets, and further market-driven regionalization. The inflow of East Asian capital throughout Southeast Asia, for instance, has worked itself out in different ways in different countries. But everywhere it has given rise to new urban middle classes.[1] Constituted through rapid global and regional industrialization driven by FDIs and finance capital, their horizontal solidarity is dependent on, but no longer solely confined to, their ability to express themselves politically through the state and culturally as a nation. Because the middle classes are constituted not solely through a homogeneous national culture but rather through networks of markets and global cultural and financial flows, middle-class consciousness is fostered through interactions between national governments and domestic and transnational markets.[2]

This concluding chapter builds on these ideas while showing that they now resonate in the broader region because modernity and its production, consumption, and representational regimes have taken root in a regionwide arena far beyond the borders of Japan. The emergent regionwide middle classes are a crucial engine of East Asian region-making.

The Making of Middle-Class East Asia

Let us first profile the emergent middle-class East Asia through an overview of the material and ideational forces and patterns that have historically shaped class formation in the region.

Middle classes in East Asia are a product of regional economic development in the postwar era. The GDP shares of Japan, South Korea, Taiwan,

---

[1] By middle classes I mean not only the middle class of each country and of the different ethnic groups within one country but the various middle class occupations within each country, e.g., business people, medical doctors, lawyers, accountants.

[2] I thank Pheng Cheah for helping me to spell out the point in this way.

Hong Kong, Singapore, Thailand, Malaysia, Indonesia, the Philippines, and China in the world GDP increased from 10 percent in 1950 to 26 percent in 1998, while the U.S. share declined from 27 to 22 percent and the West European share from 24 to 18 percent in the same period (Sugihara 2003, 5). Regional economic development took place within the context of the American informal empire in "Free Asia," with the U.S.-led regional security system and the triangular trade system as its two major pillars. Furthermore, it was actively promoted by national states in the region, whether under democratic or authoritarian developmentalist regimes, both of which espoused the politics of productivity, a politics that transformed political issues into problems of output and sought to neutralize class conflict in favor of a consensus on economic growth (Maier 1978, 23). The first wave of regional economic development took place in Japan from the mid-1950s to the early 1970s and led to the emergence of a middle-class Japan by the early 1970s. The second wave took place between the 1960s and 1980s in South Korea and Taiwan (as well as in Hong Kong and Singapore) and led to the formation of middle-class societies in these countries by the 1980s. The rise of middle classes in Thailand and Malaysia, and to a lesser extent in Indonesia and the Philippines, represents the third wave of class formation following economic development in the region from the mid-1980s to the late 1990s. We are currently witnessing the fourth wave of middle-class formation in urban centers in China.

Two salient points stand out in the history of East Asian middle-class formation. First, while middle classes in Japan as well as in South Korea and Taiwan were largely created by developmental states and national capitalism, middle-class formation in Southeast Asia was driven by global and regional transnational capitalism working in alliance with national states. From the mid-1980s to the early 1990s when global financial transactions were expanding exponentially, these countries liberalized their banking and portfolio investment regimes and made it easier for foreign banks to set up shop and for foreign institutional investors to enter their stock markets. These countries also deregulated the FDI regimes at a time when the 1985 Plaza Accord led to the appreciation of the Japanese yen, Korean won, Taiwanese dollar, and Singaporean dollar, forcing firms to move their production facilities to Southeast Asia. This led to the expansion and deepening of business networks, whether Japanese, Korean, or "overseas Chinese," and to the increasing integration of national economies in East Asia.[3] Through this process of global finance- and FDI-led regional economic development, Southeast Asia's

[3] How "Chinese" are "overseas Chinese" is of course a contentious issue, hence the recourse to quotation marks. Southeast Asia's ethnic Chinese are differently positioned in their respective domiciles—whereas Sino-Thais now constitute the mainstream middle class in Thailand, Sino-Indonesians, who are seen to dominate the economy but who remain politically marginal, occupy a more problematic place in Indonesia's political economy and cultural politics.

major urban centers were increasingly integrated into the global and regional system of finance and production (Katzenstein 2000, 4–15). Multinational corporations headquartered in global centers such as New York and Tokyo established their regional headquarters in Singapore and country headquarters in Bangkok, Kuala Lumpur, Jakarta, and Manila. The country headquarters of multinational corporations performed management, international finance, trade, and production service functions, operationalizing and translating central decisions and, if necessary, negotiating with governments, while establishing their factories in newly developed industrial estates in suburban areas, normally located near international container port facilities. The division of labor informed the transformation of Southeast Asia's major urban centers and their suburbs. The increasing integration of Thailand, Malaysia, Indonesia, and the Philippines into the global system of finance and the regional system of production created jobs for business executives and managers, engineers and technicians, bankers and stock analysts, consultants, lawyers, accountants, and white-collar office workers in city centers, while jobs for factory managers and workers were created in their suburbs.

Second, new urban middle classes in East Asia, whether in Japan, South Korea, Taiwan, or Southeast Asia, with their middle-class jobs, education, and income, have in turn created their own new lifestyles commensurate with their middle-class income and status. They may be Japanese, Korean, Minnan Taiwanese, pribumi (indigenous) Indonesians, Chinese Filipinos, Thais, Singaporeans, or Malay Malaysians, but they share a lot more in common than their parents' generation did in business, lifestyle, taste, fashion, and aspirations. They work as business executives and managers, government officials, consultants, doctors, lawyers, accountants, journalists, and other professionals; earn above average income; are highly educated and often bilingual, sometimes trilingual; live in suburban new towns or urban condominiums; own their own cars; shop in shopping centers and malls; eat out in American fast-food stores and posh Italian and Japanese restaurants; enjoy new urban lifestyles; and invest some of their savings in the stock market. Most middle-class people attained their present status in their generation, but their children, who watch TV anime and Hollywood films, read Japanese comics, play Nintendo games, and eat out at McDonald's and KFC, take their affluence for granted.

The middle-class cultures in East Asia are best understood by reference to the different historical experiences and trajectories of nation-building projects in the United States and Japan. As Ryuichiro Matsubara (2000, 52–58) tells us, class formation went hand-in-hand with Americanization in the United States. The middle class in America that came into being in the 1920s took as the object of their social consumption and self-representation the idea of the "standard package." Ownership of cars, radios, refrigerators, washing machines, cosmetics, and others made people middle class, even as people no longer believed in an enduring class structure. At the same time, class formation and self-definition were bound up with the national project of Americanization, which involved turning populations into "good" American citizens "without histories" and meant, for people both locally born and migrant, forgetting their class, ethnic, and linguistic past and living and raising a family in the same way as everyone else. Since there was no objective standard in this middle-class society, because people no longer accepted the conspicuous consumption of the upper class as the model for emulation and there was no traditionally defined and accepted American way of life, the standard package, the set of things a household owns—a suburban house, a car, a TV set, a refrigerator, a washing machine, and well-known brands of packaged food, clothing, and cosmetics—came to define what it meant to live like everyone else. The arrival of television in the 1950s revolutionized the marketing of the standard package. Through mass media, the American way of life, transcending sex, age, class, racial, ethnic, and regional differences, became representable as a standard package. TV programs, Hollywood films, and department stores displayed the American way of life as the standard package and educated people on how to dress, how to furnish their houses, and how to enjoy their leisure as Americans.

American hegemony in the East Asian region sought to contain Communism by making the creation of middle classes part of its ideological vision and crafting of "Free Asia" in collaboration with Asian developmental states. This project of creating middle classes was particularly effective in postwar Japan, though middle-class formation occurred in a context where there already existed "Japanese" citizens. If in the United States making the population middle class occurred at the same time the population had to be turned into *Americans,* in Japan, the project consisted of making Japanese *middle class.* This making of Japanese into middle classes was mediated by the Japanese embrace of the American way of life. Television was the most important agent of Americanization. The "typical" American breakfast of toast, milk, and jam as well as the American "system kitchen" displayed in American TV dramas fascinated the Japanese. But because American products could not be imported to dollar-short Japan and American services could not be provided by English-speaking Americans, Japan opted for import-substitution and relied on Japanese firms to meet these market demands. Urbanization and the increase in nuclear families expanded market demands and translated into the growing demand for TVs, refrigerators, washing machines, and other consumer durables. Urbanization also changed the Japanese notion of the house. Kitchen and bedrooms as well as parents' and children's bedrooms were now separated. Bathroom and toilet were now attached to the house. The house became a self-contained family space, the shell in which family life was lodged. Interactions with neighbors became less important, while TVs, radios, and mass-circulation national newspapers became the prime media for social communication. By the 1970s, thanks to the phenomenal growth of the economy, the great majority of Japanese had a middle-class income that enabled them to live like everyone else and to have a family like everyone else's.

In a population that already considered itself Japanese, the cultural homogeneity implied by the standard package quickly lost its appeal once the majority of Japanese could live a comfortable life. Japanese firms started to propose and market new lifestyles. The phrase "new family," coined in the early 1970s by a department store chain, created an image of family life in which people dressed in jeans and T-shirts enjoyed listening to music, viewing films, and dining out, and lived like friends, as husband and wife, parents and children, in a house furnished smartly as a stage for the "new family" life. It was also in the 1970s that new fashion and lifestyle magazines were published such as *an an, Popeye,* and *BRUTUS,* which displayed fashionable goods in a fashion catalog. Collective dreams that people had about middle-class life were represented in housing advertisements, TV dramas, and interior-design journals and were given concrete expression in new suburban towns (Matsubara 2000; Wakabayashi 2000; Miura 2000; Uchida 2000). The American way of life was thus appropriated and made part of new hybridized middle-class *ways* of life in Japan, where people now enjoy both toast and miso soup, live in a house with a tatami room and a "Western" room with a table and chairs, listen to both American pop music and Japanese-style popular songs (*kayo-kyoku*), and buy "Asian" goods such as a rice cooker and instant ramen. Hybridization also took place in the service sector, in education, health care, and leisure, because all the services were import-substituted and provided by Japanese using Japanese language.

Americanization and East Asian hybridization are twin processes that shape middle-class consumer cultures. But far from being defined solely by their capacity to consume, the East Asian middle classes have also been constituted as political subjects. Their ascendancy in South Korea and Taiwan (representing the second wave of middle-class formation) had important political consequences in reshaping their states and articulating new nationalisms.

New Nationalists in South Korea and Taiwan

South Korea and Taiwan followed the arc of Japan's trajectory in that these developmental states relied on the politics of productivity to turn existing populations, defined as "Koreans" and (more problematically) "Chinese," into middle classes. But the ascendancy of the middle classes manifested itself politically in the growing pressure to democratize the state and the assertion of new nationalisms.

South Korea underwent an enormous social transformation in one generation. In 1960, when Park Chung Hee came to power, the per capita GDP was $80; only 28 percent of the population was urban; 58 percent of the rural population was illiterate; and the middle class constituted only 15 percent of the population. But by 1980 the urban population constituted 69 percent of the total population, and by 1990, 82 percent. In 1963, 63 percent of the working population was in the primary sector (agriculture and other natural resources), while 9 percent was in the secondary sector (manufacturing), and 28 percent was in the tertiary sector (services). In 1994, the percentage in the primary sector fell to 14 percent, while the secondary sector rose to 24 percent and the tertiary sector to 63 percent. Enrollment in higher education expanded from 5 percent in 1960 to 42 percent in 1992. The middle-class population expanded from 15 percent in 1960 to 26 percent in 1980 to 32 percent in 1985. Periodicals including daily newspapers increased from 344 in 1961 to 3,898 in 1989, while the gross sales of the four largest dailies expanded from 86 billion won in 1980 to 280 billion won in 1987, with a combined circulation reaching ten million. TV ownership expanded from 6.4 percent of households in 1970 to 99.1 percent in 1985 (Moriyama 1998, 68, 76, 121, 220–21).

This enormous social transformation was brought about by rapid industrialization under Park Chung Hee. In 1973, Park embarked on heavy industrialization, above all in steel production, shipbuilding, and car production, and achieved his objectives in 1977 with per capita GDP reaching $1,000 and exports surpassing $10 billion. Park was assassinated in 1979, but in 1981 his successor Chun Doo Hwan succeeded in making Korea the host of the 1988 Olympics in Seoul. In the wake of the 1985 Plaza Accord, the depreciating U.S. dollar (to which the won had been initially pegged), coupled with low interest rates in the international financial market, and cheap oil increased South Korean industrial competitiveness in the international market. Korean products flooded overseas markets. South Korea was hailed as a "little dragon" (Vogel 1991). From 1985 to 1990, the stock market in Korea increased sixfold (Moriyama 1998, 105–6, 117).

Social transformation led to political changes. This does not mean that expanding middle class spearheaded the democratization movement, however. Seizing power in 1980, Chun fashioned his military regime after the Park regime. Middle-class Koreans initially supported the Chun regime because they wanted political stability. But the legitimacy of the regime was fragile owing to the violent manner in which it had seized state power, and middle-class people—increasingly unhappy with the economic downturn in the early 1980s—soon started to complain about injustice and corruption under Chun. The political opposition, represented by the New Korea Democratic Party led by Kim Dae Jung and Kim Yung Sang, spearheaded the movement, which demanded that the constitution be amended and the president elected directly by popular vote. This movement was galvanized by the reported death by torture of a Seoul University student. Middle-class Koreans who had been on the political sidelines now joined the movement, which initially had consisted mainly of students and workers. The movement in June 1987 mobilized 1.8 million people in street rallies and demonstrations, and led to an internal schism within the government and the emergence of Roh Tae Woo as the governing party's presidential candidate. President Chun was forced to decide whether to clamp down on the opposition by force or to compromise. The U.S. government intervened and opposed military suppression. The presence of middle-class people in the movement prevented the government from staging a showdown with the opposition. On June 29, Roh—who had won the intragovernmental struggle—announced that the government would agree to the constitutional amendment and direct presidential election (Moriyama 1998, 118–19).

South Korean economic development also changed consumption patterns in the 1980s. In the early years of industrialization, people saved for retirement, emergencies, major-item shopping, and their children's education. But with the appreciation of the won in the late 1980s and the increasing value of assets, especially in stocks and real estate, Koreans began to spend more. In the 1990s, South Korea became a mass consumer society. With the expansion of mass media and telecommunications, young Koreans provided an expanding market for cultural products such as music, TV dramas, movies, and comics.

In sum, the combination of economic development, social transformation, political change, and the emergence of young, affluent consumers led to the formation of what Koreans call the "386 generation." Born in the 1960s (6), joining the student democratic movement in the 1980s (8), and in their thirties in the 1990s (3), this generation is the first to have no direct experience of Japanese colonial rule and the Korean War, is suspicious of the authoritarianism and developmentalism espoused by older generations, and now supports Roh Moo Hyun's nationalist attempt to carve a semiautonomous space for South Korea vis-à-vis the United States in the international arena.

Taiwanese economic development started earlier and lasted longer than that in Korea. Taiwan registered an average of 11.1 percent economic growth from 1964 to 1973, 8.4 percent from 1974 to 1979, and 7.1 percent from 1980 to 1986. Chiang Ching Kuo, who became the premier in 1972, shifted the government's development policy from building a base in Taiwan to take back Mainland China from the Communist Party to that of industrial development for Taiwan itself. In the 1980s, labor-intensive export-oriented industries lost international competitiveness while technology-intensive industries powered Taiwanese industrial development (Wakabayashi 1992, 149).

This economic development transformed Taiwanese society. Per capita GNP increased from $144 in 1960 to $384 in 1970 to $2,293 in 1980 to $6,053 in 1988. The working population in the primary sector declined from 50 percent in 1960 to 18 percent in 1985, while the secondary sector increased from 21 percent to 41 percent and the tertiary sector from 29 percent to 41 percent. Taiwanese who obtained university-level educations increased from 1.9 percent of the total population in 1960 to 10.1 percent in 1988. The middle classes also expanded from 12 percent in 1963 to 40 percent in 1983 as Taiwanese joined the ranks of military personnel, public servants, and school teachers that had been initially dominated by Mainlanders. But more importantly, in the 1970s and 1980s, small- and medium-scale entrepreneurs increased along with engineers, business executives, and managers (Wakabayashi 1992, 151, 154).

Taiwan was under the control of the Guomindang party-state that for a long time served as the instrument of Mainland exiles' political dominance over native Taiwanese. Before the mid-1980s, the kind of division of labor imposed by the Guomindang government put politics in the hands of Mainlanders and the economy in the hands of Taiwanese. For a long time, this division generated tension but did not spark outright conflict between Mainlanders and Taiwanese, in part because of state power and also because rising per capita income did not widen income gaps among the population.

Unlike Korea, whose economy was dominated by chaebols (Korean business conglomerates), Taiwanese economic development was primarily led by small- and medium-scale industries. Economic development created sizeable Taiwanese middle classes that were effectively excluded from politics. Whereas democratization was brought about in South Korea largely by pressure from below, in Taiwan the initiative came from the very center of the Guomindang party-state. In his final years, Chiang Ching Kuo initiated political liberalization, which allowed the establishment of an opposition party in 1986, lifted martial law in 1987, and paved the way for the rise of Lee Teng Hui as the first Taiwan-born president. The Silent Revolution continued under Lee, who declared the end of the civil war against the Communists in 1991, retired "permanent" parliamentary members, and in 1996 captured the presidency in the first direct election in the country. In the meantime, the opposition Democratic Progressive Party formally called for Taiwanese independence in its party program in 1991, and has made the question of unification with China and Taiwanese sovereignty major political issues (Wakabayashi 1992, 157–61, 177–78, 261–62; Honda 2004, 135).

The Taiwanese middle classes that grew alongside Taiwanese economic development are primarily made up of export-oriented, small- and medium-scale entrepreneurs and their business executives and managers. They speak Minnan (as well as Hakka) as their mother tongue but are literate in Mandarin because of Chinese-language education and have extensive networks abroad owing to educational, friendship, family, and business ties. Political entrepreneurs have emerged from among these people and now call for Taiwanese independence. Cultural entrepreneurs have made Taiwan one of the centers for Chinese-language-based culture industries. The Mainland Chinese and Southeast Asian markets account for shifts in pop music trends, for example, with the erstwhile dominant Cantonese pop music giving way to Mandarin-based music, and Taiwan replacing Hong Kong as the arbiter of taste in Chinese pop music (Chua 2005).

If the political and cultural ascendancy of South Korea's new middle classes is embodied by a single generation, the so-called 386 generation, the rise of Taiwan's middle classes manifests itself in a politics of ethnicity that pits the economic and, more recently, growing cultural and political power of the Taiwanese—especially Minnan speakers—against the formerly dominant Mainlander Taiwanese and against Mainland China. Both South Korea and Taiwan have seen the rise of new nationalisms with the new middle classes as privileged subjects of history. But whereas South Koreans' new nationalism is defined generationally with younger Koreans favoring a more autonomous South Korean position in international politics vis-à-vis the United States, Taiwan's new nationalism is defined politico-ethnically with Taiwanese advocating an independent and, more important, a democratic Taiwan against both Mainlander Taiwanese and Communist China.

As in South Korea and Taiwan, the creation of middle-class Indonesians, Malaysians, Thais, and Filipinos in Southeast Asia was conceived and put into effect in specific political and social structures, and has proceeded along variable paths with different rates of success and failure. The next three sections compare and contrast the emergence of middle classes within the specific political and social structures of Thailand, Indonesia, Malaysia, and the Philippines.

Thailand's Ascendant Middle Classes

Thailand benefited from a long period of economic development from the late 1950s to the late 1990s that culminated in the economic boom in 1987–95 and led to the emergence and expansion of middle classes that are socially coherent, culturally and intellectually hegemonic, and politically ascendant.

The Thai economy grew by 8 percent on average in 1987–95. The Bangkok Metropolitan Area—the capital of Bangkok and its five neighboring provinces—emerged as a world city in this period. Global finance and foreign direct investments drove the process. The finance, insurance, and real estate sectors in the Bangkok Metropolitan Area grew by 160 percent from 1989 to

1993. The boom produced middle-class jobs in manufacturing; finance and insurance; real estate development; legal, information, accounting, translation, and marketing services; and in the hotel, restaurant, and entertainment industries.

But professionals, whether business executives, managers, engineers, bankers, accountants, lawyers, or others, were in short supply. In the boom years, therefore, their pay shot up, rising several times higher than civil service pay. Thai university graduates, most of whom previously joined the government as career civil servants, started to go into the private sector in the 1980s. This trend dramatically accelerated in the boom years. Government officials migrated to the private sector as well. The middle-class population in Bangkok (those classified as professionals and technicians, executives and managers, and white-collar office workers) increased from 310,000 in 1985 to 710,000 in 1994.[4]

The Thai new urban middle classes also were a product of educational expansion. The number of university students increased enormously from 1975 to 1985, from 316 to 2,009 for every 100,000 population. The expansion in university education benefited the traditional Sino-Thai Bangkok middle classes disproportionately. A survey in 1994 found that 61 percent of those Bangkok upper-middle-class professionals making more than twenty thousand baht a month were Bangkok-born and that 59 percent were university graduates with fourteen years of schooling (Funatsu and Kagotani 2002, 216; Matsuzono 1998, 203).

They are also younger. According to a 1990 study, 56.2 percent of the Bangkok middle-class working population belonged to the 20–34 age group (Matsuzono 1998, 193). They are also predominantly Sino-Thai. Bangkok traditionally was a "Chinese" city. A 1960 study showed that 16.2 percent of those in their thirties, 32.6 percent of those in their forties, and 37.2 percent of those in their fifties had Chinese nationality, while only 0.6 percent of the Bangkok population under age nine as well as 0.7 percent of those aged 10–14 did. To put it in another way, the traditional Bangkok middle classes, still very much of Chinese nationality in 1960, worked as store owners, small traders, and small factory owners. But their children, born from 1945 to 1955, had become Sino-Thais (Asami 1998, 313–14). These same people, Sino-Thais born in Bangkok during the postwar years to traditional, often Chinese, middle-class parents, are the ones who benefited most from the educational expansion in the 1960s and 1970s, spearheaded the student revolution in 1973, and emerged as the new urban middle classes in the past twenty years.

---

[4] Another study suggests that the middle-class working population constituted 33.4 percent of the working population in Bangkok in 1990, compared to 15 percent in 1960 (Matsuzono 1998, 193).

The rise of middle classes as a social formation transformed Bangkok's spatial structure and its social and cultural life. Condominiums were built in city centers. Suburban housing complexes were developed with shopping centers, hospitals, and schools. In 1985–1992 alone, thirty-six department stores were opened (there were only twenty-five before 1985). With deteriorating traffic conditions in the early 1990s, middle- and high-income category middle-class people also developed a new lifestyle, in which they stayed in one-room city condos on weekdays (the first city condo was developed in 1993) and went back to their suburban homes on the weekends. They also obtained "standard package" items. In 1984, 48 percent of white-collar workers in Bangkok owned cars and 53 percent had telephones. Ten years later, more than 70 percent of white-collar workers owned cars, 80 percent had telephones, and 40 percent owned cell phones (Matsuzono 1998, 203–4). Newspapers and TV programs also catered to their interests, publishing feature articles about cars, condos, electronic gadgets, and fashions.

Traditionally, the middle classes in Thailand were very small. In 1960, the middle-class population constituted only 2.6 percent of the working population, and of those more than 60 percent were in the government. Allied with the United States and enlisting support from technocrats trained there and in Britain, Sarit Thanarat, the strongman in those years (1957–63), laid the foundation for future Thai economic development with the creation of a middle-class Thailand as his nation-building objective (Funatsu and Kagotani 2002, 204–5). But the subsequent development did not meet his dream in two important respects.

First, students, mainly children of those Sino-Thai traditional middle-class people in Bangkok and products of the developmental state that Sarit fashioned, destroyed the authoritarian regime in the student revolution in 1973 and initiated a long process of political transformation that eventually led to the establishment of Thai middle-class cultural hegemony and its successful translation into political power in the 1990s. This history is well known. Open politics, which the student revolution ushered in and in which the small urban middle classes along with peasants and workers for the first time in history emerged as political forces, was truncated with the counterrevolutionary coup in 1976. It was replaced by power sharing, often called half-democracy, because the military and bureaucratic elite could no longer ignore the urban middle classes at a time when Indochina went Communist and thousands of student activists joined the Communist insurgency in the jungle to fight for the revolution. The military and the bureaucratic elite were willing to share power with party politicians and the business elite. Though neither Kriangsak Chomanand nor Prem Tinsulanond had been elected members of the parliament before each was chosen as prime minister, the stability of their governments depended on their success in forming and sustaining a governing coalition of political parties as much as on obtaining and maintaining the support of the military. In this period of half-democracy, local bosses emerged as party politicians and came to dominate agrarian-based parties, mobilizing agrarian support with public works and outright vote buying and making politics a money-making business.

The half-democracy reached a major turning point in 1991 with Chatichai Choonhavan's ascendancy to power. While the military was the senior partner and political parties the junior partner under Prem, the rise of party politician Chatichai as prime minister threatened to relegate the military to the junior partner position. The military under Suchinda Kraprayoon struck back, staging a successful coup for the first time in more than a decade. Middle-class people in Bangkok neither supported nor opposed the coup, because they were dismayed by the corruption that was the hallmark of Chatichai and his lieutenants—local bosses turned party bosses—and because Suchinda promised a return to civilian rule in the near future. When Suchinda threatened to prolong the military dominance in politics, however, they rose in opposition. In the February 1992 elections, parties in support of Suchinda obtained 195 parliamentary seats out of 350, but won only 2 out of 35 in Bangkok. There were huge demonstrations in Bangkok in May 1992, culminating in troops shooting and killing demonstrators and in Suchinda's resignation as prime minister. This development was hailed as a successful "middle-class revolt," reminiscent of the student revolution nineteen years earlier, though studies show that the middle classes did not provide major troops for demonstrations and that the idea of a middle-class revolt was created more in subsequent journalistic representations than on the streets. Yet it was the same people, Bangkok-born Sino-Thai students in 1973–76 and middle-aged urban Thai middle-class executives and professionals in 1992, who had cultural and intellectual hegemony and told the story of the "successful middle-class revolt" in 1992 (Pasuk and Baker 1995, 355–61; Asami 1998, 320–21; Ockey 1999).

But this middle-class hegemony was far from complete. Middle-class Thailand as Sarit envisioned it—with the great majority of Thais enjoying a middle-class status, income, and life—has not occurred. Those who have benefited from economic development have remained limited to the urban middle classes in Bangkok, while those in the provinces, above all the peasants and farmers that form more than half of the population, have remained outside the sphere of prosperity. This was due to the economic structure. Thai economic development mainly took place in Bangkok and its vicinity and benefited the Bangkok middle classes in the making. Denied opportunities for high school, let alone a university education, peasants and farmers in the provinces either remained in the agricultural sector of declining productivity or migrated to Bangkok as unskilled workers on a short-term contract basis. The Thai agricultural population constituted more than 50 percent of the working population even in the 1990s (while the GDP share of the agricultural sector declined to 11 percent in 1995). This resulted in a huge and expanding per capita income disparity between the provinces and the Bangkok Metropolitan Area. The per capita regional GDP in Bangkok was nine times larger than that in the northeast, the poorest region, which had one-third of the Thai population in the 1990s. The generals and bureaucrats could thus claim to be the "true" representatives and protectors of the silent majority of peasants and farmers. In the institutions of representative democracy, peasants and farmers dominated the franchise. At elections, their votes were influenced by the bureaucratic power of the army and the Ministry of Interior, and by the money and influence of local bosses (Pasuk and Baker 1995, 364; Funatsu and Kagoya 2002, 206).

It is not surprising then that the urban-rural gap divided parties in the 1990s. In the July 1995 elections, for instance, the Thai National Party, with politicians known for their corruption and vote buying, emerged as the majority party in the provinces and that its party president, Banharn Silpa-archa, was elected as prime minister. But the party did not win even a single seat in Bangkok. This was repeated in the 1996 elections, in which the New Aspiration Party under Chavalit Yongchaiyudh emerged victorious, but won only one seat in Bangkok. The major issues in these elections were corruption and vote buying. It was natural for agrarian voters to sell their votes for whatever money they could get when they knew they could not get any benefit from parliamentary politics in any other way. It was also natural that politicians, once elected, tried to get their investment return through corruption and money making. But the Bangkok middle classes found it repugnant, and respectable Bangkok newspapers exposed corruption scandals.

In the mid-1990s, this war was fought in the process of constitution-making. Middle-class cultural hegemony, however, worked in favor of the middle classes from the beginning. It was decided that the committee for a constitutional amendment would be composed of university graduates, even though university graduates formed only 2.5 percent of the Thai population aged twenty and above (Asami 1998, 321–22). The parliament dominated by parties and party bosses representing agrarian interests was expected to oppose constitutional revisions drafted by the committee.

It was at this moment that the currency crisis hit Thailand. Financial inflow that started with the establishment of an offshore banking facility in 1993 turned into a flood in 1993–95 with the out-in transactions, which had been 27.6 billion baht in 1987, reaching 650.4 billion baht in 1995. The money went to the stock market and to consumer loans. It also went to real estate development (Shindo 1999, 118–21). In 1994 alone, 250,000 housing units, three times as many as in 1993, were built. This real estate bubble popped in 1995–96. A state bank estimated that there were 275,000 housing units left unsold at the end of 1996 and 338,000 at the end of 1997. Industrial estates and shopping centers also remained unsold and unrented (Tasaka 1998, 13). In this crisis situation, parties could not afford to vote down constitutional revisions and deepen the economic crisis into a political crisis. The constitutional revisions were passed. The new constitution required parliamentary members and cabinet ministers to have university degrees, making it hard for local bosses who made money in illegal gambling, prostitution, and the hotel business and dominated agrarian-based parties to become parliamentary members and cabinet ministers. Furthermore, it prohibited parliamentary members from serving as cabinet ministers, making it hard for politicians to make money in public works and corruption. And members of the senate who had previously been appointed were chosen through elections, denying the military the parliamentary arena.

But the crisis hit the Bangkok middle classes as well as other classes all the same. Many financial and banking institutions closed, and with multinational corporations shutting down their operations, more than one million workers lost their jobs (Funatsu and Kagotani 2002, 227). Middle-class people were as scared as everyone else. This provided a rare opportunity for business-tycoon-turned-political-entrepreneur Taksin Sinawatra to bridge the urban-rural division. He presented himself to the Bangkok middle classes as a CEO capable of overcoming the crisis with domestic demand-led development (instead of the FDI- and global finance-led development of the past), while calling for equitable and autonomous agrarian development in the provinces. He also presented himself to the bureaucratic elite as the strongman who could restore their statist dreams. His new party, Thai Rak Thai, which means Thais Love Thailand, won the 2001 elections by a large margin. Yet it is the performance of the Thai economy in the years to come on which Taksin's staying power and Thai middle-class cultural hegemony will depend.

Malaysia and Indonesia's Divided and Dependent Middle Classes

If the Thai urban middle classes have emerged as reasonably coherent, culturally hegemonic, and politically ascendant in a generation, their Malaysian and Indonesian counterparts, which have also emerged in a generation, remain divided ethnically, dependent on the state, and unable to reshape Malaysian and Indonesian politics in any fundamental way.

In Malaysia, as in Thailand, the middle classes were a product of regional economic development in the boom years from 1986 to 1997, during which the Malaysian economy grew by 8.6 percent annually. The Malaysian middle classes (which are divided ethnically among Malays, Chinese, and Indians), above all the Malay middle class, also were a product of the Malaysian developmental state. Malaysia has been under the National Front (NF) government since the early 1970s. It is a governing coalition of ethnic and regional parties led and dominated by the United Malay National Organization (UNMO). The NF has controlled more than two-thirds of the parliamentary seats, while the UMNO has controlled more than half of the parliamentary seats the NF holds. The UMNO has thus run the NF government for the past thirty years and made it its stated objective to create a Malay middle class.

Its New Economic Policy as well as its successor National Development Policy have been geared in part to achieving this objective, improving Malay social and economic positions and creating a Malay middle class with state-led economic and educational development, while lulling non-Malays with FDI-led export-oriented economic growth. Quotas were introduced for Malay employment in business and Malay enrollment in universities. Malay replaced English as the language of instruction at the high school and university levels. A Malay corporate share of 30 percent was targeted. Many public corporations were established by the central and state governments to create a Malay business elite. A Malay middle class was thus produced in the public sector in the 1970s.

But the Malaysian economy slowed down shortly after Mahathir Mohamad came to power in 1981. Oil revenues collapsed, public corporations performed badly, and government debt, both central and state, mounted. This forced Mahathir to modify the New Economic Policy developmental strategy. In alliance with Japanese corporations, he embarked on heavy industrialization with the establishment of the HICOM, Heavy Industry Corporation of Malaysia (Torii 2002, 154–55). He also shifted his developmental emphasis from the public to the private sector and started privatizing public corporations. Government officials as well as executives and managers of public corporations migrated from the public to the private sector and were transformed into a Malay business elite. The number of Malay executives and managers increased from five thousand in 1970 to fifty-four thousand in 1990 (Torii 2002, 158).

The Malay middle class also was a product of state-led educational development. University education expanded steadily. There were 266 university students for every ten thousand people in 1975. The number increased to 419 in 1980, 679 in 1990, and 971 in 1995. The educational development benefited Malays disproportionately. While 3,084 Malays and 3,752 Chinese, out of the total enrollment of 7,677 students, entered universities in 1970 (with hardly anyone going abroad for university education), 22,271 Malays (37 percent of the students who went to universities) and 9,142 Chinese (15 percent) went to Malaysian universities and 6,034 Malays (10 percent) and 13,406 Chinese (22 percent) went abroad for university education in 1985 (Torii 2002, 161).

The economic development and the rise of Malay and Chinese new urban middle classes drastically changed the cityscape of Kuala Lumpur in the pre-crisis years (1981–97). Hotels, shopping centers, and office buildings were built in Kuala Lumpur's central business district. The development of the Multimedia Super Corridor was announced in 1996. The Kuala Lumpur metropolitan area expanded with the development in the suburbs. The commercial development of suburban housing complexes and new towns took place along the newly built North-South highway. The increase in nuclear families accelerated real estate development, expanding demand for urban condos and suburban houses and apartments (Takayama 2000, 82). Shopping centers, malls, and leisure facilities with huge parking lots also were developed in suburbs. Japanese and American retailers became key tenants in shopping centers.

A new lifestyle was displayed in department stores and shopping centers, newspapers and magazines, and TV programs and commercials, which, though sensitive to ethnic and religious preferences and prohibitions in food and clothing, looked as if it transcended ethnic boundaries. Whether Malay or non-Malay, middle-class people have a lot in common. They are confronted with housing problems, from defective housing developments to problematic sales practices. They want good English-language education for their children. And they are concerned about environmental problems and feminist issues. Mass media responded by reporting on rising middle-class concerns, interests, and questions in 1990s. *New Straits Times* published feature articles in its Lifestyle section, while the *Star*'s Section 2 covered culture, art, environment, women, leisure, and entertainment. Glossy women's magazines publicized a new type of women, dressed in Western clothes but wearing a head scarf, and a new style of life in a smartly furnished apartment or a suburban house. Cars, consumer durables, furniture, and brand-name food, clothing, cosmetics, and lifestyle goods as well as condos, townhouses, and resort villas were offered on TV, in newspapers and magazines, and in department stores and shopping centers. Car ownership expanded from 19 percent of all households in 1980 to 32 percent in 1991, TV ownership from 49 percent to 78 percent, and refrigerator ownership from 27 percent to 32 percent. Urban youth culture also developed with fast-food restaurants, cafés, discos, brand-name clothing, cars, tourism, and theme parks.

Yet ethnic boundaries remain. Suburban housing complexes and new towns are ethnically segregated. Malays, Chinese, and Indians have different tastes in fashion, film, and music. All may enjoy American popular music, Hollywood films, and Japanese anime, but Malays enjoy Malay Pop as well as Indonesian pop music and films, while Chinese enjoy Hong Kong films and music and Indians Hindi and Tamil films and Indian music.

Ethnic divisions thus remain the most important division in Malaysian politics. But the rise of Malay and non-Malay middle classes also made its impact felt in Malaysian politics in other ways. In the first place, UMNO became more business-oriented. Its traditional social bases had been among peasants and farmers, civil servants, and schoolteachers. By the late 1980s, however, business executives and managers emerged as a major force in the party. In the 1987 party congress, 25 percent of the delegates were business executives and managers, while 19 percent were schoolteachers and 23 percent civil servants, though only 1.4 percent of the Malay working population was classified as executives and managers even in 1990 (Torii 2001, 115–16).

. The UMNO became business-oriented in yet another sense in the 1980s and 1990s. With the establishment of Fleet Holdings as its business arm, UMNO went into business in a major way, investing in food processing, hotels, and real estate development. Its branches followed suit. As a result, more than 160,000 firms were established by the UMNO central leadership, its branches, and its party leaders by the mid-1990s. Mahathir's privatization policy and the BOT (Build-Operate-Transfer)scheme he introduced for large-scale infrastructure development projects (such as the North-South highway) helped UMNO, with its business orientation. The logic that informed it was straight-forward. The UMNO leadership, which controlled the government, distributed business opportunities to its supporters. To obtain business in public works, government-funded development projects, and BOT projects, business executives and managers joined the party to control important positions in the party organization at the state, branch, and district levels. To get elected to important party positions, these businessmen spent money on election campaigns, and once elected, they tried to recoup their investment by establishing new UMNO firms, obtaining business opportunities in public works, government-funded development projects, and BOT projects, and demanding that the government and the party central leadership distribute more business opportunities to UMNO members and business entities.

In the second place, the Islamic revival among the rising Malay middle class also deeply affected the UMNO. Not only Malay- and Arabic-educated Malays but also and more significantly an increasing number of English-educated Malays have come to follow the straitlaced, Arab-type Islam (Shamsul 1999, 110–11). The Parti Agama Se-Malaysia (PAS), the only significant Malay opposition party, which came under the control of Middle East–educated "Young Turks" with their power base in Islamic dakwah propagation and education groups in the 1980s, called for changing the federal constitution to bring it more in line with Islamic law, and attacked the UMNO leadership as "kafir," infidel. Islamic student movements also became active in the 1970s and 1980s, above all ABIM (Angkatan Belia Islam Malaysia, Malaysian Islamic Youth Movement), which under the leadership of Anwar Ibrahim called for the improvement the Malay position in the economy and society and underlined the importance of Islam for Malay identity. It expanded its influence in the 1970s among students and urban youth (Shiraishi 2002, 15–16).

The UMNO leadership capitalized on the PAS's Islamic "fundamentalist" orientation to alarm the public, while clamping down on hard-core Islamists. It also tried to co-opt Islamic revivalist forces. Anwar Ibrahim, ABIM chairman, joined the UMNO, ran successfully for the parliament in the early 1980s, was awarded a cabinet post, and rose in the party hierarchy to become deputy prime minister in 1993.

The UMNO in the 1980s and 1990s thus presented itself to the Malay community as the guardian of Malay economic interests and Malay Islamic identity. The UMNO leadership under Mahathir and Anwar Ibrahim in the 1993–98 period embodied this double guardianship. But all was not well with the UMNO and its central leadership. For one thing, Malays remained dependent on the state and did not become as competitive as the Chinese, as Mahathir had hoped. For another, ethnic divisions remained. In 1991, Mahathir announced Vision 2020, which established the goal that Malaysia would join the group of advanced industrial countries by 2020, with 7 percent annual growth for the coming twenty years and nation-building based on Malaysian national consciousness. The nexus between high economic growth and nation-building was easy to see: mobilizing non-Malay human resources and capital was imperative to achieve the 7 percent annual economic growth. In a symbolic move, the government deregulated and liberalized the university system and approved the establishment of private university educations for non-Malay students in the mid-1990s.

Yet it was generational power struggle that almost wrecked the UMNO and the UMNO-dominated NF government. This started with the rise of Anwar Ibrahim as deputy prime minister in 1993. Former ABIM activists and young business executives and entrepreneurs rose on his coattails, obtaining business opportunities in public works, government-funded development projects, and BOT projects. But it was Mahathir, not Anwar, who had the final say on the distribution of business opportunities. When the financial crisis started in 1997, the UMNO Youth was at the forefront of the anti-Mahathir forces, declaring their support for Anwar and attacking the Malay-first policy as a "crony economy." This incensed Mahathir, not only because he was attacked but also because those who attacked him and his New Economic Policy/National Development Policy were the very products and beneficiaries of his policy and the "crony economy."

What followed is well known. Anwar Ibrahim was ousted from his position as deputy prime minister and arrested. His supporters were kicked out of the UMNO. Young middle-class Malays were outraged at this development and the way Anwar was treated—being arrested, tried for sodomy, and sentenced to imprisonment. A new party, Keadilan (the Justice Party), was established with Anwar's wife as party president, and allied itself with the PAS to form the Alternative Front. In the 1999 elections, the generational division in the Malay community manifested itself. The NF obtained 148 seats, more than two-thirds of the parliamentary seats, though it was down from the 162 it had won in the 1995 elections. But the UMNO won only 72 seats, down from the 89 it won in 1995. More significantly, the UMNO now controlled less than half of the NF seats. UMNO also lost control over three northern states to the PAS. Its defeat was due to the alienation of Malay voters from UMNO. In the 40 constituencies where more than 80 percent of the voters were Malays, the UMNO won only 12, while the PAS and Keadilan won the rest. In the 58 constituencies where Malay voters constituted 50–80 percent of voters, the UMNO won 56 seats. Clearly the UMNO won the seats it did thanks to non-Malay votes. Malaysian society has been divided communally. Now the Malay community is divided along generational and ideological lines, while remaining dependent on the Malaysian developmental state. But both the ethnic peace and middle-class Malay support for the UMNO depend on the performance of a Malaysian economy that is presided over by the NF government and transnational capitalism.

Like their counterparts in Malaysia, Indonesia's new urban middle classes also emerged in a generation under Suharto's New Order. Suharto fashioned his regime with the state as his power base and the army as its backbone. It was centralized, militarized, authoritarian, and brutal. Army officers dominated the military and occupied strategic positions in the civilian arm of the state as district chiefs, mayors, provincial governors, secretaries general, and ministers. The Indonesian state was only in part funded by the formal budget; its informal or "off-budget" funding—sourced from state corporations and agencies such as Pertamina and Bulog and more recently from joint venture businesses with Suharto's lieutenants, crony business tycoons, and family members—was of crucial importance. It was tightly controlled by Suharto and served as the basis of the New Order's huge centrally controlled and directed patronage networks.

With the state as his power base, Suharto imposed his "national consensus" of Panca Sila democracy (Panca Sila means five principles on which the republic was built) on the Indonesian populace and banned all public discourses on religion, ethnicity, class, and ideologies other than his Panca Sila democracy in the name of stability and development. "Islamic" parties and organizations were forced to accept Panca Sila as their sole organizational principle. Islamist activists were monitored, harassed, arrested, and forced to go underground. Ethnic differences were put on display in museums and celebrated. With religious and ethnic divisions thus contained, the government addressed the question of class divisions through the politics of political stability and economic development.

This kind of politics, combined with the depoliticization and containment of religious and ethnic divisions, served Suharto's New Order regime well. The Indonesian economy grew by 7.7 percent annually during the decade from 1971 to 1981. Economic growth slowed down to 4 percent in 1982–1986, but the economy posted 6.7 annual growth in the post–Plaza Accord boom years from 1987 to 1997. This second boom, which was in part led by Japanese, Korean, and "overseas Chinese" FDI and in part by the inflow of global finance capital, saw the expansion of the private sector dominated by Sino-Indonesian business groups and foreign capital, overshadowing the state sector that had been the mainstay of the Indonesian economy in the 1970s and early 1980s.

New urban middle classes were born during these boom years. According to 1996 census data, those classified as professionals and technicians, executives and managers, and white-collar office workers totaled 7.4 million and constituted 8.6 percent of the working population. Given Indonesia's five million civil servants, most of the middle classes in the provinces was in the state sector. In Jakarta, however, new middle-class jobs were created in the rapidly expanding private sector during the 1987–97 period. This economic development, together with the rise of new urban middle classes, transformed Jakarta into an emergent middle-class city with a population of ten million. It combined the central city district with its business and banking headquarters, first-class hotels, and shopping centers and the suburbs with their industrial estates and new towns into an integrated structure.

From 1987 to 1997, the Jakartan economy came to be built on three sectors: manufacturing, commercial, and banking. In the city center, financial liberalization in 1988 opened the floodgates for global financial capital. Banking assets expanded from 63 trillion rupiah in 1983 to 484 trillion in 1992, and the number of banks increased from 91 in 1988 to 214 in 1993. But banking professionals were in short supply. Since English was a must in the banking business, those in their twenties and thirties who had working experiences in U.S. and British banks or were educated in the United States or Australia emerged as young banking professionals. They were employed as executives and managers at private banks and were paid five million rupiah a month (the pay for a new university graduate in the manufacturing sector was one-half to one million rupiah). The banking and real estate booms led to the expansion and redevelopment of the Jakartan central business district, the Golden Triangle. Business and banking headquarters, both Indonesian and foreign, were established there. New office buildings, shopping centers and malls, hotels and upper-end condos were also built there.

In the expansion of the Jakartan suburbs, on the other hand, the industrial estate and new town development played the key roles. Industrial estates were developed by Sino-Indonesian business groups and Japanese trading companies along the 150-kilometer East-West highway linking Karawan, Bekasi, Jakarta, Tangerang, and Serang (Sato 1999, 131–33). Japanese and Korean firms established their factories there. In 1998 there were about 150 industrial estates in Indonesia, of which 60 percent were located in Jakarta and its suburbs. New towns were also built along the East-West highway. Industrial estates and new towns were developed at each highway interchange like a bunch of grapes. The population in the Jakartan suburbs of Bogor, Tangerang, and Bekasi increased by 5.08 percent annually in the 1980s and by 4.47 percent from 1990 through 1994, far surpassing the city's growth rate of 2.41 percent in the 1980s and 2 percent in 1990–91 (Konagaya 1999, 99). The increasing population moved into commercially developed new towns.

The emerging urban middle classes in the Jakartan metropolitan area figured prominently in mass media representations. Professionals—business executives, bankers, journalists, architects, lawyers, and university professors—were featured in weekly and monthly magazines and appeared on TV talk shows at a time when the television industry was being liberalized and new private TV stations opened. Young banking professionals, dressed in brand-name suits, driving expensive cars, and eating out in posh Italian, French, and Japanese restaurants, came to symbolize new professionals in an era of private-sector-led economic development. Their ascendancy also changed the image of the middle classes. If they were non-pribumi (non-"native") and non-Muslim in the 1980s, now they could be pribumi or non-pribumi, Muslim or non-Muslim. Though they were a product of political patronage to a large extent, "being rich" became cool. Nearly 70 percent of Jakartan middle-class respondents to a survey conducted by the weekly Tiara said that they wished to be successful businessmen (Ariel 1999, 162–63, 177).

Yet the middle classes were small in number in a vast country with a population of 220 million. Moreover, they were divided in many ways, though not as segregated as in Malaysia. There were tensions between Sino- and pribumi-Indonesians and between those dependent on Suharto's family and crony businesses and independent-minded professionals and executives. There were also tensions between those in the public and private sectors and between pious Muslims and nominal/statistical Muslims. As in Malaysia, the Islamic revival deeply affected middle-class Indonesians in the making. Thousands of books about Islamic theology, politics, political theory, history, law, and revolution were translated from Arabic and Farsi into Indonesian. University lecturers and students organized discussion groups on campus and dakwah missionary activities in mosques nearby. Parents sent elementary school children to Islamic summer schools. Prayer halls were built in fancy office buildings, shopping centers, hotels, and restaurants. Real-estate firms offered "Islamic real estate" in West Java for the better-off. Islam is no longer associated exclusively with rural poverty, religious dogmatism, the Middle

East, anti-Chinese and anti-West sentiments, and with fundamentalists seek-ing to establish an Islamic state. It is now also associated with television talk shows, mobile telephones, and the consumption of *ketupat* (rice cake) during Ramadan at McDonald's (Ariel 1999, 174–76). In an attempt to exploit the Islamic revival for his own political advantage, Suharto established the Asso-ciation of Indonesia's Muslim Intellectuals (ICMI), tolerated Islamic and Is-lamist political activism, promoted pious Muslim officers in the army, and alarmed nominal Muslims and non-Muslims.

By the 1990s, it had become clear that social divisions could no longer be contained as the regime itself underwent significant transformation in those years. This change can best be summed up as a shift from a military regime to a personalistic/autocratic regime; having outlived all the rivals of his gen-eration, Suharto emerged as the unrivalled strongman in the final decade of his rule. Army officers who had served as his personal confidants dominated the military. His family members, each building his or her own business em-pire, openly plundered the state with impunity. And Suharto's lieutenants—his ministers, commanders, governors, district chiefs, and mayors—followed their superior's example in "privatizing" the state. The state thus became in-creasingly rotten, while retaining enormous power vis-à-vis society. In the meantime, secret wars were going on in Aceh and Irian Jaya (as well as in East Timor), killing Indonesians in the name of the republic and destroying what-ever popular trust the republican state still enjoyed in those places. Jakartan control of powers and resources as well as Javanese domination of the state led to the rising demand for local autonomy and the appointment of "local sons" in the strategic positions of provincial governors, district chiefs, and mayors.

The currency crisis that hit Indonesia in 1997 threatened the business em-pires, including those established and owned by Suharto's family members, cronies, and lieutenants, with bankruptcy. It also destroyed the state's infor-mal funding mechanism, a mainstay of Suharto's long-staying patronage power. The banking sector, which had already been in trouble and saddled with mounting bad loans, went into a systemic crisis. Sixteen banks were closed in the fall of 1997. More than 80 percent of the companies listed on the Jakarta Exchange went bankrupt by early 1998. Anti-Chinese riots took place in more than one hundred places in 1997–98, including massive riots that destroyed many shopping centers in Medan (northern Sumatra), Ja-karta, and Solo (central Java) in May 1998. Students demonstrated. Intra-military power struggles increasingly split the army. Suharto tried to blame the Chinese and global financial institutions for the crisis. But the military and bureaucratic elite concluded that the only way to overcome the crisis was to cut out from the body politic the cancer that was Suharto and his family and his cronies. The new urban middle classes played only a marginal role in the regime change. They were outraged at the killing of university students, which triggered the massive riots in Jakarta in mid-May 1998, but they were stunned and horrified by the violence and anarchy of the urban poor.

The fall of Suharto clearly marked the end of an era. His politics of stability and economic development was now clearly bankrupt. The republican state was in a deep legitimacy crisis. Its financial base was in tatters, ethnic and religious divisions could no longer be contained and depoliticized, and class divisions were threatening to tear apart Indonesian society. It is not surprising then that B. J. Habibie, the third president, with a weak presidential mandate and power base, tried to preempt the opposition, presenting himself as a reformer and initiating measures that, combined, led to the transformation of the regime from a centralized autocracy to a decentralized democracy. The parliament has emerged as a new power center along with the presidency and the military. Party politicians joined the government along with military officers and career bureaucrats. "Local" men with middle-class backgrounds along with the bureaucratic elite captured state powers, and resources devolved from the central government to the district and city.

Democratic politics has thus worked to the advantage of the middle classes, even though they are divided among themselves along religious and ethnic lines. Those divisions have led to the peaceful distribution of government positions (and hence resources) in accordance with ethnic and religious affiliations in some places and to violent ethnic and religious confrontations in other places. Yet democratic politics, let alone decentralized democratic politics, is shortsighted by nature. Whether in the center or in the district, the government is not in a position to proactively take policy initiatives to address long-term problems, because it is dependent on parliamentary support for budget approval and on military and police support for the maintenance of law and order.

More important, class divisions have deepened since the crisis of 1997–98 and threaten to tear apart the social fabric, because the crisis hit the poor hard and because not enough jobs have been created since for the 2.5 to three million people who enter the labor market every year. (The jobless increased from 4.2 million in 1997 to 5.06 million in 1998 and 6.03 million in 1999 according to government reports, while the poor as defined by the government expanded from 22.5 million in 1996, 11 percent of the population, to 48 million in 1999, 24 percent.) With the state structure fragmented and its power diffused and weakened, no president can hope to preside over political life as Suharto did. Social divisions along religious, ethnic, and class lines that have shaped national and local politics in many ways can no longer be contained by the state. The middle classes, still small, divided, and very much dependent on the state, remain fragile and vulnerable to the deepening social crisis.

The Megawati Sukarnoputri government has been successful in achieving macroeconomic stability, but not in improving the investment climate, achieving high economic growth, and creating jobs. If the decentralized democratic regime fails to address this question, it is not hard to see what would happen to the current regime and to whom the people, above all middle-class people, would turn for the protection of their own class interests and against the forces that their politics of ethnicity and religion might unleash.

The Philippines' Dispersed Middle Classes

If Thai, Malaysian, and Indonesian middle classes came into being in a generation in the 1980s and 1990s, Filipino middle classes have been around for at least two generations. This is due to the simple fact that Philippine industrialization started earlier, in the 1950s, though it has remained stunted ever since. This is evident in census data. Those in middle-class jobs (professionals and technicians; executives and managers; and white-collar office workers) formed 9.4 percent of the working population in 1956 and 11.5 percent in 1965 on the eve of Ferdinand Marcos's rise to power. The Philippine economy posted a 6.2 percent annual growth rate in the 1970s, but remained stagnant in the first half of the 1980s, a development that would slowly undermine the legitimacy of the Marcos dictatorship in the eyes of the middle classes. Throughout the Marcos era, those in middle-class job categories remained proportionately unchanged at 11–12 percent of the working population. Even in the post-Marcos era, Philippine economic growth remained modest, posting a 4.1 percent annual growth rate from 1986 to 1997. Those in middle-class jobs remained proportionately constant at 11.5 percent in 1995. (Their numbers, however, have increased over the years. Those as "professionals and technicians" and "executives and managers" numbered 1,264,000 in 1985, but increased to 2,185,000 in 1997.) They have also remained dependent on the state. In 1985, 67 percent of those classified as "professionals and technicians" and "executives and managers" were employed in the public sector, and 63 percent still were in 1994.

But this is only part of the story. To understand the Philippine middle classes, it is important to remember that educational development started earlier and proceeded steadily there more than in any other Southeast Asian country. The number of students in higher education for every 100,000 population was 1,808 in 1975, 2,641 in 1980, and 2,760 in 1995. (In contrast, it was 316 in 1975 and 2,096 in 1995 in Thailand and 266 in 1975 and 971 in 1995 in Malaysia [Hattori et al. 2002, 299].) This educational development, combined with the stunted economic development in the Philippines, explains why the Philippines has emerged as an exporter of professionals as well as domestic helpers and entertainers in the 1980s and 1990s and why Filipino labor has become deterritorialized. In 2002, an estimated 7.4 million Filipinos, about 10 percent of the population and 21 percent of the labor force, in 182 countries remitted $7.4 billion or the equivalent of 9 percent of the Philippine GNP for the year. It is estimated that 22.5 million to 35 million Filipinos, or roughly half the country's population, are directly or indirectly dependent on these remittances. The deterritorialization of Filipino labor was also due to developments outside the Philippines. The oil boom in the Middle East during the 1970s, and the rapid growth experienced by East Asian economies in the 1980s and 1990s, made countries such as Saudi Arabia, Japan, Malaysia, Hong Kong, Taiwan, and Singapore major sources of employment for overseas Filipino workers. Filipino labor tended to fill gender and occupational niches vacated by the "reserve army" of each labor-receiving country. Scholars have also pointed to the increasingly feminized and "domesticated" nature of Filipino overseas work: from 12 percent of deployed workers in 1975, the percentage of female overseas Filipino workers increased to 47 percent in 1987, 58 percent in 1995, 61 percent in 1998, and 72 percent in 2001 (Hau 2005).

In brief, then, it can be generally argued that stunted economic development has kept the Philippine middle classes small in number, socially stable (and separate from peasants, workers, and the urban poor), politically visible but insignificant, and in the past two decades dispersed, as university graduates often have gone abroad to work or migrated to the United States, Canada, and Australia. Moreover, with the Philippine political system long dominated by the landed oligarchy, the government has never made it its political objective to create a viable middle class in the Philippines.

This, however, does not mean that things have remained unchanged in the Philippines. Financial globalization and the regionalization of production affected the Philippines, above all Manila and Cebu. After the Plaza Accord in 1985, Japanese trading companies invested in industrial estate development in view of the appreciation of the yen, won, and Taiwanese dollar. But the timing was not quite right. The post-Marcos political instability, as evidenced by a series of unsuccessful coups and the deteriorating infrastructure (above all, power shortages), discouraged Japanese firms from moving their production facilities to the Philippines. By the early 1990s, however, East Asia was in a boom. There was no need for the Philippine government to campaign for foreign investment because surplus capital was not only pouring into the country from the NIEs but from Thailand, Malaysia, and Indonesia. This more than made up for the lack of foreign investment from Japan, the United States, and Europe. President Fidel Ramos was quick to tap the potential of these Asian capital flows, and he immediately moved toward the further liberalization of the economy. One major strategy was the breakup of monopolies, such as the telecommunications industry, which witnessed the emergence of telecommunications companies including cellular phone. The government also considerably loosened nationality restrictions on foreign investment, with 100 percent equity allowed in all but a few sectors; even the retail trade sector was opened (Tadem 2003, 468, 472–73).

The post-1986 era also witnessed the arrival of new politicians in national politics. The social backgrounds of the post-1986 party leaders differed from those of the pre-1972 party elites. While the pre-1972 party politicians were associated with the landed oligarchy whose rent-seeking and careers were anchored to state patronage and intervention, the post-1986 party elites came from a broader economic base and diverse career backgrounds. This made them more disposed toward free enterprise and limited government. Having experienced the Marcos dictatorship and become allies during the 1986 "people power" revolution, they were also convinced of the virtues of democratic politics. This included their support for liberalization to counteract the flaws and costs of economic protectionism before 1973 and the adverse effects of crony capitalism during the Marcos regime. Furthermore, changes in the political economy had eroded the power base of the old landed elites: the importance of export crops had declined while that of manufacturing and service industries had markedly increased (Tadem 2003, 471).

New urban middle classes have thus emerged in the post-1986 Philippines. They were created through growth in retail trade, manufacture, banking, real estate development, and an expanding range of specialist services such as accounting, advertising, computing, and market research. Fostered by government policies of liberalization and deregulation, the development of these new enterprises has been oriented both toward the export and domestic markets, and has entailed increasingly diverse sources of foreign investment and variable subcontracting, franchise, and service relationships, with a noticeable expansion of ties connecting the Philippines to other countries in East and Southeast Asia. A substantial stimulus for many capitalists, small and large, new and old, has been the growth of the domestic consumer market around the repatriated earnings of the Filipino workers abroad (Pinches 1999, 278). As Michael Pinches notes, the most significant change came in these years as ethnic Chinese entrepreneurs made substantial inroads into areas formerly controlled by the old Spanish or mestizo elite, and established conglomerates that surpassed those of some of the old rich. A major factor making this and related developments possible was the opening up of citizenship to Filipino Chinese in 1975. Increasingly, the Chinese taipans employed more educated middle-class non-Chinese as they professionalized their corporations. Equally important, the younger generations of Philippines-born Chinese are increasingly speaking English, Tagalog, and other Filipino languages in preference to Hokkien; many are entering prestigious schools and universities that had formerly been the almost exclusive domain of non-Chinese, particularly mestizo Filipinos; and large numbers have been moving out of the old Chinatowns into more ethnically mixed middle-class and elite suburbs (Pinches 1999, 285).

The Philippine middle classes are thus less divided than their counterparts in Malaysia and Indonesia (though animosities remain), less dependent on the state than in Malaysia, Indonesia, and Thailand, but smaller than in Thailand and Malaysia and less hegemonic than in Thailand. Politics in the post-Marcos, democratic Philippines thus shows an interesting contrast with post-1992 democratic politics in Thailand. Devoid of cultural hegemony and unable to capture the parliament and the government, middle-class forces vacillated between pro- and antigovernment positions. NGOs proliferated under Corazon Aquino and Ramos, increasing from twenty thousand in 1990 to fifty-eight thousand in 1993, in part thanks to the accord NGOs worked out with the Aquino administration in the arena of decentralization and participatory development. And yet middle-class people took to the streets when there arose major national political issues such as the ratification of U.S. bases agreement in the late 1980s, the question of constitutional amendments toward the end of the Ramos administration, and the move to oust President Joseph Estrada.

Regional Implications of Middle-Class Formation in East Asia

New urban middle classes in East Asia have been shaped by complex historical forces. They are a product of regional economic development, which has taken place in waves under the U.S. informal empire over half a century, first in Japan, then in South Korea, Taiwan, Hong Kong, and Singapore, subsequently in Thailand, Malaysia, Indonesia, and the Philippines, and now in China. They are a product as well of developmental states, whether democratic or authoritarian, and their politics of productivity. Their lifestyles have been shaped in very complex ways by their appropriation of things American, Japanese, Chinese, South Korean, Islamic, and others, and of American, Japanese, "overseas Chinese," Islamic, and other ways of life, often mediated by the market.

The political consequences of the rise of East Asian middle classes vary: though created in one generation, they have evolved along different historical trajectories, nationally occupy different social, political, and cultural positions, and exercise varying levels of political influence. The cultural and political hegemony of the South Korean middle classes is embodied by a single generation, while that of the Taiwanese middle classes manifests itself in the political assertiveness of an ethnic majority. Southeast Asian middle classes also exemplify the diversity and complexity of class formation: Thai middle classes are coherent socially, hegemonic culturally, and ascendant politically; their counterparts in Malaysia and Indonesia are socially divided, dependent on the state, politically assertive but vulnerable; and Philippine middle classes are socially coherent, less dependent on the state, culturally ascendant, but politically vacillating.

These middle classes' long-term cultural hegemony and political ascendancy are largely dependent on the economic performance of their respective countries, because high economic growth means not only their survival, prosperity, and expansion but also the promise of a life of plenty and consumption for lower classes. In this respect, the long-term development and stability of the Indonesian and Philippine middle classes appear problematic. The Indonesian economy has grown less than 4 percent a year since the end of the economic crisis, while the Philippine economy has performed anemically for the last twenty-five years. This has resulted in deepening social and political crises that routinely manifest themselves in the outflow of workers (now more than eight million people from the Philippines alone); increasingly polarized class politics playing out in the national arena; corruption and capture by rent-seekers of the state apparatus; challenges against the state by Communist revolutionary and Islamic separatist movements in the Philippines; violent anti-Chinese riots, widespread ethnic and religious conflict, and the expansion of Islamist forces in Indonesia.

This combination of middle-class assertion and vulnerability is visibly concretized by enclaves such as Lippo Karawaci, a new town developed in the 1990s in a Jakarta suburb, with a university, a huge shopping center, and a golf course in its town center, which epitomizes this emerging middle-class East Asia. The gated and police-patrolled community of Lippo Karawaci demonstrates that the middle classes live in constant fear of the lower classes, who are allowed to come into the new town as domestic workers, shop clerks, waiters, janitors, caddies, and others or sneak in as criminals. Moreover, as Hall argued earlier in this book, the emergence of Japan as a consumption superpower may have made its shadow ecology less contentious and more devastating, less Southeast Asia–centered and more China-centered and global, but the rise of middle-class Asia in South Korea, China, Taiwan, and Southeast Asia now promises to make Asia's shadow ecology potentially far more devastating.

At the same time the regionwide middle classes constitute expanding regional markets for multinational corporations. If it was Japanese, South Korean, Taiwanese, and "overseas Chinese" foreign direct investments, geared to a significant extent to the markets outside the region, that drove East Asian regionalization in the 1980s and 1990s, multinational corporations now target the middle-class markets within the region. The purchasing and consumption power of the middle class is borne out by an April 22, 2002, report in the *Financial Times,* which pointed out that in 2002, personal consumption in East Asia stood at about $5 trillion, on par with the figure for the European Union, and not that far behind the $6.9 trillion figure for the United States. Furthermore, consumption growth is very high, spurred by the fact that consumer banking remains one of the few profitable areas left for the growth of East Asian financial institutions (Thornhill 2002, 14).

Whether in fashion, lifestyle, music, or other businesses, firms that are successful in capturing regional markets thrive. Goods need to be tailored to the market. Korean entertainment companies, for instance, have done so by promoting generically "Asian"-looking boy and girl bands with at least one English-speaking member and others who speak Japanese or Mandarin. Their names are often English acronyms (NRG, HOT), their songs' refrains are in simple English ("I am your girl," "I will be back"), and they perform in Mandarin, Cantonese, or Japanese (*Far Eastern Economic Review,* October 18, 2001). The novelty of the familiar, best represented by generic Asian-looking boys and girls in films, TV commercials, and pop music, is the key to capturing regional markets or their segments.[5]

Regional middle-class markets thus open up the possibility of constructing market-mediated national and regional cultural identities. As Kasian Tejapira persuasively argues about Thai middle-class consumption and identity: "Thai-ness, unanchored, uprooted, and freed from the regime of reference to commodities signifying national or ethnic Thai identity, is now able, as it were, to roam freely around the commodified globe, to coexist and copulate with Italian earrings, American fragrance, English wool, a Swiss-made watch, Seiko, Sanyo, Toyota, Wacoal, or any other un-Thai commodities and sundries" (Kasian 2001, 153). Markets, in other words, are there, and now safely Thai (or Malay Malaysian or Sino-Indonesian or Filipino) because national identity is now spectral and undefined. Commodities can be assembled and reassembled by cultural entrepreneurs and politicians to construct an "Asianness" that is not opposed to national identities.

Two examples are instructive here. Periplus, a publisher based in Singapore, has carved out a niche for itself as a purveyor of the "Asian style," publishing books about everything from *Bali Style* to *New Asian Architecture.* Eric Oey, the owner, published the first such title, *Tropical Asian Style,* in 1995. "The

---

[5] This of course does not mean that there are pan–East Asian markets for all the commodities. Markets are segmented nationally, linguistically, and in many other ways. Giordano, for instance, emerged as one of the region's biggest fashion retail operations with more than one thousand outlets in Greater China, Southeast Asia, South Korea, and Japan in 1994–2001. In contrast, TVB, a Hong Kong TV producer, has captured the Cantonese language TV programming market and emerged as the largest television program producer in East Asia outside Japan, because of its vast fifty-thousand-hour Cantonese TV program library.

books," *Asiaweek* reports, "reflect the rise of a new crop of talented designers across the region who have been finding fresh expression for Asian artistry." At the same time, Oey taps "into the middle class's increasingly sophisticated tastes and yearning for luxurious lifestyles." Periplus's catalog includes martial arts books (including all those written by Bruce Lee) and highly rated cookbooks and travel guides. In 1996 Oey acquired Tuttle Publishing, a company his American mother's cousin founded in Tokyo, and now Periplus, with more than one thousand titles in print, ranks among the top five English-language publishers in Asia (*Asiaweek* 2001). Anwar Ibrahim, now out of jail and planning a comeback, also demonstrated his savvy political entrepreneurship when he said: "It will not be too difficult for Asian countries to gain control of the communication technologies to mount a counteroffensive. But this will be meaningful only if we can offer cultural products that compete successfully for the free choice of a universal audience. This is a challenge to Asian creativity and imagination" (*Straits Times*, February 1, 1994, quoted in Ang 2001, 32). What is important here is not his self-assertiveness but the point he makes that "Asians" will have "Asian" culture and identity if successful in cultural commodities markets. Markets are there. What remains to be seen is who produces what to further integrate the region economically and to construct an Asian identity for economic and political gain.

Over the past fifty years, successive waves of economic development, driven by national and transnational capitalism working with national states, have created middle classes across the region. Prosperous Japan—or, for that matter, South Korea, Taiwan, Hong Kong, and Singapore—does not any longer stand apart from "peasant" Asia. Manifold and variegated interactions between Japan and the rest of East Asia are embedding Japan far more deeply in the region. Global competition is forcing Japanese firms to employ non-Japanese engineers, managers, and researchers. Japanese farmers look for their wives in the Philippines. More generally, "international marriages" are on the rise. More senior Japanese are staying in retirement communities in Southeast Asia. More young Japanese, above all women, are looking for jobs abroad. More East Asians (including Mainland Chinese) are coming to Japan as tourists, students, and workers. Japanese TV melodramas now often set their stages in Asia outside Japan. And economic partnership agreements that Japan is negotiating with Malaysia, the Philippines, Thailand, Indonesia and South Korea and with ASEAN as a group will open up the professional labor market of caregivers, nurses, and others to non-Japanese people.

Japan's interaction with the rest of East Asia is also changing the assumptions on which contemporary understanding and analysis of Japan's engagement with East Asia are based. Two arguments have often been made about Japan in the 1980s and precrisis 1990s and are now being made about China: first, that regionalization is essentially a process by which one single country—

whether it is the United States, or Japan or China—creates a region in its own image; second, that regionalism is led by one country, hence the idea that China now is poised to take over the leadership from stagnant Japan and a narrowly focused United States. In light of the data presented in this chapter and more generally in this book, these two arguments are untenable. As much as Japan is deeply embedded in East Asia, so are other countries in the region, and so will China—above all its coastal provinces—be in the foreseeable future. Ideas such as "soft power" that assume unidirectional hegemonic influence by a single nation not only smack of chauvinism (as Leheny argues in chapter 9) but elide the crucial processes of creative translation and appropriation (including productive "misunderstandings") by which different peoples make sense of and use cultural products not their own.

Interactions among states, markets, and societies are now laying the social foundations for an East Asian regional integration that is rooted in specific national formations and, possibly as well, regional identification across national borders. Regional integration and growing regional identification are changing the parameters of state initiatives toward region-making while redefining nations, nationalisms, and national projects.

References

ADB (Asian Development Bank). 2003. "Progress and Institutional Arrangements for the Chiang Mai Initiative." Regional Economic Monitoring Unit, February 26. http://aric.adb.org.

——. 2002a. "A Regional Early Warning System Prototype for East Asia." Regional Economic Monitoring Unit, report prepared for the Kobe Research Project, May. http://www.mof.go.jp/jouhou/kokkin/tyousa/kobe_e.htm.

——. 2002b. "Study on Monetary and Financial Cooperation in East Asia (Summary Report)." Regional Economic Monitoring Unit, report prepared for the Kobe Research Project, May. http://www.mof.go.jp/jouhou/kokkin/tyousa/kobe_e .htm.

Adorno, Theodor. 1991. *The Culture Industry: Selected Essays on Mass Culture.* Edited and with an introduction by J. M. Bernstein. London: Routledge.

AEM (ASEAN Economic Ministers). 1991. "Joint Press Statement of the 23rd ASEAN Economic Ministers Meeting." Malaysia, October 7–8.

Allison, Anne. 2004. "Cuteness as Japan's Millennial Product." In *Pikachu's Global Adventure: The Rise and Fall of Pokemon,* edited by Joseph Tobin, 34–49. Durham: Duke University Press.

Amsden, Alice. 2001. *The Rise of "the Rest": Challenges to the West from Late-Industrializing Economies.* Oxford: Oxford University Press.

Amyx, Jennifer. 2004a. *Japan's Financial Crisis: Institutional Rigidity and Reluctant Change.* Princeton: Princeton University Press.

——. 2004b. "Japan and the Evolution of Regional Financial Arrangements in East Asia." In *Beyond Bilateralism: U.S.-Japan Relations in the New Asia-Pacific,* edited by Ellis Krauss and T. J. Pempel, 198–218. Stanford: Stanford University Press.

——. 2003a. "The Ministry of Finance and the Bank of Japan at the Crossroads." In *Japanese Governance: Beyond Japan Inc.,* edited by Jennifer Amyx and Peter Drysdale, 55–76. London: Routledge Curzon.

——. 2003b. "A New Face for Japanese Finance? Assessing the Impact of Recent Reforms." Manuscript, University of Pennsylvania, February.

Amyx, Jennifer, and Peter Drysdale, eds. 2003. *Japanese Governance: Beyond Japan Inc.* London: Routledge Curzon.

Anderson, Benedict. [1983] 1991. *Imagined Communities: Reflections on the Origin and Spread of Nationalism.* New York: Verso.

Ang, Ien. 2001. "Desperately Guarding Borders: Media Globalization, 'Cultural Imperialism,' and the Rise of 'Asia.'" In *House of Glass: Culture, Modernity, and the State in Southeast Asia,* edited by Yao Souchou, 27–45. Singapore: Institute of Southeast Asian Studies.

Aoki, Masahiko. 1988. *Information, Incentives and Bargaining in the Japanese Economy.* Cambridge: Cambridge University Press.

Aoki, Tamotsu. 2001. "'Miwaku Suru Chikara' to Bunka Seisaku" ["The Power to Fascinate" and Cultural Policy]. In *Posuto IT Kakumei 'Sofuto Pawa' Nihon Fukken e no Michi* [Soft Power after the Information Technology Revolution: The Road to Japan's Rehabilitation], edited by Takenaka Heizo, 146–76. Tokyo: Fujita Institute of Future Management.

APEC (Asia Pacific Economic Cooperation). 1997. "APEC Economic Leaders Declaration: Connecting the APEC Community." Vancouver, November 25.

——. 1995. "The Osaka Action Agenda: Implementation of the Bogor Declaration." Adopted by the Economic Leaders' meeting, Osaka, November 19.

——. 1994. "APEC Economic Leaders' Declaration of Common Resolve." Bogor, Indonesia, November 15.

APEC-EPG (Eminent Persons Group). 1995. "Implementing the APEC Vision: Executive Summary." *Selected APEC Documents 1995.* Eminent Persons Group Report. http://www.apecsec.org.sg/apec/publications/free_downloads/1997–1993. MedialibDownload.v1.html?url=/etc/medialib/apec_media_library/downloads /sec/pubs/1995.Par.0002.File.v1.1.

——. 1994. "Achieving the APEC Vision: Free and Open Trade in the Asia Pacific." August. http://www.apec.org/apec/publications/free_downloads/1997–1993. MedialibDownload.v1.html?url=/etc/medialib/apec_media_library/downloads /misc/pubs/1994.Par.0001.File.v1.1.

——. 1993. "A Vision for APEC: Towards an Asia Pacific Economic Community." Eminent Persons Group Report, November. http://www.apec.org/apec/publications /free_downloads/1997–1993.MedialibDownload.v1.html?url=/etc/medialib /apec_media_library/downloads/misc/pubs/1994.Par.0002.File.v1.1.

Apter, David, and Nagayo Sawa. 1986. *Against the State: Politics and Social Protest in Japan.* Cambridge: Harvard University Press.

Araki, Jun'ichi. 2000. "Japan's Security Strategy and the Relevance and Difficulties of New Roles for the Japan Self-Defense Force." *USJP Occasional Paper 00–01.* Cambridge: Harvard University, Program on U.S.-Japan Relations.

Arase, David. 1995. *Buying Power: The Political Economy of Japanese Foreign Aid.* New York: Lynne Rienner.

Ariel, Heryanto. 1999. "The Years of Living Luxuriously: Identity Politics of Indonesia's New Rich." In *Culture and Privilege in Capitalist Asia,* edited by Michael Pinches, 159–87. London: Routledge.

Aris, Azam. "KL to Push for East Asia Pact." *Business Times,* (December 11), 1.

Ariyoshi, Sawako. 1984. *The Twilight Years*. Translated by Mildred Tahara. Tokyo: Kodansha International.

Armacost, Michael H., and Kenneth B. Pyle. 2001. "Japan and the Engagement of China: Challenges for U.S. Policy Coordination." *NBR Analysis* 12, no. 5 (December).

Arndt, Sven W., and Henryk Kierzkowski. 2001. Introduction to *Fragmentation: New Production Patterns in the World Economy*, edited by Sven W. Arndt and Henryk Kierzkowski, 1–16. Oxford: Oxford University Press.

Asahi Shimbun. 2004. "Screening Cuts Chinese Student Numbers." March 8.

———. 2003a. "Anti-Missile Deal Ties Japan to U.S. Vision of Global Defense." December 20–21, 19.

———. 2003b. "N. Korean Threat Spurs Missile Defense Action." December 20–21, 19.

———. 2003c. "Death Benefit to Rise for Troops Sent to Iraq." October 27, 15.

———. 2003d. "Kaijikan Haken Encho o Kettei" [Decision Made to Extend Dispatch of MSDF Ships]. October 21, evening, 4th ed., 1.

———. 2003e. "NPA to Bulk Up, Target Gangs." August 27.

———. 2003f. "Tight Inspections for N. Korean Ship." June 2.

———. 2002a. "Deal Sees Sanyo, Haier as Equals." January 10.

———. 2002b. "Machine Tools: A Shrinking Domestic Market." February 6.

———. 2002c. "Spy Ship, Drug Smuggling Boat 'One and the Same.'" December 7.

———. 1998. "Nichi-Bei-Chu no Anpo Taiwa Shido" [Japan-U.S.-China Security Dialogue Starts]. July 16, 14th ed.

Asami, Yasuhito. 1998. "Chukan-so no Zodai to Seiji-ishiki no Henka" [The Rise of Middle Classes and Changes in Political Consciousness]. In *Ajia no Dai Toshi: Bangkok* [Asian Primate Cities: Bangkok], edited by Toshio Tasaka, 305–28. Tokyo: Nihon Hyoron-sha.

Asiaweek. 2001. "The Business of Style." October 12.

Asudei Nihon [Japan Earth Day]. 1992. *Yutakasa no Uragawa: Watashitachi no Kurashi to Ajia no Kankyo* [The Other Side of Abundance: Our Lifestyles and the Asian Environment]. Tokyo: Gakuyo Shobo.

Awata, Fusaho. 2003. "'Kankoryoku' no Kozo to Wa: Sofuto Pawa to shite no 'Nippon Burando Senryaku' o Kangaeru" [What is the Structure of "Tourism Power"? Considering the "Japan Brand Strategy" as "Soft Power"]. *Unso to Keizai* [Transportation and Economy] 63, no. 7 (July): 53–62.

Baker, Gerald. 1998. "Fed Official Confident over China Currency." *Financial Times* (June 24), 4.

Baker, James A. 1991–1992. "America in Asia: Emerging Architecture for a Pacific Community." *Foreign Affairs* 70, no. 5 (Winter): 1–18.

———. 1991. "The U.S. and Japan: Global Partners in a Pacific Community." Text of remarks by U.S. Secretary of State James A. Baker to the Japan Institute of International Affairs, Tokyo, November 11.

———. 1989. "A New Pacific Partnership: Framework for the Future." Address to the Asia Society, June 26.

Baldwin, Carliss Y., and Kim B. Clark. 1997. "Managing in an Age of Modularity." *Harvard Business Review* 75, no. 5: 84–93.

Bandai Group. 2002. *Annual Report 2002*. Tokyo: Bandai Group.

Barrett, Christopher B., Edward B. Barbier, and Thomas Reardon. 2001. "Agro-industrialization, Globalization, and International Development: The Environmental Implications." *Environment and Development Economics* 6, no. 4: 419–33.

Barrett, H. R., A. W. Browne, P. J. C. Harris, and K. Cadoret. 2002. "Organic Certification and the UK Market: Organic Imports from Developing Countries." *Food Policy* 27, no. 4: 301–18.

BBC Online. 2002. "Japanese Hit Cartoon Gets US Release." April 19. http://news.bbc.co.uk/2/hi/entertainment/1939090.stm (accessed October 23, 2003).

Beattie, Alan. 2004. "US Holds the Cards in Dealing with the Dollar." *Financial Times* (January 20), 8.

Bello, Walden. 1993. "Trouble in Paradise." *World Policy Journal* 10, no. 2 (Summer): 33–39.

Bergsten, C. Fred, and Yung Chul Park. 2002. "Toward Creating a Regional Monetary Arrangement in East Asia." ADB Institute Research Paper Series No. 50, Tokyo, December.

Bernard, Mitchell. 1996. "Regions in the Global Political Economy: Beyond the Local-Global Divide in the Formation of the Eastern Asian Region." *New Political Economy* 1, no. 3: 335–53.

Bestor, Theodore C. 2004. *Tsukiji: The Fish Market at the Center of the World*. Berkeley: University of California Press.

———. 2001. "Supply-Side Sushi: Commodity, Market, and the Global City." *American Anthropologist* 103, no. 1: 76–95.

Bhattasali, Deepak, and Masahiro Kawai. 2002. "Implications of China's Accession to the World Trade Organization." In *Japan and China: Cooperation, Competition, and Conflict*, edited by H. G. Hilpert and R. Haak, 72–102. Houndmills: Palgrave.

BIS (Bank for International Settlements). 2003. "Consolidated Banking Statistics for the Second Quarter of 2003." http://www.bis.org.

———. 2002. "International Consolidated Banking Statistics for the Third Quarter of 2001." http://www.bis.org.

Blyth, Mark. 2003. "The Political Power of Financial Ideas: Transparency, Risk, and Distribution in Global Finance." In *Monetary Orders: Ambiguous Economics, Ubiquitous Politics*, edited by Jonathan Kirshner, 239–59. Ithaca: Cornell University Press.

Boeicho. 2000. *Boei Hakusho* [Defense White Paper]. Tokyo: Okurasho Insatsu-kyoku.

Borden, William S. 1984. *The Pacific Alliance: United States Foreign Economic Policy and Japanese Trade Recovery, 1947–1955*. Madison: University of Wisconsin Press.

Bowles, Paul. 2002. "Asia's Post-Crisis Regionalism: Bringing the State Back In, Keeping the (United) States Out." *Review of International Political Economy* 9, no. 2 (March): 244–70.

Brinton, Mary C. 2000. "Social Capital in the Japanese Youth Labor Market: Labor Market Policy, Schools, and Norms." *Policy Sciences* 33, nos. 3–4: 289–306.

Brooke, James. 2004. "China Fears Once and Future Kingdom." *New York Times* (August 25), A3.

Brooke, James, and Keith Bradsher. 2004. "Dollar's Fall Tests Nerve of Asia's Central Bankers." *New York Times* (December 4), A1.

Brouwer, Gordon de. 2002. "Does a Formal Common-Basket Peg in East Asia Make

Economic Sense?" In *Financial Markets and Policies in East Asia,* edited by Gordon de Brouwer, 286–314. London: Routledge.

Bunker, Stephen, and Paul S. Ciccantell. 1995. "Restructuring Space, Time, and Competitive Advantage in the Capitalist World-System: Japan and Raw Materials Transport after World War II." In *A New World Order? Global Transformations in the Late 20th Century,* edited by D. Smith and J. Borocz, 109–30. Westport, Conn.: Greenwood Press.

Burpee, Geoff. 1997. "Dreams Come True Gets Asia to Perk Up Its Ears to Japanese Pop." *Billboard,* Asia-Pacific quarterly section (March 1), 1.

Buruma, Ian, and Avishai Margalit. 2004. *Occidentalism: The West in the Eyes of Its Enemies.* New York: Penguin.

Bush, George. 1990. "Remarks Announcing the Enterprise for the Americas Initiative." *Weekly Compilation of Presidential Documents* 26, no. 26: 1009–13.

Business Times. 2004. "Tokyo Unveils Radical Blueprint to Build Financial Giants." December 27.

——. 2003a. "Problem Loans at Tokyo Banks Down 7%." February 8.

——. 2003b. "New Japan Body Vows to Restore Industrial Glory." June 28.

——. 2003c. "Japanese Banks Raise Earnings Forecasts." November 26.

Business World. 1996. "Western Visayas' Prawn Industry: Sunset Too Soon?" February 12.

Calder, Kent E. 1988. *Crisis and Compensation: Public Policy and Political Stability in Japan.* Princeton: Princeton University Press.

Calvo, Guillermo, and Carmen Reinhart. 2002. "Fear of Floating." *Quarterly Journal of Economics* 117, no. 2: 379–408.

Campbell, John Creighton. 2000. "Changing Meanings of Frail Old People and the Japanese Welfare State." In *Caring for the Elderly in Japan and the US,* edited by Susan O. Long, 82–97. London: Routledge.

——. 1992. *How Policies Change: The Japanese Government and the Aging Society.* Princeton: Princeton University Press.

Carothers, Thomas. 1999. *Aiding Democracy Abroad: The Learning Curve.* Washington, D.C.: Carnegie Endowment for International Peace.

Chandler, A. D. 1977. *The Visible Hand: The Managerial Revolution in American Business.* Cambridge: Harvard University Press.

Chen, Xiaomei. 2002. *Occidentalism: A Theory of Counter-Discourse in Post-Maoist China.* Lanham, Md.: Rowman and Littlefield.

Cheng, L. K., and H. Kierzkowski, eds. 2001. *Global Production and Trade in East Asia.* Boston: Kluwer Academic Publishers.

CHI/MIT. 2003. "Report on 'Innovation Scores' survey." CHI.com. http://www.chiresearch.com/.

ChinaHR.com. 2003. "The Most Popular Employers in Chinese Students' Eyes" (in Chinese). http://www.chinahr.com/promotion/investigate/.

Chirot, Daniel, and Anthony Reid, eds. 1997. *Essential Outsiders: Chinese and Jews in the Modern Transformation of Southeast Asia and Central Europe.* Seattle: University of Washington Press.

Cho, Kyo. 1998. "Bunka ga Joho ni Natta Toki" [When Culture Becomes Information]. *Sekai* (April): 82–91.

Choi, Chang-Hee. 2003. "The China Strategies of Korea's Winning Companies." *NRI Papers* No. 67 (August 1). Tokyo: Nomura Research Institute.

Chua, Beng Huat. 2005. "Placing Singapore in East Asian Popular Culture." *Proceedings of the Core University Program Workshop on Middle Classes and Flows and Movements in Southeast Asia.* Center for Southeast Asian Studies, Kyoto University, October 6–8.

Ciccantell, Paul S., and Stephen G. Bunker. 2002. "International Inequality in the Age of Globalization: Japanese Economic Ascent and the Restructuring of the Capitalist World-Economy." *Journal of World-Systems Research* 8, no. 1: 62–98.

Clinton, William J. 1993. "Building a New Pacific Community." Speech at Waseda University (Japan), July 7. http://www.mofa.go.jp/region/n-america/us/archive/1993/remarks.html.

Council on Foreign Relations. 2003. *Chinese Military Power: Report of an Independent Task Force Sponsored by the Council on Foreign Relations Maurice R. Greenberg Center for Geoeconomic Studies.* New York: Council on Foreign Relations.

Cumings, Bruce. 1987. "The Origins and Development of the Northeast Asian Political Economy: Industrial Sectors, Product Cycles, and Political Consequences." In *The Political Economy of the New Asian Industrialism,* edited by F. C. Deyo, 44–83. Ithaca: Cornell University.

Curtis, Gerald. 1999. *The Logic of Japanese Politics: Leaders, Institutions, and the Limits of Change.* New York: Columbia University Press.

——. 1988. *The Japanese Way of Politics.* New York: Columbia University Press.

Daily Yomiuri. 2003. "NPA Plans Steps against Terrorist Gangs." December 23.

——. 2001a. "Smuggling of People Doubles since January." April 30.

——. 2001b. "Arrests Made Over Marriage Scam." July 17.

——. 2001c. "NPA Unveils Plan to Increase Officers by 10,000 in 3 Years." August 27.

——. 1998. "China to Crack Down on Arms, Drug Smuggling." May 7.

Darling, Michael. 2001. "Plumbing the Depths of Superflatness." *Art Journal* 60, no. 3 (Fall): 76–89.

Dasgupta, S., N. Mamingi, and C. Meisner. 2001. "Pesticide Use in Brazil in the Era of Agroindustrialization and Globalization." *Environment and Development Economics* 6, no. 4: 459–82.

Dauvergne, Peter. 1997. *Shadows in the Forest: Japan and the Politics of Timber in Southeast Asia.* Cambridge: MIT Press.

——. 2001. "The Rise of an Environmental Superpower? Evaluating Japanese Environmental Aid to Southeast Asia." In *Japan and East Asian Regionalism,* edited by S. Javed Masood, 51–67. London: Routledge.

Davies, A., P. Tuang, T. Brady, M. Hobday, H. Rush, and D. Gann. 2001. *Integrated Solutions — the New Economy between Manufacturing and Services.* Report by Science Policy Research Unit (SPRU), University of Sussex, December.

Defense Agency. 2000. *Defense of Japan 1999.* Tokyo: Japan Times.

Dejitaru Kontentsu Kyokai. 2003. *Deijitaru Kontentsu Hakusho 2003* [Digital Contents White Paper 2003]. Tokyo: METI/Digitaru Kontentsu Kyokai.

Department of Justice (DOJ). 2003. "United States-Japan Mutual Legal Assistance Treaty Signed to Enhance Law Enforcement Cooperation." Department of Justice Press Release #443 (August 5). http://www.usdoj.gov.

Destler, I. M. 1995. *American Trade Politics.* 3rd ed. Washington, D.C.: Institute for International Economics with the Twentieth Century Fund.

De Vos, George A. 1992. *Social Cohesion and Alienation: Minorities in the United States and Japan.* Boulder: Westview.

Diamond, Larry. 1999. *Developing Democracy: Toward Consolidation.* Baltimore: Johns Hopkins University Press.

Dieter, Heribert, and Richard Higgott. 2003. "Exploring Alternative Theories of Economic Regionalism: From Trade to Finance in Asian Co-operation?" *Review of International Political Economy* 10, no. 3 (August): 430–54.

DiMaggio, Paul, and Walter Powell. 1991. *The New Institutionalism in Organizational Analysis.* Chicago: University of Chicago Press.

Dore, Ronald. 1986. *Flexible Rigidities: Industrial Policy and Structural Adjustment in the Japanese Economy 1970–1980.* London: Athlone Press.

Dore, Ronald P., and Sako Mari. 1989. *How the Japanese Learn to Work.* London: Routledge.

Doremus, Paul N., William W. Keller, Louis W. Pauly, and Simon Reich. 1998. *The Myth of the Global Corporation.* Princeton: Princeton University Press.

Dörrenbächer, Christoph. 1999. *Vom Hoflieferanten zum Global Player: Unternehmensreorganisation und nationale Politik in der Welttelekommunikationsindustrie.* Berlin: Edition Sigma, Rainer Bohn Verlag.

Douglass, Mike, and Glenda S. Roberts, eds. 2000. *Japan and Global Migration: Foreign Workers and the Advent of a Multicultural Society.* London: Routledge.

Drifte, Reinhard. 2003. "Transboundary Pollution as an Issue in Northeast Asian Regional Politics." Unpublished paper, Asia Research Centre, London School of Economics.

Dunning, John. 1981. *International Production and the Multinational Enterprise.* London: George Allen and Unwin.

East Asia Vision Group. 2001. "Towards an East Asian Community—Region of Peace, Prosperity and Progress." http://www.infojapan.org/region/asia-paci/report2001.pdf.

Economist. 2003. "IT in Japan: Watching the World Scroll By." April 19, 55–56.

Elger, Tony, and Chris Smith. 1994a. Introduction to *Global Japanization: The Transnational Transformation of the Labour Process,* edited by Tony Elger and Chris Smith, 1–24. London: Routledge.

——. 1994b. "Global Japanization? Convergence and Competition in the Organization of the Labour Process." In *Global Japanization: The Transnational Transformation of the Labour Process,* edited by Tony Elger and Chris Smith, 31–59. London: Routledge.

Elliott, Lorraine. 2003. "ASEAN and Environmental Cooperation: Norms, Interests, and Identity." *Pacific Review* 16, no. 1: 29–52.

Encarnation, Dennis J., ed. 1999. *Japanese Multinationals in Asia: Regional Operations in Comparative Perspective.* New York: Oxford University Press.

Endo, Hajime. 1998. "Ote-Ryutsu-Shihon no Chiho Shinshutsu to Chiho-Ryutsu-Kigyo no Soshiki-ka" [Penetration into Provinces by Major Retail Capital and the Reorganization of Local Retail Firms]. In *Ajia no Dai Toshi: Bangkok* [Asian Primate Cities: Bangkok], edited by Toshio Tasaka, 163–90. Tokyo: Nihon Hyoron-sha.

Ernst, Dieter. 2005a. "Complexity and Internationalisation of Innovation: Why Is Chip Design Moving to Asia?" Special issue, *International Journal of Innovation Management* 9, no. 1 (March): 47–73. An earlier version was published as *East-West Center Economics Working Paper* No. 64.

———. 2005b. "The New Mobility of Knowledge: Digital Information Systems and Global Flagship Networks." In *Digital Formations, IT and New Architectures in the Global Realm,* edited by R. Latham and S. Sassen (Princeton: Princeton University Press and Social Science Research Council).

———. 2004. "Pathways to Innovation in Asia's Leading Electronics Exporting Countries—A Framework for Exploring Drivers and Policy Implications." *International Journal of Technology Management* 29, nos. 1–2: 6–20.

———. 2003. "Digital Information Systems and Global Flagship Networks: How Mobile Is Knowledge in the Global Network Economy?" In *The Industrial Dynamics of the New Digital Economy,* edited by J. F. Christensen. Cheltenham: Edward Elgar.

———. 2002a. "The Economics of the Electronics Industry: Competitive Dynamics and Industrial Organization." In *The IEBM Handbook of Economics,* edited by William Lazonick, 319–39. Part of the *International Encyclopedia of Business and Management* handbook series. London: International Thomson Business Press.

———. 2002b. "Global Production Networks and the Changing Geography of Innovation Systems: Implications for Developing Countries." *Journal of the Economics of Innovation and New Technologies* 11, no. 6: 497–523.

———. 2000. "Evolutionary Aspects: The Asian Production Networks of Japanese Electronics Firms." In *International Production Networks in Asia: Rivalry or Riches?,* edited by M. Borrus, D. Ernst, and S. Haggard, 80–109. London: Routledge.

———. 1997. "From Partial to Systemic Globalization: International Production Networks in the Electronics Industry." Report prepared for the Sloan Foundation, jointly published as *The Data Storage Industry Globalization Project Report 97–02.* San Diego: University of California, Graduate School of International Relations and Pacific Studies.

Ernst, Dieter, and Paolo Guerrieri. 1998. "International Production Networks and Changing Trade Patterns in East Asia: The Case of the Electronics Industry." *Oxford Development Studies* 26, no. 2 (June): 191–212.

Ernst, D., P. Guerrieri, and S. Iammarino. 2005. *Pathways to Asian Regionalism: Global Production Networks, Trade, and Clusters.* Manuscript, East-West Center, Honolulu, and Science Policy Research Unit (SPRU), Sussex.

Ernst, Dieter, and Linsu Kim. 2002. "Global Production Networks, Knowledge Diffusion, and Local Capability Formation." Special issue, *Research Policy* 31, nos. 8–9: 1417–29.

Ernst, D., and B. Naughton. 2005. "China's Emerging Industrial Economy—Insights from the IT Industry." Paper prepared for the East-West Center Conference on China's emerging capitalist system, August 10–12, Honolulu, Hawaii.

Ernst, Dieter, and David O'Connor. 1989. *Technology and Global Competition: The Challenge for Newly Industrialising Economies.* Paris: Organisation for Economic Co-operation and Development.

Ernst, Dieter, and John Ravenhill. 2000. "Convergence and Diversity: How Globalization Reshapes Asian Production Networks." In *International Production Networks in Asia: Rivalry or Riches?* edited by M. Borrus, D. Ernst, and S. Haggard, 226–56. London: Routledge.

Far Eastern Economic Review. 2001. "Swept Up On a Wave." October 18, 92–94.

FAS Online. 2001. "Organic Perspectives." May. http://www.fas.usda.gov/agx/organics/2001/may01.htm.

Feenstra, Robert. 1998. "Integration of Trade and Disintegration of Production in the Global Economy." *Journal of Economic Perspectives* 12, no. 4: 31–50.

Field, Norma. 1991. *In the Realm of a Dying Emperor: Japan at Century's End.* New York: Vintage.

Flannagan, Scott, Shinsaku Kohei, Ichiro Miyake, Bradley M. Richardson, and Joji Watanuke. 1991. *The Japanese Voter.* New Haven: Yale University Press.

Focus Japan. 2003. "An Anime Culture Blossoms in Japan." March.

Fong, Leslie. 2003. "China's Not in Competition with Japan." *Straits Times* (December 19).

Frankel, Jeffrey, and Andrew Rose. 2002. "An Estimate of the Effect of Common Currencies on Trade and Income." *Quarterly Journal of Economics* 117, no. 2: 437–66.

Fratianni, Michele, Paolo Savona, and John Kirton, eds. 2002. *Governing Global Finance: New Challenges, G7 and IMF Contributions.* Aldershot: Ashgate.

Frederick, Jim. 2003. "What's Right with Japan?" *Time Asia,* August 11. http://www.time.com/time/asia/2003/cool_japan/story.html (accessed October 26, 2003).

Frieden, Jeffry, and Ronald Rogowski. 1996. "The Impact of the International Economy on National Policies: An Analytic Overview." In *Internationalization and Domestic Politics,* edited by Robert Keohane and Helen Milner, 25–47. New York: Cambridge University Press.

Friedman, Edward. 1997. "The Asianization of the World?" Unpublished paper, University of Wisconsin, Madison.

Friman, H. Richard. 2004. "The Great Escape? Globalization and Immigrant Entrepreneurship in the Criminal Economy." *Review of International Political Economy* 11, no. 1 (February): 98–131.

——. 2003. "Evading the Divine Wind through the Side Door: The Transformation of Chinese Migration to Japan." In *Globalizing Chinese Migration: Trends in Europe and Asia,* edited by Pal Nyri and Igor R. Saveliev, 9–33. Hampshire: Ashgate Press.

——. 2001. "Immigrant Smuggling and Threats to Social Order in Japan." In *Global Human Smuggling: Comparative Perspectives,* edited by David Kyle and Rey Koslowsky, 294–317. Baltimore: Johns Hopkins University Press.

——. 1999. "Obstructing Markets: Organized Crime Networks and Drug Control in Japan." In *The Illicit Global Economy and State Power,* edited by H. Richard Friman and Peter Andreas, 173–97. Boulder: Rowman and Littlefield.

——. 1996. *NarcoDiplomacy: Exporting the U.S. War on Drugs.* Ithaca: Cornell University Press.

Fruin, W. Mark. 1997. *Knowledge Works: Managing Intellectual Capital at Toshiba.* New York: Oxford University Press.

Fujimoto, Takahiro. 2002. "Nihon-gata Sapuraiyaa Sisutemu to Mojuru-ka—Jidousha Sangyo o Jirei toshite" [The Japanese Supplier System and Modularity—A Case Study of the Automobile Industry]. In *Mojuru-ka—Atarashii Sangyo Akite-*

kucha no Honshitsu [Modularity—the Essence of New Industrial Architecture], Keizai Seisaku Rebyu [Economic Policy Review], edited by Masahiko Aoki and Haruhiko Ando, 169–202. Tokyo: Research Institute of Economy, Trade and Industry (RIETI), Toyo Keizai Shimpo-Sha.

Fujishima, Hiroji. 1997. *Yunyu Yasai San-Byaku-Man Ton Jidai* [The Age of Three Million Tons of Vegetable Imports]. Tokyo: Ienohikari Kyokai.

Fujita, Masahisa, Paul Krugman, and Anthony J. Venables. 2001. *The Spatial Economy: Cities, Regions, and International Trade*. Cambridge: MIT Press.

Fukao, Kyoji. 2001. "How Japanese Subsidiaries in Asia Responded to the Regional Crisis: An Empirical Analysis Based on the MITI Survey." In *Regional and Global Capital Flows: Macroeconomic Causes and Consequences; East Asia Seminar on Economics*, vol. 10, edited by Takatoshi Ito and Anne O. Krueger, 267–310. Chicago: University of Chicago Press.

Fukao, Kyoji, Hikari Ishido, and Keiko Ito. 2003. "Vertical Intra-Industry Trade and Direct Investment in East Asia." *RIETI Discussion Papers* 03–E-001, January. http://www.rieti.go.jp/jp/publications/dp/03e001.pdf.

Fukui, Haruhiro, and Shigeko N. Fukai. 1996. "Pork Barrel Politics, Networks, and Local Economic Development in Contemporary Japan." *Asian Survey* 36: 268–86.

Fukunaga, Kazuhiko. 2003. "*Konbini* Culture Hits Asia." *Look Japan* 48, no. 563 (February): 12–14.

Fukuoka, Yasunori. 2000. *Lives of Young Koreans in Japan*. Melbourne: Trans-Pacific Press.

Funabashi, Yoichi. 1995. *Asia Pacific Fusion: Japan's Role in APEC*. Washington, D.C.: Institute for International Economics.

Funatsu, Tsuruyo, and Kazuhiro Kagotani. 2002. "Tai no Chukanso: Toshi Gakureki Erito no Seisei to Shakai Ishiki" [Thai Middle Classes: The Formation and Social Consciousness of Urban Educated Elite]. In *Ajia Chukan-so no Seisei to Tokushitu* [The Formation and Characteristics of Asian Middle Classes], edited by Tamio Hattori, Tsuruyo Funatsu, and Takashi Torii, 201–34. Tokyo: Ajia Keizai Kenkyusho.

Gaiko Forum [Foreign Affairs Forum]. 1999. Special issue "Security in the 21st Century: Japanese Diplomacy at the Crossroads" (November).

Gaimusho. 2002. *Gaiko Seisho* [Foreign Affairs Blue Book]. Tokyo: Zaimusho Insatsu-kyoku.

Gellert, Paul K. 2003. "Renegotiating a Timber Commodity Chain: Lessons from Indonesia on the Political Construction of Global Commodity Chains." *Sociological Forum* 18, no. 1: 53–84.

Gemünden, Gerd. 1998. *Framed Visions: Popular Culture, Americanization, and the Contemporary German and Austrian Imagination*. Ann Arbor: University of Michigan Press.

Gilboy, George J. 2004. "The Myth behind China's Miracle." *Foreign Affairs* 83, no. 4 (July): 33–48.

Gill, Stephen. 1992. "Economic Globalization and the Internationalization of Authority: Limits and Contradictions." *Geoforum* 23, no. 3: 269–83.

Gilpin, Robert. 2001. *Global Political Economy: Understanding the International Economic Order*. Princeton: Princeton University Press.

———. 1975. *U.S. Power and the Multinational Corporation*. New York: Basic Books.

Goh, Robert. 1990. "PM Calls for Asia Pacific Trade Bloc." *New Straits Times* (December 11), 1.

Goka, Kazumichi. 1999. *Koyo no danryokuka to rodosha haken: Shokugyo jigyo* [Employment Flexibility and Temporary Workers: The Employment Introduction Business]. Tokyo: Otsuki shoten.

Goodman, David. 2001. "Ontology Matters: The Relational Materiality of Nature and Agro-Food Studies." *Sociologia Ruralis* 41, no. 2: 182–200.

Goodman, Peter S. 2004. "Booming China Devouring Raw Materials: Producers and Suppliers Struggle to Feed a Voracious Appetite." *Washington Post* (May 21), A1.

Government of Japan. 1991. *Environment and Development: Japan's Experience and Achievement*. Tokyo: Government of Japan.

Green, Michael. 2001. *Japan's Reluctant Realism: Foreign Policy Challenges in an Era of Uncertain Power*. New York: Palgrave.

Hall, Derek. 2004a. "Japanese Spirit, Western Economics: The Continuing Salience of Economic Nationalism in Japan." *New Political Economy* 9, no. 1 (March): 79–99.

———. 2004b. "Explaining the Diversity of Southeast Asian Shrimp Aquaculture." *Journal of Agrarian Change* 4, no. 3: 315–35.

———. 2002. "Environmental Change, Protest, and Havens of Environmental Degradation: Evidence from Japan–Southeast Asia Relations." *Global Environmental Politics* 2, no. 2: 20–28.

———. 2001. "Japan's Role in the Asian Environmental Crisis: Comparing the Critical Literature and the Environment Agency's White Papers." *Social Science Japan Journal* 4, no. 1: 95–102.

Hamilton-Hart, Natasha. 2004. "Capital Flows and Financial Markets in Asia: National, Regional, or Global?" In *Beyond Bilateralism: U.S.-Japan Relations in the New Asia-Pacific*, edited by Ellis Krauss and T. J. Pempel, 133–53. Stanford: Stanford University Press.

———. 2003. "Co-operation on Money and Finance: How Important? How Likely?" *Third World Quarterly* 24, no. 2: 283–97.

Hardacre, Helen. 2003. "After Aum: Religion and Civil Society in Japan." In *The State of Civil Society in Japan*, edited by Frank J. Schwartz and Susan Pharr, 135–53. Cambridge: Cambridge University Press.

Harney, Alexandra. 2001. "Japan Drafts Law to Allow Its Military to Operate Overseas." *Financial Times* (October 17), 2.

Harris, Owen. 1993. "The Collapse of 'The West.'" *Foreign Affairs* 72, no. 4 (September–October): 41–53.

Hashimoto, Akiko. 1996. *The Gift of Generations: Japanese and American Perspectives on Aging and the Social Contract*. Cambridge: Cambridge University Press.

Hashimoto, Ryutaro. 1995a. "Next Task for the WTO System and the APEC Process." *Journal of Northeast Asian Studies* 14, no. 4 (Winter): 25–32.

———. 1995b. "Challenges for the World Economy in a Transitional Period and Development in the Asia-Pacific Region." Speech in Vancouver, May 2.

Hatch, Walter Frank. 2002a. "Regionalizing the State: Japanese Administrative and Financial Guidance for Asia." *Social Science Japan Journal* 5, no. 2: 179–97.

——. 2002b. "Japanese Production Networks in Asia: Extending the Status Quo." In *Crisis and Innovation in Asian Technology,* edited by William W. Keller and Richard J. Samuels, 23–56. Cambridge: Cambridge University Press.

——. 2000. "Rearguard Regionalization: Protecting Core Networks in Japan's Political Economy." PhD diss., University of Washington.

Hatch, Walter, and Kozo Yamamura. 1996. *Asia in Japan's Embrace: Building a Regional Production Alliance.* New York: Cambridge University Press.

Hattori, Tamio, Tsuruyo Funatsu, and Takashi Torii, eds. 2002. *Ajia Chukan-so no Seisei to Tokushitu* [The Formation and Characteristics of Asian Middle Classes]. Tokyo: Ajia Keizai Kenkyusho.

Hau, Caroline Sy. 2005. *On the Subject of the Nation: Filipino Writings from the Margins, 1981–2004.* Manila: Ateneo de Manila University Press.

Hayami, Masaru. 2002a. "Statement by the Hon. Masaru Hayami, Governor of the Bank of Japan, for Japan at the Joint Annual Discussion." Statement at the Joint Annual Meeting of the IMF and World Bank, September 29. http://www.mof.go.jp.

——. 2002b. "Statement by the Hon. Masaru Hayami, Governor of the Bank of Japan and Alternate Governor of the IMF, for Japan at the Sixth Meeting of the International and Monetary Committee." September 28. http://www.mof.go.jp.

——. 2000. "Statement by the Hon. Masaru Hayami, Governor of the Bank of Japan, at the Joint Annual Discussion." Statement at the Joint Annual Meeting of the IMF and World Bank, September 26. http://www.mof.go.jp.

Heilbron, Selwyn, and J. T. Larkin. 1997. *Food Market Channel Development in Japan and Korea: A Report for the Rural Industries Research and Development Corporation and Supermarket to Asia Limited.* Barton, A.C.T., Australia: Rural Industries Research and Development Corporation.

Hemmer, Christopher, and Peter J. Katzenstein. 2002. "Why Is There No NATO in Asia? Collective Identity, Regionalism, and the Origins of Multilateralism." *International Organization* 56, no. 3 (Summer): 575–607.

Henning, C. Randall. 2002. *East Asian Financial Cooperation.* Policy Analyses in International Economics 68. Washington, D.C.: Institute for International Economics.

Herbert, Wolfgang. 2000. "The Yakuza and the Law." In *Globalization and Social Change in Contemporary Japan,* edited by J. S. Eades, Tom Gill, and Harumi Befu, 143–58. Melbourne: Trans Pacific Press.

——. 1996. *Foreign Workers and Law Enforcement in Japan.* London: Kegan Paul.

Hill, Peter. 2003. *The Japanese Mafia: Yakuza, Law and the State.* Oxford: Oxford University Press.

Hirado, Mikio. 2000. "Jinko to Sangyo-Shokugyo no Kosei" [Population and The Structure of Industrial Occupations]. In *Ajia no Dai-toshi: Kuala Lumpur and Singapore* [Asian Primate Cities: Kuala Lumpur and Singapore], edited by Masato Ikuta and Toshio Matsuzawa, 147–71. Tokyo: Nihon Hyoron-sha.

Hirayama, Takasada. 1974. "Watashi to Nichi-Tai Seinen Yuko Undo" [The Japan-Thailand Youth Friendship Movement and Me]. *Nichi-Tai Seinen Yiko Undo Nyusu* [Japan-Thailand Youth Friendship Movement News] 3: 5–7.

Hirst, Paul, and Grahame Thompson. 1996. *Globalization in Question: The International Economy and the Possibilities of Governance.* Cambridge: Polity Press.

Hiwatari, Nobuhiro, and Mari Miura. 2002. *Ryudoki no Nihon Seiji* [The Lost Decade and Beyond: Japanese Politics in the 1990s]. Tokyo: University of Tokyo Press.

Honda, Yoshihiro. 2004. *Taiwan Soto Retsuden: Beichu Kankei no Rimen-shi* [Biographies of Taiwan's Presidents: Inside Story of U.S.-China Relations]. Tokyo: Chuokoron Shinsha.

Honda, Yuki. 2003. "The Reality of the Japanese School-to-Work Transition System at the Turn of the Century: Necessary Disillusionment." *Social Science Japan* (February): 8–12.

Horiuchi, Akiyoshi. 2003. "The Big Bang Financial System Reforms: Implications for Corporate Governance." In *Japanese Governance: Beyond Japan Inc.*, edited by Jennifer Amyx and Peter Drysdale, 77–95. London: Routledge Curzon.

Hoshino, Kanehiro. 1994. *Organized Crime and Its Origins in Japan*. Tokyo: National Research Institute of Police Science.

Howells, Jeremy, and Michelle Wood. 1993. *The Globalisation of Production and Technology*. London: Belhaven Press.

Hu, Yao-Su. 1992. "Global or Stateless Corporations Are National Firms with International Operations." *California Management Review* 34, no. 2 (Winter): 107–26.

Huang, Sophia Wu. 2002. "China Increases Exports of Fresh and Frozen Vegetables to Japan." *Electronic Outlook Report from the Economic Research Service of the USDA*. Washington, D.C.: U.S. Department of Agriculture, August.

Hughes, Christopher. 2000. "Japanese Policy and the East Asian Currency Crisis: Abject Defeat or Quiet Victory?" *Review of International Political Economy* 7, no. 2 (April): 219–53.

Huntington, Samuel P. 1996. "The West, Unique, Not Universal." *Foreign Affairs* 75, no. 6 (November–December): 28–46.

Igarashi, Akio. 1997. "From Americanization to 'Japanization' in East Asia." *Journal of Pacific Asia* 4: 3–19.

IIF (Institute of International Finance). 2003. "Capital Flows to Emerging Market Economies." September 21. http://www.iif.com.

IMF (International Monetary Fund). 2003a. "IMF Executive Board Recommends to Governors Conclusion of Quota Review." *Press Release No. 03/02,* January 10. http://www.imf.org.

———. 2003b. "Japan: Financial System Stability Assessment and Supplementary Information." *IMF Country Report No. 03/287,* September.

———. 2002a. "Guidelines on Conditionality." September 25. http://www.imf.org.

———. 2002b. "Reforming the IMF: Progress Since Prague." December. http://www.imf.org.

Inada, Juichi. 2002. "Japan's ODA: Its Impacts on China's Industrialization and Sino-Japanese Relations." In *Japan and China: Cooperation, Competition and Conflict,* edited by H. G. Hilpert and R. Haak, 121–39. Houndmills: Palgrave.

Inoguchi, Takashi. 2000. "Three Frameworks in Search of a Policy: U.S. Democracy Promotion in Asia-Pacific." In *American Democracy Promotion: Impulses, Strategies, and Impacts,* edited by Michael Cox, G. John Ikenberry, and Takashi Inoguchi, 267–86. Oxford: Oxford University Press.

Institute of Social Science, University of Tokyo. 1998. "Okinawa." Special issue, *Social Science Japan* 14 (November).

Interfax China IT & Telecom Weekly. 2004. January 31, 3.

Ishi, Hiromitsu. 1993. "The Fiscal Investment and Loan Program and Public Enterprise." In *Japan's Public Sector: How the Government Is Financed,* edited by Tokue Shibata, 82–102. Tokyo: University of Tokyo Press.

Ishida, Hiroshi. 2001. "Industrialization, Class Structure, and Social Mobility in Postwar Japan." *British Journal of Sociology* 52, no. 4: 579–604.

———. 1993. *Social Mobility in Contemporary Japan: Educational Credentials, Class, and the Labour Market in a Cross-National Perspective.* Stanford: Stanford University Press.

Ishiyama, Yoshihide. 1999. "Is Japan Hollowing Out?" In *Japanese Multinationals in Asia: Regional Operations in Comparative Perspective,* edited by Dennis J. Encarnation. New York: Oxford University Press.

Itabashi, Isao, Masamichi Ogawara, with David Leheny. 2002. "Japan." In *Countering Terrorism: Strategies of Ten Nations,* edited by Yonah Alexander, 337–73. Ann Arbor: University of Michigan Press.

Ito, Takatoshi. 2002. "A Case for a Coordinated Basket for Asian Countries." Paper prepared for the report of the study group on Exchange Rate Regimes for Asia, Kobe Research Project. http://www.mof.go.jp/jouhou/kokkin/tyousa/kobe_e.htm.

ITTO (International Tropical Timber Organization). 2002. *Annual Review and Assessment of the World Timber Situation 2002.* Yokohama: ITTO.

———. 2004. *Annual Review and Assessment of the World Timber Situation 2004.* Yokohama: ITTO.

Iwabuchi, Koichi. 2002. *Recentering Globalization: Popular Culture and Japanese Transnationalism.* Durham: Duke University Press.

———. 1998. "Gurobarizeshon no Naka no Nihon Bunka no Nioi" [The Odor of Japanese Culture under Globalization]. *Sekai* (April): 69–81.

Iwai, Tomoaki. 1990. *Seiji Shikin' no Kenkyu* [A Study of 'Political Money']. Tokyo: Toyo Keizai.

Jackson, Patrick Thaddeus. N.d. "Defending the West: Occidentalism and the Formation of NATO." Manuscript, American University, Washington, D.C.

———. 2001. "Occidentalism: Rhetoric, Process, and Postwar German Reconstruction." PhD diss., Columbia University.

Japan Economic Newswire. 1990. "Li Peng is Supportive of East Asia Market Idea." December 13.

Japan Society, National Institute for Research Advancement (Tokyo), and Research Institute for Peace and Security (Tokyo). 2001. "New Approaches to U.S.-Japan Security Cooperation: Conference Report." In *New Approaches to U.S.-Japan Security Cooperation: Terrorism Prevention and Preparedness,* edited by Michael Green, 11–37. New York: Japan Society.

Japan Times. 2003a. "The Zeit Gist: Time to Come Clean on Foreign Crime Wave." October 7.

———. 2003b. "Two Held in China over Fukuoka Killings." September 21.

———. 2003c. "Show of Force Greets North Korean Ferry." August 26.

———. 2002a. "Shinjuku's Boom-Bust Underground Economy." February 3.

———. 2002b. "Drug Ring Bugged." May 24.

———. 2002c. "Nation at Crime and Punishment Crossroad." July 24.

———. 2002d. "Osaka Seminar Clarifies Provision of U.N. Crime Convention." August 24.

——. 2002e. "U.S. Urges Signing of Bilateral Treaty for Exchanging Crime Information." October 22.

——. 2002f. "Chinese, Japanese Clash in 'Mafia Town.'" October 27.

——. 2001a. "The Diet That Set a Precedent." December 11.

——. 2001b. "Ministry Opens Counterterrorism Office." December 13.

——. 1997a. "China Pushed on Illegal Entry." March 2.

——. 1997b. "China to Curb Illegal Immigrants." March 20.

Japan Today. 2003a. "PM: Influx of Foreign Workers Will Cause Security Problems." September 20.

——. 2003b. "Two Hundred Officers to Crack Down on Illegal Residents." December 30.

——. 2003c. "Police Start Probe in China on Fukuoka Family Murder." October 2.

——. 2002a. "U.S. Presses Japan to Crack Down on Human Trafficking." June 6.

——. 2002b. "Police Bust Counterfeit Passport Ring." August 27.

——. 2002c. "Japan, U.S. to Block Weapons Smuggling." September 26.

——. 2002d. "Drug Smuggling to Be on Japan–N. Korea Agenda." September 27.

——. 2002e. "Japan Suspects N. Korea Abducted 70–80 More Japanese." November 18.

——. 2002f. "Police Arrest Iranians in Undercover Drug Sting." November 26.

——. 2002g. "Ship Smuggled $2.5 Bil from Japan to North Korea." December 6.

Jarausch, Konrad H., and Hannes Siegrist. 1997. "Amerikanisierung und Sowjetisierung: Eine Vergleichende Fragestellung zur Deutsch-Deutschen Nachkriegsgeschichte." In *Amerikanisierung und Sowjetisierung in Deutschland, 1945–1970,* edited by K. Jarausch and H. Siegrist, 3–24. Frankfurt: Campus.

JBICI (Japan Bank for International Cooperation Institute). 2003. *Survey Report on Overseas Business Operations by Japanese Manufacturing Companies — Results of JBIC FY 2002 Survey.* Tokyo: Japan Bank for International Cooperation Institute.

——. 2001. *Survey Report on Overseas Business Operations by Japanese Manufacturing Companies — Results of JBIC FY 2000 Survey.* Tokyo: Japan Bank for International Cooperation Institute.

Jepperson, Ron. 1991. "Institutions, Institutional Effects, and Institutionalism." In *The New Institutionalism in Organizational Analysis,* edited by Paul J. DiMaggio and Walter W. Powell, 143–63. Chicago: University of Chicago Press.

JETRO (Japan External Trade Organization). 2004. *2004 JETRO White Paper on International Economy and Trade — Towards a "New Value Creation Economy."* Tokyo: Japan External Trade Organization.

——. 2003a. *Ajia Nikkei Seizogyo no Keiei Jittai — 2002 Nendo Chosa* [The Business Condition of Japanese Manufacturing in Asia—FY 2002 Report]. Tokyo: Japan External Trade Organization, March.

——. 2003b. *Chugoku Deta Fairu 2002/03* [China Data File]. Tokyo: Japan External Trade Organization.

——. 2003c. *2003 JETRO White Paper on International Trade and Foreign Direct Investment.* Tokyo: Japan External Trade Organization.

——. 2002. *2002 JETRO White Paper on International Trade and Investment.* Tokyo: Japan External Trade Organization.

Jinakul, Apichit. 2003. "Farmers Angry over Threat to Livelihood: Cheap Imports Push Down Local Demand." *Bangkok Post* (July 2).

Job, Brian L. 2000. "Non-Governmental Regional Institutions in the Evolving Asia Pacific Security Order." Paper prepared for the Second Workshop on Security Order in the Asia Pacific, Bali, May 30–June 2.

Johnson, Chalmers. 1997. "The Failure of Japanese and American Leadership after the Cold War: The Case of Okinawa." *Occasional Paper No. 74* (February 6). Washington, D.C.: Woodrow Wilson International Center for Scholars, Asia Program.

Joho Tsushin Sofuto Kondankai [Information Transmission and Software Discussion Council]. 2003. *Dejitaru Kontentsu WG no Kento Jokyo* [Investigative Conditions for the Digital Content Working Group]. http://www.soumu.go.jp.

Jones, David Martin. 1997. *Political Development in Pacific Asia*. Cambridge: Polity Press.

Jonquières, Guy de. 2002. "As Countries Clamour for Bilateral Agreements, the Prospects of Creating a Truly Open Global Economy Recede." *Financial Times* (November 19), 11.

JSE (Jakarta Stock Exchange). 2003. *JSX Statistics, 3rd Quarter 2003*. Jakarta: JSE.

Kabashima, Ikuo. 2004. *Sengo Seiji no Kiseki* [The Tracks of Postwar Politics]. Tokyo: Iwanami Shoten.

———. 1994. "Shinto no Tojo to Jiminto Itto Yuitaisei no Hokai" [The Rise of New Parties and the End to the Liberal Democratic Party's Single-Party Dominance]. *Leviathan* 15: 7–31.

Kahler, Miles. 2000. "The New International Financial Architecture and Its Limits." In *The Asian Financial Crisis and the Architecture of Global Finance*, edited by Gregory Noble and John Ravenhill, 235–60. Cambridge: Cambridge University Press.

Kamiya, Matake. 2001. "Sofuto Pawa to wa Nani Ka?" [What Is Soft Power?]. In *Posuto IT Kakumei 'Sofuto Pawa' Nihon Fukken e no Michi* [Soft Power after the Information Technology Revolution: The Road to Japan's Rehabilitation], edited by Heizo Takenaka, 31–64. Tokyo: Fujita Institute of Future Management.

Kanko Rikoku Kondankai. 2003. *Kanko Rikoku Kondankai Hokokusho: Sundeyoshi, Otozureteyoshi no Kuni Zukuri* [Final Report of the Japan Tourism Advisory Council: Making a Country Good for Living and Visiting]. Tokyo: Prime Minister's Office.

Kaplan, David E., and Alec Dubro. 2003. *Yakuza: Japan's Criminal Underworld*. Berkeley: University of California Press.

Kapur, Devesh. 2002. "The Changing Anatomy of Governance at the World Bank." In *Reinventing the World Bank*, edited by Jonathan Pincus and Jeffrey Winters, 54–75. Ithaca: Cornell University Press.

Kariya, Takehiko. 2001. *Kaisoka Nihon to kyoiku kiki: Fubyodo saiseisan kara iyoku (insentibu dibaido) kakusa shakai e* [Education in Crisis and Stratified Japan: From the Reproduction of Inequality to an 'Incentive-Divide' Society]. Tokyo: Yushindo.

Kariya, Takehiko, and James E. Rosenbaum. 1999. "Bright Flight: Unintended Consequences of Detracking Policies in Japan." *American Journal of Education* 107 (May 3): 210–30.

Kasian, Tejapira. 2001. "The Post-Modernization of Thainess." In *House of Glass: Culture, Modernity, and the State in Southeast Asia*, edited by Yao Souchou, 150–70. Singapore: Institute of Southeast Asian Studies.

Katada, Saori. 2001. "Japan's Approach to Shaping a New Financial Architecture."

In *New Directions in Global Economic Governance: Managing Globalisation in the Twenty-first Century*, edited by John Kirton and George von Furstenberg, 113–26. Aldershot: Ashgate.

Katzenstein, Peter J. 2005. *A World of Regions: Asia and Europe in the American Imperium.* Ithaca: Cornell University Press.

——. 2003a. "Same War—Different Views: Germany, Japan, and Counter-Terrorism." *International Organization* 57, no. 4 (Fall): 731–60.

——. 2003b. "Japan, Technology and Asian Regionalism in Comparative Perspective." In *The Resurgence of East Asia: 500, 150 and 50 Year Perspectives,* edited by Giovanni Arrighi, Takeshi Hamashita, and Mark Selden, 214–58. London: Routledge.

——. 2002. "September 11 in Comparative Perspective: The Counterterrorist Campaigns of Germany and Japan." *Dialogue-Io* (Spring): 45–56.

——. 2000. "Varieties of Asian Regionalisms." In *Asian Regionalism,* edited by Peter J. Katzenstein, Natasha Hamilton-Hart, Kozo Kato, and Ming Yue, 1–34. Ithaca: Cornell University, East Asia Program.

——. 1997. "Introduction: Asian Regionalism in Comparative Perspective." In *Network Power: Japan and Asia,* edited by Peter J. Katzenstein and Takashi Shiraishi, 1–44. Ithaca: Cornell University Press.

——. 1996. *Cultural Norms and National Security: Police and Military in Postwar Japan.* Ithaca: Cornell University Press.

Katzenstein, Peter J., and Nobuo Okawara. 2001–2002. "Japan and Asian-Pacific Security: Analytical Eclecticism, Not Parsimony." *International Security* 26, no. 2 (Winter): 153–85.

Katzenstein, Peter J., and Takashi Shiraishi, eds. 1997. *Network Power: Japan and Asia.* Ithaca: Cornell University Press.

Kawaguchi, Yoriko. 2003. "Henka Suru Anzen Hosho Kankyo to Nihon Gaiko" [The Changing National Security Environment and Japan's Diplomacy]. *Ronza* (March): 180–89.

——. 2002. "Common Opportunities: Japan and Canada in the 21st Century." Speech to Vancouver Board of Trade, Vancouver, Canada, June 14. http://www.mofa.go.jp/region/n-america/canada/p_ship21/fmspeech.html (accessed October 27, 2003).

Keck, Margaret, and Kathryn Sikkink. 1998. *Activists beyond Borders.* Ithaca: Cornell University Press.

Keisatsucho. Annual. *Keisatsu Hakusho* [White Paper on Police]. Tokyo: Zaimusho Insatsu-kyoku.

Keller, William W., and Richard J. Samuels. 2003. "Innovation and the Asian Economies." In *Crisis and Innovation in Asian Technology,* edited by William W. Keller and Richard J. Samuels, 1–22. Cambridge: Cambridge University Press.

Kelly, William W. 2002. "At the Limits of New Middle Class Japan: Beyond Mainstream Consciousness." In *Social Contracts under Stress: The Middle Classes of America, Europe, and Japan at the Turn of the Century,* edited by Olivier Zunz, Leonard Schoppa, and Nobuhiro Hiwatari, 232–54. New York: Russell Sage Foundation.

Kennedy, Paul M. 1988. *The Rise and Fall of the Great Powers.* New York: Random House.

Kim, Ah Young. 2003. "End North Korea's Drug Trade Addiction." *Japan Times* online, June 26.

Kim, Elisa. 2000. "Korea Loosens Ban on Japanese Pop Culture." *Billboard* (July 22), 68–77.

Kim, Samuel S., ed. 2004. *The International Relations of Northeast Asia*. Lanham, Md.: Rowman and Littlefield.

Kim, Sun-Bae. 2002. "Regional Commentary: Asia's Brave New Business Cycle Part II: Intra-regional Trade." *Asia-Pacific Economics Analyst* No. 2002/15, Goldman Sachs, September 2.

Kimura, Masataka. 2002. "Firipin no Chukanso Soshutsu to Seiji Henyo" [The Creation and Political Changes of Philippine Middle Classes]. In *Ajia Chukan-so no Seisei to Tokushitu* [The Formation and Characteristics of Asian Middle Classes], edited by Tamio Hattori, Tsuruyo Funatsu, and Takashi Torii, 169–200. Tokyo: Ajia Keizai Kenkyusho.

Kina, Shoukichi, and Sugok Shin. 1998. "Nihon Bunka tte Nan Da?" [What the Hell Is Japanese Culture?]. *Sekai* (April): 115–29.

Kindleberger, Charles. 1973. *The World in Depression, 1929–1939*. Berkeley: University of California Press.

King, Michael. 2001. "Who Triggered the Asian Financial Crisis?" *Review of International Political Economy* 8, no. 3 (September): 438–66.

King, Michael, and Timothy Sinclair. 2003. "Private Actors and Public Policy: A Requiem for the New Basel Capital Accord." *International Political Science Review* 24, no. 3: 345–62.

Kinsella, Sharon. 1998. "Japanese Subculture in the 1990s: Otaku and the Amateur Manga Movement." *Journal of Japanese Studies* 24, no. 2 (Summer): 289–316.

Kitschelt, Herbert. 2000. "Linkages between Citizens and Politicians in Democratic Polities." *Comparative Political Studies* 33: 845–79.

Kobayashi, Yoshiaki. 1991. *Sengo Nihon no Senkyo* [Postwar Japanese Elections]. Tokyo: Tokyo Daigaku Shuppan.

Kojima, Kiyoshi. 1986. "Japanese-Style Direct Foreign Investment." *Japanese Economic Studies* 14, no. 3: 52–82.

———. 1978. *Direct Foreign Investment: A Japanese Model of Multinational Business Operations*. London: Croom Helm.

Kokubun, Ryosei, and Jisi Wang, eds. 2004. *The Rise of China and a Changing East Asian Order*. Tokyo: Japan Center for International Exchange.

Kokusai Koryu Kenkyukai [International Exchange Research Group]. 2003. *Arata na Jidai no Gaiki to Arata na Kokusai Koryu no Yakuwari* [Diplomacy in a New Era, and a New Role for International Exchange]. April. Tokyo: Japan Foundation.

Kompas. 2003. "TNI AL Dukung Riau Beli Kapal Perang" [Indonesian Navy Supports Purchase of Warship]. August 30.

Konagaya, Kazuyuki. 1999. "Toshi Kozo." In *Ajia no Dai-toshi: Jakarta*, edited by Kensuke Miyamoto and Kazuyuki Konagaya, 87–116. Tokyo: Nihon Hyoron-sha.

Konno, Yasuaki. 1999. "Shakai Kaikyu-Kaiso no Hendo" [Changes in Social Classes/ Strata]. In *Ajia no Dai-toshi:* Jakarta [Asian Primate Cities: Jakarta], edited by Kensuke Miyamoto and Kazuyuki Konagaya, 307–33. Tokyo: Nihon Hyoron-sha.

Konomoto, Shingo. 2002. "China's Rapidly Growing Infocom Industry and Approaches by Japanese Companies." *NRI Papers* No. 53, August 1. Tokyo: Nomura Research Institute.

———. 2000. "Problems of Japanese Companies in East and Southeast Asia." *NRI Papers* No. 18, November 1. Tokyo: Nomura Research Institute.

Kralev, Nicholas. 2003. "U.S. Seeks Asian Aid for Ship Searches." *Washington Times* (June 18), A1.

Krause, Elizabeth L. 2001. "'Empty Cradles' and the Quiet Revolution: Demographic Discourse and Cultural Struggles of Gender, Race, and Class in Italy." *Cultural Anthropology* 16, no. 4: 576–611.

Krauss, Ellis S., and T. J. Pempel. 2004. *Beyond Bilateralism: U.S.-Japan Relations in the New Asia-Pacific.* Stanford: Stanford University Press.

Kroes, Rob. 1996. *If You've Seen One, You've Seen the Mall: Europeans and American Mass Culture.* Urbana: University of Illinois Press.

Kumagai, Tetsuya. 2003. "In Limbo." *Asahi Shimbun* (December 6–7), 19.

Kunikawa, Kyoko. 2004. "Japan Meets Korian Mubi" [Japan Meets Korean Film]. *Pia* 1039 (February 16): 28–31.

Kuroda, Atsuo. 2001. *Meido in Chaina* [Made in China]. Tokyo: Toyo Keizai Shimposha.

Kuroki, Fumiaki. 2002. "Cross-Shareholdings Decline for the 11th Straight Year (FY 2001 Survey)." *NLI Research,* October 1. http://www.nli-research.co.jp/eng/resea/econo/eco021001.pdf.

Kuwahara, Satoshi. 2004. "Higashi Ajia oyobi Tonan-Ajia Chiiki ni okeru Sangyoshuseki Keisei patan no Henka to Boeki-Kozo ni okeru Kyogo-Hokan-kankei ni tsuite" [Changes in the Pattern of Formation of Industrial Clusters and Competitive and Complementary Relationships in Trade Structure in East and Southeast Asia]. In *Gendai Ajia no Furontia* [The Frontiers of Asia Today], edited by Hideo Kobayashi, 83–108. Tokyo: Shakaihyoronsha.

———. 2003. "ASEAN no Keizai-Hatten Senryaku to Nichi ASEAN Kankei" [ASEAN's Strategy for Economic Development and Japan-ASEAN Relations]. Manuscript.

Kwan, C. H. 1996. "A Yen Bloc in Asia." *Journal of the Asia Pacific Economy* 1, no. 1: 1–21.

Kwan, Chi Hung. 2003. "Why Japanese Firms are Unpopular." *China in Transition,* April 2. http://www.rieti.go.jp/en/china/03040201.html.

———. 2002. "China's Immiserizing Growth." *China in Transition,* August 16. http://www.rieti.go.jp/en/china/02081601.html.

———. 2001. *Yen Bloc: Toward Economic Integration in Asia.* Washington, D.C.: Brookings Institution Press.

Kyodo News Service. 2002. "Japanese Animated Movie 'Spirited Away' Big Hit in Korea." July 18.

Laurence, Henry. 2001. *Money Rules: The New Politics of Finance in Britain and Japan.* Ithaca: Cornell University Press.

Lawrence, Geoffrey, and Frank Vanclay. 1994. "Agricultural Change and Environmental Degradation in the Semi-Periphery: The Case of the Murray-Darling Basin in Australia." In *The Global Restructuring of Agro-Food Systems,* edited by Philip McMichael, 76–103. Ithaca: Cornell University Press.

Lee, Simon. 2002. "Global Monitor: The International Monetary Fund." *New Political Economy* 7, no. 2: 283–98.

Leheny, David. 2003. *The Rules of Play: National Identity and the Shaping of Japanese Leisure.* Ithaca: Cornell University Press.

———. 2001–2002. "Tokyo Confronts Terror." *Policy Review* 110 (December–January): 37–47.

Linhart, Sepp, and Sabine Frühstück, eds. 1998. *The Culture of Japan as Seen Through Its Leisure.* Albany: State University of New York Press.

Liu, Meng-Chun, and Shin-Horng Chen. 2003. *International R&D Deployment and Locational Advantage of Developing Countries: A Case Study of Taiwan.* Taipei: Chung-Hua Institution for Economic Research.

Long, Susan Orpett, ed. 2000. *Caring for the Elderly in Japan and the U.S.: Practices and Policies.* London: Routledge.

Long, Susan Orpett, and Phyllis Braudy Harris. 2000. "Gender and Elder Care: Social Change and the Role of the Caregiver in Japan." *Social Science Japan Journal* 3, no. 1: 21–36.

Maase, Kaspar. 1997. "'Amerikanisierung der Gesellschaft': Nationalisierende Deutung von Globalisierungsprozessen." In *Amerikanisierung und Sowjetisierung in Deutschland 1945–1970,* edited by K. Jarausch and H. Siegrist, 219–41. Frankfurt: Campus.

MacIntyre, Andrew, and Barry Naughton. 2004. "The Decline of a Japan-Led Model of the East Asian Economy." In *Remapping East Asia: The Construction of a Region,* edited by T. J. Pempel, 77–100. Ithaca: Cornell University Press.

MacNeill, Jim, Peter Winsemius, and Taizo Yakushiji. 1991. *Beyond Interdependence: The Meshing of the World's Economy and the Earth's Ecology.* New York: Oxford University Press.

Maeda, Tetsuo. 2002. "Kaijo Hoancho Ho no kaitei to ryoiki keibi" [Territorial Security and the Revision of the Japanese Coast Guard Law]. In *Yuji hosei o kento suru* [Investigating the Emergency Laws], edited by Yamauchi Toshihiro, 184–200. Tokyo: Horitsubunkasha.

Mahathir, Mohamad, and Shintaro Ishihara. 1995. *The Voice of Asia: Two Leaders Discuss the Coming Century.* Tokyo: Kodansha International.

Maier, Charles S. 1978. "The Politics of Productivity: Foundations of American International Economic Policy after World War II." In *Between Power and Plenty: Foreign Economic Policies of Advanced Industrial States,* edited by Peter J. Katzenstein, 23–50. Madison: University of Wisconsin Press.

Mainichi Daily News. 2003. "Japan Denies 90% of Chinese Students Resident Permits." December 4.

———. 2001. "Gang Boss Gunned Down as Yakuza War Escalates." August 21.

———. 1997. "Osaka Authorities to Crack Down on Fake Chinese 'War Orphans.'" December 17.

Mainichi Shimbun. 2004. "Shushoku Setsumeikai ni Ni-Man-Nin" [Twenty Thousand Attend Job-Seeking Explanation Meeting]. *Jakarta Shimbun,* January 29. http://www.mainichi.co.jp/asia/news/Indonesia/200401/29-1.html (accessed February 12, 2004).

———. 2003. "Seme no Nogyo, Yushutu Shiko" [Agriculture Getting Aggressive and Export-oriented]. Morning edition, July 5, 11.

Manila Times. 2003. "RP to Exit from IMF Program in a Huff, Says Buenaventura." February 3.

Manning, Robert A., and Paula Stern. 1994. "The Myth of the Pacific Community." *Foreign Affairs* 73, no. 6 (November–December): 79–93.

Martinez, D. P., ed. 1998. *The Worlds of Japanese Popular Culture: Gender, Shifting Boundaries, and Global Culture.* Cambridge: Cambridge University Press.

Marukawa, Tomoo. 2002. "Japanese FDI and China's Industrial Development in the Automobile, Electronics and Textile Industries." In *Japan and China: Cooperation, Competition and Conflict,* edited by Hanns Guenther Hilpert and Rene Haak, 174–93. Basingstoke: Palgrave.

MAS (Monetary Authority of Singapore, Economic Policy Department). 2003. *Macroeconomic Review* 2, no. 1 (January). http://www.mas.gov.sg/resource/download/MRJan2003_upload.pdf.

Mathews, Gordon. 2004. "Seeking a Career, Finding a Job: How Young People Enter and Resist the Japanese World of Work." In *Japan's Changing Generations: Are Young People Creating a New Society?,* edited by Gordon Mathews and Bruce White, 121–36. London: Routledge Curzon.

Matsubara, Hiroshi. 2003. "Justice Minister Pledges to Make Japan 'Safe Again,' Tighten Border Controls." *Japan Times* online, September 28.

Matsubara, Ryuichiro. 2000. *Shohi Shihonshugi no Yukue* [Whither Consumer Capitalism?]. Tokyo: Chikuma Shinsho.

Matsushita Annual Report. 2003. Matsushita Corp., Osaka.

Matsuzono, Yuko. 1998. "Shugyo Kozo to Jumin Seikatsu" [Occupational Structure and People's Lives]. In *Ajia no Dai Toshi: Bangkok* [Asian Primate Cities: Bangkok], edited by Toshio Tasaka, 191–209. Tokyo: Nihon Hyoron-sha.

Maull, Hans W. 1991. "Japan's Global Environmental Policies." *Pacific Review* 4, no. 3: 254–62.

McClure, Steve. 2000. "Japanese Pop Sweeps across Asia." *Billboard* (January 8), 42.

McCormack, Gavan. 1999. "Modernism, Water, and Affluence: The Japanese Way in East Asia." In *Ecology and the World-System,* edited by W. L. Goldfrank, D. Goodman, and A. Szasz, 147–63. Westport, Conn.: Greenwood Press.

McGray, Douglas. 2002. "Japan's Gross National Cool." *Foreign Policy* (May–June): 44–54.

McMichael, Philip. 2000. "A Global Interpretation of the Rise of the East Asian Food Import Complex." *World Development* 28, no. 3: 409–24.

McNicoll, Geoffrey. 2004. "Demographic Factors in East Asian Regional Integration." In *Remapping East Asia: The Construction of a Region,* edited by T. J. Pempel, 54–74. Ithaca: Cornell University Press.

Menasveta, Piamsak. 1997. "Mangrove Destruction and Shrimp Culture Systems." *World Aquaculture* 28, no. 4: 36–42.

METI (Ministry of Economy, Trade and Industry). 2003. *Summary of the 32nd Survey of Overseas Business Activities,* June 16. Tokyo: METI.

——. 2002a. *White Paper on International Trade.*

——. 2002b. *Summary of the 31st Survey of Overseas Business Activities,* May 17.

——. 2001. *White Paper on International Trade 2001.*

Meyer-Ohle, Hendrik, and Katsuhiko Hirasawa. 2000. "Marketing Strategies of Japanese Firms: Building Brands with a Regional and Long-Term Perspective." In *Corporate Strategies for Southeast Asia after the Crisis: A Comparison of Multinational Firms from Japan and Europe,* edited by Jochen Legewie and Hendrik Meyer-Ohle, 141–62. Basingstoke: Palgrave.

Midford, Paul. 2003. "Japan's Response to Terror: Dispatching the SDF to the Arabian Sea." *Asian Survey* 43, no. 2 (March–April): 329–51.

Ministry of Public Welfare, ed. 1998. "Sho shi shakai o kangaeru" [Thinking about a Society with Few Children]. *Ministry White Paper for Heisei* No. 10. Tokyo.

MITI (Ministry of International Trade and Industry). 1993. *Prospects and Challenges for the Upgrading of Industries in the ASEAN Region.*

——. 1989. "Hirakareta 'Kyoryoku ni yoru Hatten no Jidai e" [Entering an Era of Development through Open Cooperation]. Ajia Taiheiyo Kyoryoku Suishin Kondan-kai [Roundtable on the Promotion of Asia Pacific Cooperation], June 15.

——. 1988. "Aratanaru Ajia Taiheiyo Kyoryoku o Motomete" [In Quest of New Asia Pacific Cooperation]. *Ajia Taiheiyo Boueki Kaihatsu Kenkyu-kai Chukan Torimatome* [Interim Report of the Study Group for Asia Pacific Trade and Development], International Economic Affairs Department, International Trade Policy Bureau. June.

Mitoro, Tomoyuki. 2000. "Shokuhin Sangyo no Kaigai Shinshutsu to Sangyo Kudoka no Tokushitsu" [Overseas Movement of the Food Products Industry and the Pros and Cons of Industrial Hollowing-Out]. In *Ajia no Shokuryo—Nosanbutsu Shijo to Nihon* [Japan and Asia's Food and Agricultural Products Markets], edited by H. Mikuni, 13–26. Tokyo: Otsuki Shoten.

Miura, Atsushi. 2000. "Kogai no Hikaku-bunka-shi to 'dai-4 yamanote'no Genzai" [Comparative Cultural Histories of Suburbs and the Modernity of the Fourth Yamanote Suburb]. In *"Kogai" to Gendai Shakai* ["Suburbs" and Modern Society], edited by Jun Kaneko, 61–99. Tokyo: Seikyusha.

Miyadai, Shinji. 1994. *Seifuku Shojotachi no Sentaku* [The Options for Girls in Uniform]. Tokyo: Kodansha.

——. 1989. *Kenryoku no Yoki Riron: Ryokai no Baikai no Sado Keisei* [Expectation Theory of Social Power: Formation of a System for the Transmission of Understanding]. Tokyo: Keioshobo.

Miyake, Ichiro. 1985. *Seito Shiji no Bunseki* [An Analysis of Political Party Support]. Tokyo: Sobunsha.

Miyasaka, Naofumi. 2001. "Terrorism and Antiterrorism in Japan: Aum Shinrikyo and After." In *Terrorism Prevention and Preparedness: New Approaches to U.S.-Japan Security Cooperation,* edited by Michael Green, 67–81. New York: Japan Society.

Miyashita, Akitoshi. 2003. *Limits to Power: Asymmetric Dependence and Japanese Foreign Aid Policy.* Lanham, Md.: Lexington Books.

Miyawaki, Raisuke. 2001. "Lessons in Fighting Terrorism: American and Japanese Perspectives ." Remarks prepared for the Global Security Roundtable, Japan Society, New York, November 7.

Miyazawa, Kiichi. 2000. "Statement by Kiichi Miyazawa, Minister of Finance of Japan." March 14. http://www.mof.go.jp.

Mo, Bangfu. 1998. "The Rise of the Chinese Mafia in Japan." *Japan Echo* 25, no. 1

(February): 44–47. Translation of "Kyuzosuru Zainichi Chugokujin Mafia no Hanzai," *Sekai* (November 1997): 240–47.

——. 1994. *Jato: Suneku Heddo* [Snake Head]. Tokyo: Shincho Bunko.

Mochizuki, Mike M. 1997. "A New Bargain for a Stronger Alliance." In *Toward a True Alliance: Restructuring U.S.-Japan Security Relations,* edited by Mike M. Mochizuki, 5–40. Washington, D.C.: Brookings Institution Press.

MOFA (Ministry of Foreign Affairs). 2002a. *Japanese Report on Implementation of the APEC Leaders Statement on Counter-Terrorism.* http://www.mofa.go.jp

——. 2002b. *Anzen hosho ni kan suru yoron chosa* [Opinion Poll on National Security]. Reported on MOFA website, http://www.mofa.go.jp/mofaj/gaiko/ah_chosa/index.html.

Mollman, Steve. 2001a. "No Fly Zones." *Asiaweek,* November 30.

——. 2001b. "Playing the Field." *Asiaweek,* November 30.

Mori, Hiromi. 1997. *Immigration Policy and Foreign Workers in Japan.* New York: St. Martin's.

Morimoto, Taiji. 1993. "Parupu-Zai no Shorai Tenbo" [Future Direction of Pulp Materials]. *Kami-pa Gikyo shi* [Paper-Pulp Technical Cooperation] 47, no. 1: 35–47.

Moriyama, Shigenori. 1998. *Kankoku Gendai Seiji* [Contemporary South Korean Politics]. Tokyo: Tokyo Daigaku Shuppankai.

Mulgan, Aurelia George. 2002. *Japan's Failed Revolution: Koizumi and the Politics of Economic Reform.* Canberra: Asia Pacific Press at the Australian National University.

Mullins, Mark R. 1997. "The Political and Legal Response to Aum-Related Violence in Japan: A Review Article." *Japan Christian Review* (Tokyo) 63: 37–46.

Munakata, Naoko. 2003a. "The Impact of the Rise of China and Regional Economic Integration in Asia—A Japanese Perspective." Testimony before the U.S.-China Economic and Security Review Commission Hearing on China's Growth as a Regional Economic Power: Impacts and Implications, December 4. http://www.uscc.gov/hearings/2003hearings/written_testimonies/031204bios/naokmun

——. 2003b. "The U.S. Should Bless the Japan-ROK Free Trade Pact." *CSIS PacNet Newsletter* No. 24, June 9. http://csis.org/pacfor/paco324.htm.

——. 2002. "Whither East Asian Economic Integration?" *RIETI Discussion Paper Series* 02–E-007, June. http://www.rieti.go.jp/jp/publications/dp/02e007.pdf.

——. 2001. "Evolution of Japan's Policy toward Economic Integration." *RIETI Discussion Paper Series* 02–E-006, December. http://www.rieti.go.jp/jp/publications/dp/02e006.pdf.

——. Forthcoming. *Transforming East Asia: The Evolution of Regional Economic Integration.* Washington, D.C.: Brookings Institution Press.

Muravchik, Joshua. 1991. *Exporting Democracy: Fulfilling America's Destiny.* Washington, D.C.: American Enterprise Institute Press.

Nabeshima, Keizo. 2004. "Northeast Asian Safety Valve." *Japan Times* online, March 8.

——. 2002. "Defense Bill Only a First Step." *Japan Times* online, April 22.

Nagae, Akira. 2003. *Tarase no Jidai: Otaku na Nihon no Supafuratto* [The Age of Flatness: Nerdy Japan's Superflatness]. Tokyo: Hara Shobo.

Nakagane, Katsuji. 2002. "Japanese Direct Investment in China: Its Effects on China's Economic Development." In *Japan and China: Cooperation, Competition and*

Conflict, edited by Hanns Guenther Hilpert and Rene Haak, 52–71. Basingstoke: Palgrave.

Nakamori, Akio, and Shinji Miyadai. 1999. "Otaku-ka" [Nerd-ization]. In *Poppu Karucha* [Pop Culture], edited by Miyadai Shinji and Matsuzawa Kureichi, 90–95. Tokyo: Mainichi Shimbunsha.

Nakanishi, Toru, Toru Kodama, and Koichi Niitsu. 2001. *Ajia no Dai Toshi: Manila* [Asian Primate Cities: Manila]. Tokyo: Nihon Hyoron-sha.

Nakano, Lynne. Forthcoming. *Community Volunteering in Japan: Everyday Stories of Social Change.* London: Curzon Press.

Nakano, Yoshiko. 2002. "Who Initiates a Global Flow? Japanese Popular Culture in Asia." *Visual Communication* 1, no. 2 (June): 229–53.

Nakano, Yoshiko, and Wu Yongmei. 2003. "Puchiburu no Kurashikata: Chugoku no Daigakusei ga Mita Nihon no Dorama" [Lifestyles of the Petit Bourgeois: How Chinese University Students Watch Japanese Dramas]. In *Gurobaru Purizumu: 'Ajian Dorimu' to Shite no Nihon no Terebi Dorama* [The Global Prism: Japanese Television Dramas as the 'Asian Dream'], edited by Iwabuchi Koichi, 183–219. Tokyo: Heibonsha.

Napier, Susan J. 2000. *Anime: From Akira to Princess Mononoke.* New York: Palgrave.

Napier, Susan, and Toshio Okada. 2003. "'Gendai Nihon no Anime' ga Amerika no Otona o Kaeru" ['Contemporary Japanese Anime' Are Changing American Adults]. *Chuo Koron* (May): 142–48.

Nectoux, François, and Yoichi Kuroda. 1990. *Timber from the South Seas: An Analysis of Japan's Tropical Timber Trade and Its Environmental Impact.* Gland, Switzerland: World Wildlife Federation International.

Ng, Francis, and Alexander Yeats. 2003. "Major Trade Trends in East Asia: What Are Their Implications for Regional Cooperation and Growth?" *World Bank Policy Research Working Paper* No. 3084, June. Washington, D.C.: World Bank.

Nihon Bengoshi Rengokai. 1991. *Nihon no Kogai Yushutsu to Kankyo Hakai: Tonan Ajia ni Okeru Kigyo Shinshutsu to ODA* [Japan's Pollution Exports and Environmental Destruction: The Advance of Companies and ODA into Southeast Asia]. Tokyo: Nihon Hyoron-sha.

Nii, Takashi. 2005. "Todai Kyodai 'Gokakuryoku' Ranku" [Entrance Examination Success Rankings for Tokyo University and Kyoto University]. *Yomiuri Weekly* (April 3), 10–18.

Nikkei Business. 2000. "Transcript of Prime Minister Goh Chok Tong's Interview with Mr. Osamu Kobayashi, Editor-in-Chief of *Nikkei Business.*" December 19. http://www.gov.sg/sgip/intervws/0101–03.htm.

Nikkei Weekly. 2002. "Sanyo-Haier Group Alliance Offers Lucrative Foothold." January 15.

Nishitani, Satoshi. 2003. "Assessing the Growth in Irregular Employment." *Japan Echo* 30 (April 2): 63–67.

Noguchi, Yukio. 1995. "The Role of the Fiscal Investment and Loan Program in Post-war Japanese Economic Growth." In *The Japanese Civil Service and Economic Development: Catalysts of Change,* edited by Hyung-ki Kim, Michio Muramatsu, T. J. Pempel, and Kozo Yamamura, 261–87. Oxford: Oxford University Press.

Noikorn, Uamdao. 2000. "Japan Agrees to Help Restore Mangroves; End of Shrimp Farm Concessions Near." *Bangkok Post* (October 7).

Noland, Marcus. 2000. "Japan and the International Economic Institutions." Paper prepared for the Centre for Japanese Economic Studies Fifth Biennial Conference, Macquarie University, Sydney, July 6–7. http://www.iie.com.

Nonaka, Ikujiro, and Hirotaka Takeuchi. 1995. *The Knowledge-Creating Company: How Japanese Companies Create the Dynamics of Innovation.* New York: Oxford University Press.

Nye, Joseph S., Jr. 2004. "The Soft Power of Japan." *Gaiko Forum: Japanese Perspectives on Foreign Affairs* 4, no. 2 (Summer): 3–7.

———. 2003. "The Velvet Hegemon: How Soft Power Can Help Defeat Terrorism." *Foreign Policy* 136 (May–June): 74–75.

———. 2002. *The Paradox of American Power: Why the World's Only Superpower Can't Go It Alone.* New York: Oxford University Press.

———. 2000. "Asia's First Globalizer." *Washington Quarterly* 23, no. 4 (Autumn): 121–24.

———. 1991. *Bound to Lead: The Changing Nature of American Power.* New York: Basic Books.

———. 1990. "Soft Power." *Foreign Policy* 80 (Fall): 153–71.

Ochiai, Emiko. 1997. *The Japanese Family System in Transition: A Sociological Analysis of Family Change in Postwar Japan.* Tokyo: LTCB International Library Foundation.

Ockey, Jim. 1999. "Creating the Thai Middle Class." In *Culture and Privilege in Capitalist Asia,* edited by Michael Pinches, 230–50. London: Routledge.

O'Hagan, Jacinta. 2002. *Conceptualizing the West in International Relations: From Spengler to Said.* New York: Palgrave.

Ohmae, Kenichi. 1990. *The Borderless World: Power and Strategy in the Interlinked Economy.* New York: Harper Business.

Okano, Kaori. 1993. *School to Work Transition in Japan: An Ethnographic Study.* Clevedon, England: Multilingual Matters.

Okawara, Nobuo, and Peter J. Katzenstein. 2001. "Japan and Asian-Pacific Security: Regionalization, Entrenched Bilateralism, and Incipient Multilateralism." *Pacific Review* 14, no. 2: 165–94.

Onishi, Norimitsu. 2004a. "This 21st-Century Japan, More Contented than Driven." *New York Times* (February 4), A4.

———. 2004b. "Just 20, She Captures Altered Japan in a Debut Novel." *New York Times* (March 27), A4.

———. 2004c. "Japan Tightens Security on Eve of Troop Deployment to Iraq." *New York Times* (February 21), A7.

———. 2003. "Letter from Asia: Japan Heads to Iraq, Haunted by Taboo Bred in Another War." *New York Times* (November 19), A4.

Orr, Robert M., Jr. 1990. *The Emergence of Japan's Foreign Aid Power.* New York: Columbia University Press.

Osawa, Mari. 2001. "People in Irregular Modes of Employment: Are They Really Not Subject to Discrimination?." *Social Science Japan Journal* 4, no. 2: 183–99.

Otake, Hideo. 1995. "Jiminto wakate kaikakuha to Ozawa guruupu—'seiji kaikaku' o mezashita futatsu no seiji seiryoku" [The LDP's Young Reformers and the Ozawa Group—Two Strands of Political Power Focusing on Reform]. *Leviathan* 17: 7–29.

——. 1990. "Defense Controversies and One-Party Dominance: The Opposition in Japan and West Germany." In *Uncommon Democracies: The One-Party Dominant Regimes,* edited by T. J. Pempel, 128–61. Ithaca: Cornell University Press.

Otsubo, Shozo. 2001. "Toshi Chukan-so no Komyuniti to Chiho Jichi" [Community and Local Government of Urban Middle Classes]. In *Ajia no Dai-toshi: Manila* [Asian Primate Cities: Manila], edited by Toru Nakanishi, Toru Kodama, and Koichi Niizu, 219–44. Tokyo: Nihon Hyoron-sha.

Ozawa, Terutomo. 2003. "Pax Americana-Led Macro-Clustering and Flying-Geese-Style Catch-Up in East Asia: Mechanisms of Regionalized Endogenous Growth." *Journal of Asian Economics* 13: 699–713.

——. 2000. "The 'Flying-Geese' Paradigm: Toward a Co-evolutionary Theory of MNC-Assisted Growth." In *The New World Order: Internationalism, Regionalism, and the Multinational Corporations,* edited by Khosrow Fatemi, 209–23. Amsterdam: Pergamon.

——. 1979. *Multinationalism, Japanese Style: The Political Economy of Outward Dependency.* Princeton: Princeton University Press.

Pacific Council on International Policy Task Force. 2002. *Can Japan Come Back?* Los Angeles: PCIP.

Pangi, Robyn. 2003. "Consequence Management in the 1995 Sarin Attacks on the Japanese Subway System." BCSIA Discussion Paper 2002–4, EDSP Discussion Paper ESDP-2002–01, John F. Kennedy School of Government, Harvard University, February.

Pasuk, Phongpaichit, and Chris Baker. 1995. *Thailand: Economy and Politics.* Kuala Lumpur: Oxford University Press.

Patrick, Hugh, and Henry Rosovsky. 1976. *Asia's New Giant: How the Japanese Economy Works.* Washington, D.C.: Brookings Institution.

Pauly, Louis W., and Simon Reich. 1997. "National Structures and Multinational Corporate Behavior: Enduring Differences in a Globalizing World." *International Organization* 51, no. 1 (Winter): 1–30.

Paxton, Midori. 1992. "Unfairways: Japan Exports Golf Woes to Hawaii." *Japan Environment Monitor* 5, no. 4: 22.

Pekkanen, Robert. 2000. "Japan's New Politics? The Case of the NPO Law." *Journal of Japanese Studies* 26, no. 1 (Winter): 111–43.

Pempel, T. J. 1999. "Structural Gaiatsu: International Finance and Political Change in Japan." *Comparative Political Studies* 32, no. 8 (December): 907–32.

——. 1998. *Regime Shift: Comparative Dynamics of the Japanese Political Economy.* Ithaca: Cornell University Press.

——. 1997. *The Politics of Economic Reform in Japan.* Canberra: Australia-Japan Research Centre.

——, ed. 1990. *Uncommon Democracies: The One-Party Dominant Regimes.* Ithaca: Cornell University Press.

People's Daily Online. 2003. "Another Major Move in China's Diplomacy: Commentary." October 10.

Perlez, Jane. 2002. "China Emerges as Rival to U.S. in Asian Trade." *New York Times* (June 28), A1.

Pharr, Susan J., and Ming Wan. 1998. "Yen for the Earth: Japan's Pro-Active China Environment Policy." In *Energizing China: Reconciling Environmental Protection and Economic Growth,* edited by M. B. McElroy, C. P. Nielsen, and P. Lydon, 601–38. Cambridge: Harvard University, Committee on Environment.

Pilling, David, and Richard McGregor. 2004. "Crossing the Divide: How Booming Business and Closer Cultural Ties Are Bringing Two Asian Giants Together." *Financial Times* (March 30), 13.

Pinches, Michael. 1999. "Entrepreneurship, Consumption, Ethnicity and National Identity in the Making of the Philippines' New Rich." In *Culture and Privilege in Capitalist Asia,* edited by Michael Pinches, 275–301. London: Routledge.

Plath, David W. 1988. "The Age of Silver: Aging in Modern Japan." *The World & I* 3 (March): 505–13.

———. 1975. "The Last Confucian Sandwich: Becoming Middle Aged." In *Adult Episodes in Japan,* edited by David W. Plath, 51–63. Leiden: E. J. Brill.

Porter, Tony. 2003. "Technical Collaboration and Political Conflict in the Emerging Regime for International Financial Regulation." *Review of International Political Economy* 10, no. 3 (August): 520–51.

Posen, Adam. 2001. "Finance and Changing U.S.-Japan Relations: Convergence without Leverage—Until Now." Working Paper, Institute for International Economics, Washington, D.C. http://www.iie.com.

Posner, M. 1961. "International Trade and Technical Change." *Oxford Economic Papers* 13: 323–42.

Prestowitz, Clyde. 1997. "What Happened to the Japanese Economic Model?" *Washington Post* (December 14), C1.

Prime Minister of Japan. 2002. "Reforms in the Prime Minister's Office." http://www.kantei.go.jp/jp/tokino-ugoki/9909/pdf9_18.pdf (accessed February 4, 2004).

Pritchard, Bill. 2000. "Geographies of the Firm and Transnational Agro-Food Corporations in East Asia." *Singapore Journal of Tropical Geography* 21, no. 3: 246–62.

Rajan, Ramkishen. 2001. "Financial and Macroeconomic Co-operation in ASEAN: Issues and Policy Initiatives." In *ASEAN beyond the Crisis: Challenges and Initiatives,* edited by Mya Than, 126–47. Singapore: Institute of Southeast Asian Studies.

Raymo, James M. 2003a. "Educational Attainment and the Transition to First Marriage among Japanese Women." *Demography* 40, no. 1 (February): 83–103.

———. 2003b. "Premarital Living Arrangements and the Transition to First Marriage in Japan." *Journal of Marriage and the Family* 65, no. 2 (May): 302–16.

Reed, Steven R. 2002. "Evaluating Political Reform in Japan: A Midterm Report." *Japanese Journal of Political Science* 3, no. 2: 243–63.

———. 1993. *Making Common Sense of Japan.* Pittsburgh: University of Pittsburgh Press.

Reynolds, Isabel. 2003. "Japan's Politicians Turn to Crime—to Win Votes." Reuters, October 27.

RIETI (Research Institute of Economy, Trade and Industry). 2002. "Kyousouryoku no Kenkyu (19)—Mojuruka" [Study on Competitiveness (19)—Modularity]. *Nohonkeizai Shimbun*, January 29, morning ed., 29.

Roach, Stephen. 2003. "The World Is More U.S.-Centric Now Than It Has Ever Been." Presentation by the chief economist of Morgan Stanley to the World Economic Forum.

Robertson, Jennifer. 1998. *Takarazuka: Sexual Politics and Popular Culture in Modern Japan*. Berkeley: University of California Press.

Rohlen, Thomas P. 2002. *Cosmopolitan Cities and Nation States: Open Economics, Urban Dynamics, and Government in East Asia*. Stanford: Stanford University, Asia/Pacific Research Center.

——. 1977. "Is Japanese Education Becoming Less Egalitarian? Note on High School Stratification and Reform." *Journal of Japanese Studies* 3, no. 2 (Summer): 37–70.

Rohter, Larry. 2004. "China Widens Economic Role in Latin America." *New York Times* (November 20), A1.

Rose, Gideon. 2000–2001. "Democracy Promotion and American Foreign Policy: A Review Essay." *International Security* 25, no. 3 (Winter): 186–203.

Rosecrance, Richard N. 1986. *The Rise of the Trading State: Commerce and Conquest in the Modern World*. New York: Basic Books.

Rosenbaum, James E., and Takehiko Kariya. 1989. "From High School to Work: Market and Institutional Mechanisms in Japan." *American Journal of Sociology* 94 (May): 1334–65.

Rosenthal, Elisabeth. 2003. "North of Beijing, California Dreams Come True." *New York Times* (February 3), A3.

Roth, Joshua Hotaka. 2002. *Brokered Homeland: Japanese Brazilian Migrants in Japan*. Ithaca: Cornell University Press.

Rozman, Gilbert. 2001. "The Northeast Asian Regional Context for Environmentalism: Assessing Environmental Goals against Other Priorities in the 1990s." *Journal of East Asian Studies* 1, no. 2: 13–30.

Rubin, Robert E. 1998. "Testimony by Treasury Secretary Robert E. Rubin" before the House Banking Committee, RR-2186, January 30. http://www.treas.gov/press/releases/rr2186.htm.

Russett, Bruce M. 1985. "The Mysterious Case of Vanishing Hegemony, or, Is Mark Twain Really Dead?" *International Organization* 38, no. 2 (Spring): 207–31.

Ryang, Sonia. 1997. *North Koreans in Japan: Language, Ideology, and Identity*. Boulder: Westview.

——, ed. 2000. *Koreans in Japan*. London: Routledge.

Ryuken Research. 2002. *Shrimp Databook 2002*. Tokyo: Ryuken Risachi.

Said, Edward W. 1978. *Orientalism*. New York: Pantheon Books.

Sakakibara, Eisuke. 2000. *Nihon to Sekai ga Furueta Hi* [The Day Japan and the World Trembled]. Tokyo: Chuo Koron Shinsha.

Samuels, Richard J. 2004. "Politics, Security Policy, and Japan's Cabinet Legislation Bureau: Who Elected These Guys Anyway?" *JPRI Working Paper* No. 99 (March).

——. 2003a. "Gunning for Reform." *Time* (Asia), September 22.

——. 2003b. *Machiavelli's Children: Leaders and Their Legacies in Italy and Japan.* Ithaca: Cornell University Press.

——. 1994. *"Rich Nation, Strong Army": National Security and the Technological Transformation of Japan.* Ithaca: Cornell University Press.

Sansoucy, Lisa. 1998. "Aum Shinrikyo and the Japanese State." Unpublished paper, Government Department, Cornell University (March 13).

Sappani, Kamatchy. 1991. "ASEAN Endorses East Asia Economic Group." *Japan Economic Newswire,* October 8.

Sasaki, Yoshitaka. 1997. "Asian Trilateral Security Talks Debut." *Asahi Evening News,* November 7.

Sassa, Atsuyuki. 2004. "Chian wo keishi shitekita tsuke o ima harawasareteiru" [We Are Now Paying the Price for Having Neglected Public Order]. *Chuo Koron* 119, no. 2 (February): 86–91.

——. 1997. *Kiki kanri* [Crisis Management]. Tokyo: Gyosei.

Sato, Hiroki. 2001. "Atypical Employment: A Source of Flexible Work Opportunities?" *Social Science Japan Journal* 4, no. 2: 161–81.

Sato, Yuri. 1999. "Sangyo to Kigyo" [Industries and Firms]. In *Ajia no Dai-toshi: Jakarta* [Asian Primate Cities: Jakarta], edited by Kensuke Miyamoto and Kazuyuki Konagaya, 117–46. Tokyo: Nihon Hyoron-sha.

Scheiner, Ethan. 2002. "Democracy without Competition: Opposition Failure in One-Party Dominant Japan." PhD diss., Duke University.

Schlesinger, Jacob M. 1997. *Shadow Shoguns: The Rise and Fall of Japan's Postwar Political Machine.* New York: Simon & Schuster.

Schodt, Frederik L. 1996. *Dreamland Japan: Writings on Modern Japan.* Berkeley: Stone Bridge Press.

Scholte, Jan Aart. 2000. *Globalization: A Critical Introduction.* New York: St. Martin's.

Schwartz, Frank, and Susan J. Pharr, eds. 2003. *The State of Civil Society in Japan.* Cambridge: Cambridge University Press.

Scollay, Robert, and John P. Gilbert. 2001. "New Regional Trading Arrangements in the Asia Pacific?" *Policy Analyses in International Economics* 63, May. Washington, D.C.: Institute for International Economics.

Scott, James C. 1985. *Weapons of the Weak.* New Haven: Yale University Press.

Searight, Amy. 2002. "International Organizations." In *U.S.-Japan Relations in a Changing World,* edited by Steven Vogel, 160–97. Washington, D.C.: Brookings Institution Press.

Segal, Gerald. 1999. "Does China Matter?" *Foreign Affairs* 78, no. 5 (September–October): 24–36.

——. 1998. "Overrating China Is a Bad American Habit." *International Herald Tribune* (June 22), 8.

Segawa, Shinpei. 1999. "Dokuritsu-go ni okeru Keikan no Henyo" [Changes in Landscape after Independence]. In *Ajia no Dai-toshi: Jakarta* [Asian Primate Cities: Jakarta], edited by Kensuke Miyamoto and Kazuyuki Konagaya, 57–83. Tokyo: Nihon Hyoron-sha.

Sellek, Yoko. 2001. *Migrant Labor in Japan.* Hampshire: Palgrave.

Shamsul, A. B. 1999. "From Orang Kaya Baru to Melayu Baru: Cultural Construction of the Malay 'New Rich.'" In *Culture and Privilege in Capitalist Asia,* edited by Michael Pinches, 86–110. London: Routledge.

Shimada, Haruo. 1997. "The Significance of the Okinawa Issue: The Experience of the Okinawa Problem Committee." In *Restructuring the U.S.-Japan Alliance: Towards a More Equal Partnership,* edited by Ralph A. Cossa, 83–97. Washington, D.C.: CSIS Press.

Shin, Kwanho, and Yunjong Wang. 2002. "Monetary Integration ahead of Trade Integration in East Asia." Paper prepared for a conference on "Linkages in East Asia: Implications for Currency Regimes and Policy Dialogue," Joint Australia-Japan Research Project on Future Financial Arrangements in East Asia, Seoul, September 23–24.

Shindo, Eiichi. 1999. *Ajia Keizai Kiki o Yomitoku* [Figuring Out the Asian Economic Crisis]. Tokyo: Nihon Keizai Hyoron-sha.

Shinoda, Tomohito. 2002. "Japan's Response to Terrorism and Implications for the Taiwan Straits Issue." *Japan-Taiwan Security Forum,* January 22. http://taiwan security.org/TS/2002/JTRF-Shinoda-0102.htm.

Shiokawa, Masajuro. 2003. "Statement by H. E. Masajuro Shiokawa, Minister of Finance of Japan and Governor of the IMF for Japan, at the Seventh Meeting of the International Monetary and Financial Committee." April 12. http://www.mof .go.jp.

Shiraishi, Saya. 1997. "Japan's Soft Power: Doraemon Goes Overseas." In *Network Power: Japan and Asia,* edited by Peter J. Katzenstein and Takashi Shiraishi, 234–72. Ithaca: Cornell University Press.

Shiraishi, Takashi, ed. 2002. *Kaihatsu to Shakai-teki Antei: Ajia no Islam o Nento ni oite* [Development and Social Stability: Viewing Islam in Asia]. Tokyo: Nihon Kokusai Mondai Kenkyusho.

———. 1999. *Hokai: Indonesia wa Doko he Yuku* [Whither Indonesia?]. Tokyo: NTT Publications.

Shultz, George P. 1988. "Address before the Association of Indonesian Economists." Jakarta, July 11.

Simon, Sheldon W. 2002. "Evaluating Track II Approaches to Security Diplomacy in the Asia-Pacific: The CSCAP Experience." *Pacific Review* 15, no. 2: 167–200.

———. 1998. "Security Prospects in Southeast Asia: Collaborative Efforts and the ASEAN Regional Forum." *Pacific Review* 11, no. 2: 195–212.

Sinclair, Timothy J. 2005. *The New Masters of Capital: American Bond Rating Agencies and the Politics of Creditworthiness.* Ithaca: Cornell University Press.

Skladany, Mike, and Craig K. Harris. 1995. "On Global Pond: International Development and Commodity Chains in the Shrimp Industry." In *Food and Agrarian Orders in the World Economy,* edited by Philip McMichael, 169–91. Westport, Conn.: Greenwood Press.

Smith, Tony. 1994. *America's Mission: The United States and the Worldwide Struggle for Democracy in the Twentieth Century.* Princeton: Princeton University Press.

Snidal, Duncan. 1985. "The Limits of Hegemonic Stability Theory." *International Organization* 39, no. 4 (Autumn): 579–614.

Spengler, Oswald. 1933. *Jahr der Entscheidung.* Munich: C. H. Beck.

State Department. 1991. "Text of Joint Ministerial Press Conference, Third APEC

Ministerial Meeting as Released by the US Department of State, Office of the Assistant Secretary/Spokesman, Shilla Hotel, Seoul, Korea." *Federal News Service,* November 14.

State Department, Bureau for International Narcotics and Law Enforcement Affairs. Annual. *International Narcotics Control Strategy Report.* Washington, D.C. http://www.state.gov/g/inl/rls/nrcrpt/.

Stead, William. 1901. *The Americanization of the World.* New York: Horace Markley.

Steinhoff, Patricia G. 1996. "From Dangerous Thoughts to Dangerous Gas: A Frame Analysis of the Control of Social Movements in Japan." Paper presented at the American Sociological Association Meetings, New York, August 16–20.

Steslicke, William E. 1987. "The Japanese State of Health: A Political-Economic Perspective." In *Health, Illness, and Medical Care in Japan: Cultural and Social Dimensions,* edited by Edward Norbeck and Margaret Lock, 24–65. Honolulu: University of Hawaii Press.

Stone, Diane. 1997. "Networks, Second Track Diplomacy, and Regional Cooperation: The Role of Southeast Asian Think Tanks." Paper presented to the 38th Annual International Studies Association Convention, Toronto, March 22–26.

Straits Times. 2003a. "New Rules Give Troubled Japanese Banks a Breather." April 5.

———. 2003b. "Japan Sets Aside $149b to Buy up Bad Loans." May 8.

Strange, Susan. 1987. "The Persistent Myth of Lost Hegemony." *International Organization* 41, no. 4 (Autumn): 551–74.

Stubbs, Richard. 2002. "ASEAN Plus Three: Emerging East Asian Regionalism?" *Asian Survey* 42, no. 3: 440–55.

Suehiro, Akira, and Susumu Yamakage, eds. 2001. *Ajia Seiji Keizai-ron* [Discourses on Asian Political Economy]. Tokyo: NTT Publications.

Sugihara, Kaoru. 2003. *Ajia Taiheiyo Keizai-ken no Koryu* [Exchanges in the Asia Pacific Economic Zone]. Osaka: Osaka Daigaku Shuppankai.

Summers, Lawrence H. 1998. "Statement of Deputy Secretary of Treasury Lawrence H. Summers, Testimony before the Committee on Finance, United States Senate." RR-1295, February 4. http://www.treas.gov/press/releases/rr1295.htm.

Summit of the Americas. 1998. "Declaration of Santiago." Second Summit of the Americas, April 18–19.

———. 1994. "Declaration of Principles: Partnership for Development and Prosperity; Democracy, Free Trade and Sustainable Development in the Americas." Miami, December.

Suzuki, Nobue. 2003. "Of Love and the Marriage Market: Masculinity Politics and Filipina-Japanese Marriages in Japan." In *Men and Masculinities in Contemporary Japan: Dislocating the Salaryman Doxa,* edited by James Roberson and Nobue Suzuki, 91–108. London: Routledge Curzon.

Suzuki, Takashi. 1997. "Nihon e no Yushutsu ga Gensanchi Gyogyo ni Ataeru Eikyo— Indonesia no Ebi Gyogyo/Yoshokugyo no Hatten o Jirei to Shite" [The Influence on Local Fisheries of Exports to Japan: With the Development of Indonesia's Shrimp Fishery/Aquaculture as an Example]. *Chiiki Gyogyo Kenkyu* [Local Fisheries Research] 38, no. 1: 57–79.

Tachiki, Dennis S. 1999. "The Business Strategies of Japanese Production Networks in Asia." In *Japanese Multinationals in Asia: Regional Operations in Comparative Per-*

spective, edited by Dennis J. Encarnation, 183–212. New York: Oxford University Press.

Tadem, Teresa S. Encarnacion. 2003. "The Philippine Technocracy and U.S.-Led Capitalism." In *Hegemony, Technocracy, Networks: Papers Presented at Core University Program Workshop on Networks, Hegemony and Technocracy,* edited by Takeshi Hamashita and Takashi Shiraishi, 445–500. Kyoto: Kyoto University, Center for Southeast Asian Studies.

Tadokoro, Masayuki. 2003. "Sofuto Pawa to iu Gaiko Shigen o Minaoese" [Rethinking Soft Power as a Diplomatic Resource]. *Chuo Koron* (May): 120–28.

Takashina, Shoji, Shinji Fukukawa, and Hiroaki Fujii. 2003. "Nihonjin wa Sofuto Pawa o motto Katsuyo Subeki" [Japanese Must Make More Use of Their Soft Power]. *Gaiko Foramu,* no. 174 (January): 18–27.

Takayama, Masaki. 2000. "Toshi Keizai Kozo no Henka to Chukan-so no Seicho" [Changes in Urban Economic Structure and the Growth of Middle Classes]. In *Ajia no Dai-toshi: Kuala Lumpur and Singapore* [Asian Primate Cities: Kuala Lumpur and Singapore], edited by Masato Ikuta and Toshio Matsuzawa, 63–68. Tokyo: Nihon Hyoron-sha.

Takenaka, Heizo. 2001a. "Nihon Keizai Saisei no Kagi" [The Key to Japan's Economic Revitalization]. In *Posuto IT Kakumei 'Sofuto Pawa' Nihon Fukken e no Michi* [Soft Power after the Information Technology Revolution: The Road to Japan's Rehabilitation], edited by Heizo Takenaka, 14–30. Tokyo: Fujita Institute of Future Management.

———. 2001b. *Posuto IT Kakumei 'Sofuto Pawa' Nihon Fukken e no Michi* [Soft Power after the Information Technology Revolution: The Road to Japan's Rehabilitation]. Tokyo: Fujita Institute of Future Management.

Takeuchi, Junko. 2003. "The Effect of Free Trade Agreements on the Activities of Japanese Companies in Asia." *RIM. Pacific Business and Industries* 3, no. 10: 2–23.

———. 2001. "Comparison of Asian Business by Japanese and American Companies in the Electronics Sector." *RIM. Pacific Business and Industries* 1, no. 3: 18–44.

Tamaki, Matsuo. 2001. "Seiji Shakai no Renzoku-sei to Henyo" [Continuity and Change in Political Society]. In *Ajia no Dai-toshi: Manila* [Asian Primate Cities: Manila], edited by Toru Nakanishi, Toru Kodama, and Koichi Niizu, 195–217. Tokyo: Nihon Hyoron-sha.

Tang, Zun, and Mary C. Brinton. 2003. "Institutional Change in the Japanese Youth Labor Market." Unpublished paper (October).

Tanimura, Shiho. 1990. *Kekkon shinai ka mo shiranai shokogun* [The 'I Might Not Get Married After All' Syndrome]. Tokyo: Shufu-no-tomo sha.

Tasaka, Toshio. 1998. "Bangkok Sekai-toshi-ka Kasetsu" [Hypotheses on the Urbanization of Bangkok]. In *Ajia no Dai Toshi: Bangkok* [Asian Primate Cities: Bangkok], edited by Toshio Tasaka, 1–41. Tokyo: Nihon Hyoron-sha.

Thang, Leng Leng. 2001. *Generations in Touch: Linking the Young and Old in a Tokyo Neighborhood.* Ithaca: Cornell University Press.

Thang, Leng Leng, and S. K. Gan. 2000. "Deconstructing 'Japanization': Reflections from the 'Learn from Japan' Campaign in Singapore." Paper delivered at the International Conference on the Japanese Model, Malaysian Association of Japanese Studies, Kuala Lumpur, March 29–30.

Thiers, Paul. 2002. "From Grassroots Movement to State-Coordinated Market Strategy: The Transformation of Organic Agriculture in China." *Environment and Planning C — Government and Policy* 20, no. 3: 357–73.

Thornhill, John. 2002. "Asia Awakes." *Financial Times* (April 22), 14.

Torii, Takashi. 2002. "Malaysia no Chukanso Soshutsu no Mekanizumu: Kokka Shudo ni yoru Ikusei" [How Have Malaysian Middle Classes Been Created?]. In *Ajia Chukan-so no Seisei to Tokushitu* [The Formation and Characteristics of Asian Middle Classes], edited by Tamio Hattori, Tsuruyo Funatsu, and Takashi Torii, 133–68. Tokyo: Ajia Keizai Kenkyusho.

——. 2001. "Malaysia no Kaihatsu Senryaku to Seiji Hendo" [Developmental Strategies and Political Changes in Malaysia]. In *Ajia Seiji Keizai Ron* [Discourses on Asian Political Economy], edited by Akira Suehiro and Yamakage Susumu, 127–55. Tokyo: NTT Shuppan.

——. 2000. "Toshi-ka to Seiji Hendo" [Urbanization and Political Changes]. In *Ajia no Dai-toshi: Kuala Lumpur and Singapore* [Asian Primate Cities: Kuala Lumpur and Singapore], edited by Masato Ikuta and Toshio Matsuzawa, 197–218. Tokyo: Nihon Hyoron-sha.

Tsuda, Takeyuki. 2003. *Strangers in the Ethnic Homeland: Japanese Brazilian Return Migration in Transnational Perspective.* New York: Columbia University Press.

Tsugami, Toshiya. 2003. *Chugoku Taito* [The Rise of China]. Tokyo: Nihon Keizai Shimbun-sha.

Tsujii, Takeshi. 1998. "Nihon Bunka wa Naze Suitai no Ka?" [Why Did Japanese Culture Decline?]. *Sekai* (April): 57–68.

Tsuru, Kotaro. 2003. "Toward Reconstruction of Banks: Can Public Bailout of Resona Bank Become Model Case? (Part 2)—Rebuilding of Governance System." *RIETI Policy Update* (June 16). http://www.rieti.go.jp/en/special/policy-update/011.html.

Tsusho Sangyosho Yoka Kaihatsutshitsu [MITI Leisure Development Office], ed. 1974. *Yoka Soran: Shakai, Sangyo, Seisaku* [Overview of Leisure: Society, Industry, and Policy]. Tokyo: Daiyamondo.

Uchida, Kenzo, Takeshige Kunemasa, and Yasunori Sone. 1996. "Nihon no kiro o to" [Japan at the Crossroads]. *Bungei Shunju* (August): 96–99.

Uchida, Ryuzo. 2000. "Kogai Nyu Taun no 'Yokubo'" ['Desires' in Suburban New Towns]. In *"Kogai" to Gendai Shakai* ["Suburbs" and Modern Society], edited by Jun Kaneko, 175–214. Tokyo: Seikyusha.

Uehara, Nobumoto. 2003. "Kako no Seifu Hokokusho ni Miru Kontentsu Seisaku no Ronten" [Topics in Digital Content Policy, as Seen through Previous Government Reports], Ministry of Public Management, Home Affairs, and Posts and Telecommunications. http://www.soumu.go.jp/s-news/2003/pdf/030725_5_b1_s5.pdf (accessed October 28, 2003).

Ueta, Kazuhiro. 1995. "Environment and Economy: Lessons of Japan's Environmental Problems and Policies." In *Development and the Environment: The Experiences of Japan and Industrializing Asia*, edited by K. Rei'itsu et al., 55–67. Tokyo: Institute of Developing Economies.

UNCTAD (United Nations Conference on Trade and Development). 2003. *World Investment Report 2003.* New York: United Nations.

Urata, Shujiro. 1999. "Intrafirm Technology Transfer by Japanese Multinationals." In *Japanese Multinationals in Asia: Regional Operations in Comparative Perspective,* edited by Dennis J. Encarnation, 143–62. New York: Oxford University Press.

U.S. Department of State. 2001. "U.S. Welcomes Japan's Anti-Terrorism Assistance Package." http://usinfo.state.gov.

U.S. Embassy. 2002. "Japan Seeks Greater Law Enforcement Cooperation." U.S. Embassy Transcript, October 22. http://usembassy.state.gov/tokyo/.

USITC (United States International Trade Commission). 1989. "The Pros and Cons of Entering into Negotiations on Free Trade Area Agreements with Taiwan, the Republic of Korea, and ASEAN, or the Pacific Rim Region in General." Report to the Senate Committee on Finance on Investigation No. TA-332–259 under Section 332 of the Tariff Act of 1930, USITC Publication 2166, March.

———. 1988. "Pros and Cons of Initiating Negotiations with Japan to Explore the Possibility of a U.S.-Japan Free Trade Area Agreement." Report to the Senate Committee on Finance on Investigation No. TA-332–255 under Section 332 of the Tariff Act of 1930, USITC Publication 2120, September.

USTR (Office of the United States Trade Representative). 2003a. "Free Trade with Central America: Summary of the U.S.–Central America Free Trade Agreement." *Trade Facts* (December 17).

———. 2003b. "Free Trade with Morocco: Helping to Solidify Economic Reforms." *Trade Facts* (January 21).

———. 2003c. "2003 Assessment of Morocco's Technical Assistance Needs in Negotiating and Implementing a Free Trade Agreement with the United States." January 21.

Utsunomiya, Yuji. 2003a. "Tokyo Sets Up Security Force." *Japan Times* online, August 2.

———. 2003b. "More Police, Immigration Officers Sought." *Japan Times* online, September 23.

Valencia, Mark J., and Guoxing Ji. 2002. "The 'North Korean Ship' and U.S. Spy Plane Incidents: Similarities, Differences, and Lessons Learned." *Asian Survey* 42, no. 5 (September–October): 723–32.

Veeck, G., and S. H. Wang. 2000. "Challenges to Family Farming in China." *Geographical Review* 90, no. 1: 57–82.

Verniere, James. 1999. "Un-American Dream: Raft of Films Made in Hollywood by Foreigners." *Chicago Tribune* (November 27).

Vernon, R. 1979. "The Product Cycle Hypothesis in a New International Environment." *Oxford Bulletin of Economics and Statistics* 41: 255–68.

———. 1966. "International Investment and International Trade in the Product Cycle." *Quarterly Journal of Economics* 80: 190–207.

Vogel, Ezra F. 1991. *The Four Little Dragons.* Cambridge: Harvard University Press.

———. 1979. *Japan as Number One: Lessons for America.* Cambridge: Harvard University Press.

Vogel, Steven. 2003. "The Re-Organization of Organized Capitalism: How the German and Japanese Models Are Shaping Their Own Transformations." In *The End of Diversity? Prospects for German and Japanese Capitalism,* edited by Kozo Yamamura and Wolfgang Streeck, 306–33. Ithaca: Cornell University Press.

——. 1999. "Can Japan Disengage? Winners and Losers in Japan's Political Economy and the Ties That Bind Them." *Social Science Journal of Japan* 2, no. 1 (April): 3–22.

——. 1996. *Freer Markets, More Rules: Regulatory Reform in Advanced Industrial Countries.* Ithaca: Cornell University Press.

Wada, Jun. 1998. "Applying Track Two to China-Japan-U.S. Relations." In *Challenges for China-Japan-U.S. Cooperation,* edited by Ryosei Kokubun, 154–83. Tokyo: Japan Center for International Exchange.

Wade, Robert. 2001. "The US Role in the Long Asian Crisis of 1990–2000." In *The Political Economy of the East Asian Crisis and Its Aftermath,* edited by Arvid John Lukauskas and Francisco Rivera-Batiz, 195–226. Cheltenham: Edward Elgar.

Wakabayashi, Masahiro. 1992. *Taiwan: Bunretsu Kokka to Minshuka* [Taiwan: Divided Nation and Democratization]. Tokyo: Tokyo Daigaku Shuppankai.

Wakabayashi, Mikio. 2000. "Toshi to Kogai no Shakaigaku" [Sociology of Cities and Suburbs]. In *"Kogai" to Gendai Shakai* ["Suburbs" and Modern Society], edited by Jun Kaneko, 13–59. Tokyo: Seikyusha.

Walsh, Kathleen. 2003. *Foreign High-Tech R&D in China: Risks, Rewards, and Implications for U.S.-China Relations.* Washington, D.C: Henry L. Stimson Center.

Wang, Ryon-guan. 2000. "Taiwan ni Okeru Nihon Muke no Butaniku Yushutsu Mondai" [Taiwan's Pork Exports to Japan]. In *Ajia no Shokuryo — Nosanbutsu Shijo to Nihon* [Japan and Asia's Food and Agricultural Products Markets], edited by H. Mikuni, 117–39. Tokyo: Otsuki Shoten.

Watson, James L., ed. 1998. *Golden Arches East: Mcdonald's in East Asia.* Stanford: Stanford University Press.

Weathers, Charles. 2001. "Changing White-Collar Workplaces and Female Temporary Workers in Japan." *Social Science Japan Journal* 4, no. 2: 201–18.

Webb, Amy L. 2001. "Shrimp Farmers Worry as Japan's Appetite Wanes." *Wall Street Journal* (July 30), 1.

Webber, Douglas. 2001. "Two Funerals and a Wedding? The Ups and Downs of Regionalism in East Asia and Asia-Pacific after the Asian Crisis." *Pacific Review* 14, no. 3: 339–72.

Weiner, Michael, ed. 1997. *Japan's Minorities: The Illusion of Homogeneity.* London: Routledge.

Weiner, Robert James. 2002. "Opposition Disappearance in Japan: Post-Realignment Evidence Supports Theoretical Pessimism." Paper delivered at the annual convention of the American Political Science Association, August 31.

Westney, Eleanor D. 1999a. "Changing Perspectives on the Organization of Japanese Multinational Companies." In *Japanese Multinationals Abroad: Individual and Organizational Learning,* edited by Schon L. Beechler and Allan Bird, 11–29. New York: Oxford University Press.

——. 1999b. "Organization Theory Perspectives on the Cross-Border Transfer of Organizational Patterns." In *Remade in America: Transplanting and Transforming Japanese Management Systems,* edited by Jeffrey K. Liker, W. Mark Fruin, and Paul S. Adler, 385–408. New York: Oxford University Press.

White House. 2003. "Statement on U.S.-Thailand FTA Negotiations." Statement by the Press Secretary, White House. October 19.

———. 2002. Office of the Press Secretary. "Fact Sheet: Enterprise for ASEAN Initiative (EAI)." October 26.

White, Merry I. 2002. *Perfectly Japanese: Making Families in an Era of Upheaval.* Berkeley: University of California Press.

Wolfers, Arnold. 1962. *Discord and Collaboration: Essays on International Politics.* Baltimore: Johns Hopkins University Press.

Yakushiji, Taizo. 1986. "Techno-Emulous Countries: Japan's Initial Conditions in Euro-American Contexts." Paper read at second International Symposium on Technological Innovation, Saitama University, Urawa, Japan, September 17–19.

Yamaguchi, Noboru. 1997. "Why the U.S. Marines Should Remain in Okinawa: A Military Perspective." In *Restructuring the U.S.-Japan Alliance: Towards a More Equal Partnership,* edited by Ralph A. Cossa, 98–110. Washington, D.C.: CSIS Press.

Yamaguchi, Yumi. 1999. *Tokyo Trash Web: The Book.* Tokyo: Bijutsu Shuppansha.

Yamamoto, Masao, ed. 1972. *Keizai kanryo no jittai: Seisaku ketteir no mekanizumu* [The Realities of the Economic Bureaucracy: The Mechanics of Policy Formation]. Tokyo: Mainichi Shimbun.

Yamazaki, Masakazu. 1996. "Asia, a Civilization in the Making." *Foreign Affairs* 75, no. 4 (July–August): 106–18.

Yano, Izumi. 2000. "Shokuryo Yunyu to Anzensei Mondai" [Food Imports and Safety Problems]. In *Ajia no Shokuryo — Nosanbutsu Shijo to Nihon* [Japan and Asia's Food and Agricultural Products Markets], edited by H. Mikuni, 41–63. Tokyo: Otsuki Shoten.

Yao, Souchou. 2001. "Modernity and Mahathir's Rage: Theorizing State Discourse of Mass Media in Southeast Asia." In *House of Glass: Culture, Modernity, and the State in Southeast Asia,* edited by Yao Souchou, 1–23. Singapore: ISEAS.

Yomiuri Shimbun. 2003a. "Nichibei de sosa kyojo joyaku, natsu ni mo teiketsu" [U.S.-Japan MLAT Expected to Be Completed This Summer]. June 20.

———. 2003b. "Kayo CD ya Gemu Sofuto mo, Kankoku ga Nihon Bunka Kaihoe" [Korea Moves Toward Openness for Japanese Culture—Popular CDs, Game Software, and the Like]. September 16. http://www.yomiuri.co.jp/entertainment/news/20030916it13.htm (accessed October 28, 2003).

———. 2003c. "Yasai, Kudamono, Ajia de Shobu" [Vegetables and Fruits Taking a Chance in Asia]. July 7.

———. 2002. "China Alliance Brings Opportunity, Problems." September 23.

Yoneyama, Shiro. 1990. "U.S. Cools to Japanese Military Presence in Gulf." *Japan Economic Newswire,* December 21.

Yoon, Suh-Kyung. 2001. "Swept Up on a Wave." *Far Eastern Economic Review* (October 18), 92–94.

Yoshihara, Hideki. 2000. "Options for Strategic Change: Screwdriver Factories of Integrated Production Systems." In *Corporate Strategies for Southeast Asia after the Crisis: A Comparison of Multinational Firms from Japan and Europe,* edited by Jochen Legewie and Hendrik Meyer-Ohle. Basingstoke: Palgrave.

Yoshimura, Mako. 2000. "Kuala Lumpur no Shugyo Kozo to Shakai no Henyo" [Changes in Occupational Structure Society in Kuala Lumpur]. In *Ajia no Daitoshi: Kuala Lumpur and Singapore* [Asian Primate Cities: Kuala Lumpur and Singapore], edited by Masato Ikuta and Toshio Matsuzawa, 173–96. Tokyo: Nihon Hyoron-sha.

Youngblood, Ruth. 1991. United Press International, February 24.

Zakaria, Fareed. 2003. *The Future of Freedom.* New York: W. W. Norton.

Zhou, Kate Xiao. 1996. *How the Farmers Changed China: Power of the People.* Boulder: Westview.

Contributors

DIETER ERNST is a Senior Fellow at the East-West Center, Honolulu, Hawaii.

H. RICHARD FRIMAN holds the Eliot Fitch Chair for International Studies at Marquette University.

DEREK HALL is Assistant Professor of International Development Studies and Political Studies at Trent University, Peterborough, Ontario, Canada.

NATASHA HAMILTON-HART is Assistant Professor in the Southeast Asian Studies Programme at the National University of Singapore.

PETER J. KATZENSTEIN is the Walter S. Carpenter, Jr. Professor of International Studies, Cornell University.

WILLIAM W. KELLY is Professor of Anthropology and Sumitomo Professor of Japanese Studies at Yale University.

DAVID LEHENY is Associate Professor of Political Science at the University of Wisconsin–Madison.

NAOKO MUNAKATA is former Senior Fellow at the Research Institute of Economy, Trade and Industry (RIETI) and currently Director, Textile and Clothing Division, Manufacturing Industries Bureau at the Ministry of Economy, Trade and Industry of the Japanese government.

NOBUO OKAWARA is Professor of Political Studies at Kyushu University.

T. J. PEMPEL is Professor of Political Science and Director of the Institute of East Asian Studies at the University of California–Berkeley.

TAKASHI SHIRAISHI is Professor at the National Graduate Institute for Policy Studies, Tokyo.

MERRY I. WHITE is Professor of Anthropology at Boston University.

311

Index

Note: Page numbers with an *f* indicate figures; those with a *t* indicate tables; those with an *n* indicate footnotes.

Acer Corporation, 183, 184n
Adorno, Theodor, 229
Afghanistan
    Japanese economic aid to, 50
    Japanese SDF in, 89, 103, 223
    U.S. armed forces in, 32, 55
Agency for Small Business (Japan), 43
"agglomerations," industrial, 136
agribusiness
    Chinese, 151, 156–57, 193, 194f, 196,
        201–4, 207–8
    ecological concerns with, 188–97, 210
    FDI in, 199–202
    genetically modified organisms and, 197
    liberalization of, 199–202
    Taiwanese, 193, 197, 204–5
    Thai, 193, 196–200, 205, 252–53
    WTO and, 209
AIDS (acquired immunodeficiency syn-
    drome), 225
Akihiko, Tanaka, 104
Alcatel Corporation, 169, 184
Allison, Anne, 6
al Qaeda, 32, 55, 103
Alternative Front (Malaysia), 259
Americanization, 2, 7–11, 33, 192, 244
    definition of, 8

globalization and, 8, 109, 153–54, 209
    hybridization and, 245
    Japanization versus, 109, 162, 164
Amnesty International, 9
amphetamines, 94
Amsden, Alice, 29
Anderson, Benedict, 231
Angel Plan (Japanese day care), 74
Angkatan Belia Islam Malaysia (ABIM),
    257–58
anime (animated films), 14, 27, 71, 243,
    256
    cultural meanings of, 218
    global success of, 214, 221
    influence on *The Matrix*, 211, 218
    otaku of, 219–22, 228
anthrax, 99
Anti-Subversive Activities Law (Japan),
    100, 101
Anti-Terrorism Special Measures Law (Ja-
    pan), 89, 105–6
Anwar Ibrahim, 257–59, 270
Aoki Tamotsu, 221
Apkindo Corporation, 199
Apple Computers, 169
Aquino, Corazon, 267
Ariyoshi, Sawako, 75